Joseph DeCamp

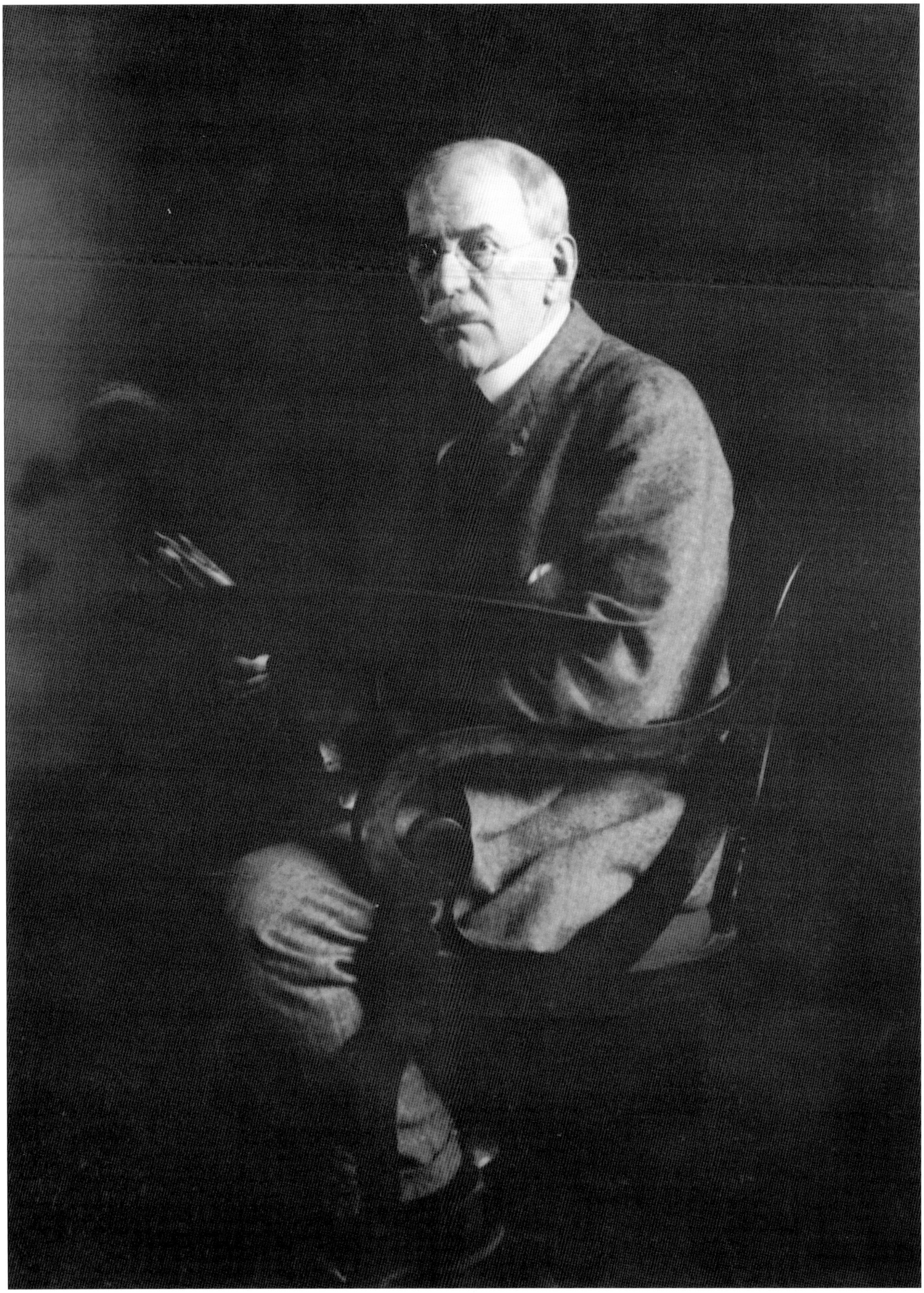

Laurene Buckley

Joseph DeCamp

Master Painter of the Boston School

Prestel
Munich · New York

Front cover: *The Hammock,* ca. 1895 (detail; plate 10)
Frontispiece: Joseph DeCamp, ca. 1920

Prestel books are available worldwide.
Please contact your nearest bookseller or write to either
of the following addresses for information concerning
your local distributor:

Prestel Verlag

16 West 22nd Street, New York, NY 10010;
Tel. (212) 627-8199, Fax (212) 627-9866

Mandlstrasse 26, D-80802 Munich, Germany;
Tel. (+49-89) 381 70 90, Fax (+49-89) 381 70 935

Designed by Knut Liese, Munich, Germany
Typeset by
Setzerei Max Vornehm, Munich, Germany
Color separations by
Scanner Studio, Scan-Tec-GmbH, Munich, Germany
Printed and bound by
Passavia Druckerei GmbH, Passau, Germany
Printed in Germany

ISBN 3-7913-1604-4

Contents

This book is dedicated to my sons
Erik and Adam

Preface

In 1956 Donald Moffat, Joseph DeCamp's son-in-law, wrote to the Assistant Director of the Pennsylvania Academy of the Fine Arts, Philadelphia, to propose an exhibition to be held two years later in celebration of the centenary of the artist's birth. "My only question," he wrote, "is whether the time is ripe, in view of current trends in painting, or whether it would be wiser to wait on the perspective of another generation or two." Moffat did not live to see the revival of many nineteenth-century artists' reputations, but he must have recognized the importance of his research on DeCamp, as he filed away the results—a list of known paintings, a biographical sketch, an appreciation of the artist's work, a chronological record of his life, and a bibliography—in the Frick Art Reference Library, New York.

Aside from the Moffat material, the data on DeCamp available when I embarked on the present study consisted of little more than a few documents held by the artist's family and a meager assortment of articles, two of them written shortly after DeCamp's death: William Howe Downes's groundbreaking "Joseph DeCamp and His Work," in *Art and Progress* (April 1913); Rose V. S. Berry's "Joseph DeCamp: Painter and Man," in *American Magazine of Art* (April 1923); and Lee W. Court's *Joseph DeCamp: An Appreciation* (1924). DeCamp also figures in such general surveys as Alvin I. Harlow's *The Serene Cincinnatians* (1950), Trevor J. Fairbrother's *The Bostonians: Painters of an Elegant Age* (1986), and William H. Gerdts *et al.*, *Ten American Painters* (1990). It was clear from the outset that any indepth study of the artist would need to draw mostly on the critical literature surrounding his exhibited works.

In 1990 the Spanierman Gallery in New York produced a catalogue to accompany its exhibition of work by the Ten American Painters, with one scholar assigned to each artist. DeCamp was the only member of the group without a scholar, and it became my task to reconstruct his life and work for the publication. Since the appearance of that catalogue, much more visual material has become available from the artist's family and from dealers, making it feasible to write a full-scale monograph on DeCamp. It has been an oft-repeated axiom about the artist that a fire in his studio in 1904 destroyed so much of his work as to preclude a comprehensive account of his oeuvre. Without a doubt, the losses hinder a close study of DeCamp's early career, but, with the reemergence of a few key figural and landscape works, some gaps have been filled.

As the first major study of DeCamp, this book was initially a daunting undertaking. A great number of potentially insurmountable hurdles had to be negotiated. Could the artist's early history in Cincinnati be reconstructed, not to mention his time in Munich, where records are at best sparse? Frank Duveneck's career in Germany has tended to overshadow the activities of the group he referred to as his "boys": Was there enough material on DeCamp in those years to define his role within the Duveneck coterie? How does this early, intensive training figure in his later work? Was there a good reason for James B. Townsend, in an article published in the December 12, 1908, issue of *American Art News*, to dub DeCamp the "Boston technician"?

DeCamp's subject matter after his move to Boston in 1884 encompassed a number of genres—landscape, portraiture, and the nude. A full appraisal of each of these had not been previously attempted. Which circumstances led DeCamp to concentrate so heavily on the male portrait and how does he fit into the tradition of portraiture in America? How does his portrait style differ from that of his contemporaries Thomas Eakins, John Singer Sargent, and Frederic Porter Vinton?

Plein air landscape painting captured DeCamp's attention from the 1880s to the early part of the twentieth century. The transition from the artist's early scenes, done at Annisquam, near Gloucester, Massachusetts, to full-blown Impressionism had hardly been known, let alone explored. What accounts for this evolution? Who were his mentors in the new style and how far did he take Impressionism in developing a personal approach? Why did he turn away from Impressionism so abruptly in the early years of the new century, to embrace a more monochromatic vision? What part did DeCamp's Impressionist works play in his role within the Ten American Painters and, even more importantly, was it Impressionism or his Vermeeresque interior scenes that established his position within the Boston School? Could a review of DeCamp's works and the criticism surrounding them contribute to a more precise characterization of that school and also help to distinguish his artistic personality more clearly from those of his colleagues?

Finally, the idealization apparent in DeCamp's female portraits contrasts sharply with the greater individualization that he accorded his male sitters. Were the female figural works done with a different perspective on the part of the artist? Were they meant to be the lasting statement of a more universal, if also specifically Bostonian, vision? The present monograph attempts to provide answers to at least some of these questions.

My deepest debt of gratitude is owed to Donald Moffat, whose researches on DeCamp form the basis of any study of the artist. Without Moffat's early detective work and his extensive correspondence with various private owners and public institutions, many of DeCamp's paintings might not have been located today.

Secondly, I must thank members of the artist's family for their constant encouragement, not to mention their patience during the many years required to complete this study. Of particular help and guidance were Mrs. Ignatius Sargent, Mrs. Edith Harding, Joseph DeCamp, James Lambert DeCamp, Jane DeCamp Stanton, Graydon DeCamp, Crane DeCamp, Corinne (Mrs. Harold C.) Van Wye, Fred DeCamp, Nancy DeCamp Bahlman, Benjamin and Sally Blake, Richard S. DeCamp, Sally Brumfield, Mrs. Earl G. De Camp, Catharine R. Erwin, Mary B. Hallett, Julia DeCamp Hobart, Stirling Moffat, Lydia DeCamp Mulligan, Dorothy Olson, Katharine E. Parsons, Betty Parsons, William Sheeline, Josephine Turner, Joan Tuttle, and Francis Welch.

This book began life as a doctoral dissertation. I was helped immensely by the continually sound counsel of my advisor at the Graduate School and University Center of the City University of New York, Professor William H. Gerdts. His concern for the broader issues kept the study from being a narrow discussion of one artist's career, and his research library was one of my most valuable resources. My thanks go to professors Sally Webster and Marlene Park, also of the Graduate School of the City University of New York, for second and third readership, and to Bruce Weber for the fourth. H. Barbara Weinberg, Curator of American Paintings and Sculpture at the Metropolitan Museum of Art, New York, read parts of the manuscript, and I am grateful to her for many insightful suggestions.

The idea of writing a monograph on DeCamp was sparked by the exhibition on the Ten American Painters at the Spanierman Gallery. The project gained momentum with the planning of an exhibition on the artist by Vose Galleries in Boston, which was unfortunately aborted for financial reasons. The year of research underwritten by Edward Shein and Bill and Terry Vose provided the basic material for the study. The staffs of both galleries are to be acknowledged for their contributions to this work. I would especially like to thank Lesley Wright and Christine Rossi-Anerella for their extremely helpful research.

Others who have been instrumental in providing information and assistance are: J. Richard Abell, Warren Adelson and the staff at Adelson Galleries, Susan and Herbert Adler, Linda Bailey, Faith Bedford, Jean N. Berry, M. Elizabeth Boone, Jeffrey Brown, Laura L. Chace, Mona Chapin, William K. Clark, A. B. Closson, Jr., William A. Coles, George L. Collord II, Barbara J. Dawson, Deborah Donovan, Ann Fisk, Anna Gabriel, Barbara Dayer Gallati, Genetta Gardner, Anne J. Gilliland, Elizabeth H. and Alan B. Harris, Mary Sayre Haverstock, Roger Howlett, Constance Cain Hungerford, Robert Douglas Hunter, Thomas Mairs, John J. McDonough, Mary Jane Neely, Barbara Ninness, Carolyn O'Connor, Charles Packard, Michael Pantazzi, Mary Ran, Charles Rettig, William Rettig, Ed Rider, Beverly Rosenthal, Grace Russell, Randy Sandler, Cathy G. Shaffer, Carol Shelton, Wendy Willison Smith, Phyllis Weston, Laurie K. Whitehill, Michelle Wilson, Nancy Coe Wixom, Leslie Yudell, and Karen Zukowski. My sincere thanks to them all.

Finally, my thanks go to the staff of Prestel for their care and professionalism at every stage in the production of this volume.

Laurene Buckley

Chapter One

Early Years, 1858–1877

Joseph Rodefer DeCamp's years in America before he embarked on a lengthy period of study abroad can be traced through family records, Cincinnati school archives, and a few extant paintings. Together, these reveal that, from an early age, he was deeply immersed in building the skills necessary to sustain a lifetime of artistic endeavor.

The artist was born on November 5, 1858, the son of Lambert and Lydia Garwood DeCamp. He belonged to the seventh generation of his family in America, a lineage originating with Laurent DeCamp, who was born in Normandy, France, around 1645 and who emigrated from Holland to New Amsterdam in 1664 with other French Huguenots. In 1811, according to Graydon DeCamp, the family historian, Laurent's great grandson and his wife, Moses and Sarah Ross DeCamp, decided to "develop new farms in the West," together with their two sons, David and Ezekiel, and the latter's children.[1] Ezekiel went ahead of the others on horseback. Passing up twenty-eight acres of property in what is now the heart of downtown Cincinnati, he chose a huge tract of timberland in Reily Township, Butler County, some forty miles north of the city, which became known as the DeCamp Homestead. Ezekiel and Mary Baker DeCamp raised seventeen children on this land, including Lambert, the father of the artist.[2]

As Lambert and each of his eleven brothers reached maturity, they were sent to Cincinnati, where they apprenticed as brick and stone masons, carpenters and plasterers. Henry, for example, worked under the sculptor Hiram Powers and later owned the company that produced stone for many of the city's major churches. Joseph DeCamp's other uncles, David, Walter, Hiram, Harvey, Joseph, Daniel, and James, as well as his father, were all later connected with the building industry. Known as the DeCamp Syndicate, they were collectively responsible for the original buildings of Miami University in Oxford, Ohio; the entire layout and development of the Cincinnati suburb of Hartwell (commemorated by the street named DeCamp Avenue); and, in Cincinnati itself, the original Pike's Opera House (which would later serve as an artists' studio for Frank Duveneck, John Henry Twachtman, DeCamp, and others); Trinity and St. Paul's Methodist Episcopal churches; the Boylan, Glenn, Carlisle, Bishop, and Cleneay business blocks; the original Post Office; the Cincinnati, Hamilton, and Dayton Railroad depot and shops; and many large private residences, including some on Wesley Avenue, where Joseph DeCamp spent his childhood.[3]

All works are oil on canvas, unless otherwise stated

His mother, Lydia Garwood, was eight years old in 1836 when her family moved from Harrisburg, Pennsylvania, to Cincinnati, then a village of a few thousand inhabitants. Educated in the public schools and at the local Wesleyan College for Young Women, she taught in public schools for twelve years, from 1845 until 1856, when she became the wife of Lambert and the stepmother of two surviving children from his first marriage.[4] Two years later, she gave birth to her second child, Joseph.

One incident from DeCamp's childhood, an indication of early artistic interests, was recounted in a memorial piece that appeared in the *Boston Evening Transcript* on January 5, 1924:

> One day when no more than twelve or thirteen years of age someone gave him a tiny color-box. It instantly became his dearest possession and he carried it about constantly, even to school, where he could not resist the temptation of dabbling with the bright colors under the cover of his desk. The teacher noticed the rapt preoccupation and sharply reprimanded the boy, demanding, "What have you got?" On seeing the color-box and little dreaming what its possession indicated, he said sternly, "Give it to me." That was the one thing above all else that the boy had no idea of doing and he immediately buttoned it inside his little round jacket. Whereupon the master descended upon the luckless pupil, who ran twice around the schoolroom closely pursued by the irrate disciplinarian. Seeing an open window and being hard pressed, the boy made one flying leap through it, clutching all the while his dearest possession. Years after, when in Cincinnati on a visit, he pointed out the very window through which he leaped—two stories to the ground—to save his first crude artist outfit. The boy was, of course, severely dealt with for such glaring disrespect of authority, but was happily reinstated by a superior master, who made allowances for budding artistic temperament.[5]

De Camp's childhood home, at 25 Wesley Avenue (now demolished), was part of the "fashionable West

End," far removed from the chaotic and bustling life of downtown Cincinnati.[6] A tribute to Wesley Avenue appeared in the *Cincinnati Times Star* of May 29, 1950, at a time when the street of formerly "well-kept gardens and rows of lombardy populars [*sic*] which lined either side of a broad, cobble-stone roadway" was a victim of redevelopment: "In all the maelstrom of brawling parents and yellowing [*sic*] children of the West End... Wesley Ave. stood quiet and genteel. Named for the father of Methodism, this block-long street of handsome smooth-stone houses was a religious stronghold until recent years.... All along the street lived the clergymen who ministered to the [Wesleyan College for Young Women] girls' intellectual and spiritual needs .... Many a well-known Cincinnati name once gave a Wesley Avenue address."[7]

By the time DeCamp began his art studies in 1873, Cincinnati was considered a major regional art center in America. A post-Civil War cultural boom was well underway, with the building of the music hall, the municipal zoo, the conservatory of music, and the public library. It was a period of railroad expansion, the beginning of telephone communication, and an extremely active time for women seeking the vote and equality in the workplace and elsewhere.[8] For the budding art student, it was reassuring to know that Cincinnati had its ample share of private collectors and generous patrons, although their purchases were often Europe-oriented. Many Cincinnati artists who had established national reputations in the earlier decades of the nineteenth century—Hiram Powers, Lilly Martin Spencer, T. Worthington Whittredge, and others—left the city for more lucrative artistic centers. In fact, when it was time to appoint a director in 1868 for the newly established School of Art and Design of McMicken College (later part of the University of Cincinnati), the trustees for the Charles McMicken estate hired an outsider, the Düsseldorf- and Paris-trained Thomas Satterwhite Noble. Noble's insistence on rigorous draftsmanship, true to the academic manner in which he had been trained, exerted a lasting influence on DeCamp.

DeCamp spent five years at the McMicken School of Art and Design, beginning with evening classes in 1873 when he was just fifteen years old and still in high school.[9] The aim of the institution, according to its mission statement of 1869, was to improve the state of the industrial arts "by spreading among the operative classes of this city a more thorough technical and scientific education in Art and Design, as applied to manufacture."[10] DeCamp's first efforts, judging by his entries in the Cincinnati Industrial Exposition of 1875 and the School of Art and Design's annuals of 1875 and 1876—four wood carvings (one a medal-winner) and an ornamental drawing—reflected this functional emphasis in his early training.[11] Developing skills in the decorative arts accorded with the DeCamp family tradition in Cincinnati. Furthermore, the decade of the 1870s was the peak of a twenty-year wood carving craze in the city, which left "hundreds of buildings, public and private, more or less decorated interiorly with carven wood."[12] A review of the 1875 annual states that 164 students were registered in the carving class, which was taught by Benn Pitman, an adherent of John Ruskin's "truth to nature" doctrine, and by his daughter, Agnes.

The department of wood carving received special attention in an otherwise scathing review of the 1876 annual that appeared in the *Cincinnati Daily Enquirer*:

> Our art school is weighted a little with sham work. The time has come for the school to rid itself of this. Drawing from the flat as a means of training eye and hand may have its advantages. Some of the very oracles in art vehemently deny this possibility and as vehemently assert that its results are only pernicious.... We have this system in the Cincinnati School of Design. Ability to copy a picture and copy it well is very different from power to draw. Power and what it involves is what we want to see coming out of the instruction given in this school. How many pupils who have taken prizes in the School of Design for drawing from the flat and from the antique can draw with tolerable accuracy and with any pleasure from nature?... We have departments in the school whose want in the very nature of the case is real work—the department of industrial design, for instance, and pre-eminently the department of wood carving. The latter had 160 specimens on exhibition, and these were only what were left after sending the best specimens off during the year to the Centennial Exhibition at Philadelphia. Yet this year's display—remnant as it was—was better than that of any previous year.[13]

The *Cincinnati Daily Enquirer* critic was no doubt aware of a new movement within the school, one that reflected the enormous impact of the teaching of Frank Duveneck, who had returned from studies at Munich's Royal Academy in 1873 and had taught a class of sixteen enterprising students at the Ohio Mechanics Institute in Cincinnati the following season (1874–75). Master of a bold, realist style based on the work of his mentor in Munich, Wilhelm Leibl, who, in turn, admired the rugged approach of Gustave Courbet, Duveneck gave his students a taste of freedom they would not soon forget. Robert Blum, Alfred Brennan, Kenyon Cox, John Henry Twachtman, and others, including the sixteen-year-old DeCamp, rallied around Duveneck. He taught them more than just the mechanics of painting a head, making it "a vitalized affair of veritable flesh and bone," and more than a doctrine of sound modeling and drawing, demonstrating for them "the spectacle of a brush flashing over the canvas as in a kind of joyous bravura," as Royal Cortissoz later remarked of Duveneck's style.[14]

After Duveneck left for Munich again in August 1875, Brennan and Cox carried on his teaching methods, receiving permission from the university to conduct a life class in a room below the School of Art and Design. In an article entitled "Revolt in the Old Art School Led By Famous Painters" Charles Elliott recalled the startling contrast between the two classes: "There was constant slashing about and slapping on of color" in the lower chamber, while "Professor Noble's students nearby painstakingly and with patience without limit copied and elaborately finished to the most finicky detail their drawings from antique casts."[15]

Another insider's view of the more progressive Mechanics Institute and its freer atmosphere was provided some years later by the Cincinnati painter John Rettig:

> The first designs made in tones of sepia or India ink washes were a revelation in the first exhibits, but were out-classed by later pupils, who benefited by all our experimenting.... Later we had a life class, at first the head only, then a nude male model (for men only) in a special room on the floor below, which was attended, among others, by Joe DeCamp.... During the models' rest we usually played ball in the life-class room. DeCamp at that time was working on an exhibition piece, an 8 x 10 foot charcoal drawing, representing a swimming group. One life-sized figure on shore in the foreground, the other, head and arm out of the water, in a swimming pose. I pitched the ball and Bill Drake swifted it through the swimmer, leaving the standing figure only, for which later he received the gold medal.[16]

Fig. 1 *Self-Portrait*, ca. 1876–77. 22⅛ x 18¼ in. (56 x 46.5 cm). Private collection

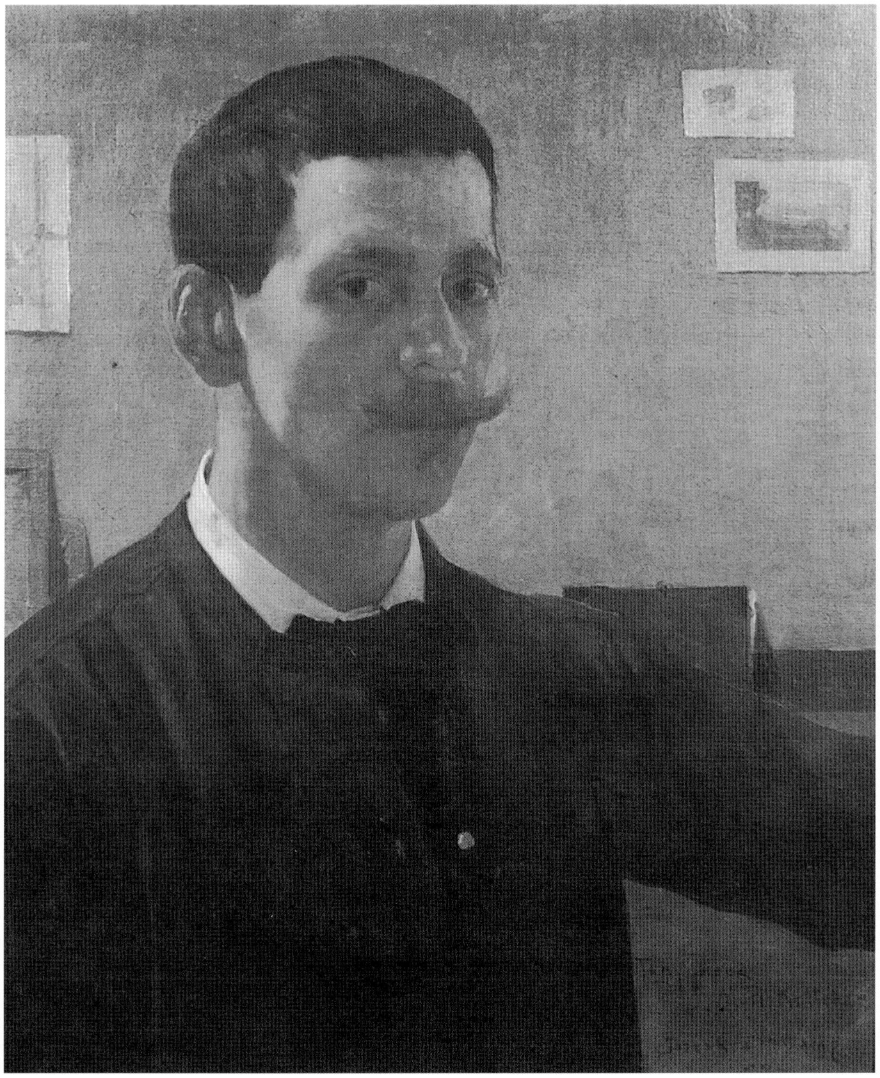

As a member of both groups, DeCamp surely benefited from the cross influences, especially in the fall of 1877, when Noble instituted life drawing classes in which "a few of the more qualified students were allowed to draw costumed models and detailed studies of human heads, hands, and still life arrangements," according to Bruce Weber, writing in 1979.[17] Now in the third year of his studies, DeCamp entered works in the 1877 annual exhibition of the School of Art and Design that reflected this change in curriculum. Besides two carved picture frames, he submitted a portrait head "after [Thomas] Couture" (Noble's teacher in Paris), a sketch from nature, a study of trees, an anatomical figure drawing, and a figure from life, the last receiving praise from a *Cincinnati Daily Enquirer* critic: "We regard it as unfortunate [that] Mr. DeCamp did not invest his superbly drawn study from life with such accessories as would have brought it under the head of original designs."[18] This may have been the salvaged "standing figure" mentioned in Rettig's article.

Two paintings exist from this early period that show the progress DeCamp made at the School of Art and Design. A self-portrait (fig. 1), inscribed as such and given later to a friend, is clearly a student work in its awkward composition and two-dimensional style. The young DeCamp, wearing an artist's smock, dominates the foreground. He stares out at us (and into the mirror), his outstretched right arm indicating the existence of an easel outside the picture area, on which he renders his own image. Several paintings are stacked along the rear wall, which is hung with carefully arranged sketches and a Japanese print.

Pears (plate 1), a still life probably done shortly before DeCamp's departure for Europe in 1878, is far more advanced technically in its depiction of three-dimensional volumes within an atmospheric space. When DeCamp was shown the tightly rendered work on a visit to Cincinnati in the 1920s, he jokingly remarked that he had "run a wire" around some of the fruit.[19]

Before going abroad, the artist is said to have taught a drawing class for women in 1876, in Chillicothe, Ohio, a town eighty miles east of Cincinnati and, at the time, a rival to that city for cultural dominance in the region.[20] If it is true that the eighteen-year-old DeCamp was considered proficient enough to be called to another city to teach, this would add credence to the statement made by him many years later to his friend R. H. Ives Gammell that, after only "two years of study, he could draw as correctly as he ever came to do."[21] The course that DeCamp would take in his art—toward firm draftsmanship and sound technique—was apparently already underway.

Notes

1 Graydon DeCamp, ed., *Record of the Descendants of Ezekiel and Mary Baker DeCamp of Butler County, Ohio* (Cincinnati: privately printed, 1976), p. 9.

2 Donald Moffat, "Joseph Rodefer DeCamp: Biographical Sketch," unpublished typescript, Frick Art Reference Library, New York, 1955–57, p. 18. Moffat points out that the artist "had no less than 124 first cousins," since "all but one of the seventeen children survived to marry." The DeCamp family home was destroyed by fire in 1936.

3 G. DeCamp, *Record of the Descendants*, pp. 11–12.

4 Hiram A. DeCamp, "Lydia Garwood DeCamp," *Cincinnati Daily Enquirer*, April 8, 1902, p. 7.

5 Harley Perkins, "Joseph DeCamp: The Man and the Artist," *Boston Evening Transcript*, January 5, 1924, p. 8.

6 Alvin F. Harlow, *The Serene Cincinnatians* (New York: E. P. Dutton & Co., 1950), p. 105. For an excellent text and bibliography on the development of cultural life in Cincinnati and other Ohio cities, see William H. Gerdts, *Art Across America: Two Centuries of Regional Painting, 1710–1920* (New York: Abbeville Press, 1990), pp. 178–229 and 369–71, and also Lyle Koehler, "Women's Rights, Society and the Schools: Feminist Activities in Cincinnati, Ohio, 1864–1880," *Queen City Heritage* 42 (Summer 1984), pp. 3–15.

7 Iphigene Bettman, "Hereabouts," *Cincinnati Times Star*, May 29, 1950, p.2.

8 Koehler, "Women's Rights, Society and the Schools," p. 13.

9 Donald Moffat, "Joseph Rodefer DeCamp: "Chronology," unpublished typescript, Frick Art Reference Library, New York, 1955–57, p. 1. Two years later, according to Moffat, DeCamp quit high school to become a full-time art student.

10 "A Circular—The School of Drawing and Design, University of Cincinnati—Board of Directors—Minutes for June 7, 1869, p. 203," Cincinnati Historical Society.

11 The medal, now in a private collection, reads: "Wood Carving by Amateur, 1875."

12 Harlow, *The Serene Cincinnatians*, p. 319.

13 "Cincinnati University: Eighth Commencement of the Cincinnati School of Design," *Cincinnati Daily Enquirer*, June 18, 1876, p. 1.

14 Royal Cortissoz, *American Artists* (New York: Charles Scribner's Sons, 1923), p. 160.

15 Charles A. Elliott, "Revolt in the Old Art School Led By Famous Painters," *Commercial Tribune*, March 21, 1915, p. 8.

16 John Rettig, "This Week in Art Circles," *Cincinnati Daily Enquirer*, October 8, 1916, sect. 4, p. 8.

17 Bruce Weber, "Frank Duveneck and the Art Life of Cincinnati, 1865–1900," in *The Golden Age: Cincinnati Painters of the Nineteenth Century Represented in the Cincinnati Art Museum*, exh. cat. (Cincinnati: Cincinnati Art Museum, 1979), p. 25.

18 "The School of Design," *Cincinnati Daily Enquirer*, June 17, 1877, p. 2.

19 Quoted from a note attached to the verso of the painting. I am grateful to Jane DeCamp Stanton for bringing this note to my attention.

20 Moffat, "Joseph Rodefer DeCamp: Biographical Sketch," p. 1. Even in a family that promoted independence at an early age (DeCamp's father and uncles were apprenticed in the building trade in their late teens), this would have been a daring adventure for an eighteen-year-old. The school was probably the Female Seminary referred to in Henry Holcomb Bennett's *County of Ross* (Madison, Wisc.: Selwyn A. Brant, 1902), p. 154. The other possibility, Dague's Collegiate Institute, was founded in 1877 and admitted both men and women. DeCamp is not listed as a teacher during the first season of the institute, nor is he listed in the city directories.

21 R. H. Ives Gammell, *The Boston Painters: 1900–1930* (Orleans, Mass.: Parnassus Imprints, 1986), p. 55.

Chapter Two

Training Abroad, 1878–1883

Munich beckoned DeCamp for many reasons, not the least of which was the sheer number of Cincinnati artists who had already chosen that city over Paris, the other major European center for artistic training in the 1870s. Thomas Noble also may have recommended the Bavarian city to DeCamp, since the older artist was himself contemplating a period of further training there. Probably the most compelling reason for DeCamp to study at Munich's Royal Academy was a desire to follow in the footsteps of Frank Duveneck, who had made such great strides at the academy in his student years and who was just then receiving enthusiastic reviews for his entries in the 1876 Philadelphia Centennial Exhibition, the 1877 annuals of the National Academy of Design and the Pennsylvania Academy of the Fine Arts, and the inaugural show of the Society of American Artists of 1878.

Against his parents' wishes and with a meager sum of five hundred dollars, borrowed from his brother, Hiram, DeCamp departed for Munich in the fall of 1878, for what would be a five-year sojourn abroad. He signed the matriculation book of the Royal Academy with his traveling companions and fellow Cincinnatians Theodore Wendel and George Hopkins on October 17, 1878; all three registered for the *Naturklasse* (life drawing class).[1]

With its visual feast of architectural styles—Gothic, Baroque, Neoclassical—Munich must have been an overwhelming experience for these young men. Museums of the caliber of the Glyptothek, the Neue Pinakothek, the Bayerisches Nationalmuseum, and, especially for aspiring artists, the Alte Pinakothek, with its masterpieces by Botticelli, Dürer, Hals, Raphael, Rembrandt, Rubens, Titian, Van Dyck, and Velázquez, were not to be found in America. Munich was then "music mad," yet, according to a writer in the 1930s, it "lavished its enthusiasm equally on pictorial art through its many museums, exhibitions . . . and schools of instruction."[2]

DeCamp and his friends were fortunate to be accepted into the Royal Academy, particularly the *Naturklasse*, at such a late date in the season. Karl Kappes, a student in Munich in the early 1880s, described a similar, albeit later, dilemma to his parents: "I wanted to get in the nature school—that is, drawing from life—but I was unsuccessful on account of the school being so crow[d]ed and I being to[o] late in the session. The school had been opened a month before I arrived so all I was to do was wait until Christmas as the Professor advised me to do, and run the chances of there being a vacancy in the Nature Class. . . . A great many students fail to get in the Academy as a good drawing must be made befor[e] you become a member."[3]

With his finely honed ability as a draftsman, DeCamp was apparently excused attendance at the preparatory school, where new students were asked to draw from Antique casts before moving on to advanced classes with such distinguished instructors as Karl von Piloty, Ludwig von Löfftz, and Wilhelm von Diez. According to Gammell, DeCamp was a student of Diez, if only for a short period.[4] At the time the young artist arrived in Munich the prevailing style taught at the academy owed much to Diez. His meticulously drawn genre scenes, based on Dutch seventeenth-century prototypes, were greatly admired by the student body.[5] Diez, who had instructed Duveneck, was also known to allow much freedom of stylistic experimentation, and this may have added to his popularity.

Diez's liberality notwithstanding, DeCamp's daily routine was far from easy. No doubt it approximated that of Kappes, who, in a letter to his parents dated November 26, 1883, wrote: "My time is all occupied from 8 to 12 and 1 to 4 . . . 4 to 5 we have lectures . . . 5 to 6 I draw from the nude figure at school, and 7–9 at night I draw from the nude at a large studio that the students have rented."[6]

A fellow student of DeCamp's at the academy, Julius Rolshoven, later recalled the rigors of their first winter in Munich: "Winter in Munich is severe; top boots and heavy coats are essential to the student while wading through snow and ice. I would encounter early mornings Joseph DeCamp, Theodore Wendel, Charles Freeman, Henry Bisbing, all rushing to get best placing for their easle [*sic*]. DeCamp started his day with a clay pipe while Wendel was a marksman with snow balls which amused the Bavarians."[7]

DeCamp stayed at the academy for the full season (fall through spring), capping off the spring term and the annual exhibition in July with the receipt of a bronze medal. A letter to his brother dated July 29, 1879, barely mentions the award, but boasts instead of the accomplishments of his friend Charles Niehaus:

> Dear Hi—I have not time to write you as long a letter as I would like to in answer to your last, but I wish to tell you about our exhibition and especially about Niehaus, a Cincinnati sculptor, and an old friend of mine, in the School of Design. Niehaus has been here about two years in the modeling school, and has just finished a large group in clay, which has been awarded the Grand Silver medal, the highest prize that the Academy can give. The judges did not attempt to criticise [*sic*] it but immediately awar[d]ed it the medal. Now, I wish you would see Brown, give him the facts in the case and have him make as much of it as possible. Niehaus is a talented fellow and has no more money than he ought to have. As a slight evidence of the way he is appreciated here, he was given the job of making a couple of figures to go over the doorway of the new Academy building. I forgot to say before, that the Academy have asked permission to have his group cast in bronze at their own expense. Hopkins took an honorable mention. Wendel and I got Bronze medals. But what I consider better than the medal, Duveneck said, after looking through our exhibition, that I had the best stuff there.[8]

Duveneck had returned to Munich in 1875, three years before DeCamp arrived, and had gathered around him some students from the McMicken class in Cincinnati, as well as other Americans and European pupils. Apparently, the young DeCamp was now fully in the Duveneck camp, along with so many of his Munich colleagues. Shortly before DeCamp's arrival in Munich (probably in September 1878), a group of American students, including John White Alexander, John O. Anderson, Louis Ritter, and others, had persuaded Duveneck to start his own school, which increased in numbers as the season progressed. "Little by little we were weaned away from the Academy classes," wrote Rolshoven, "for there was one who had captured our admiration—Duveneck. . . . We younger fellows . . . at last became convinced that no one in Munich possessed the gift which Duveneck had. To see him lay in a head made us breathless. We stood amazed for there was the model and on the easel a flat surface upon which each touch recounted an unmistakable truth."[9]

For a minimal fee of five dollars per month plus living expenses, DeCamp could become part of this avant-garde movement, led by a wizard of the brush and a man whom he trusted and greatly admired.[10] Rolshoven would later recall that DeCamp was "possessed" by even the "personal mannerisms of Duveneck . . . he [DeCamp] too wore his hat toward his nose and walked with his feet apart."[11]

DeCamp was probably also a member of the American Art Club in Munich, where Duveneck held court with his "boys," as he referred to them. The group met often to discuss art, usually with the aid of reproductions of Old Masters, but also to sketch and engage in festive activities that included costume balls and musical events. During the summers, Munich art students scattered to the outlying villages of Dachau, Schleissheim, and Polling, the latter being the choice of the Duveneck coterie. Located thirty miles southwest of Munich, near Weilheim, Polling had become something of an international art colony by this time, with Duveneck as one of the most sought-after teachers. DeCamp probably joined the group after the Royal Academy's exhibition of July 1879. He had been to the village the previous Christmas, signing the guest book of the local inn on December 23, 1878, along with Anderson, Hopkins, Wendel, Edward H. Dwight, and Charles H. Freeman.[12]

Expenses in Polling were extremely low compared to those in Munich. Models were available at the equivalent of five or ten cents per day and a "combined studio and sleeping arrangement could be had for three dollars per month," according to a newspaper account of 1883.[13] This was mostly due to the makeshift character of the artists' community that took over the unoccupied ruins of a walled monastery on the outskirts of the village. Donald Moffat, DeCamp's first biographer, lists one example of the artist's work during the Munich/Polling period, a portrait entitled *Cavalier*, which is now lost.

As the fall of 1879 approached, the Duveneck group headed back to Munich, but the highly structured Academy had lost its appeal. The artists may have been aware that an even more stringent course of study was to be instituted "by royal decree" the following year.[14] Duveneck had expressed his own disenchantment with the Bavarian city two years earlier in a letter to his friend John M. Donaldson: "Munich is very plead [*sic*] out in the way of art," he wrote. "No pictures [are] bought at all and I don't know but what I would do better to get out of Munich as soon as possible."[15] At the beginning of October 1879 he decided to move his school to Florence. He, Alexander, and Ritter went ahead of the others to rent a villa on the Poggio Imperiale and to make arrangements for the students who were to follow in November, among them Anderson, Freeman, Hopkins, Rolshoven, Wendel, Otto Bacher, Charles A. Corwin, Oliver D. Grover, Charles E. Mills, Albert Reinhart, Henry Rosenberg, Ross Turner, and DeCamp.[16] A description of the exodus appears in Josephine Duveneck's 1970 biography of her father-in-law: "A motley crew they were when they leaped forth from their fourth class railroad compartments at stations along the way [from Munich to Florence] in pursuit of beer and pretzels. . . . They were dressed in all manner of styles and costumes . . . some in frayed and faded corduroys, some in the latest fashion, others in no fashion ever seen before or since . . . such as a frock coat with tails, kneed breeches and tam-o-shanter or an

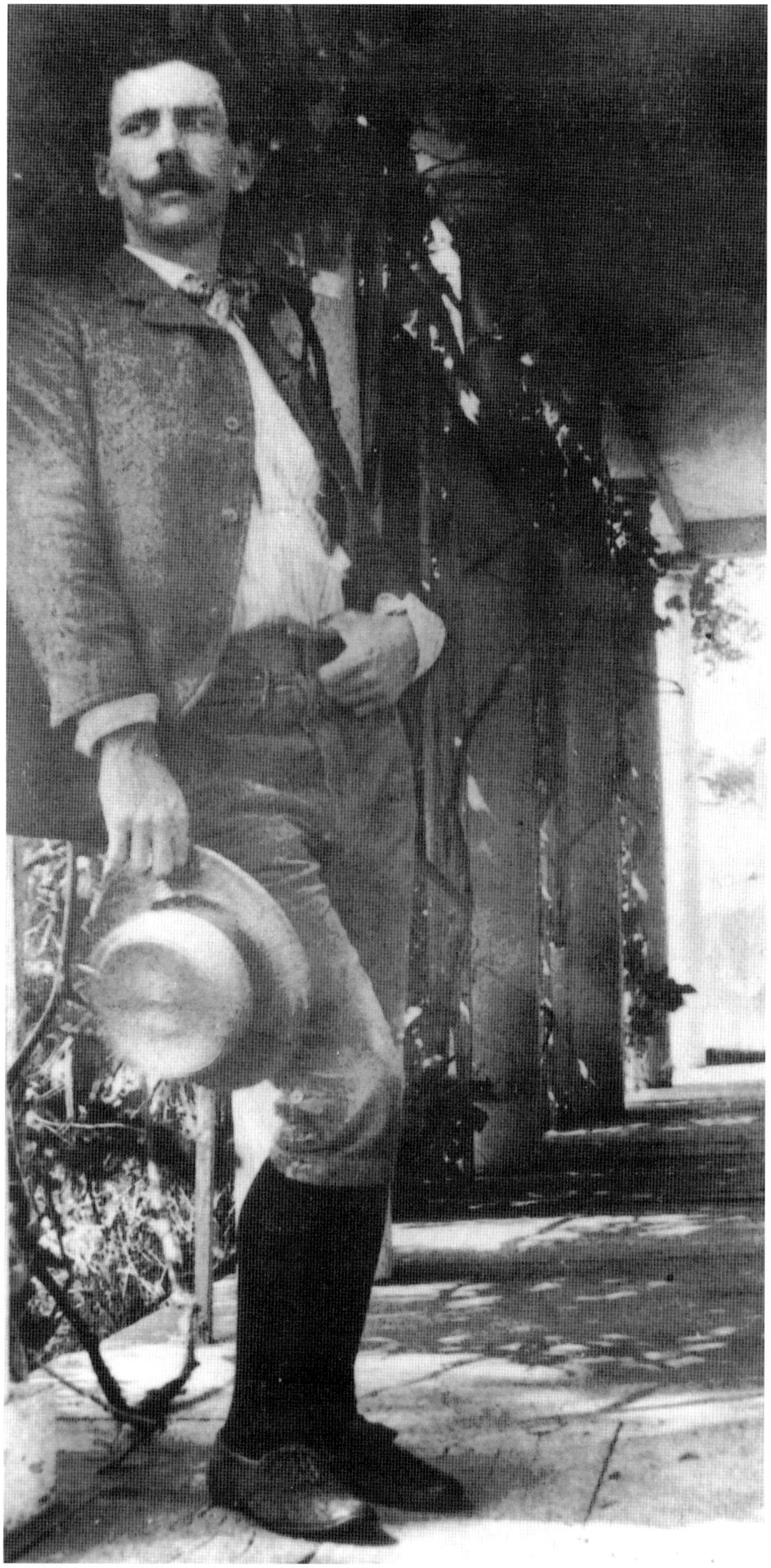

Fig. 2 The artist abroad, ca. 1880

ancient pea-jacket with silk hat worn jauntily on the side.... DeCamp carried a flute and Hopkins had a fiddle."[17] A photograph of DeCamp (fig. 2) gives an idea of his appearance at about this time.

Thanks to Duveneck's wealthy student and future wife Elizabeth Boott, whose well-connected family rented rooms in the Villa Castellani outside of Florence every year, the "boys" were privy not only to the rich cultural experience of the city, but also to a cosmopolitan world that included expatriate American patrons and artists, among them the sculptor Thomas Ball.

Mills wrote home in December 1879 that there were fifteen members in the group the first winter in Florence and so many more applicants that Duveneck could not accommodate everyone. A decision was then made that the number could only be "increased by unanimous vote or the request of the 'old man.'"[18] Two studios were arranged, one for ten students, the other for five. The less experienced group was dubbed the "Kindergarten," but, according to Rolshoven, the more "advanced fellows grew sick of prolonged picture painting and finally came to us [in the Kindergarten] where fresh impressions were done without concerns." Rolshoven remembered DeCamp as the "early bird," at work a good hour before the others: "Joe came to breakfast with an air of indifferent ease trying to make believe that painting is easy in the hands of talent."[19] Expenses were minimal. According to Mills, a "little more then one dollar per diem furnished meals, clothes, operas, theatre and artist materials." Yet the routine was intense. "We paint from models every day," he wrote, "the hours being from 8:30 to 12:00 and 1 to 4. Then we draw in the evening from 7 to 9. The Prof comes in to see us as often as he can, generally twice or three times a week.... When he has a day [he] will come and paint a half day or all day for us."[20]

As spring approached, the group headed to the Adriatic coast. By the end of April 1880 DeCamp, and probably most of the others, were in Venice, where they would spend the next two or three summers. Hopkins, Rosenberg, Wendel, and DeCamp occupied two rooms on the Fundamenta San Biagio in the east end. They were not far from the Riva degli Schiavoni, where the rest were staying—Duveneck at the Casa Kirsch, and Bacher, Twachtman, Robert Blum, and, later, James McNeill Whistler, at the Casa Janowitz.

In a letter to his brother Hiram in Cincinnati, DeCamp described his situation in Venice, including his deteriorating finances:

I have been here just a week and have been busy doing nothing.... You can imagine how it is yourself, going into a new place. Two or three days were occupied in find[ing] a room, and the rest of the time in staring about like a Hoosier. I have made a couple of color sketches just to keep my hand in, so to speak, but tomorrow the business will begin in earnest. Wendel, Hopkins, Rosenberg of Chicago, and I have two rooms on the Fundamento [*sic*] San Biagio, which is the west end [*sic*] of Venice and [which] open out on the harbour, with the island of San Giorgio just opposite and the famous palace of the Doges in full view from our west window. . . . We can see the whole harbour at a glance. We had expected to get rooms in the Pallazzo [*sic*] Ressonico [*sic*] [John Singer Sargent was there at the time], but they were too far from where we wished to work and were a little expensive. Some afternoon when I get time, I'll take a Guide Book and write you a description of Venice and its attractions. I could not do it now if I wished to, as I know little more about it, historically, than you do; and the only thing that interests me particularly is its picturesqueness. . . . I am expecting a letter daily and relying on your having gotten my letter telling you that I was in debt and needed clothes. The last money you sent me cleared me, but as I was fully a month behind . . . it could not last as long and I am needy again. I am rapidly getting seedy. . . . I made a calculation last night and find that the item of materials will be more than a third of my expenses this summer so that you may know that I'm not very extravagant in my way of living. To prove this, we get our own dinner at home. Although at first we used newspapers and such like to eat from, we now have each a plate which cost three cents, and Ed has an eight cent knife, the two edges of which are so nearly alike that, he says he only knows which side to cut with by the position of the handle.[21]

Hiram had been diligently sending money to his younger brother all along. Years later, he stated in a letter to DeCamp's widow that he was able to sell about twenty of the artist's European canvases in the Cincinnati area.[22] Two Venice scenes and an etching produced during this first visit are known, all demonstrating DeCamp's interest in the "picturesque" areas of the city as opposed to the more popular sites frequented by tourists. Both *Bridge in Venice* (fig. 3) and *Venetian Street* (private collection) retain the dark tonalities and thick impasto of the Munich style, which is applied to vignettes of the old city that focus on the buildings themselves and the play of light across their richly textured surfaces.

Another major influence on the American artists in Venice was Whistler, who had been working in the city since September 1879, trying to restore his finances after the empty victory of the Ruskin trial. He had been commissioned by the Fine Arts Society of London to do a series of etchings of Venice, many of which are views of inner niches of the city, similar to DeCamp's oils. The etching craze affected all the "boys," especially when Bacher became the proud owner of a printing press. One etching by DeCamp is known from the Venetian period, a Whistlerian view of an antique door and window, not unlike the impressions done at the time by Bacher, Hopkins, and others.[23]

A friendly encounter between Whistler and DeCamp, suggesting that the older artist was not pleased with DeCamp's treatment of outlines, was recalled by Gammell in his *Twilight of Painting* of 1946: "Joseph DeCamp told me that he, when a young student, once showed Whistler a painting representing the profile of an old woman. DeCamp had indicated the edge of this profile with a dark outline. Whistler turned to him with a snicker and asked, 'What did you put a shoestring around the old lady's face for? Did she have one there?'"[24]

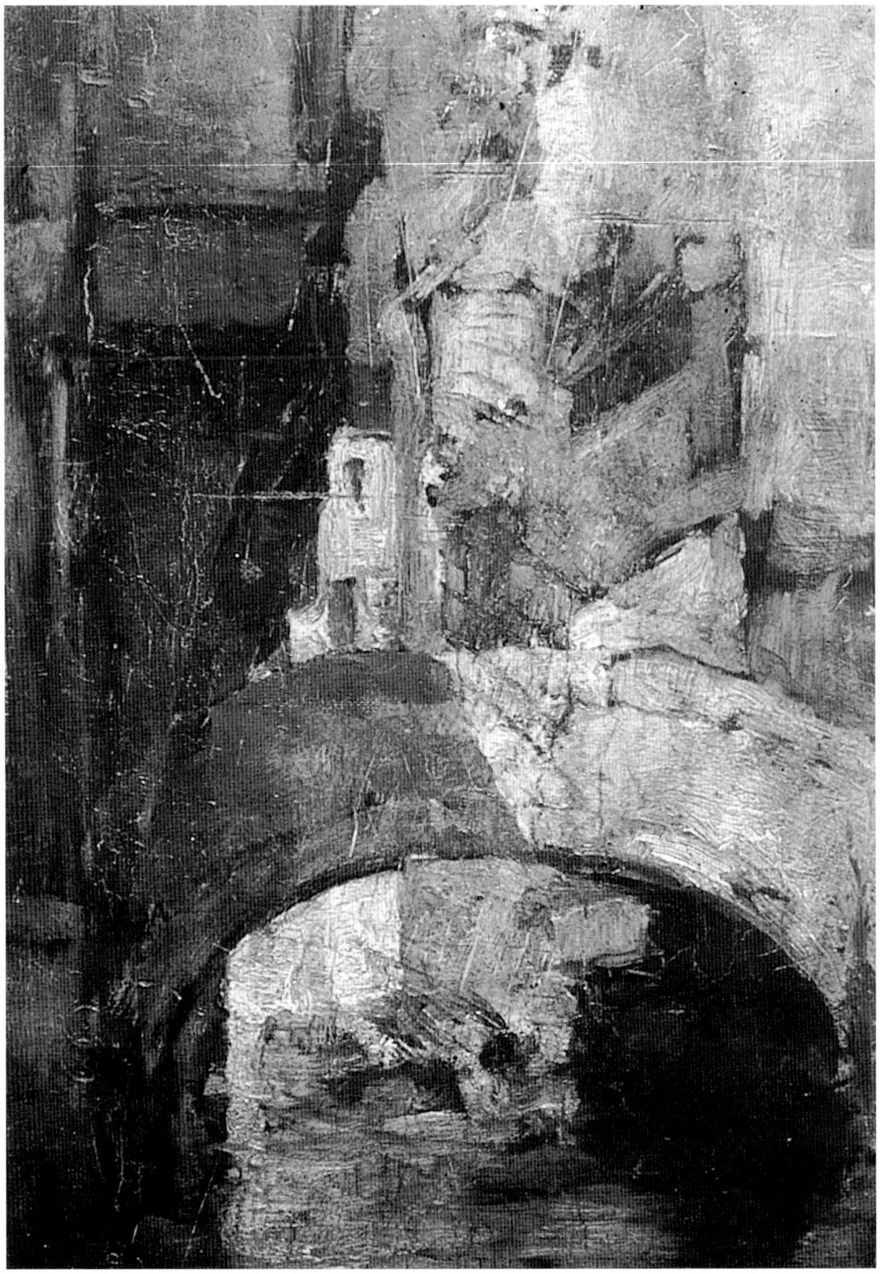

Fig. 3 *Bridge in Venice*, ca. 1879. Oil on panel, 15½ x 10¼ in. (39.5 x 26 cm). Private collection

Life in Venice had its carefree moments. The "boys" often rented gondolas for an evening frolic on the canals. Dinner was the best meal of the day, according to Bacher, because they would be joined by Duveneck and, frequently, Whistler. It was not unusual to spot other notables, including Robert Browning, George Eliot, Franz Liszt, Jean-Louis Meissonier, Richard Wagner, and Martin Rico, the last a Spanish artist whose genre scenes with backdrops of highly textured buildings and panoramic views of Venice influenced many of the Americans. As for DeCamp, he was "just 'Joe'"

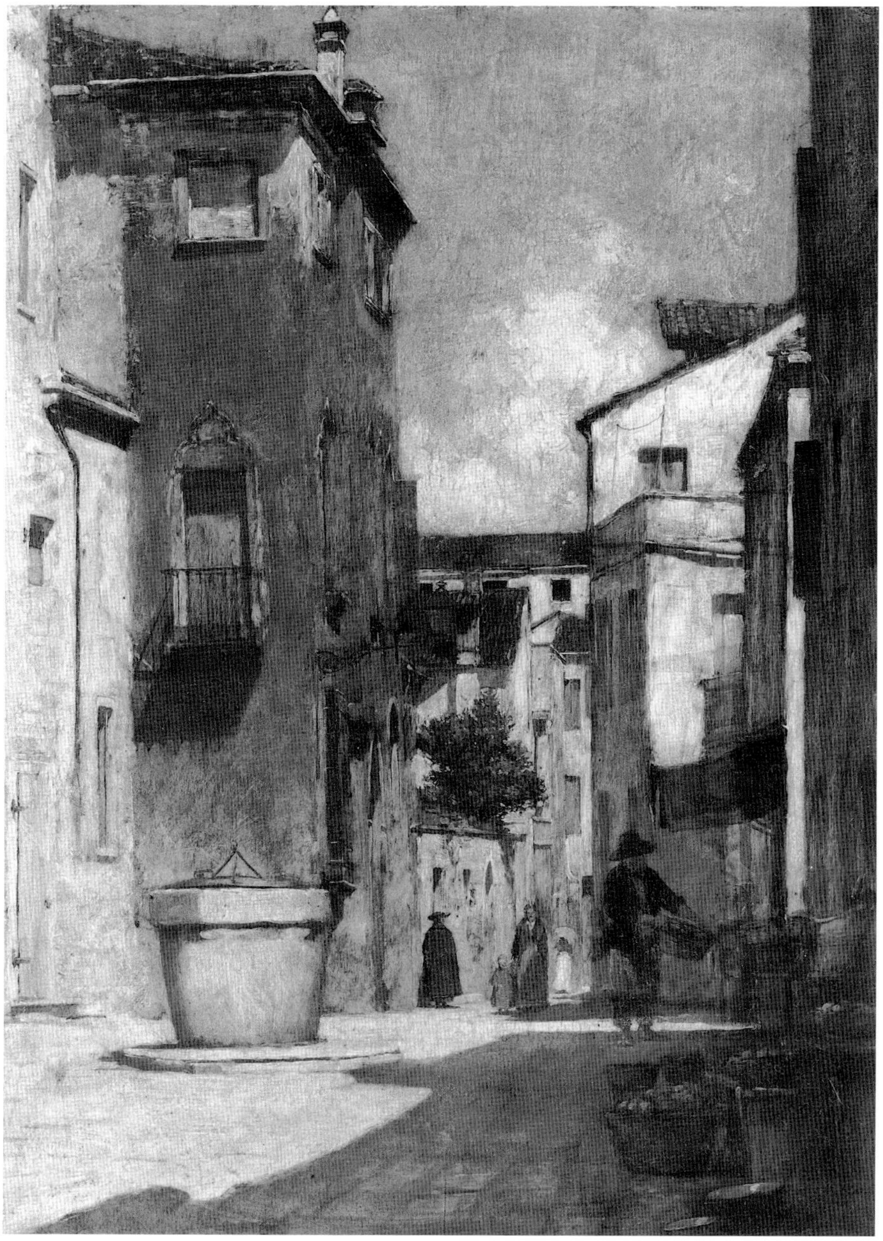

Fig. 4 *A Street Scene, in Venice,* 1881.
Oil on panel, 16⅛ x 11$\frac{1}{16}$ in. (41 x 28 cm). Cincinnati Art Museum, Bequest of Mrs. Hugh Smythe and Miss Rebecca Scarborough

and, according to Grover, "the breeziest, cheekiest, warmest hearted Bohemian in Venice. He was the pioneer, the discoverer of the company. Filled with curiosity, he investigated everything, learned everything. Full of life, energy and ambition he worked unceasingly and intelligently, and gave and took many a hard knock."[25]

In the autumn of 1880, the Duveneck group began to yearn for Florence and, in Rolshoven's words, "one by one and in groups, they packed their studies and were off to 'the city of flowers.'"[26] Their arrival did not go unnoticed, according to William Dean Howells, who thinly disguised the group as the Inglehart boys in his 1886 novel, *Indian Summer*: "They were here all last winter, and they've just got back. It's rather exciting for Florence.... They had their own school for a while in Munich, and then they all came down into Italy in a body. They had their studio things with them, and they travelled third class, and they made the greatest excitement everywhere, and had the greatest fun. They were a great sensation."[27] Later, again through his hero Colville, Howells describes a typical gathering of the boys at a *trattoria*: "Colville could recognize several of them in the vigorous burlesques on the walls.... They all talked at once, each man of his own interests, except when they joined in a shout of mockery and welcome for some new-comer. Colville... could hear what they thought, one and another, of Botticelli and Michelangelo; of old Piloty's things at Munich... of the overrated coloring of some of those Venetian fellows."[28]

This was probably the same *trattoria* later described by Harper Pennington, who joined the group in the summer of 1880 in Venice and followed its members to Florence:

> There was a little *trattoria* in the Via Guelfa where we ate, and drank the wine of our host's vineyard—with songs and laughter.... We had in a piano, appropriating a back room of the little restaurant to it and to ourselves. One of the boys played well... and another "beat the box".... We made a fake exhibition at Christmas, decorated our small dining-room fantastically, and let in the polite public, the American colony, and whoever was curious about us or our impromptu show. Little by little the whitewashed walls were covered by Duveneck himself with astonishingly clever caricatures of all the class and of the very few outsiders who were sometimes admitted to our board.[29]

For the "fake exhibition" mentioned by Pennington, the group issued a brochure, entitled "Academy Notes," compiled by "the Duveneck Boys for the Duveneck Boys about the Duveneck Boys," and dated December 25, 1880.[30] Rough caricatures of works by contemporary Europeans, Old Masters, and the Duveneck circle are included, few escaping the sarcastic commentaries of the editor J. Rushing (probably a pseudonym for one of the group's members). A drawing after a work by Frank Currier (no. 5697) was declared a "double-ended, back-action painting," one that the committee had difficulty knowing "which end ought to go uppermost," the result being that "on Tuesdays & Fridays" it was reversed.[31] Whistler was the butt of several jokes: "Mr. Whistler has again flung a pot of paint in the public's face!! In regard to this picture [no. 6835] critics are considered unnecessary evils." His *Gold Girl* (no. 1086) was subtitled *Come into the Garden Mud*, with the added comment, "This picture is beyond praise: Whistler says so himself."[32] Meissonier's *Charge of the Chillicothians* (no. 5878) was said to have been "purchased by Mr. Vanderbilt at some fabulous sum."[33] Rosenberg's *Apotheosis of Duyweneck [sic]—Saint & Martyr—surrounded by the inmates of his "hospital for incurables"* was "purchased by James Jackson Jarvis, but not paid for."[34] Manet's entry

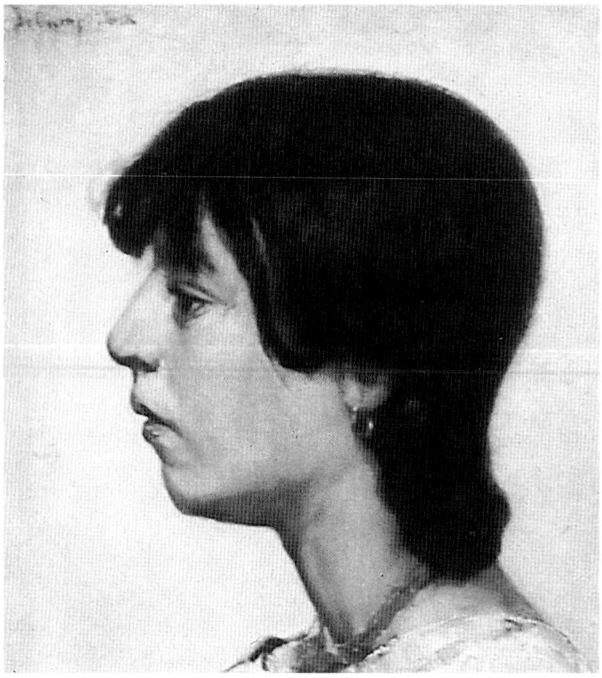

Fig. 5 *Head of a Young Woman,* 1881. Oil on panel, 9¼ x 8¼ in. (23.5 x 21 cm). Private collection

(no. 4.11.44) received the "grand Leather medal of Honor" for its "simple naivete [which] fascinates the most fastidious," but a Corot work (no. 6) received the greatest praise: "Before him we are mute."[35]

Despite an even greater round of activities during the second winter in Florence, and despite additional income from teaching a women's class, Duveneck decided to disband the school, declaring that it was "better for the students to go to some large place, such as Paris or Munich."[36] Mills, who would be with DeCamp later in Rome, stated in a letter of December 13, 1880, to his parents: "Beyond this winter there is no definite plan for the school as a number of the boys expect to return home to stay. Duveneck talks somewhat of going to Rome in which case we will go with him."[37] Duveneck did pay a brief visit to that city in late December 1880, but by the following February he had "reconsidered on Rome," according to Mills, and was planning to return to America in the fall.[38] Before his trip home, however, Duveneck spent some time in England. That DeCamp followed him could be inferred from a letter written years later by Mrs. DeCamp when she and her husband were visiting London in 1909. "We went to Chelsea," she states, "and saw Whistler's house, where Joe visited him."[39]

Tracing DeCamp's whereabouts after the dispersal of the group is difficult, but not impossible, since there are five dated paintings that locate him in Venice or Rome before his return to the United States in 1883. *A Street Scene, in Venice* (fig. 4) and *Venetian Courtyard* (unlocated) are both inscribed "'81." Two other oils, *Venetian Boatyard* and *Venice Canal Scene* (both private collection), probably belong to the same summer's work, given their similarity in approach and technique. Except for *Venetian Courtyard,* which is still almost claustrophobic in its selected view and extreme vertical format, the subjects are seen from relatively distant vantage points, offering spatially relieving foregrounds of water or pavement, with glimpses of blue skies at the top. These four pictures by DeCamp, while tonal and earthbound in their coloration, evince a more mature handling of paint and an increased awareness of compositional balance.

It seems probable that the artist spent the winter of 1881 in Rome, since his *Head of a Young Woman* (fig. 5) is inscribed "Rome Xmas '81." The work emulates the stark profiles of fifteenth-century Italian portraits and also reveals the influence of Duveneck's Italian style in its thin application of paint and crisp coloration (see fig. 6). DeCamp spent the summer of 1882 in Venice, judging by the inscribed date on *Venice* (plate 2), a

Fig. 6 Frank Duveneck, *Head of an Oriental Woman,* ca. 1880. 11⅝ x 7⅛ in. (29.5 x 18 cm). Cincinnati Art Museum, Gift of Harold W. Nichols

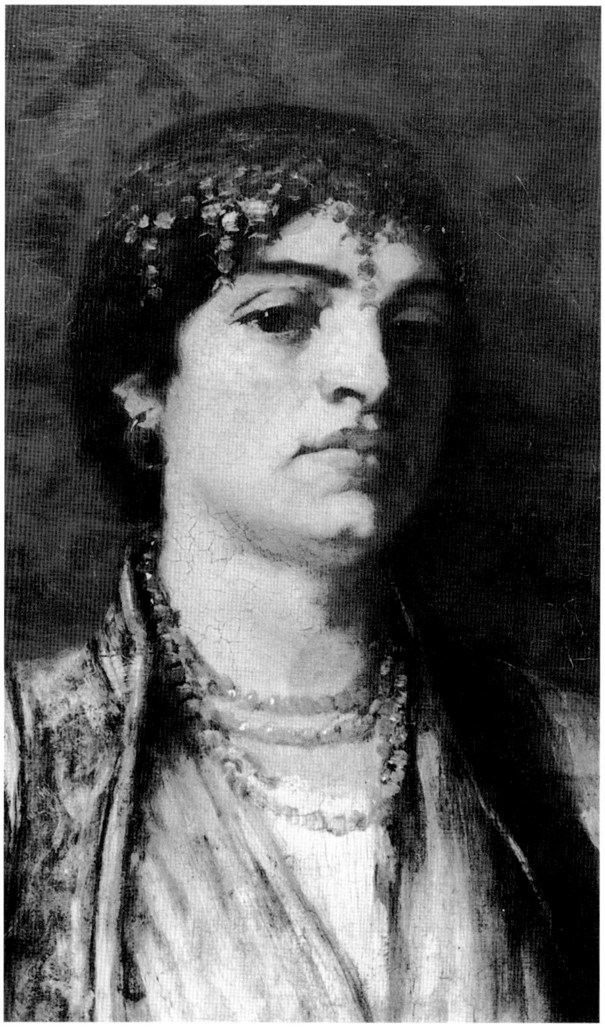

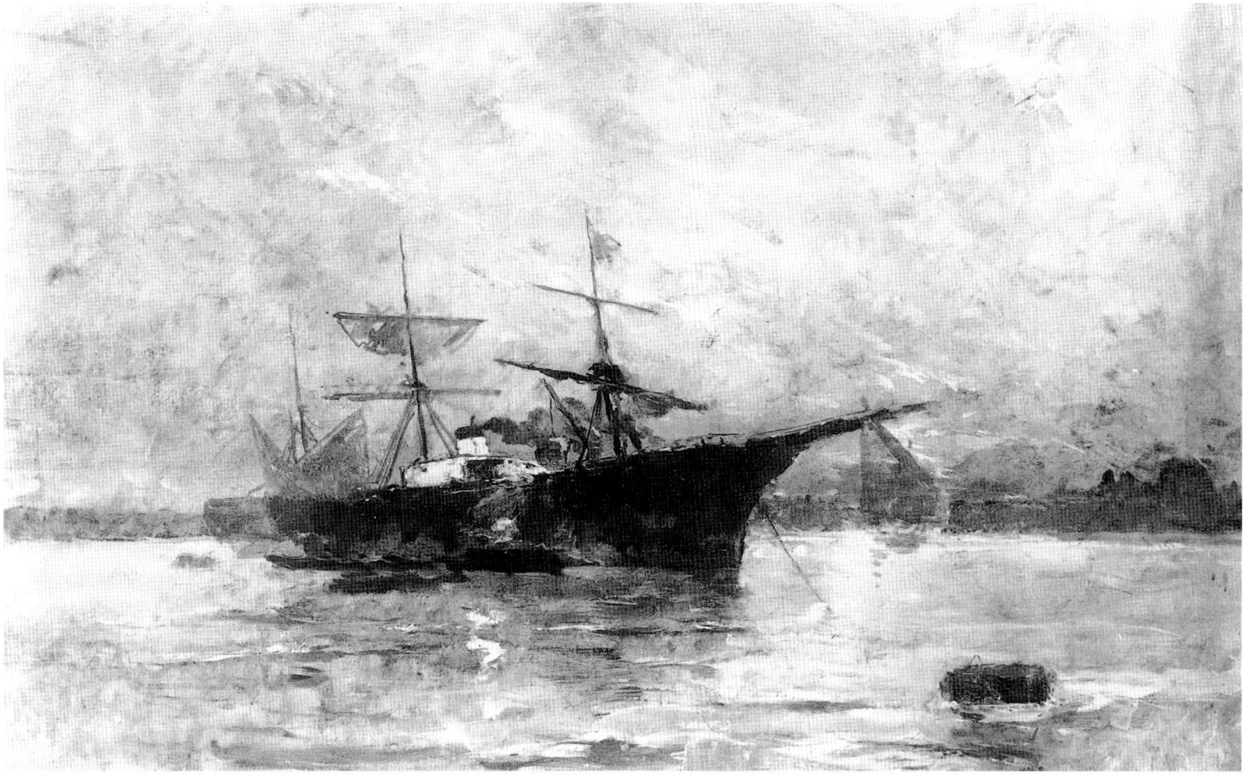

Fig. 7 Frank Duveneck, *Steamer at Anchor, Twilight, Venice*, ca. 1884. 42 x 66 ⅛ in. (106.5 x 168 cm). Cincinnati Art Museum, Gift of the artist

light-filled sunset view, ablaze with purple skies and red sailboats. The work brings to mind Duveneck's contemporary marines of Venice, with their rich hues and heavily impastoed skies reflected in large expanses of sparkling water (see fig. 7).[40]

The inscription "Roma, 1883" on the reverse of *Italian Girl* (fig. 8) would seem to indicate that, for the winter of 1882–83, DeCamp's choice was once again Rome. A highly accomplished profile view of a seated girl, the painting is the first of a number of delicate character studies of children in DeCamp's oeuvre. It reflects Duveneck's figural studies of Italian peasants of the same period.

By 1883 DeCamp had been away from his family for four and a half years. No doubt he was nearing the end of his limited resources and, faced with the scare of a Europe-wide cholera epidemic, he must have felt that the time had come to test his advanced artistic skills in his homeland. The two subjects that DeCamp explored while studying abroad—landscape and portraiture—would dominate his work for some time after his return to America. His Venetian experience with the etching medium would stand him in good stead in fostering his early teaching career.

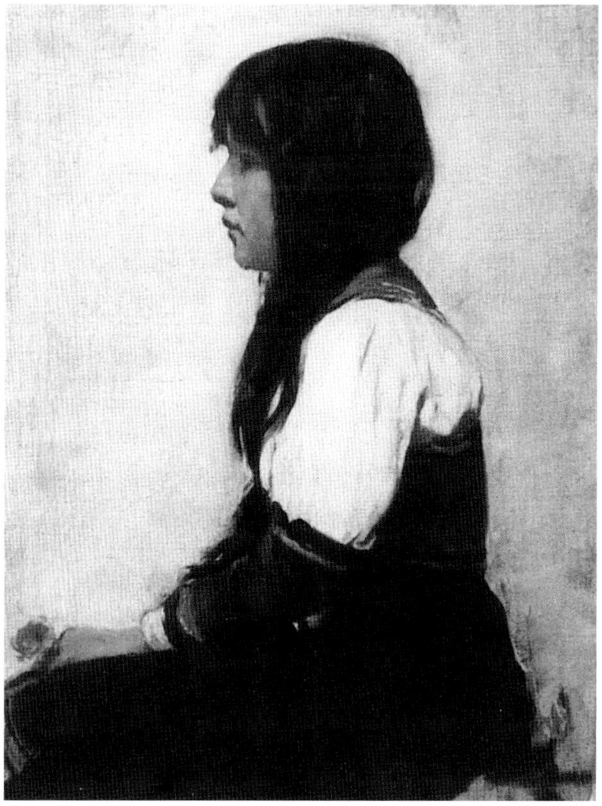

Fig. 8 *Italian Girl*, 1883.
Oil on panel, 13½ x 10½ in. (34.5 x 26.5 cm).
Mr. and Mrs. Thomas A. Rosse

Notes

1 "Matrikelbuch der Jahrgänge 1841–1884," Akademie der Bildenden Künste, Munich: No. 3602, Theodore Wendel, Washington [Ohio], (father) Protestant, (age) 21, Naturklasse, October 17, 1878; No. 3604, Joseph R. DeCamp, Cincinnati, (father) Protestant, (age) 20, Naturklasse, October 17,⅝ 1878; No. 3605, George E. Hopkins, Cincinnati, (father) Protestant, (age) 23, Naturklasse, October 17, 1878.

2 William Henry Fox, "Frank Currier's Place," Brooklyn Museum Quarterly 18 (January 1931), p. 2.

3 Karl Kappes to his parents, January 13, 1884; quoted in Randolph C. Downes, ed., "An American Art Student Abroad: Selections from the Letters of Karl Kappes, 1883–85," Northwest Ohio Quarterly 23 (Winter 1950–51), p. 30.

4 R. H. Ives Gammell, The Boston Painters: 1900–1930 (Orleans, Mass.: Parnassus Imprints, 1986), pp. 55–56.

5 William H. Gerdts, Louis Moeller, N. A.: A Victorian Man's World, exh. cat. (New York: Grand Central Art Galleries, 1984), p. 4.

6 Karl Kappes to his parents, November 26, 1883; quoted in Downes, "An American Art Student Abroad," p. 28.

7 Julius Rolshoven, "Autobiography," unpublished MS., p. 39; William H. Gerdts Art Reference Library, New York.

8 Joseph DeCamp to Hiram DeCamp, July 29, 1879; Joseph DeCamp scrapbook, family of the artist.

9 Rolshoven, "Autobiography," p. 39.

10 Royal Cortissoz, "The Field of Art," Scribner's Magazine 81 (February 1927), p. 222.

11 Rolshoven, "Autobiography," p. 68.

12 "Fremdenbuch," guesthouse, Polling, Germany. DeCamp and his friends registered on December 23, 1878, nos. 1044 through 1051. A facsimile of the guestbook (the original is in a private collection) is in the collection of the Heimatmuseum (local history museum), which is situated in one of the restored buildings of the former Holy Cross Monastery (founded 1010). The director of the museum, Dr. Hans-Joachim Büchler, has gathered many artifacts that remain from the guild workshops of the medieval period as well as the later artists' colonies. A school now occupies another of the monastery buildings; adjoining it is a cottage said to be the one in which Duveneck and his group worked, using the surfaces of the walls for their impromptu sketches. Artists and craftspeople are again living in the outbuildings of the monastery.

13 W. R. H., "Art," Spectator, December 8, 1883.

14 "Schools and Academies," American Art Review 1 (1880), pp. 134–35.

15 Frank Duveneck to John M. Donaldson, February 17, 1877; John M. Donaldson Papers, Archives of American Art, Smithsonian Institution, Washington, D.C.

16 Charles E. Mills, "Notes compiled by Charles E. Mills on the Duveneck students, 1879–1881"; Joseph DeCamp scrapbook, family of the artist. John Henry Twachtman was with the group, not as a student, but as an occasional substitute teacher for Duveneck.

17 Josephine Duveneck, Frank Duveneck: Painter and Teacher (San Francisco: John Howell Book Publishers, 1970), p. 75. A photograph of DeCamp (reproduced here as fig. 2) was probably taken in Florence.

18 Charles E. Mills to his father, December 13, 1879; Frank Duveneck Papers, Archives of American Art, Smithsonian Institution, Washington, D.C.

19 Rolshoven, "Autobiography," pp. 67–68.

20 Mills to his father, December 13, 1879 (see note 18).

21 Joseph DeCamp to Hiram DeCamp, April 25, 1880. I am most grateful to Dorothy Olson, Hiram DeCamp's granddaughter, for sending me a copy of this letter.

22 Hiram DeCamp to Edith (Mrs. Joseph) DeCamp, May 4, 1923; Joseph DeCamp scrapbook, family of the artist.

23 The etching, Doorway (1880), was owned by Frank Duveneck, who gave it to the Cincinnati Art Museum in 1913.

24 R. H. Ives Gammell, Twilight of Painting (New York: G. P. Putnam's Sons, 1946), p. 100.

25 Oliver Dennett Grover, "Duveneck and His School," typescript, lecture to Woodlawn, Cincinnati, Women's Club, January 18, 1915, p. 15; quoted in Norbert Heermann, Frank Duveneck (Boston: Houghton Mifflin & Co., 1918), p. 46.

26 Rolshoven, "Autobiography," p. 61.

27 William Dean Howells, Indian Summer (Boston: Ticknor & Co., 1886), p. 41.

28 Ibid., pp. 73–74.

29 Harper Pennington, "Artist Life in Venice," Century Magazine 69 (October 1902), p. 837.

30 J. Rushing, ed., "Academy Notes," unpublished exh. cat. (Florence, Italy: Duveneck School, 1880). I am grateful to Drs. Ben and A. Jess Shenson for sending me a copy of this catalogue.

31 Ibid., p. 2.

32 Ibid., p. 4.

33 Ibid., p. 15.

34 Ibid., p. 6.

35 Ibid., pp. 2, 14.

36 Frank Duveneck, quoted posthumously in "Resolutions Read in a Meeting Held in Memory of Frank Duveneck by His Students," unpublished pamphlet, 1919, p. 2; Cincinnati Museum Association, Cincinnati.

37 Charles E. Mills to his parents, December 13, 1880; quoted in Christine T. Evans, "Frank Duveneck: The Italian Years," M. A. thesis, University of Cincinnati, 1981, p. 64.

38 Charles E. Mills to his parents, February 13, 1881; quoted in Evans, "Frank Duveneck," p. 64.

39 Donald Moffat, "Joseph Rodefer DeCamp: Biographical Sketch," unpublished typescript, Frick Art Reference Library, New York, 1955–57, p. 22.

40 For a discussion of Duveneck's marines of the period, see Evans, "Frank Duveneck," pp. 86–88.

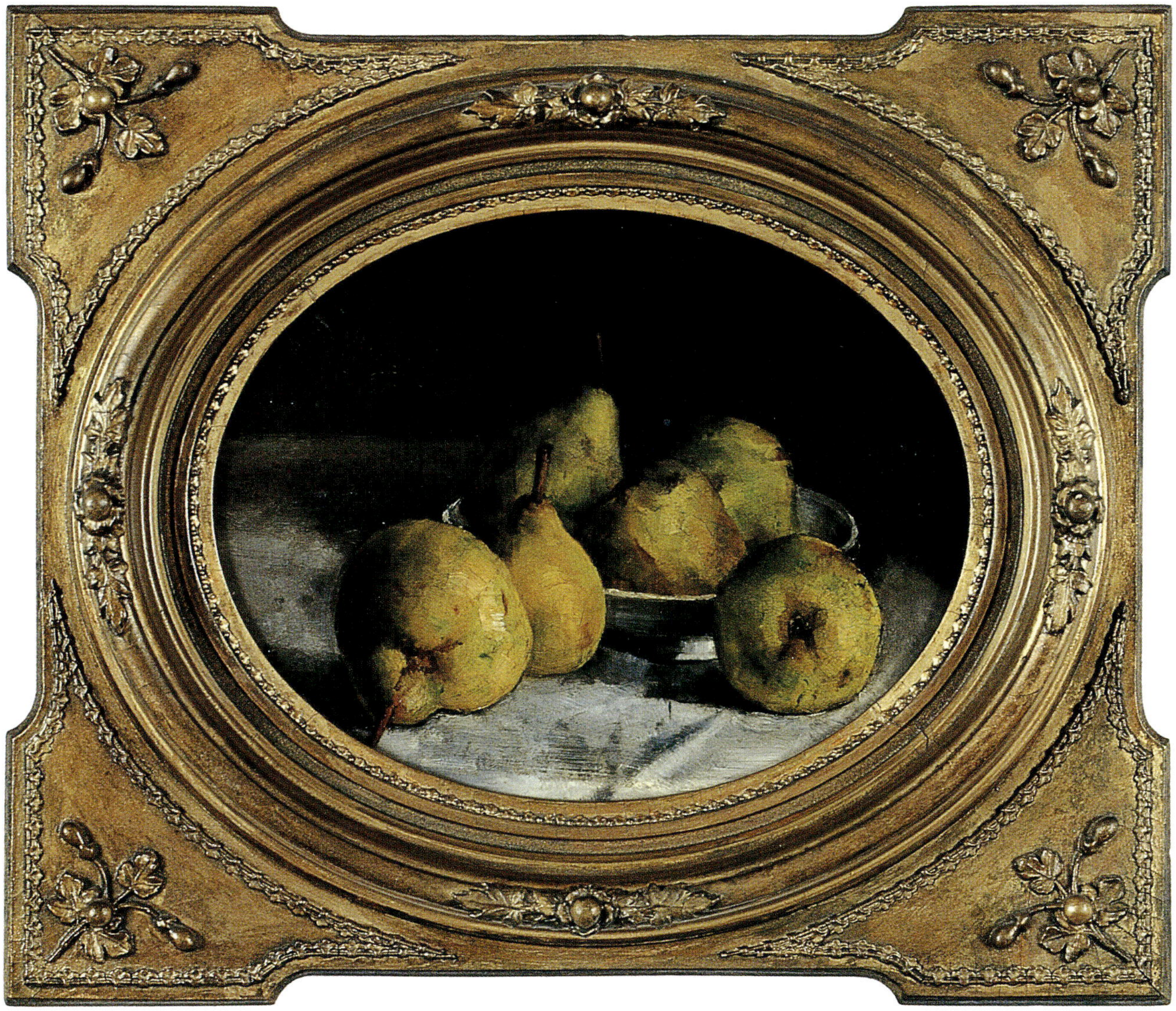

1 *Pears*, ca. 1877–78. Oil on panel, 8 x 9½ in. (20.5 x 24 cm). Jane DeCamp Stanton

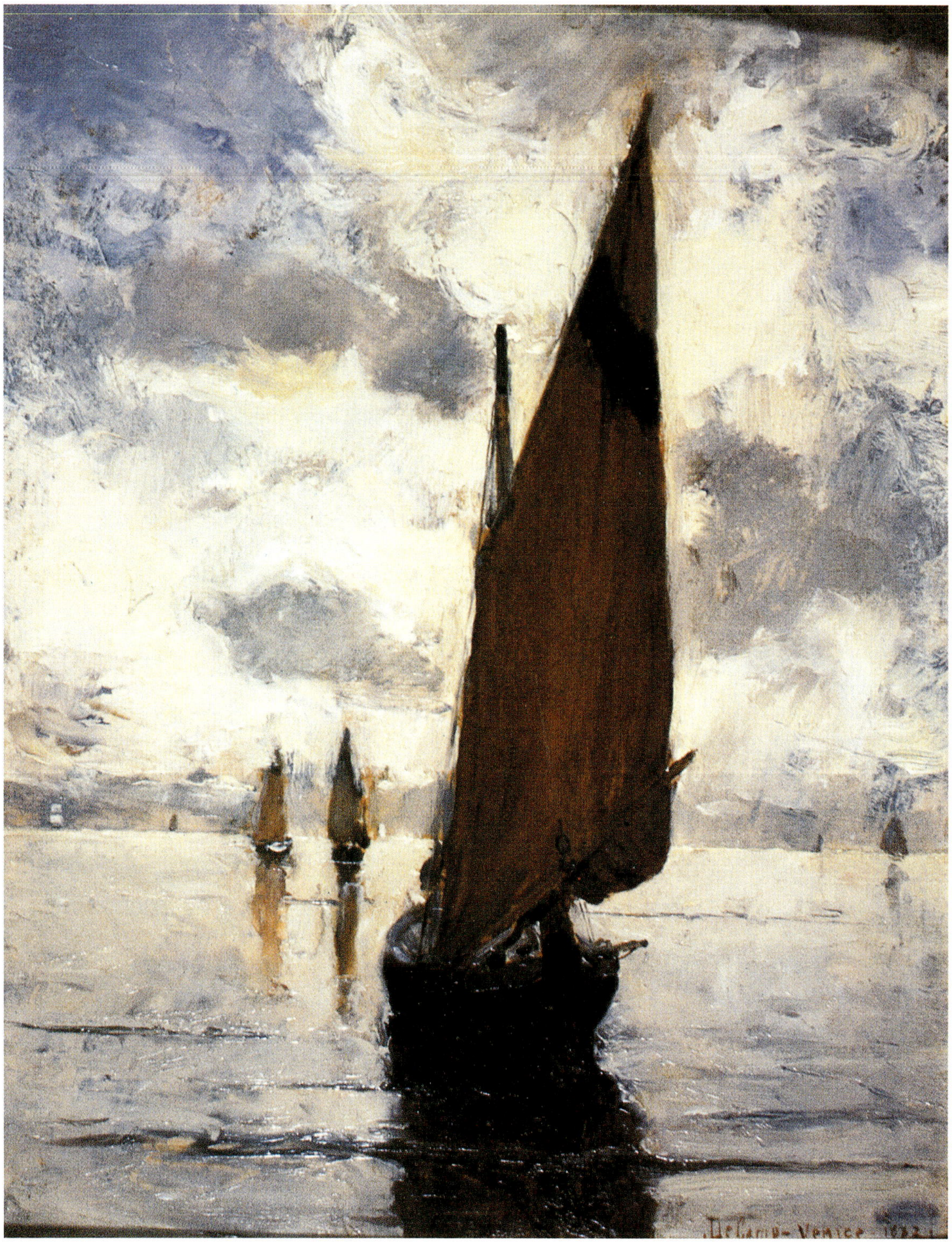

2 *Venice* (*Becalmed*), 1882. Oil on panel, 12¼ x 9⅜ in. (31 x 24 cm). Private collection

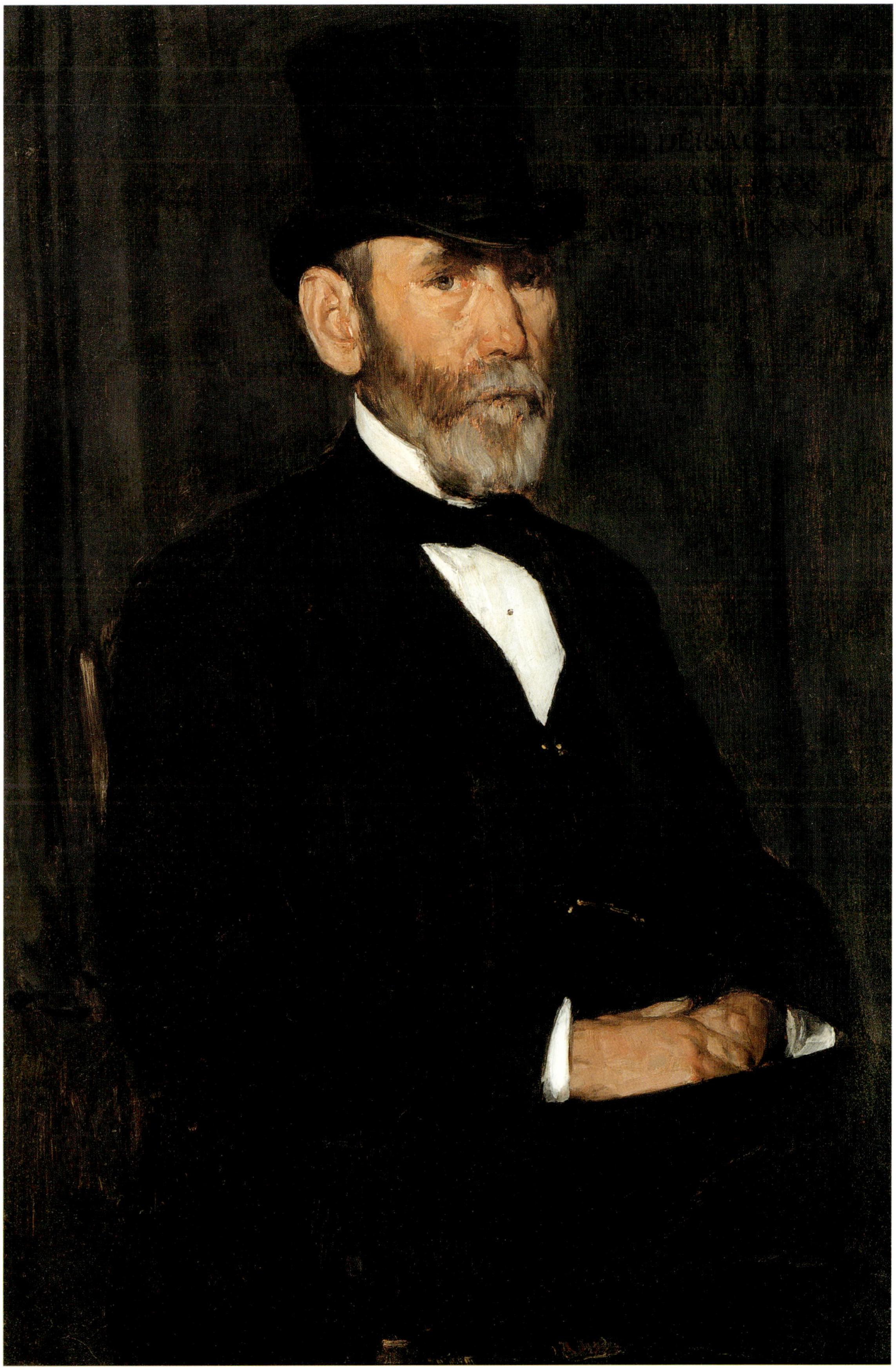

3 *Lambert DeCamp*, 1883. 19¾ x 12¼ in. (50 x 31 cm). Richard S. DeCamp

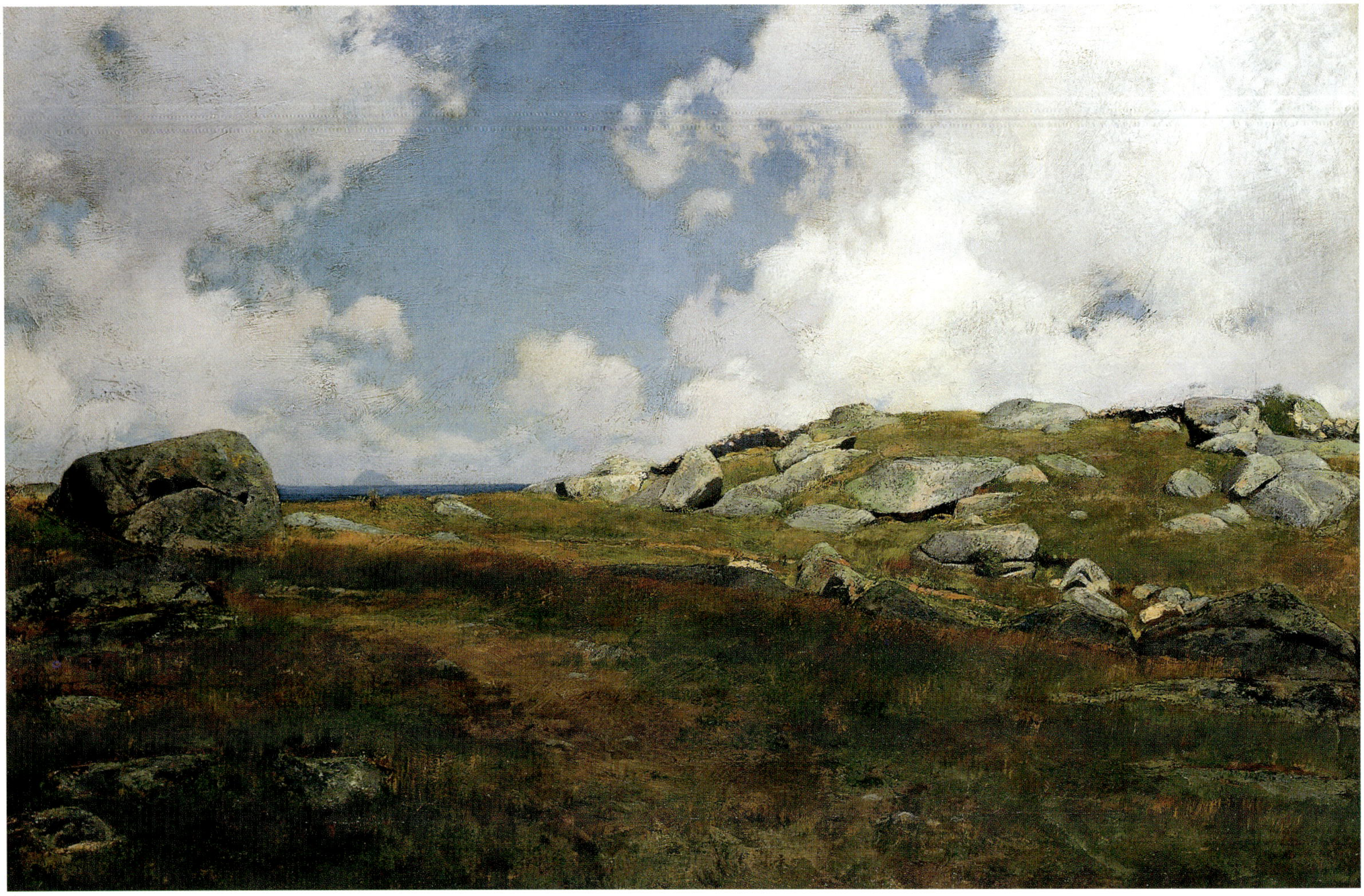

4 *A Murky Day*, 1886. 28 x 42 in. (71 x 106.5 cm). Mr. and Mrs. Thomas A. Rosse

Chapter Three

Return to Ohio, 1883–1884

Equipped with four and a half years of further training and a wealth of experience in painting the figure and landscape, the twenty-five-year-old DeCamp returned to America early in 1883. His parents were still living at 25 Wesley Avenue in Cincinnati. According to the city directory of 1883, which lists DeCamp as an artist, he was working at 65 Pike's Building, where many of the colleagues who had been with him recently in Europe also took studios: Kenyon Cox, George Hopkins, Louis Ritter, John Henry Twachtman, and Theodore Wendel.[1]

This group lost no time in assembling an exhibition of its work, which was held at Cincinnati's A. B. Closson Gallery during February. Asa Burton Closson, a native of New Hampshire, had opened a print shop in Cincinnati in 1866, specializing in prints of Civil War generals; even as late as 1883, his gallery was one of very few exhibition venues in the city.[2] The 1883 show, although not well patronized, was in general favorably reviewed by the local press. The *Commercial Gazette* applauded the enthusiasm of the newly formed group: "Twenty years ago, when the old Sketch Club was in existence, when Eastman Johnston [*sic*] and other famous artists dwelt in our midst, exhibitions were common, but fully a decade has passed by since a sufficient number of Cincinnati artists could be induced to combine in an undertaking of similar character.... Joseph DeCamp, George Hopkins, Louis Ritter, J. H. Twachtman and Theo. Wendel are part of a little itinerant colony, that wandered as far over as the lagoons of Venice, with Duveneck as their Nestor."[3]

Although the exhibition included recent Venetian work by Cox, DeCamp, Wendel, and Martha Twachtman, there were also still lifes by Ritter "painted in a manner which reminds one of Duveneck," according to a *Cincinnati Daily Enquirer* critic; portraits by Hopkins, among them "a head of an old woman in monochrome"; and other works that apparently still bore remnants of the Munich style in their painterliness and subdued hues.[4] Twachtman was mistakenly called a "confirmed impressionist" for his atmospheric, but still dark, winter views of nearby Avondale. The same critic recognized a new spirit in the work of this group, applauding their "audacity to see nature with their own eyes and not through Düsseldorf spectacles."[5] The vigorous technique and *plein air* approach used by these artists contrasted markedly with the work of an older generation of Cincinnatians, such as James H. Beard, Henry Mosler, John R. Tait, T. Worthington Whittredge, and Alexander Wyant, many of whom also were trained in Germany, but predominantly in Düsseldorf. At this time nearly all the major collections in Cincinnati included works of the Düsseldorf School.[6]

The brighter palette and looser technique employed by the Closson group must have appeared quite distinct also from the styles of the resident artists. Among these, Thomas Lindsay produced highly detailed, somber landscapes and animal studies reflecting his training in Düsseldorf; Charles T. Webber, although apparently self-taught, created sweet genre subjects and hand-tinted photographs in a similar manner; and Thomas Noble painted portraits in a dry style, also a reflection of Düsseldorf training, that continued to be practiced by his protégés, even though he had ventured to Munich for further training in 1881.[7]

Among the eighty works on view at Closson's were DeCamp's *Calle Stretto*, *After the Rain*, and *On the Lagoons* (all unlocated), which the *Commercial Gazette* critic characterized as proving the artist's "fondness for the gay colors and bright water of the city of the sea." "DeCamp is airy and light," he wrote. "He seems to have lingered lovingly about Venice."[8] The paintings in the Closson show must, therefore, have been similar in style and coloration to *Venice* (plate 2).

The exhibition also included a self-portrait of DeCamp at work in his studio (unlocated), said to be "treated with considerable freedom" by a reviewer for the *Cincinnati Daily Enquirer*, who described a portrait of the artist's father (plate 3) as being "painted with more attention to detail" than most of the other pictures in the show.[9] Given that DeCamp's other exhibits were light and airy landscapes, he apparently did not hesitate to show work done in two different styles. He would continue to do so in later life, exhibiting both highly modeled, often dark, portraits alongside lighter, more painterly figures in interiors.

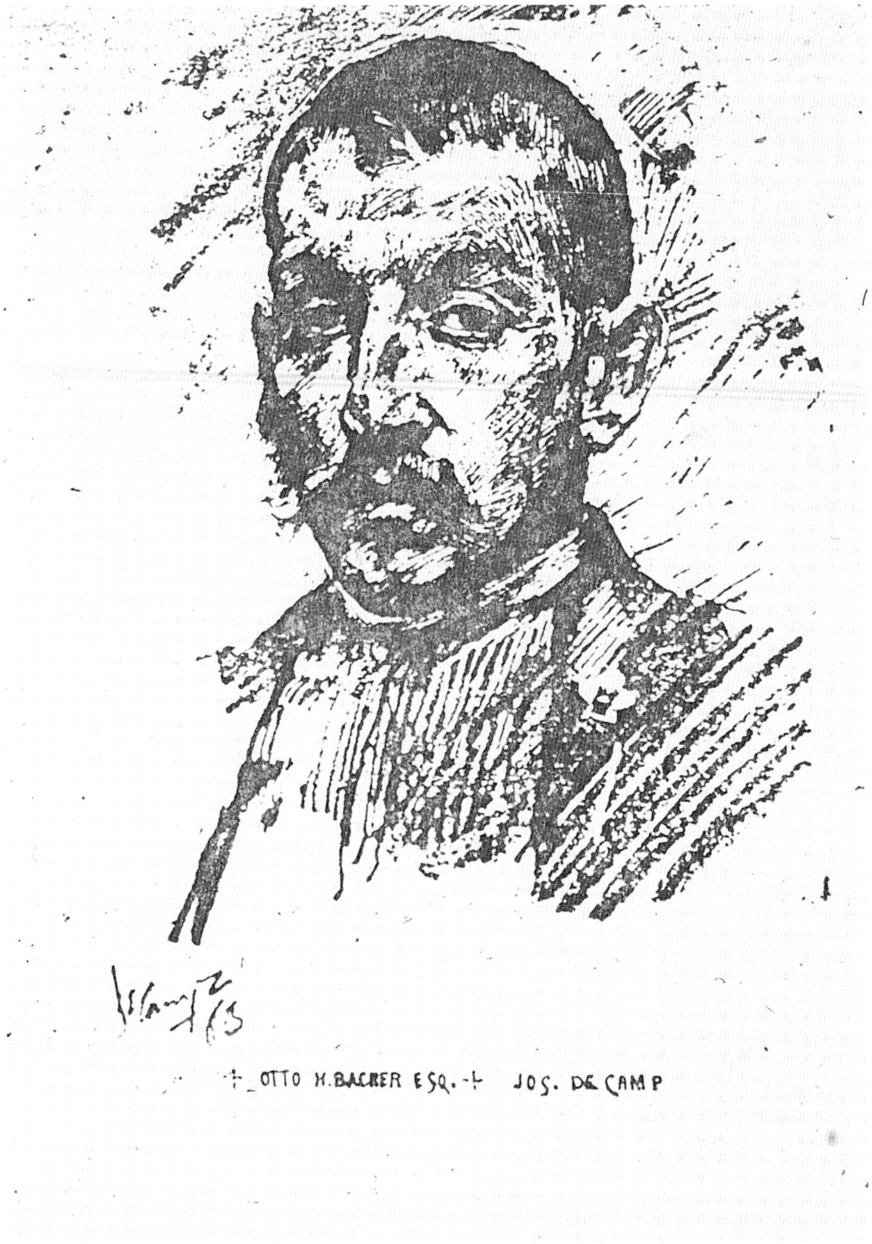

Fig. 9 *Otto Bacher*, 1883. From *Sketch Book* (April 1883), p. 38

DeCamp took great pains with the sensitive portrayal of his father displayed in the Closson exhibition, perhaps to impress a family not yet thoroughly convinced of his aptitude for an artistic career. The sixty-two-year-old Lambert, dressed in his best suit and top hat, is revealed as the stern family patriarch, posed against an equally severe backdrop. DeCamp's debt to the Munich style is still apparent in his use of dark tonalities and thick, impastoed pigment, especially in the flesh areas. The portrait also pays homage to realism in sparing no unsightly details'—for example, the sitter's disfigured left hand, the result of a construction accident. In large Roman letters at the upper right, the sitter is identified as a builder, despite his formal attire.

DeCamp showed the work again, at the eleventh Cincinnati Industrial Exposition in September 1883. A review of that exhibition mentioned the painting's subtle coloration, a demonstration of that tonal approach to developing a portrait which DeCamp was to pursue throughout his career: "A picture may contain nothing but gray, yet be a work of color, if the grays are distinguished among themselves, having their proper shadows and aerial distances, and may contain all the primary colors and have no color, if these have not their proper shadows and distances. Mr. DeCamp's portrait of his father, for instance, is painted in uniform gray tones, yet it is a work in color. It is also a strong bit of portraiture, thoroughly characterized, yet dignified."[10]

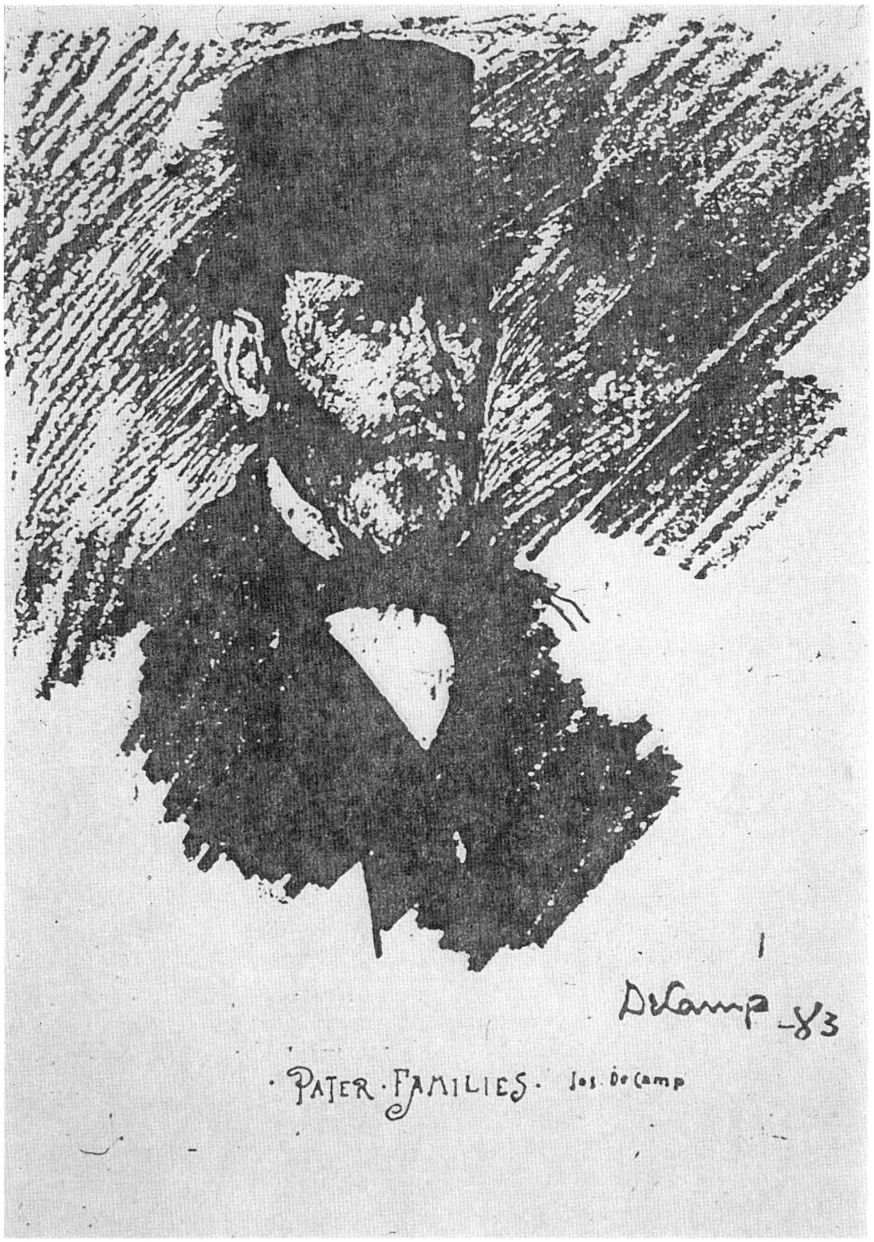

Fig. 10 *Pater Families*, 1883. From *Sketch Book* (May 1883), p. 60

Another family member whom DeCamp painted at this time was his maternal grandmother, Mary Garwood Mitchell (private collection). Grandmother Mitchell, described by Hiram DeCamp as a woman of "sturdy Pennsylvania German stock," dominates the space in which she is seated, yet her bulk contrasts markedly with the spare, spindly table at her side, as if to underscore the fragility of old age.[11]

DeCamp did not tarry long in Cincinnati, nor did his fellow exhibitors. The Twachtmans left for Paris, Cox went to New York, and Ritter and Wendel moved to Boston. Despite a few favorable reviews, the general public was not enthusiastic about the "new" art and certainly did not back it financially.[12] In April 1883 DeCamp was asked to teach at the recently opened Western Reserve School of Design for Women in Cleveland. He may have been recommended for the post by a fellow Duveneck "boy," Otto Bacher, who returned to his hometown of Cleveland at this time, but was already committed to another teaching assignment.

A reporter for the Cleveland *Plain Dealer* who visited the school a week after it was in session found a lively atmosphere:

In a large, well lighted room on the top floor of the City Hall building a forest of easels, arranged in such a manner that each of the young lady pupils—and there were some forty of them—has in full view the object from which perhaps half a dozen others may be drawing at the same time.... The reporter inspected the work being done by the students and was surprised at the advanced state of the sketches. Crayon

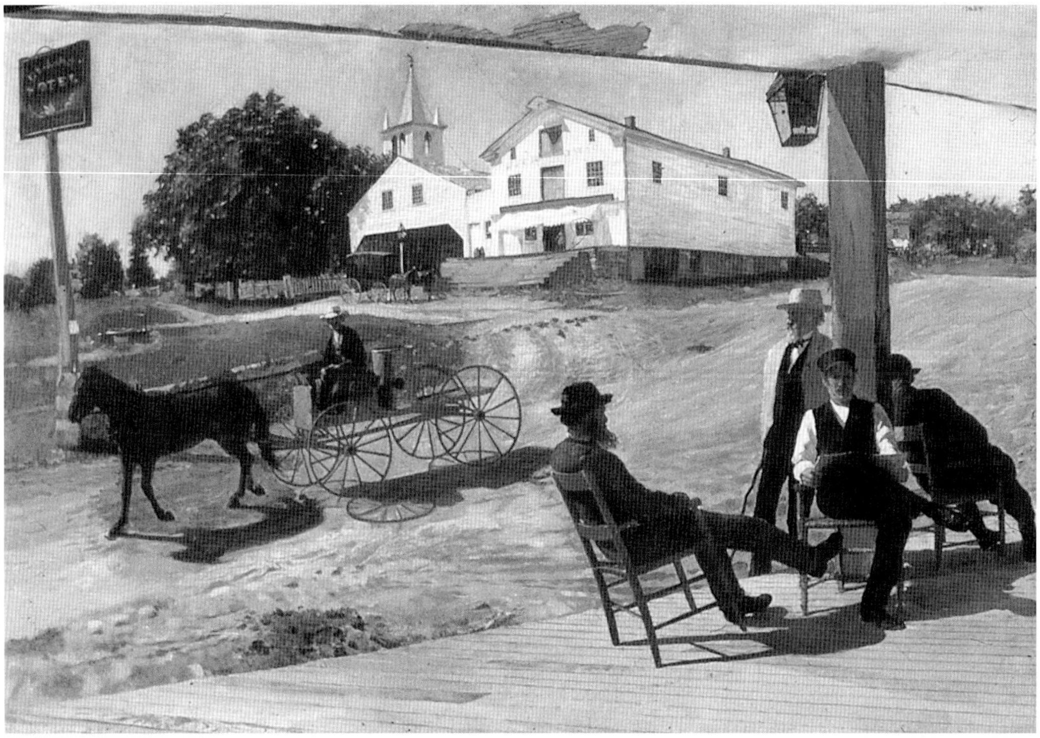

Fig. 11
Otto Bacher,
Ella's Hotel, Richfield Center, 1885.
31 x 42½ in.
(78.5 x 108 cm).
Private collection

drawing is not permitted and while a little more care is required at first to learn the handling of oil, it teaches the students the use of the brush and makes them familiar with mixing color, thus preparing them for after studies.[13]

DeCamp was obviously instilling in his students the methods he had learned in Munich, including sketching in oil rather than laboriously working out a composition in preliminary drawings. The seriousness with which the women were being taught professional painting techniques also sheds some light on DeCamp's attitude toward female students, regardless of the school's declared intent "to prepare [a] woman to do the work for which she is especially endowed by nature, found in the many departments of the industrial arts."[14]

The classrooms for the school shared the upper floor of the city hall with the Cleveland Academy of Art, which had been founded as the Old Bohemians in 1876 by the history and landscape painter Archibald Willard. From this coterie of artists, which included Bacher, Max Bohm, George L. Grossman, Herman and John Herkomer, and Adam Lehr, a sketch club was organized, complete with its own journal, *Sketch Book.* Its staff of artists included Bacher, DeCamp, Grossman, Willard, John W. Bell, Amelia Duerringer, DeScott Evans, George C. Groll, and R. Way Smith. A work by DeCamp—a portrait of Bacher (fig. 9)—first appeared in the journal in April 1883. Reproductions of *Pater Families* (*sic*; fig. 10), a sketch done after the artist's first painting of his father, and *"Misery"—Jack's heir,* a sketch of a dog, followed, in the May and June issues respectively.

Continuing their European experience in *plein air* work, Bacher and DeCamp, in July 1883, instituted a month-long sketching class in the scenic northern Ohio country near Richfield. The students were most likely women from their regular classes. One pupil recalled that amusing activities far outweighed "any honest to goodness sketching": "I can always see us rushing about the place in our huge Mother Hubbard painting aprons and scandalizing the natives. It must have given them a fine bit of gossip."[15] "Whether the sketching or the picnic feature of the movement predominates," one local reporter speculated, "is an open question which can only be determined on exhibition of sketch books upon the return of the class."[16] Bacher would soon produce his important *Ella's Hotel, Richfield Center* (private collection, fig. 11), a composition of well-modeled forms, especially in the figures, and architectural elements that is bathed in brilliant sunlight. According to Richard Love, Bacher's approach underwent a significant change from "broad, spontaneous execution" to a technique in which he applied "his pigment with smaller, more delicate, juxtaposed dashes of color."[17] With no paintings by DeCamp having survived from the month at Richfield, we can only speculate that his work at this time may have been done in a similar fashion.

In August 1883 the Sketch Club was invited to Chautauqua, New York, by the Cleveland Grays, a Civil War militia that by this time had become a social club. Located on scenic Lake Chautauqua, midway between Jamestown and Mayville, the Chautauqua Institute, which began in 1874 as a Methodist campground for

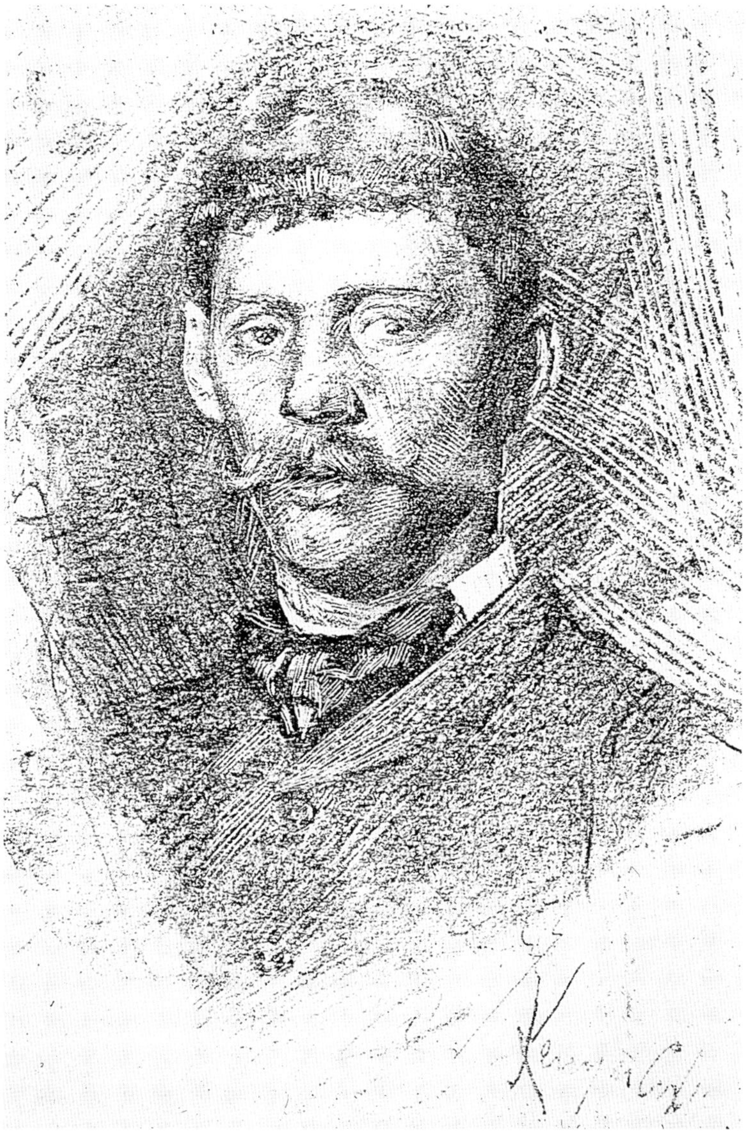

Fig. 12 Kenyon Cox, *Joseph DeCamp*, 1883. From *Sketch Book* (September 1883), p. 10

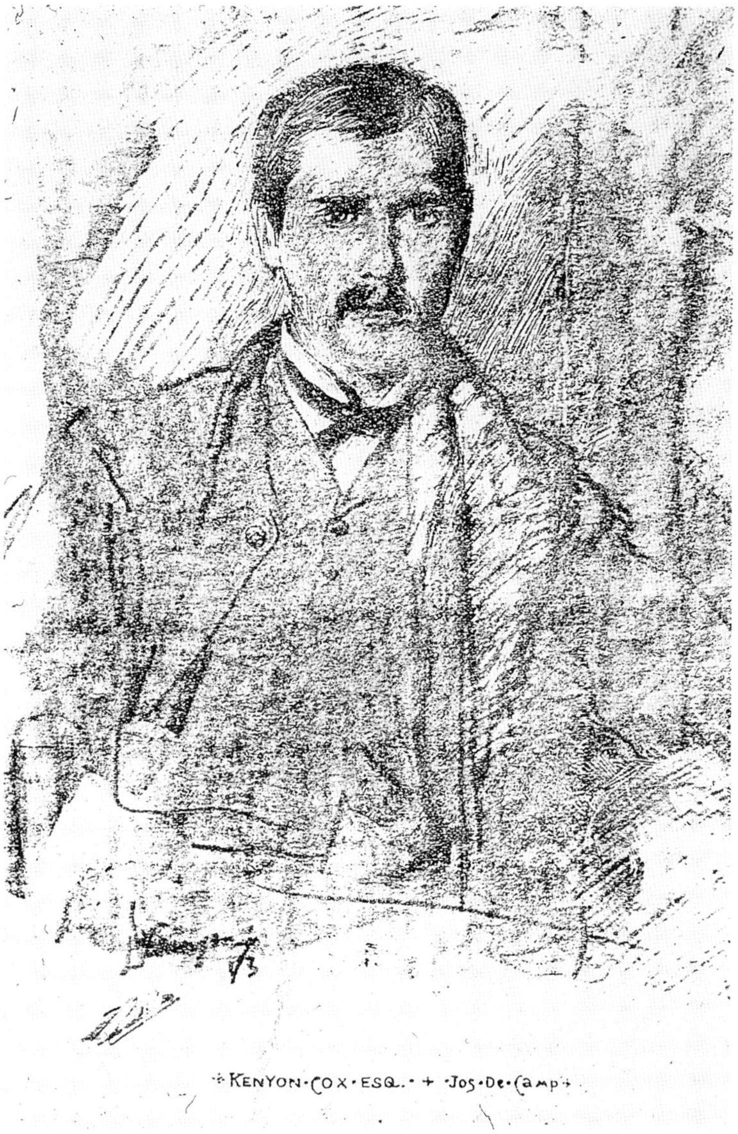

Fig. 13 *Kenyon Cox*, 1883. From *Sketch Book* (September 1883), p. 26

yearly revival meetings, had by 1883 reduced its religious focus to become a major center for cultural activities in America. The mix of hunting and sketching was not entirely successful, with Grossman narrowly escaping a bullet that lodged in his sketchbook![18] The Grays and the members of the Sketch Club were joined by the Canoe Club and the Oriental Commandery Knights Templar, whose camp was drawn by DeCamp and reproduced in the August issue of *Sketch Book*.

Earlier in the summer, DeCamp had returned briefly to Cincinnati to visit his family.[19] This may have been the occasion for the dual portrait sketches—one of DeCamp by Cox (fig. 12), and one of Cox by DeCamp (fig. 13)—that appeared in *Sketch Book* in September.

Before departing for Richfield in July, DeCamp had helped Bacher to assemble canvases and secure loans for the Cleveland Room of the Detroit Art Loan Exhibition, which was to be hung in August. That fall DeCamp apparently joined the faculty of the Cleveland Art Academy for the term running from September 1883 through June 1884. He taught portraiture, figure painting, landscape in oil, and drawing in black and white on Saturdays, and etching on Tuesdays.

Following a revival of original etching by artists associated with the Barbizon School in France—Charles Daubigny, Charles Jacque, Charles Meryon, Jean François Millet, and others—an etching movement had been started in America in the 1870s by Henry Farrer, Stephen Parrish, and James Smillie. This American revival received added vigor from Whistler's circle in Venice, which, as mentioned above, included Bacher and DeCamp. In 1883 Cleveland's Sion Wenban was beginning to establish himself in Munich as a major etcher and DeCamp's own skill in the medium was the subject of a lengthy *Sketch Book* commentary:

Joseph R. DeCamp, who has accepted the position of Instructor in Painting and Etching in the Academy, is a native of Cincinnati. He was for some years, previous to his coming to this city last summer, a pupil of Mr. Frank Duveneck in Venice and Florence. The Duveneck class has very justly come to be regarded by American students who go abroad as a most desirable one, and as Mr. DeCamp took high rank in the class, we are fully assured of his ability to direct so important a class. During his stay abroad Mr. DeCamp enjoyed a close intimacy with Mr. Whistler, the eccentric painter-etcher, and with Mr. Otto Bacher, both of whom are recognized as among the best living etchers; such intimacy couldn't but have its influence upon the work of a student so earnest as Mr. DeCamp, and in placing him in charge of the class in etching the student may be amply assured that the instruction received will be grounded upon the best principles of the beautiful art.[20]

Other instructors at the Cleveland Art Academy were Bell, Duerringer, Evans, Grossman, Lehr, George Bradley, C. M. Buxbaum, and Otto Ruetenik. Whether DeCamp fulfilled his Tuesday and Saturday schedule at the academy is questionable, as is suggested by two fragments of conflicting information printed in *Sketch Book*. In September 1883 it was announced that "Mr. Joseph DeCamp, having concluded to remain in the city during the winter, has organized a special class in Oil Painting, which will be in session daily, from 9 a.m. to 4 p.m., Mr. DeCamp being in attendance on Mond. Tues. Thurs. and Frid. This class, owing to lack of accommodations, is limited in numbers."[21] In the December issue it was noted that Bacher and DeCamp were about to open a joint class in drawing and painting.[22]

Despite these apparent demands for DeCamp's teaching skills, and despite Cleveland's tremendous growth during the artist's residence there, the opportunities for exhibiting his art, much less selling it, were meager, as they had been in Cincinnati. Not until 1894 was there a significant show of work by local artists. The *Sketch Book* issue of November 1883, in fact, had included a lengthy diatribe on Cleveland's lack of support for artists returning from Germany and France.

The next notice of DeCamp's whereabouts occurs in the Cleveland *Plain Dealer* of September 30, 1884, in which it was announced: "Mr. Joseph R. DeCamp, the well known and talented young artist, has been appointed teacher of painting at the Wellesley Female Academy in Boston, and will leave for The Hub on Saturday."[23] In November the same newspaper included a last mention of the artist, in its column "Rents Due the City": "Several debtors have 'vacated,' and the city is their creditor for the following sums: . . . J. DeCamp, $68.60."[24]

Notes

1 City directory, Cincinnati, Ohio, 1883. The following year, DeCamp's parents are listed in Winton Place and, in 1885, at the suburb of Hartwell.

2 I am grateful to A. B. Closson, Jr., the great-grandson of the original owner, for this information. See also Margaret Josten, "The Carriage Trade: Closson Family Caters to Art, Antique Buyers, for 126 Years," *Cincinnati Enquirer*, May 25, 1992, sect. D, pp. 1, 3.

3 "Art Exhibit," *Commercial Gazette*, February 6, 1883, p. 8.

4 "Cincinnati Art," *Cincinnati Daily Enquirer*, February 6, 1883, p. 8.

5 *Ibid.*

6 William S. Groesbeck, Nicholas Longworth, George K. Shoenberger, and Reuben R. Springer were just some of those who collected representative work by artists of the Düsseldorf School. For more information on Cincinnati collectors of the Golden Age, see Joseph E. Holliday, "Collectors' Choice of the Gilded Age," *Cincinnati Historical Society Bulletin* (Winter 1970), pp. 294–315.

7 For more information on the cultural life of Cincinnati at this time, see Bruce Weber, "Frank Duveneck and the Art Life of Cincinnati, 1865–1900," in *The Golden Age: Cincinnati Painters of the Nineteenth Century Represented in the Cincinnati Art Museum*, exh. cat. (Cincinnati: Cincinnati Art Museum, 1979).

8 "Art Exhibit," p. 8. With more accurate descriptions, these works could probably be identified among DeCamp's extant Venetian paintings. One other European picture, *S. Vio, Venice* (unlocated), was sent to the 1883 annual exhibition of the Society of American Artists, to be termed "sincere and delicate" by a Boston reviewer when the show traveled to that city ("Notes About the Art Museum Exhibition," *Boston Evening Transcript*, May 31, 1883, p. 6). DeCamp had entered the national exhibition arena earlier, with his *A Street Scene, in Venice* (fig. 4), which was accepted for an 1881 show, entitled "Special Exhibition of Paintings by American Artists at Home and in Europe," at the Pennsylvania Academy of the Fine Arts, Philadelphia.

9 "Cincinnati Art," p. 8.

10 "The Cincinnati Exposition," *Sketch Book*, no. 9 (September 1883), p. 110. A year earlier, while still in Europe, DeCamp had produced a small portrait of his father facing in the opposite direction. This must have been executed after a photograph, a practice that the artist continued sporadically in later years.

11 Hiram DeCamp, "Lydia Garwood DeCamp," *Cincinnati Daily Enquirer*, April 8, 1902, p. 7.

12 Weber, "Frank Duveneck," p. 27.

13 "Western Reserve School of Design," *Plain Dealer*, April 27, 1883, p. 4.

14 Nancy Coe Wixom, *Cleveland Institute of Art: The First Hundred Years, 1882–1982* (Cleveland: Cleveland Institute of Art, 1983), p. 14. The 1880s was a particularly intense period in the promotion of women's education. In Cleveland alone the number of women graduating from high school was double that of men.

15 Letter from an unidentified pupil to Mary H. Bacher, January 5, 1938; quoted in William H. Andrew, *Otto H. Bacher* (Madison, Wisc.: Education Industries, 1973), unpaginated.

16 Unidentified newspaper, July 1883; quoted in Andrew, *Otto H. Bacher*, unpaginated.

17 Richard Love, *Otto Bacher, 1856–1909*, exh. cat. (Chicago: R. H. Love Galleries, 1991), p. 6.

18 "Camp Notes," *Sketch Book*, no. 8 (August 1883), p. 98.

19 Unidentified newspaper, June 1883; cited in Andrew, *Otto H. Bacher*, unpaginated.

20 "Personal," *Sketch Book*, no. 6 (June 1883), p. 78.

21 "Personal," *Sketch Book*, no. 9 (September 1883), p. 111.

22 "Volume I—Finis," *Sketch Book*, no. 12 (December 1883), p. 145.

23 "Personal and Society," *Plain Dealer*, September 30, 1884, p. 4. I am indebted to Mary Sayre Haverstock for drawing my attention to information contained in *Plain Dealer*.

24 "Rents Due the City," *Plain Dealer*, November 6, 1884, p. 8.

CHAPTER FOUR

Boston Beckons, 1884–1890

DeCamp will scarcely have expected to spend the rest of his days in Boston when he arrived in the city in 1884. Yet in no time at all he was able to establish a reputation as a superb technician, a significant teacher, and a painter of landscape, the subject that Bostonians favored long before they acquired a penchant for figurative art.

The prevailing image of Boston during the Gilded Age, between 1873 and 1893, used to be that the city had suffered a cultural paralysis after the golden era represented, at mid-century, by the presence of such literary geniuses as Ralph Waldo Emerson, Nathaniel Hawthorne, and Henry David Thoreau.[1] Recent studies, however, have explored the extraordinary richness of the later period, with its technological growth, educational and feminist reforms, and assimilation of vast numbers of immigrants.[2]

If the literary output fell short of the peak reached at mid-century, advances in the other arts more than made up for this shortcoming. The artistic circles of Boston that DeCamp encountered in 1884 had been revitalized after the Civil War, mostly through the efforts of the influential painter William Morris Hunt. Just as Washington Allston had established a taste for a figurative and historical tradition based on European ideals, so Hunt promoted the Old Masters and the French Barbizon painters.

A popular lecturer on the arts, Hunt first "discovered" for Boston the work of George Inness, John LaFarge, and Elihu Vedder, as well as the Munich style of Frank Duveneck, seen at a show of the Cincinnatian's work at the Boston Art Club in 1875. Duveneck's resounding success laid the foundation for the city's understanding and appreciation of the Munich style. Paintings such as the *The Whistling Boy* (1872; Cincinnati Art Museum), *Circassian Soldier* (1870; Museum of Fine Arts, Boston), *Lady with a Fan* (1873; Metropolitan Museum of Art, New York), and *The Old School Master* (1871; Museum of Fine Arts, Boston) were hailed by critic Henry James as works of "vigor, frankness and comprehensive simplicity" by "an unsuspected man of genius."[3]

The knowledge of Duveneck's enthusiastic reception in Boston must have been comforting to DeCamp, but the main attraction of the city to him was probably the security offered by a job as instructor of drawing from the Antique and painting from life at Wellesley College. Since none of the names associated with the school, including those of his fellow instructors, Ida Bothe, Agnes Hastings, John B. Johnston, and Alice Mills, is familiar from DeCamp's earlier history, it would seem that the recommendation for the position came from another source. Harley Perkins, in his 1924 memorial piece on DeCamp, posited that the artist went to Boston "possibly at the request of Ross Turner or some of the other [Duveneck] 'boys' who had preceded him."[4] Turner had settled in Boston in 1882 and was already firmly entrenched in the city's artistic circles, teaching classes in watercolor at his studio and at the Massachusetts Institute of Technology. Another of the "boys" who had moved to Boston was Charles E. Mills, with whom DeCamp had spent the last months of his European sojourn and who was now living in Dedham, a short distance from Wellesley. DeCamp stayed with Mills and Mills's sister at least from the fall of 1884 through the spring of 1886.[5]

The five-year curriculum at the women's college was quite advanced for its time and was strongly oriented toward the arts, especially music. In the School of Art two years were devoted to the study of form and light and shadow before the student could move on to painting and color studies. There were specific goals for each year, as spelled out in the calendars for the season of 1884–85: "First Year—Form (drawing from objects and casts, design, geometrical drawing, lectures on perspective); Second Year—Light and Shade (drawing and shading from objects, models and casts, perspective, artistic anatomy, lecture on Egyptian and Greek Art); Third Year—Color (drawing from casts [head], historic ornament, painting from still life, lectures on Italian art); Fourth Year—Color (drawing from casts [head, figure], painting from still life and life model, lectures on German, French and English art); Fifth Year (drawing and painting from life models, compositions and style)."[6] It is not surprising that, with the abundance of courses in art history, Wellesley was the first college in America to award a degree in that field.[7]

Midstream in his tenure at Wellesley, DeCamp returned briefly to the Midwest, in November 1885, to attend a family reunion in Hartwell, the Cincinnati suburb where his parents were then living. It may have been during this visit that he painted his brothers Arthur and Hiram, as well as a small self-portrait (all private collection). From this early Boston period there also survive a study of a youth in a fur cap (1884, unlocated) and one of Mills, dated 1885 (fig. 14). All these works exhibit the typical dark tonalities, rapid execution, and thick impastoes that were so much a part of DeCamp's Munich portrait style, but they also capture the essential features of his sitters, a characteristic of all his later work in the genre.

In the fall of 1885 DeCamp took on the additional responsibility of teaching at the prestigious School of Drawing and Painting at the Museum of Fine Arts in Boston. Founded in 1876, the school offered one of the city's very few courses of study for artists, the others being the Drawing School of the Lowell Institute, the Boston Atheneum, with its collection of casts, the Cowles Art Institute, and the State Normal Art School, where art teachers in public schools were trained and where DeCamp would later be a faculty member. His fellow instructors at the Museum School included Otto Grundmann, a German painter of solidly modeled portraits and interior genre scenes; Robert Vonnoh, who, trained at the Académie Julian in Paris, taught the painting course; Lilian Greene, DeCamp's assistant; Dr. Edward Waldo Emerson, who taught anatomy; and Ernest Wadsworth Longfellow, a painter and son of the poet.

As the head instructor of the school, Grundmann set its standards, which were surely the result of his own years of academic training in Antwerp, Paris, and Düsseldorf. The curriculum centered around the portrait and the human figure, especially the nude, but also placed great emphasis on developing a student's skills before he or she was permitted to progress to painting in color.[8] DeCamp was hired as the first instructor to supervise a large, mixed group of students whose common trait was that they were not yet ready for admission to the life class taught by Grundmann. According to the annual report of 1885, there were "beginners of various degrees... and those who after showing, or acquiring in the school, some skill in the simpler work of the course, are studying from the antiques in the galleries of the museum as a last preparation for the life class."[9] Bernice Leader, in her 1980 dissertation "The Boston Lady as a Work of Art," explains the grueling procedure in drawing from the casts: With each new medium, the student was first asked to master the rendering of separate parts of the body before working from the full-length statue, then to return to the individual parts for the next medium, and so on.[10]

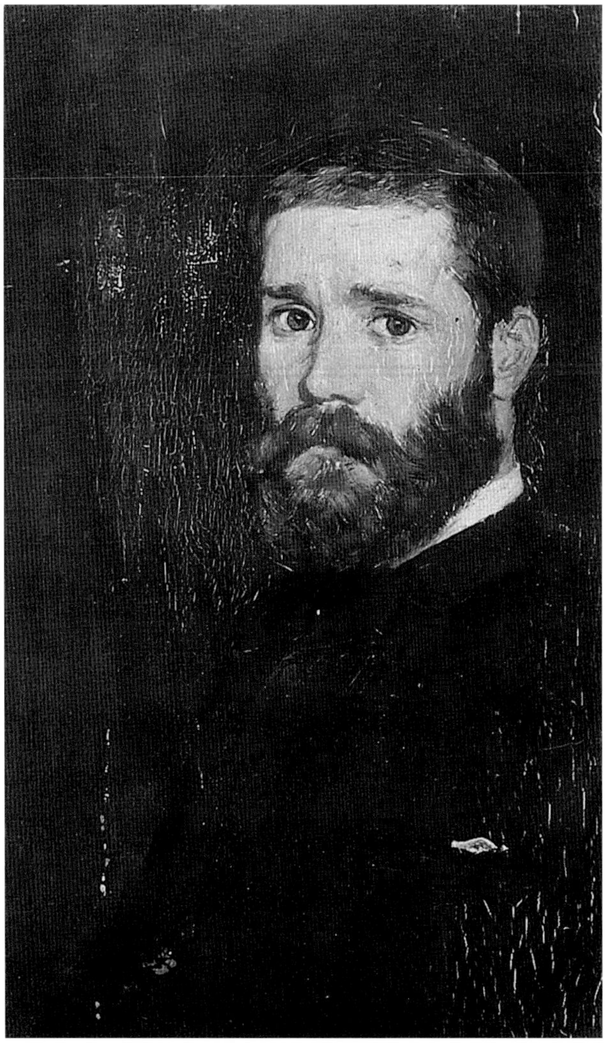

Fig. 14 *Charles Mills*, 1885.
Oil on panel, 16½ x 9¼ in. (42 x 23.5 cm). Unlocated

This conservative approach was clearly at odds with DeCamp's method of teaching at Wellesley. That he felt cramped by the Museum School's approach is suggested by a statement of his that appeared in the annual report of 1886: "The object of the system of instruction has been mainly to train the pupil's sense of action and proportion, and to make the department a place of study rather than, as is too often the case, a mere manufactory of drawings."[11] H. Winthrop Peirce, in his 1930 reminiscence *The History of the School of the Museum of Fine Arts, Boston*, remembered DeCamp as a man of "rough and ready frankness [and] independence of... character" who displayed "indifference to formal convention."[12]

In spite of the pressures of teaching both at Wellesley and at the Museum School, DeCamp did manage to exhibit his work during this period. Three portraits, "a life-size picture of a middle-aged gentleman" and two "small half-lengths," were shown at Boston's Chase Gallery, according to the *Boston Morning Journal* of

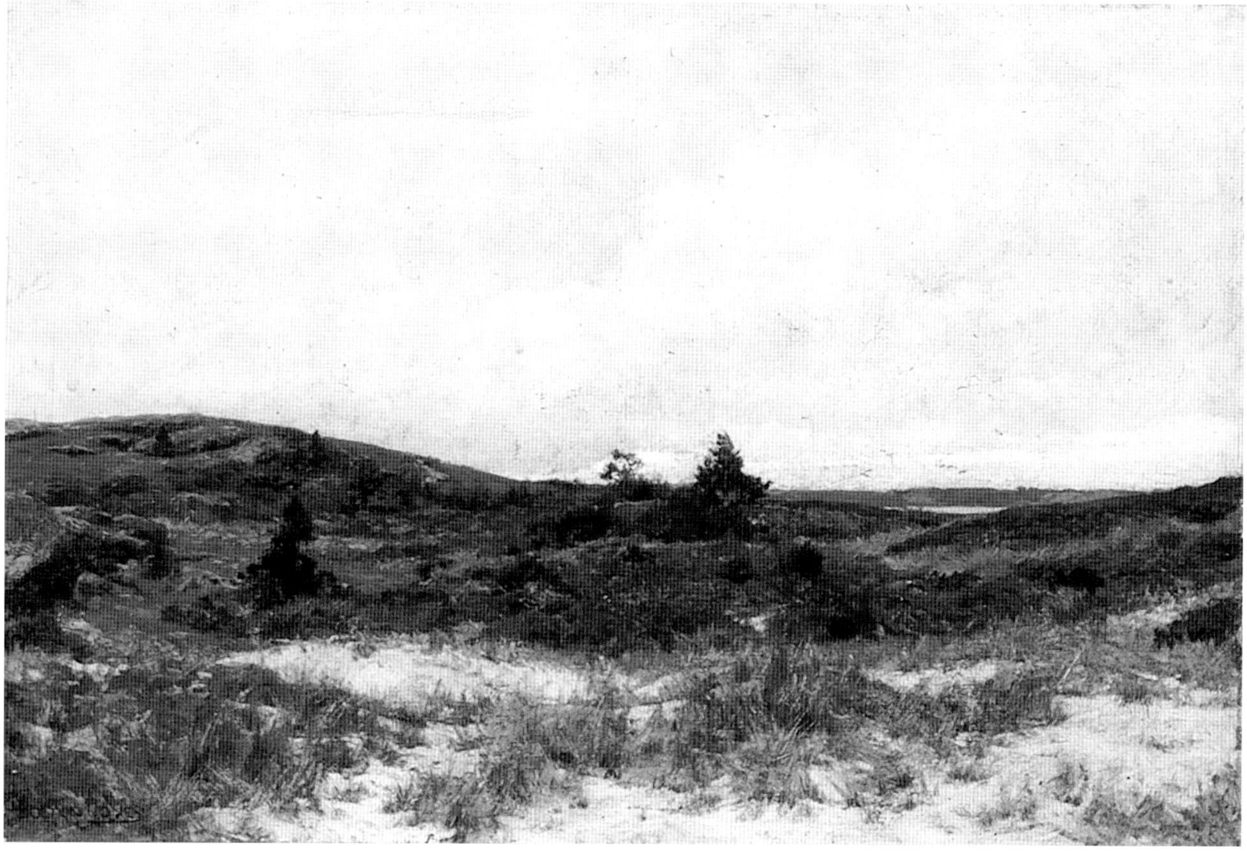

Fig. 15 Hugh Bolton Jones, *The Dunes*, ca. 1885. 22 x 32¼ in. (56 x 82 cm). Memorial Art Gallery of the University of Rochester, New York, Gift of Mr. and Mrs. Hollister Spencer

February 13, 1885. The reviewer bemoaned the fact that the portraits were "none of them what we might expect from a draughtsman of Mr. DeCamp's ability" and called the colors "hard and cold,"[13] indicating that what was anticipated of the artist was the freer, Munich style. Since its inception in the 1870s, the Chase Gallery had been primarily known for its promotion of European art, but it also showed the work of Winslow Homer and other contemporary Americans. As early as 1886, J. Eastman Chase, the gallery's owner, displayed the paintings of John Henry Twachtman, and, by the 1890s, Chase's would be one of the leading galleries in Boston for Impressionism. (DeCamp's later portrait of Chase [ca. 1900, unlocated] documents his friendship with the dealer.) It was at the Chase Gallery in 1891 that the figural work of Frank W. Benson and Edmund C. Tarbell began to be reviewed together, later leading to the appellation "Tarbellites" for these two artists and their close associates, who included DeCamp.

One of DeCamp's entries in the 1885 Chase exhibition may have been a portrait of Edward C. Cabot (unlocated), the architect of the Boston Atheneum, a watercolorist, and the chairman of the Permanent Committee of the Museum School during DeCamp's tenure there. The portrait was also shown at the Fifth Annual Exhibition of Contemporary American Art, held at the Museum of Fine Arts in May 1885, and perhaps it was the same reviewer for the *Boston Morning Journal* who called it "hard and cold in color and inexcusably disagreeable in its presentation of the subject." "An artist," he claimed, "should certainly possess sufficient cleverness to overcome by an arrangement of light, or a choosing of position, or an introduction of accessories, those characteristics which tend to caricature."[14] It would be a few more years before DeCamp would again submit his formal portraits to the exhibition circuit—and to critical review.

At this time DeCamp returned to landscape as a subject, especially in 1886, after he had spent the first of many summers at Annisquam on the Massachusetts coast, near Gloucester. No doubt he had seen, at the Williams & Everett Galleries in Boston and in other exhibitions in the city, the work of a group of artists who had established a summer colony at the village—most notably, William Lamb Picknell, Hugh Bolton Jones, and his brother Francis Coates Jones, all of whom were veterans of an earlier gathering of Americans at Pont-Aven in Brittany. Their *plein air* landscapes, rich in color, celebrate the bright and sunny days at "'Squam," as the village was called, but also the misty, gray tones of the nearby low-lying marshes and dunes. These paintings owe much to William Morris

Hunt, whose tonal landscapes of the 1870s, executed at nearby Magnolia, became the standard for landscape interpretations of the area for some time to come.[15]

DeCamp's first depictions of 'Squam landscapes indicate that he knew the work of Picknell and Jones quite well. *A Murky Day* of 1886 (plate 4), in its elemental rendering of rocky earth and cloud-filled sky, recalls the thickly painted surfaces of Picknell's canvases, in which light is concentrated in certain areas, rather than dissolved, as in Impressionism. Compositionally, the painting bears a strong resemblance to Jones's *The Dunes* (fig. 15), recently acquired by the Memorial Art Gallery, Rochester, New York. Indeed, both landscapes are probably views of Halibut Point, a stretch of barren land at the northernmost point of Cape Ann, just north of Annisquam, where local artists still go to view the open sea at its most dramatic moments, especially during a nor'easter.[16]

Fig. 16 *St. John the Baptist*, 1886.
13½ x 11½ in. (34.5 x 29 cm). James L. DeCamp

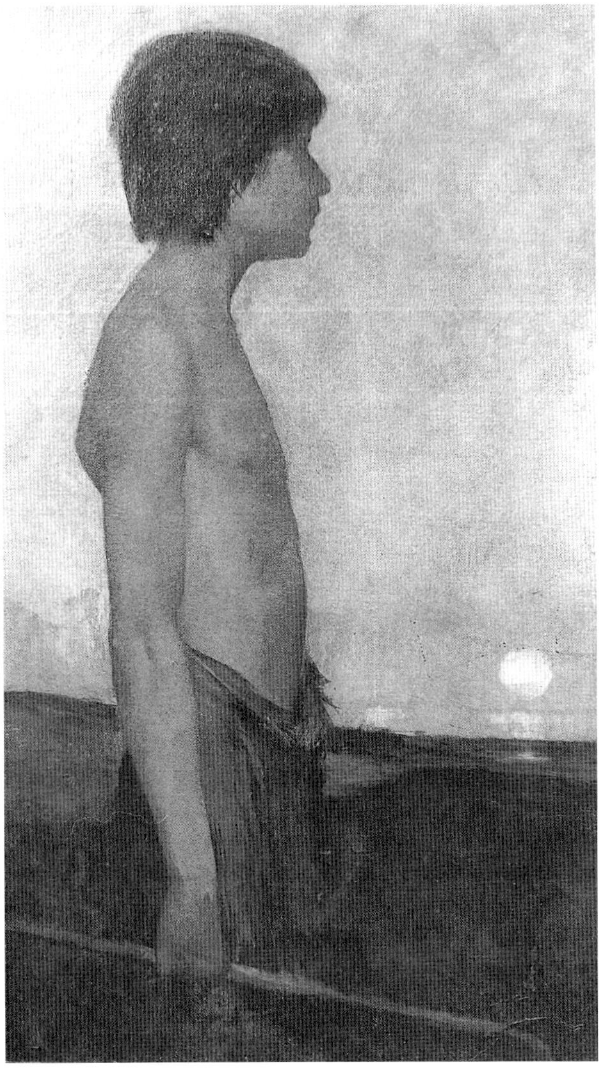

A Murky Day was DeCamp's first entry in a National Academy of Design annual, that of 1888, and a companion picture executed at the same time, *Moorland-Cape Ann* (probably identical with the present fig. 17), was shown at the exhibition of the rival organization in New York, the Society of American Artists, of which DeCamp had just been elected a member. *A Murky Day* was described by one critic as "a strongly painted effect of sunlight on rocky ground near the sea-coast, which is exceedingly realistic, but is without much quality of color."[17] At the end of May *Moorland-Cape Ann* traveled to the first annual to be held at the Art Institute of Chicago and, in September, to the Ohio Centennial Exposition in Columbus.

The year he painted *A Murky Day* DeCamp was boarding at One St. James Avenue, according to the Boston city directory of 1886, and was maintaining an atelier at 110 Chauncy Street.[18] He took into his studio one of the hundreds of immigrant children roaming the streets, a bootblack named Joe Cavagnaro, who assisted him in his painting and, at times, served as a model for his canvases.[19] Cavagnaro was the sitter for DeCamp's *St. John the Baptist* of 1886 (fig. 16), a spare image of a youth set against the austere Annisquam dunes.[20] It met with mixed reviews when shown at the American Art Association galleries in New York and, subsequently, at Boston's Museum of Fine Arts. "DeCamp will send an important painting to the prize exhibit [Prize Fund Exhibition of the American Art Association, New York]," it was announced in the *Boston Evening Transcript* of February 28, 1886. "It represents St. John as the young evangelist. The figure is nearly nude, and is seen advancing with a staff in the outstretched right hand and a scroll in the left. The advocate of Christ is proclaiming to the priests and Levites, 'I am the voice of one crying in the wilderness.'"[21] The reviewer for the *Boston Daily Advertiser* was far less generous: "'St. John the Baptist' (51) is nothing more than an academical study, not of surpassing merit even as such, for the coloring is dull and lifeless. The New York critic who called this 'a pie crust child in a sole leather land,' meant to display his cheap wit at the artist's expense, but was not this, in some sort, a just retribution upon Mr. DeCamp for trying to show his cleverness at the expense of St. John the Baptist?"[22] This, and a slightly later work entitled *Magdalene*, would be the artist's only forays into religious subject matter. The late nineteenth century witnessed an international revival of religious painting that often, like DeCamp's *St. John the Baptist*, combined traditional sacred narratives with contemporary settings. In France the work of Jules Bastien-Lepage, for example, was highly influential, especially among his American followers George Hitchcock, Robert Vonnoh, J. Alden Weir, and others. During his stay in Germany, DeCamp may have seen the naturalistic religious imagery produced by artists of the Wilhelm Leibl circle, such as

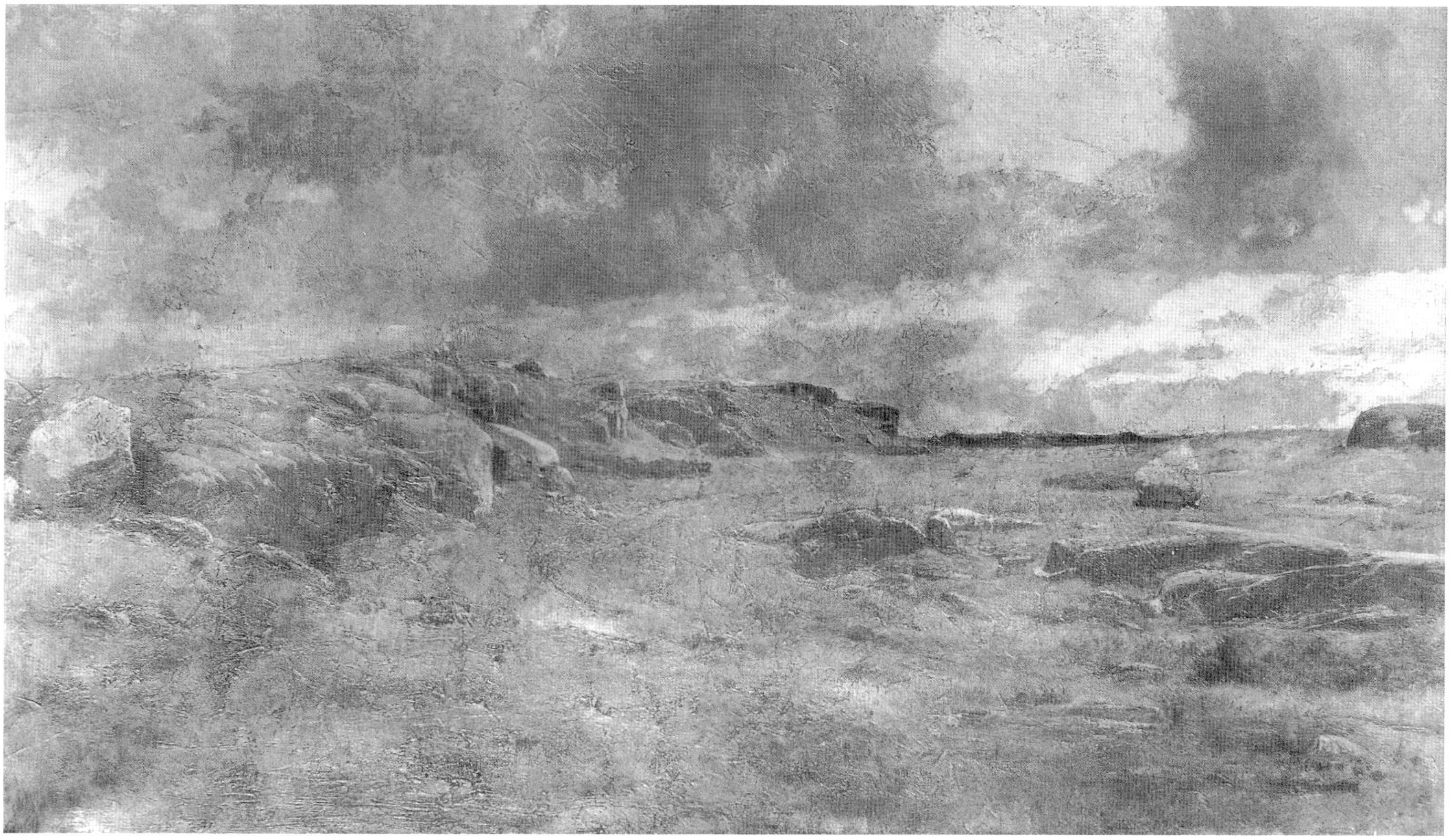

Fig. 17 *Landscape*, ca. 1886. 29 x 50 in. (73.5 x 127 cm). Private collection

Gabriel Max and Fritz von Uhde. The importance of *St. John the Baptist* is that it shows DeCamp experimenting with the figure outdoors before Benson and Tarbell, the other members of the Boston triad. It would be another year or so before Benson painted *In Summer* (unlocated), and Tarbell did not create *Three Sisters—A Study in June Sunlight* (Milwaukee Art Museum) until 1890.

DeCamp continued to teach at the Museum School for two years, through the spring of 1889. The institution's annual reports indicate favorable results from the pupils under his tutelage, at least at the outset. In subsequent years there are hints of pressure from the students for more painting classes and for a separate unit for decorative design, along with constant concerns about the school's financial future.[23] The minutes for the annual meeting of May 23, 1889, reveal additional in-house problems. Frank H. Tompkins, a Cleveland artist lately returned from studies in Munich, had replaced Vonnoh as the instructor for painting and was now himself to be replaced by Tarbell, who had earlier been a pupil of Grundmann at the school. Tarbell was to be offered a salary of one thousand dollars per year and, when it was recommended that DeCamp's salary be increased to that level, objections were raised "on the grounds that Mr. DeCamp's teaching, though valuable in many respects, had not been entirely satisfactory." It was then "voted that the resolution reappointing Mr. DeCamp be recommended with instructions to consider whether another and more satisfactory candidate cannot be found." Discussion continued with a recommendation to "dispense with the services" of Miss Green, DeCamp's assistant. One committee member stated that her teaching was "not satisfactory and was not in accord with that of the other teachers," but another supported her, stating only that her teaching did "not agree with that of Mr. DeCamp."[24] Six days later the committee met again to hear the report of a special subcommittee assigned to "engage Mr. Tarbell and to nominate a successor to Mr. DeCamp." After Willard Metcalf and "Emmett"(?) had both declined, Benson, another Grundmann disciple who, with Tarbell, had recently returned from study in France, was suggested as a candidate. The committee was empowered to offer him DeCamp's position at a salary of one thousand dollars, which Benson accepted.[25] Despite this, DeCamp would remain close to Benson and Tarbell, both of whom taught at the school until 1912.

Without a job, DeCamp apparently moved back to Dedham sometime in 1889 to stay with Mills. He kept his contacts in Boston, however, serving as a critic for the newly established composition class of the Boston Art Students' Association, along with Duveneck and Turner.[26] He maintained a studio at the Mechanics' Fair Building at 135 Huntington Avenue, where he, Mills, and Dennis Miller Bunker sketched from the nude model.[27] Bunker had been trained in Paris in the academic manner under Jean-Léon Gérôme before teaching at the newly established Cowles Art School in Boston from 1885 to 1889. His connections in the city included the prominent art patron Mrs. Jack Gardner and John Singer Sargent, who visited Boston in 1887 and 1888. Bunker had spent the summer of 1888 with Sargent at Calcot, England, and DeCamp must have been struck by Bunker's new, Impressionist style upon the latter's return from working outdoors with the older artist. As Hamlin Garland later observed, Bunker had accomplished a transition from "the school of mud to the school of the open air."[28]

About this time, DeCamp's landscapes underwent a similar transformation. This development came on the heels of a new wave of Impressionism, as seen at the 1889 annual of the Society of American Artists in New York, at which the Monet-inspired views of Theodore Robinson, Henry Fitch Taylor, and Theodore Wendel were exhibited for the first time. Unfortunately, DeCamp's entry in the show, *Portrait of Miss J.* (unlocated), was not discussed in any known review. It may have been similar in style to the artist's submission to the next year's annual, *At the Piano*, which was described as "a half-life size of another young woman in yellow [Tarbell had entered a similar work] at her piano."[29]

Whether DeCamp was actually in New York for the 1889 Society show is not known, but press reactions to his work of the following summer clearly indicate that he had acquired a new awareness of the Impressionist style. He again stayed in Annisquam, at his usual abode, the boarding house run by Charlotte Lane. She was the daughter of a ship's captain and ran one of two houses in the village for summer visitors, who often included college professors, authors, and a considerable number of artists.[30] According to the local newspaper, *Cape Ann Breeze*, DeCamp was in 'Squam "for a few hours" in late June 1890, probably to make arrangements for a group of women students from Philadelphia who called themselves the "Lavender Club."[31] By July 26 Miss Lane had "a snug little family of 36," including presumably the Lavender Club's members: Miss Gertrude Neil and the Misses Goodman, Trutt, Lee, Maxwell, Hunt, Fox, and [Margarette] Lippincott, "matronized by Mrs. [J. R.] Snowden and Mrs. [L. F. T.] Mitchel of Philadelphia."[32] "The artists are everywhere," announced the *Cape Ann Breeze*. "They occupy every point of advantage.... Everything odd, bizarre and picturesque is grist for their mill. Men of national fame are here, who add year by year to their already assured reputation, and gay young amateurs."[33]

Nearby East Gloucester, like Annisquam, was also "never so full of artists," according to Helen Knowlton, a student of William Morris Hunt who surveyed the north shore in July 1890 for *Studio* magazine. She noted DeCamp's class, one taught by Arthur Wesley Dow at Ipswich, a watercolor class of "a dozen or more" pupils under Rhoda Holmes Nicholls, and a group from Boston who had come to study with Duveneck. The biggest news in Knowlton's report was the visit of Wendel, one of DeCamp's closest friends from Munich and Venice, who had taken over Duveneck's class for a week. After visiting Italy, Wendel had become one of the first-generation American members of the artists' colony near Monet's home at Giverny. He was still "studying deeply into the mysteries of light upon color," Knowlton observed. "No browns and black enter into his scheme of... pure color, fresh from the tub [*sic*]."[34] He and DeCamp were working alongside each other at 135 Huntington Avenue, Boston, and, evidently, at Annisquam.

When DeCamp left Cape Ann in late September 1890, he carried with him "several landscapes and bits of Annisquam scenery," according to the *Gloucester Daily Times* critic.[35] One picture, *A Cape Anne Lane* (unlocated), would win a silver medal at the Triennial Massachusetts Charitable Mechanics Association fair in October of that year. Two months later, DeCamp's entries in an exhibition at Boston's St. Botolph Club, *Mill Pond* and *On the Marsh, Medford* (both unlocated), were among those cited in the *Boston Post* as "representing some of the most advanced ideas of the time."[36] Work by Wendel was included in the show, and he and DeCamp were singled out as "two painters whose color schemes indicate more or less complete adherence to the impressionist 'idea.'"[37] DeCamp would now seem to have directed his talents fully toward Impressionism, yet a precise characterization of his first essays in the style is impossible, because none has survived.

In the summer of 1890, Duveneck, who had been finishing a bronze memorial to his wife in Boston before he left for Cape Ann, was planning to return to his teaching career in Cincinnati. His letter of May 8, 1890, to Mrs. Maria Longworth Storer, who was forming an art class at the city's art academy, outlined his expectations if he were to be hired and also recommended DeCamp as his assistant. "DeCamp," he wrote, "had considerable experience in teaching" and was "a conscientious draughtsman and a clever painter." Duveneck also stated in the letter that he had found no one who would accept the position of assistant at a salary of $1,000.[38]

Perhaps that is why DeCamp did not return to Cincinnati. In any case, Boston offered better patronage and exhibition possibilities, and he is next recorded, in October 1890, as a teacher at the Cowles Art School on Dartmouth Street.[39] Along with the Museum School, Cowles was considered to be one of the "two most excellent and completely equipped schools with life classes in Boston."[40] Established in 1883 by Frank M. Cowles, a former student at the Museum School, it was called the "Julian's" of Boston because, like the Académie Julian in Paris, its teaching was informal and emphasized life and modeling classes. As described in the *Boston Art Guide and Artists' Directory* of 1893, the school was flexibly organized to meet the "needs of a considerable number of earnest students who are not able to attend for long periods at a time, or who have been obliged to gain their instruction in an irregular and unequal way, and need to have their deficiencies made up in special lines of study."[41]

Bunker had established the excellence of the school and, on his departure for New York in 1889, may have recommended DeCamp for the position. "It may be said that the beginning of the Cowles Art School's success dates from 1885, when Dennis Miller Bunker was engaged as teacher," wrote a reviewer for the *Boston Transcript*. "The standard to which his valuable and well-directed endeavors raised it is fully maintained today under the efficient and conscientious labors of Ernest L. Major and Joseph DeCamp. Students come to it from almost every State in the Union, as well as from Canada, the provinces, South America and the Sandwich Islands."[42] In private, Bunker had complained about the Cowles School's management and its student body (and about Boston in general), but DeCamp, who appears to have continued teaching there at least through the 1898–99 season, apparently enjoyed an atmosphere that was more relaxed than that at the Museum School.[43]

Notes

1 See, for example, Robert Newton Linscott, *State of the Mind: A Boston Reader* (New York: Farrar, Straus & Co., 1948).

2 See also John Higham, *Writing American History: Essays on Modern Scholarship* (Bloomington, Ind.: Indiana University Press, 1970); Neil Harris, "The Gilded Age Reconsidered Once Again," *Archives of American Art Journal* 23 (1983), pp. 9–11; and Donald D. Keyes, *The Genteel Tradition*, exh. cat. (Winter Park, Fla.: George D. and Harriet W. Cornell Fine Arts Center, Rollins College, 1985).

3 Henry James, "Exhibition Review," *The Nation* 20 (June 3, 1875), pp. 376–77.

4 H[arley]. P[erkins]., "The Fine Arts," *Boston Evening Transcript*, January 8, 1924, p. 13.

5 DeCamp is listed in the Wellesley calendars for 1884–85 and 1885–86. His residence with Mills is mentioned in Donald Moffat, "Joseph DeCamp: Biographical Sketch," unpublished typescript, Frick Art Reference Library, New York, 1955–57, p. 23.

6 Tenth Annual Calendar, 1884–85, Wellesley College Archives, Wellesley, Mass., unpaginated.

7 *Wellesley College, 1875–1975: A Century of Women* (Wellesley, Mass.: Wellesley College, 1975), p. 132.

8 For a summary of the school's practices, see H. Barbara Weinberg, "Robert Reid: Academic Impressionist," *Archives of American Art Journal* 15 (1975), pp. 2–11; Bernice Kramer Leader, "The Boston Lady as a Work of Art: Paintings by the Boston School at the Turn of the Century," Ph. D. diss., Columbia University, 1980, pp. 12–16; and the annual reports of the Museum of Fine Arts, School of Drawing and Painting, Library Archives, School of the Museum of Fine Arts, Boston.

9 *Museum of Fine Arts: School of Drawing and Painting, Ninth Annual Report* (Boston: Alfred Mudge & Son, 1885), p. 9.

10 Leader, "The Boston Lady as a Work of Art," p. 14.

11 Joseph DeCamp to W. P. P. Longfellow, Esq., August 1886; published in *Museum of Fine Arts: School of Drawing and Painting, Tenth Annual Report* (Boston: Alfred Mudge & Son, 1886), p. 12.

12 H. Winthrop Peirce, *The History of the School of the Museum of Fine Arts, Boston* (Boston: T. O. Metcalf Co., 1930), p. 41.

13 "The Fine Arts," *Boston Morning Journal*, February 13, 1885, p. 2. Other thriving galleries in Boston at this time were Doll & Richards, J. Lowell & Co., Noyes & Blakeslee, and Williams and Everett.

14 "The Fine Arts," *Boston Morning Journal*, May 9, 1885, p. 2.

15 See William H. Gerdts, "John Twachtman and the Artistic Colony in Gloucester at the Turn of the Century," in *Twachtman in Gloucester: His Last Years, 1900–1902*, exh. cat. (New York: Spanierman Gallery, 1987), p. 27.

16 See Harrison Cady, "Cape Ann: America's Oldest Art Colony," *American Artist* 16 (May 1952), p. 62.

17 "Fine Arts: Society of American Artists—II," *The Nation* 46 (May 3, 1888), p. 374.

18 City directory, Boston, Massachusetts, 1886. In 1887 he was boarding at 57 Chestnut Street. Donald Moffat ("Joseph Rodefer DeCamp: Chronology," unpublished typescript, Frick Art Reference Library, New York, 1955–57, p. 2) also locates him at Mount Vernon Street some time between 1885 and 1890.

19 Munich street children, especially young boys, were the subjects of numerous paintings by Duveneck, William Merritt Chase, Frank Currier, and others. For more details on Joe Cavagnaro, see Moffat, "Joseph Rodefer DeCamp: Biographical Sketch," pp. 23–25. DeCamp supposedly offered a job to the boy if he could outdistance him in a foot race. Cavagnaro later joined the Boston police department and subsequently became chief of the Italian division of the detective force.

20 A letter from Joseph L. Cavagnaro to Mrs. Joseph DeCamp, dated January 11, 1924, written shortly after her husband's death, states that, in the four years that he was with the artist, Cavagnaro had "posed for DeCamp on Chauncy Street and at Annisquam and cared for him at his room on Mount Vernon Street when he was ill." Joseph DeCamp scrapbook, family of the artist.

21 "Art and Artists," *Boston Evening Transcript*, February 28, 1886, p. 6.

22 "The Fine Arts," *Boston Daily Advertiser*, February 24, 1886, p. 4.

23 See the eleventh through thirteenth annual reports of the School of Drawing and Painting of the Museum of Fine Arts, published by Alfred Mudge & Son, Boston, from 1887 to 1889.

24 "23rd May 1889—(Annual Meeting). Minutes of the Annual Meeting of the Permanent Committee, School of Drawing and Painting of the Museum of Fine Arts, Boston," unpublished MS., unpaginated; Library Archives, School of the Museum of Fine Arts, Boston.

25 "29th May 1889. Adjourned Annual Meeting of Permanent Committee of the School of Drawing and Painting of the Museum of Fine Arts, Boston," unpublished MS., unpaginated; Library Archives, School of the Museum of Fine Arts, Boston.

26 Annual Report of the Secretary and Treasurer with a List of Officers for the Tenth Year of the Boston Art Students' Association, November 1889; clippings files, Boston Public Library.

27 R. H. Ives Gammell, *The Boston Painters: 1900–1930* (Orleans, Mass.: Parnassus Imprints, 1986), p. 59.

28 Hamlin Garland, *Roadside Meetings* (New York: Macmillan Press, 1930), p. 31. Moffat ("Joseph Rodefer DeCamp: Biographical Sketch," p. 15) relates the story of DeCamp's one and only encounter with Mrs. Gardner. Apparently, she asked DeCamp's opinion of a newly acquired work said to be by Titian (*Portrait of Juana of Austrai, with Her Niece Margaret*, now attributed to Alonso Sanchez Coello). DeCamp, after a thorough examination of the work, called it a "truly great painting ... a beautiful thing," but added, to the detriment of any hopes he may have entertained of receiving commissions from Gardner: "Titian never painted it."

29 "The Society of American Artists' Exhibition," *Art Amateur* 23 (June 1890), p. 3.

30 Morris R. Robinson, "Some Artists Who Called 'Squam, Lanesville and The Folly Home," unpublished MS., 1973, p. 5; Annisquam Historical Society, Massachusetts.

31 "Squibs from 'Sqam," *Cape Ann Breeze*, June 27, 1890, p. 4.

32 "Squibs from 'Squam," *Cape Ann Breeze*, July 26, 1890, p. 4, and "Annisquam," *Gloucester Daily Times*, July 7, 1890, p. 2. Of this group, only Margarette Lippincott, a painter of floral landscapes and still lifes, appears in surveys of American art. Philadelphia-born, she studied at the Pennsylvania Academy of the Fine Arts, exhibited there and with the Plastic Club of Philadelphia, and was a member of the New York Watercolor Club.

33 "Squibs from 'Squam," *Cape Ann Breeze*, July 29, 1890, p. 4.

34 Helen M. Knowlton, "A Home-Colony of Artists," *Studio* 5 (July 14, 1890), pp. 326–27.

35 "Annisquam," *Gloucester Daily Times*, October 2, 1890, p. 2.

36 "At the St. Botolph," *Boston Post*, January 7, 1891, p. 4.

37 "The Fine Arts," *Boston Evening Transcript*, December 30, 1890, p. 6.

38 Frank Duveneck to Maria Longworth Storer, May 8, 1890; Duveneck file, Library Archives, Cincinnati Art Museum.

39 The *Boston Evening Transcript* for October 29, 1890, p. 9, announced that "Mr. Joseph DeCamp has been engaged as an instructor in the Cowles Art School."

40 Greta, "The Art Season in Boston," *Art Amateur* 19 (June 1888), p. 5.

41 Quoted in Peirce, *History of the School of the Museum of Fine Arts*, p. 35.

42 "The Fine Arts," *Boston Evening Transcript*, June 22, 1891, p. 6.

43 For Bunker's relationship to the Cowles School, see R. H. Ives Gammell, *Dennis Miller Bunker* (New York: Coward-McCann, 1953), and Charles B. Ferguson, "Dennis Miller Bunker," in *Dennis Miller Bunker Rediscovered*, exh. cat. (New Britain, Conn.: The New Britain Museum of American Art, 1978). The length of DeCamp's tenure at the school can be inferred from the fact that he is mentioned in connection with the institution in 1890 (see note 40), 1891 ("The Fine Arts," *Boston Evening Transcript*, June 22, 1891, p. 6), 1893 (*Boston Art Guide and Artists' Directory* [Boston: Wheat Pub. Co., 1893], p. 78), 1897 (Frank T. Robinson, "An American Art School," *Art Interchange* 34 [July 1898], pp. 12–13), and 1898–99 (Cowles Art School: 1898–99; clippings file, Boston Public Library).

Chapter five

Emergence as a National Figure, 1890–1899

The decade of the 1890s was a crucial one for DeCamp and an eclectic one in terms of subject matter. He continued to exhibit paintings devoted to each of his established themes—portraiture, the figure outdoors (now in an Impressionist mode), and the pure landscape (also fully Impressionistic)—but began also to show his indoor figural work, including nudes.

In the early 1890s the name "Medford" starts to appear in the titles of DeCamp's paintings. *Medford Marshes* (unlocated) was exhibited at the St. Botolph Club, Boston, in January 1890 and, in December of that year, *On the Marsh, Medford* (unlocated) was shown at the same club. According to Moffat, DeCamp had fallen in love with Edith Franklin Baker of Medford, Massachusetts, in the late 1880s when she was his pupil at the School of Drawing and Painting at Boston's Museum of Fine Arts.[1] An early portrait of Edith by DeCamp, known in the family by the title *Edith As a Student,* shows her as a winsome young woman with sparkling eyes and confident smile (fig. 18). By 1891 DeCamp was actually living in Medford, at a boarding establishment called the Medford House.[2] That year he had again summered at Annisquam, teaching the women of the Philadelphia Lavender Club for a second time.[3] At the season's close, the *Cape Ann Breeze* announced that "Mr. DeCamp the well known artist... will enter the ranks matrimonial."[4]

On September 21, 1892, with Edmund C. Tarbell as a witness,[5] Joseph and Edith were married at Medford's Grace Episcopal Church. Their union did not receive the whole-hearted approval of her family, which, Moffat acknowledged, "favored a daughter's security to her marriage with a wild young painter from the West."[6] However, Edith, at age twenty-two, was totally in awe of her thirty-three-year-old spouse, "still addressing him respectfully as Mr. DeCamp when they married."[7]

The couple lived for a time with her family at 14 Water Street and, later, at 107 High Street in Medford.[8] Their household included Edith's two brothers, one of whom would later become the postmaster of Boston;[9] her mother, Sarah Franklin; and her father, Joseph E. Baker, a well-known lithographic artist and a lifelong friend of Winslow Homer, having apprenticed with him at Bufford's lithography firm in Boston.[10] Probably in 1894 the DeCamps purchased a house at 283 West Medford in order to accommodate their own expanding family. That year saw the birth of their son, Ted; he had been preceded by Sally, born in 1892, and would be followed by Lydia (1896) and Pauline (1899).[11] A former farmhouse dating to the Federal period (fig. 19), the DeCamps' new home was said to have been situated on the route taken by Paul Revere to Lexington.[12] Here the family led a fairly withdrawn life, although, when DeCamp later was commissioned to paint a portrait of President Roosevelt, the artist was described in a local newspaper as a "thorough-going loyal citizen of this historic old municipality and a member of our local school committee."[13] In the 1890s, West Medford was a "country village of decent Yankee stock—friendly folk, good neighbors, self-respecting and self supporting. Mrs. DeCamp thought nothing of stopping the horse-car and asking Mr. Standish the conductor to match a spool of thread for her in Medford Square and drop it off at the house on his return trip. There was a brook at the foot of the hill, elms and dirt roads, back yards and stone walls, a neighbor always ready to help deliver a baby... and Grace Episcopal Church down High Street, where... Mrs. DeCamp was a loyal member of the congregation."[14]

DeCamp regularly commuted to Boston by the "'electric cars' in the early days," arriving "never later than eight o'clock" at his studio, which, from 1889 to 1893, was at 135 Huntington Avenue, a building in which Charles E. Mills, Theodore Wendel, and the landscapist Arthur Wesley Dow also had studios.[15] In 1894 and 1895 DeCamp was working at 20 St. Botolph Street with his friends Tarbell and Frank W. Benson.[16] The latter were still teaching at the Museum School and, in mid-April 1893, they sent a letter to the board of the school, urging the appointment of another teacher to the staff, since the number of pupils had nearly doubled during their tenure.[17] Their recommendation of DeCamp was accepted by the nominating committee in May, but, by the time the

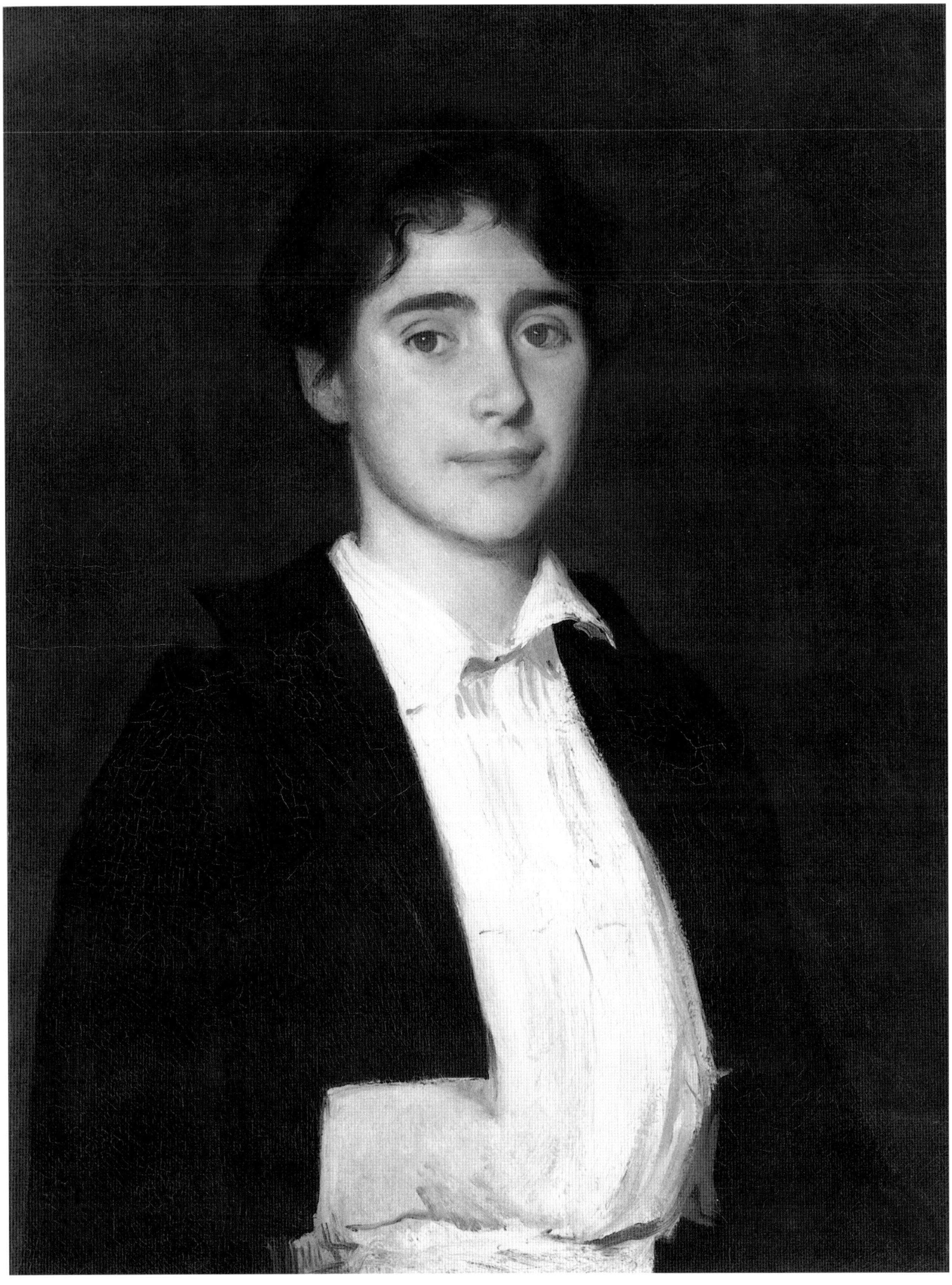

Fig. 18 *Edith As a Student*, ca. 1891. 24 x 18 in. (61 x 45.5 cm). Private collection

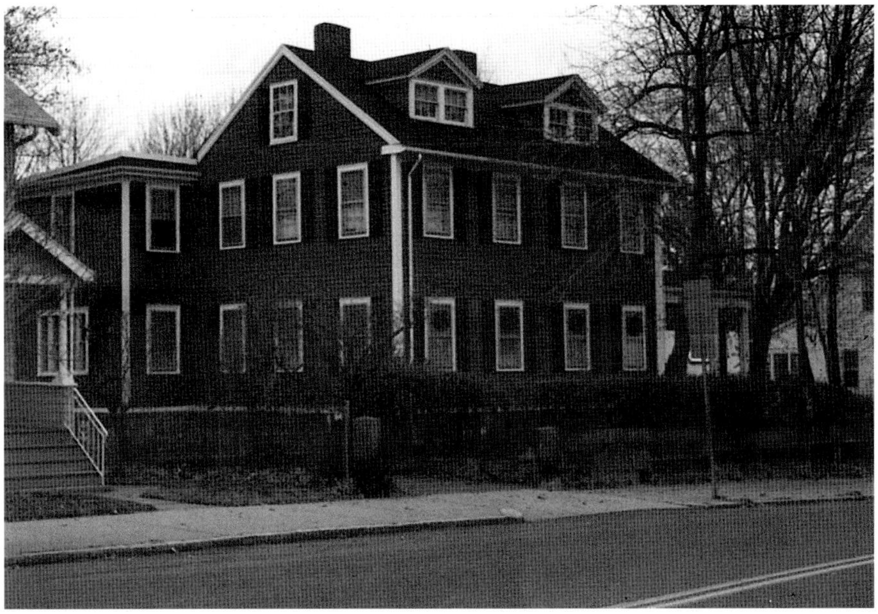

Fig. 19 The DeCamps' house at 283 West Medford, Massachusetts

board met in November, it was clear that he had refused the offer.[18] Perhaps he was still upset by his dismissal from the school in 1889. He continued to teach at the Cowles Art School, where his fellow instructors were Wendel and Ernest Major, a Boston figural artist who visited Annisquam at the same time as DeCamp in 1894 and 1895.

Annisquam, Lanesville, and Folly Cove on Cape Ann were often the subjects of DeCamp's vibrant landscapes of the early to mid-1890s, which, judging by their critical reception, became increasingly Impressionistic as the decade advanced. That Impressionism was already accepted in Boston is proven by the fact that an exhibition of Monet's landscapes, held at the St. Botolph Club in 1892, consisted entirely of loans from ten local collectors.[19] It was DeCamp's *plein air* work that first caught the attention of the national press and placed him among the avant-garde painters of his day. Even the French critic S. C. de Soissons, who in 1894 expressed his surprise at the quality of the arts in America, noticed DeCamp, remarking that he had "lately made much progress, and paints pictures vibrating with air and light."[20]

Bay Bushes (unlocated), exhibited at the Society of American Artists annual of 1892, was adduced as an example of the "inquisitive, experimental and scientific" branch of contemporary American Art "in the hands of the Impressionists," as opposed to the "spiritualized, imaginative and psychological" viewpoint represented by another school (probably the Tonalists).[21] Applauding its "atmospheric effect" and "vivid blue" water, a *Boston Daily Advertiser* critic noted its overall diffusion when the painting was shown at the St. Botolph Club in December of the same year: "The middle distance is no farther from the eye than the foreground," he observed.[22] *In the Arbor* (unlocated) and *September Afternoon* (possibly identical with the present plate 5) were exhibited first at the fourth annual show of the Art Club of Philadelphia of 1892 and later grouped with *New England Garden, The Hammock*, and *Study, September Morning* (all unlocated) at the Society of American Artists annual of 1893 to gain DeCamp the distinction of being one of the "*plein-air* men."[23] The *New-York Daily Tribune* critic singled out *New England Garden* at the society's show as proof that DeCamp was "in the Monet advance."[24] Difficult as it is to determine the location of the scenes depicted in these works of the 1890s, one can assume that the paintings with coastal titles were done at Cape Ann. Artists generally stayed there until mid- or late September and those pictures that suggest the fall season could, therefore, also have been executed at Annisquam or Lanesville.

The Hillside (unlocated), an "autumnal" scene,[25] was one of DeCamp's five entries in an exhibition held at the St. Botolph Club in 1894. The other artists represented were Benson, Tarbell, Frederic Porter Vinton (the leading Boston portraitist at the time),[26] and four painters who were certainly part of the "Monet advance," having worked alongside the French master in Giverny: Wendel, Dawson Dawson-Watson, Philip Leslie Hale, and Lila Cabot Perry. A *Boston Daily Advertiser* review of the show offered a perceptive comparison between Boston's more restrained Impressionism and its New York counterpart. "There is manifest in this exhibition," the critic observed, "a respect for drawing, an eye to the softening of the sheen of sunlight and a moderation in the use of unbended colors that sharply separate it in character from the ultra-Impressionism shown in the exhibits of Weir and Twachtman."[27] This was an important exhibition for DeCamp, not only because he was included among the Boston School of Impressionists, but also because reviews accorded him a leading role within the group. The *Boston Evening Transcript* critic found that Tarbell's "impressionistic mantle" had "fallen upon Mr. DeCamp, who wears it with more harmony and grace."[28] This was a compliment indeed, as Tarbell had just completed a number of important outdoor figural works, beginning in 1890 with *Three Sisters—A Study in June Sunlight* and including *In the Orchard* of 1891 and *Mother and Child in a Boat* of 1892. (Benson was at this time immersed in a series of indoor firelight scenes.) When shown in New York at the Society of American Artists annual in March 1894, *Hillside* further established DeCamp as one of the "younger painters... walking in the iridescent and more or less uncertain footsteps of the sunlightists."[29] *Edge of the Cliff* (unlocated), DeCamp's entry in the Art Club of Philadelphia annual of 1895, was described as an "impressionist study of green trees, purple shadows and blue sea."[30]

Several pure landscapes of the 1890s by DeCamp have survived. *Summer Landscape* (plate 6) was titled

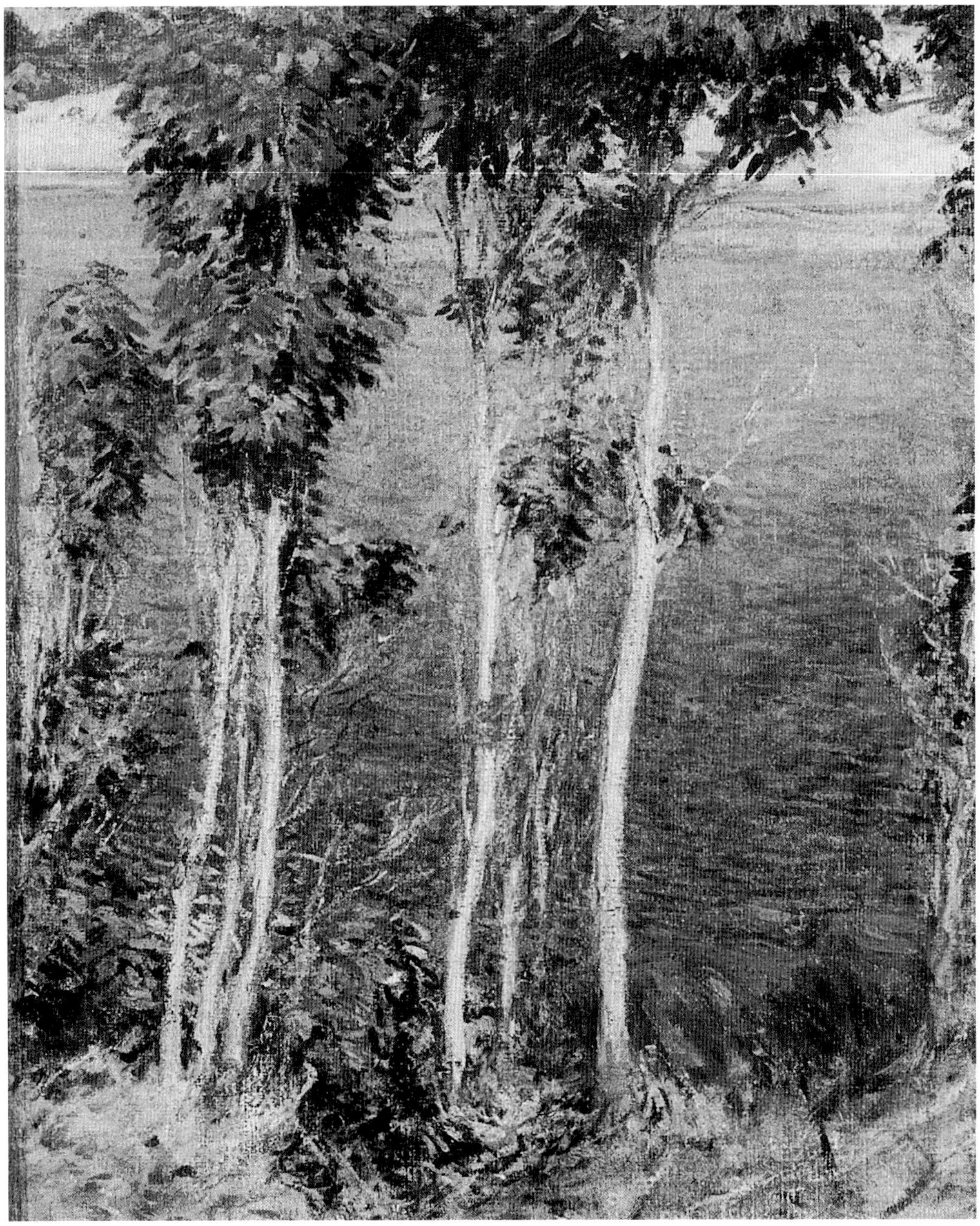

Fig. 20 *Birches By the Sea*, ca. 1895. 23 x 19 in. (58.5 x 48.5 cm). Unlocated

simply *Summer* when lent by the artist's brother Arthur to the sixteenth annual of the St. Louis Exposition and Music Hall Association in 1899. A fairly traditional view, with a standardized use of local color, the painting illustrates a convention that appears often in DeCamp's landscapes—a foreground pathway and screen of trees that allow glimpses of distant vistas. The drybrush technique employed for the foliage also became a feature of his work at about this time. *A Glimpse of the Sea*, lent to the same St. Louis show by another of the artist's brothers, Frank Baker DeCamp, is no doubt identical with one of the two paintings that have descended to members of that family: *Birches By the Sea* (fig. 20), which further explores the screening effect of trees against a distant seascape, and *Granite Cove* (fig. 21), a cliffside view of Folly Cove, just north of Lanesville, where the artist taught a group of women staying at the Folly Cove Cottage in the summer of 1895.[31] The latter painting shows DeCamp's love of rich vegetation, rendered in vibrant colors and swirling, diagonal brushstrokes that contrast with the more feathered treatment of sea and sky. Along the opposite shore of the quiet cove are sandy beaches, their edges lined by the familiar granite rocks of the area.

Halibut Point, further up the coast, appears to have been the site for two other extant landscapes: *Bayberry Bushes* (private collection), which, in its elemental view of land, sea, and sky, employs the same coloration and

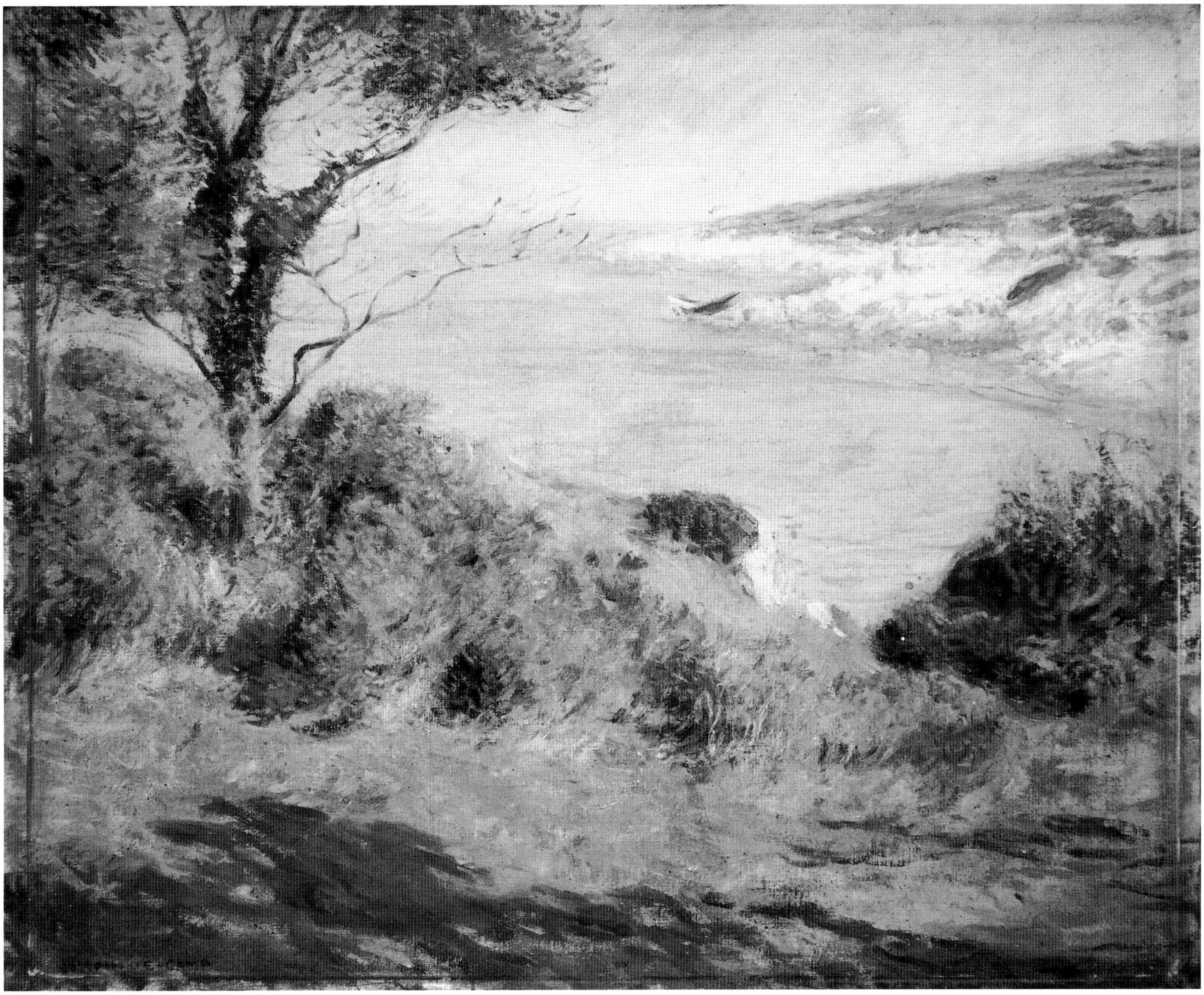

Fig. 21 *Granite Cove*, ca. 1895. 20⅛ x 24⅛ in. (51 x 61.5 cm). Private collection

technique as *Granite Cove* to render windswept shrubs, and *Seascape* (plate 7), which superbly captures the wildness for which the spot is known.

Trees Along the Coast (formerly *Road to the Sea*, plate 8), with its exploration of the "screen of trees" effect and its rich coloration, must belong to this period. The painting was formerly owned by Dwight Blaney and may date to the summer of 1894, when Blaney, DeCamp, and the other members of a group that called itself "The Big Five" (fig. 22) were together at a yet to be determined location.[32] Blaney's landscape work of this time—for example, *Across the River* of 1895 (fig. 23)—comes very close to that of DeCamp in its feathery trees and its choice of colors. The others in the group were John Leslie Breck, Ross Turner, and George C. Wales. Breck's technique during this period, as seen in *Near Annisquam, Autumn* of about 1894 (fig. 24), is also similar to DeCamp's. Rapid strokes, often applied in curvilinear daubs and drybrush overlays, characterize the work of both men. Breck's particular brand of Impressionism, the result of years spent working under the influence of Monet at Giverny, will have provided DeCamp with authentic knowledge of the French style, and indeed, through this exposure to the work of Breck and, earlier, to that of Wendel, DeCamp's Impressionism was linked more directly to Monet than that of many of his colleagues. In 1892 DeCamp painted a portrait of Breck (fig. 25) that was given to the St. Botolph Club in 1899, following the younger artist's death there from asphyxiation.[33]

Portraiture for DeCamp was still limited to family and friends, Edith being a favorite model. She appears as a mature woman in an oval canvas of circa 1895 (plate 9) and later is shown, either alone or with one of her infants, in numerous extant charcoal, pastel, and silverpoint studies. Pauline ("Polly") at birth is the center of attention in an oil of the same period (fig. 26).

In the 1890s DeCamp also continued his experiments with the figure outdoors, picking up where he had left off with *St. John the Baptist* of 1886. *The Hammock* of about 1895 (plate 10), which shows Edith and the couple's first two children, Sally and Ted, is made up of triangular shapes throughout—in the lines leading from the mother to her children (harking back to Renaissance prototypes); in the outlines of each of the children; and in the encompassing form of the hammock itself. The rather "unnatural" feel of the surroundings suggests that the work may have been "landscaped" in the studio. Foliage is treated individually, leaf by leaf, to form an arboreal canopy for the intimate family unit below. The painting bears a certain

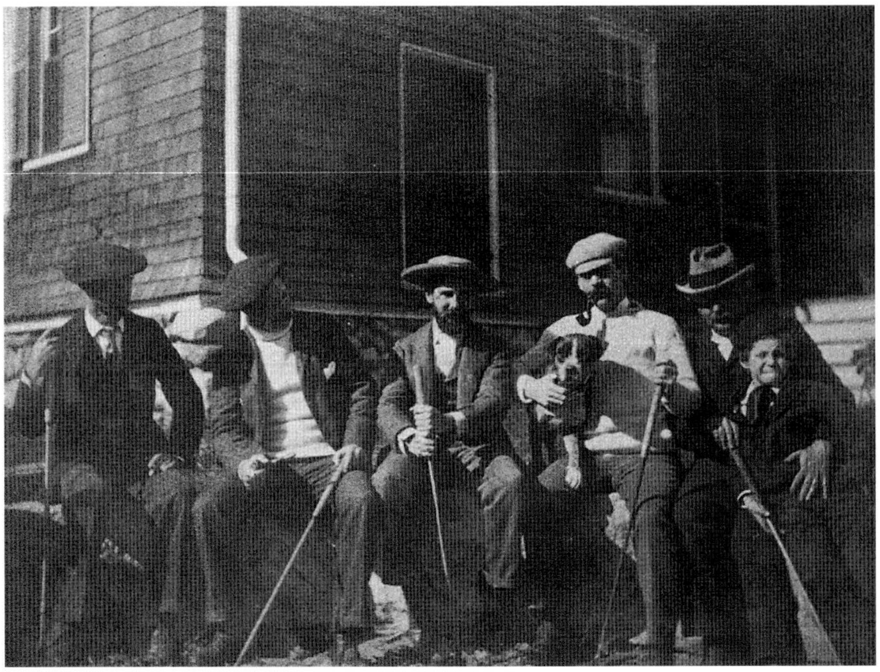

Fig. 22 "The Big Five," 1894. Left to right: George C. Wales, Dwight Blaney, John Leslie Breck, DeCamp, Ross Turner

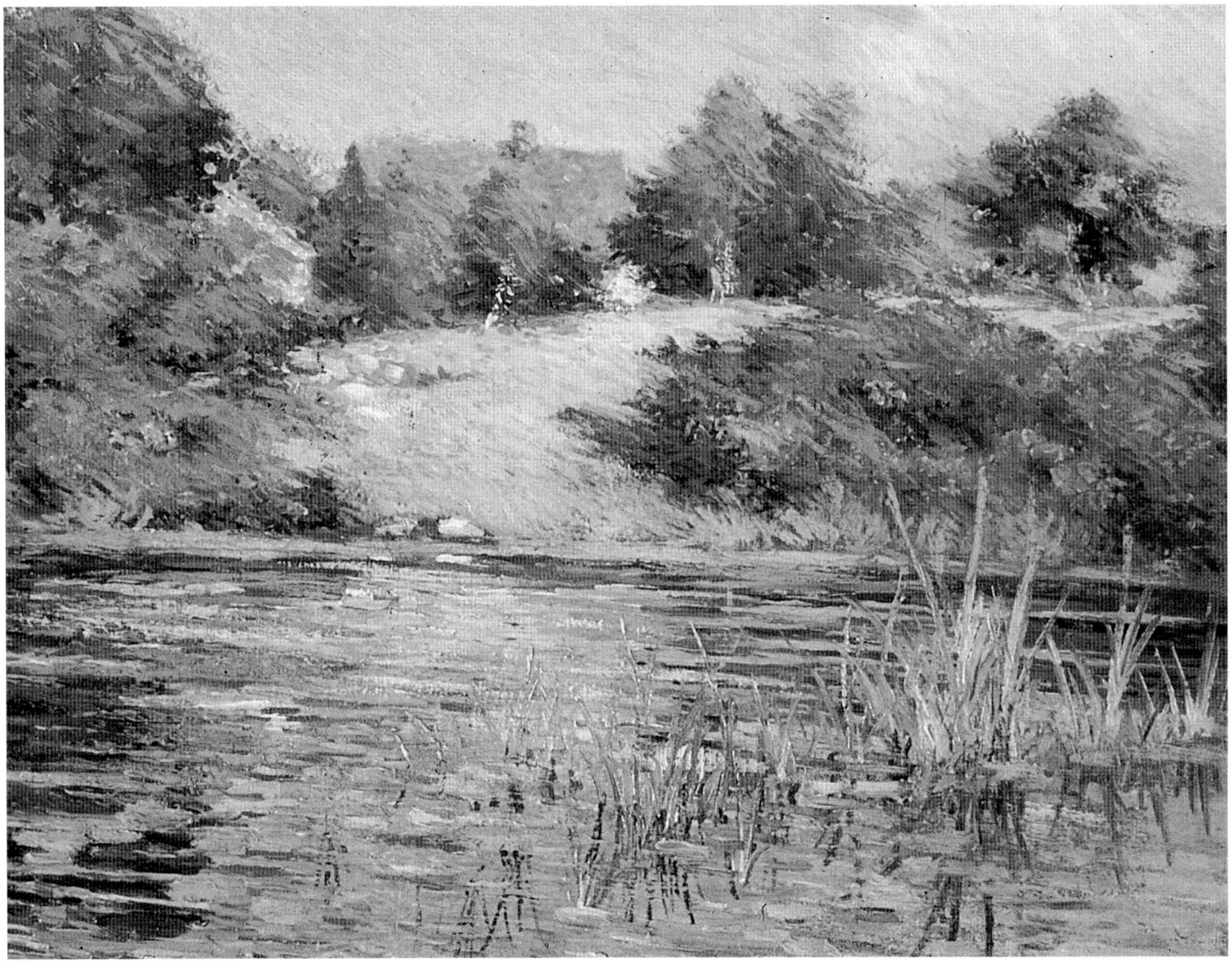

Fig. 23 Dwight Blaney, *Across the River*, 1895. 18 x 22 in. (45.5 x 56 cm). Collection of Joel and Lois Heller

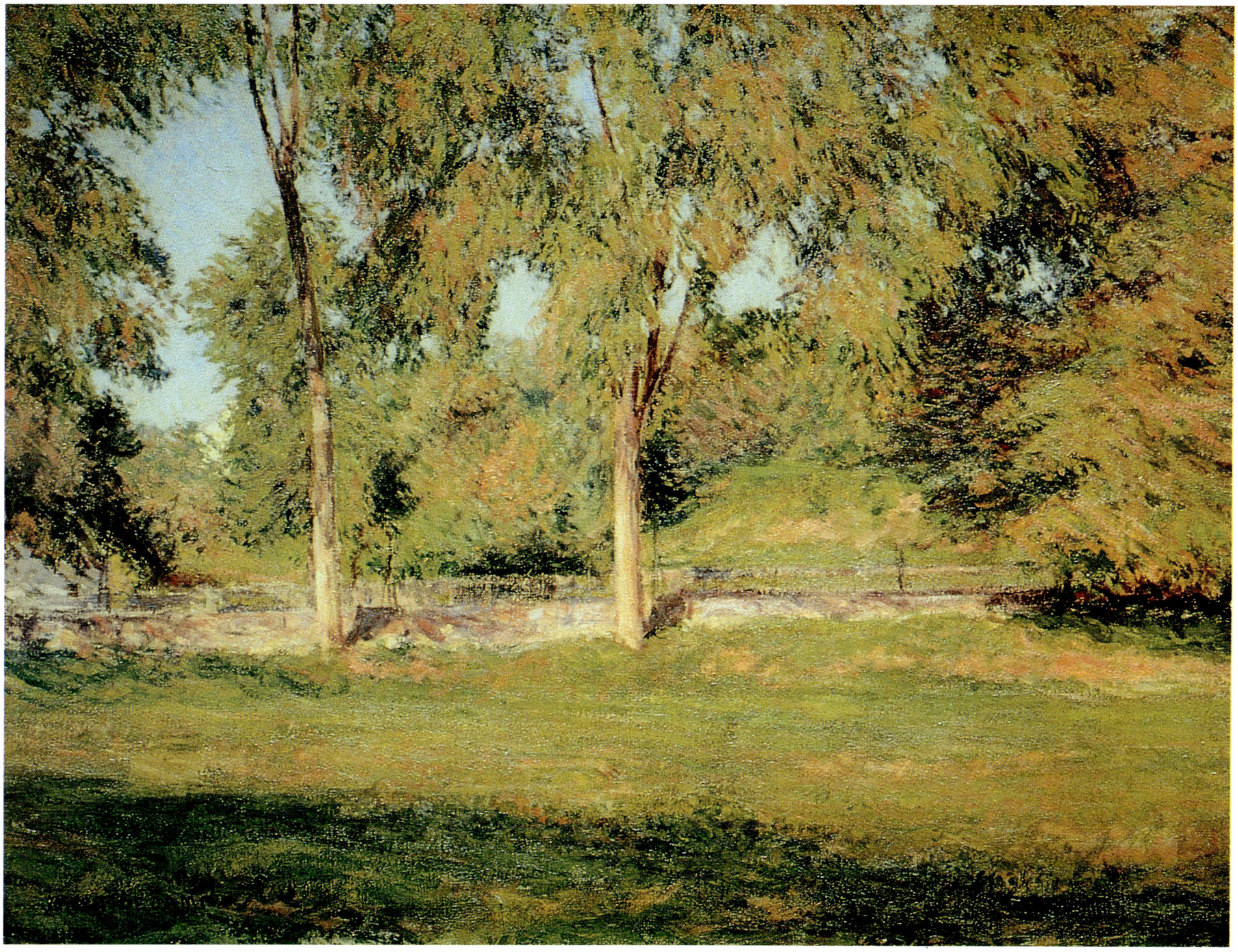

5 *September Afternoon—Road in Milton, Massachusetts,* early 1890s. 20 x 27 in. (51 x 68.5 cm). Vose Galleries of Boston, Inc.

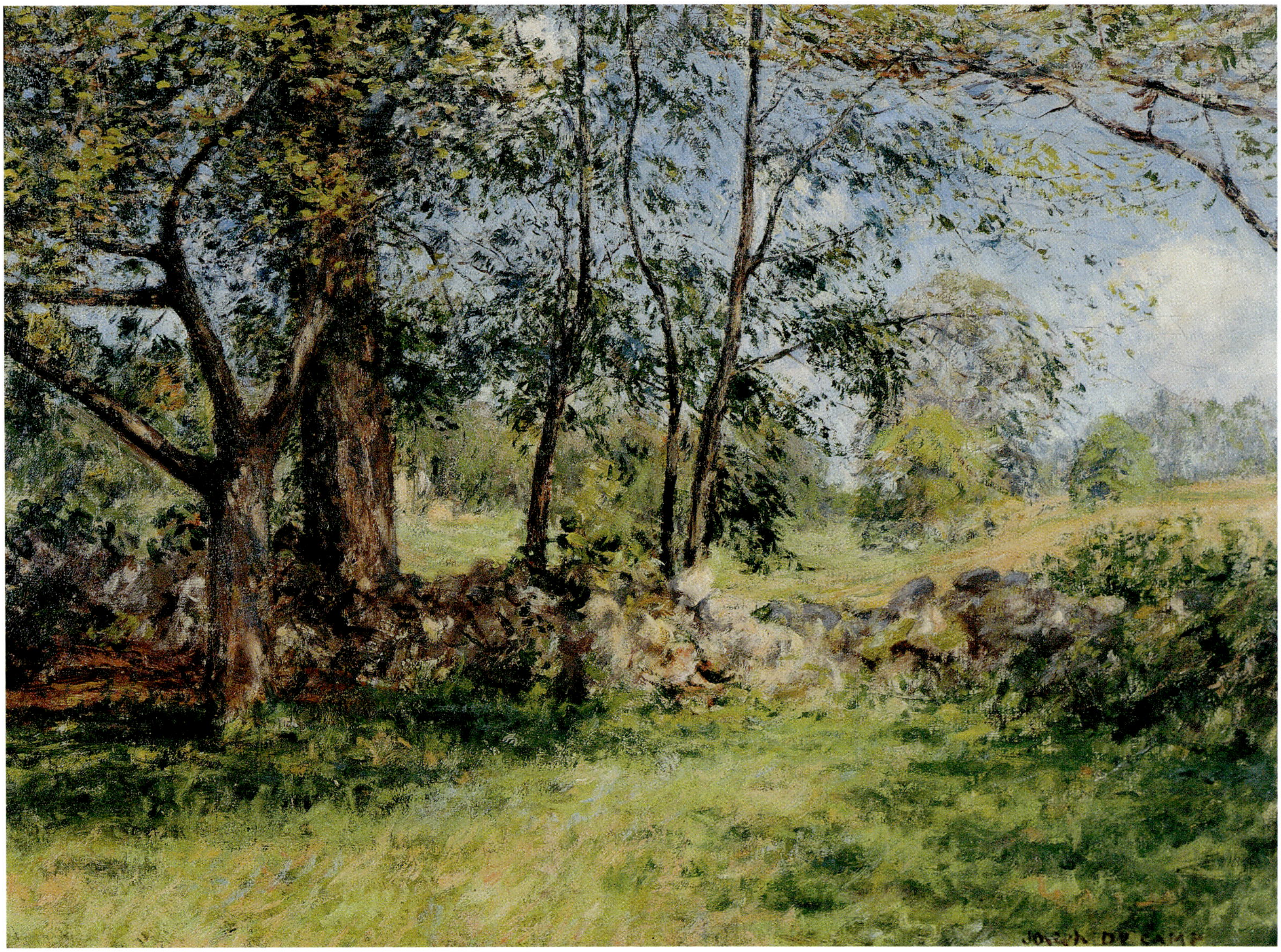

6 *Summer Landscape* (*Summertime*), mid-1890s. 20 x 27 in. (51 x 68.5 cm).
The Warner Collection of Gulf States Paper Corporation, Tuscaloosa, Alabama

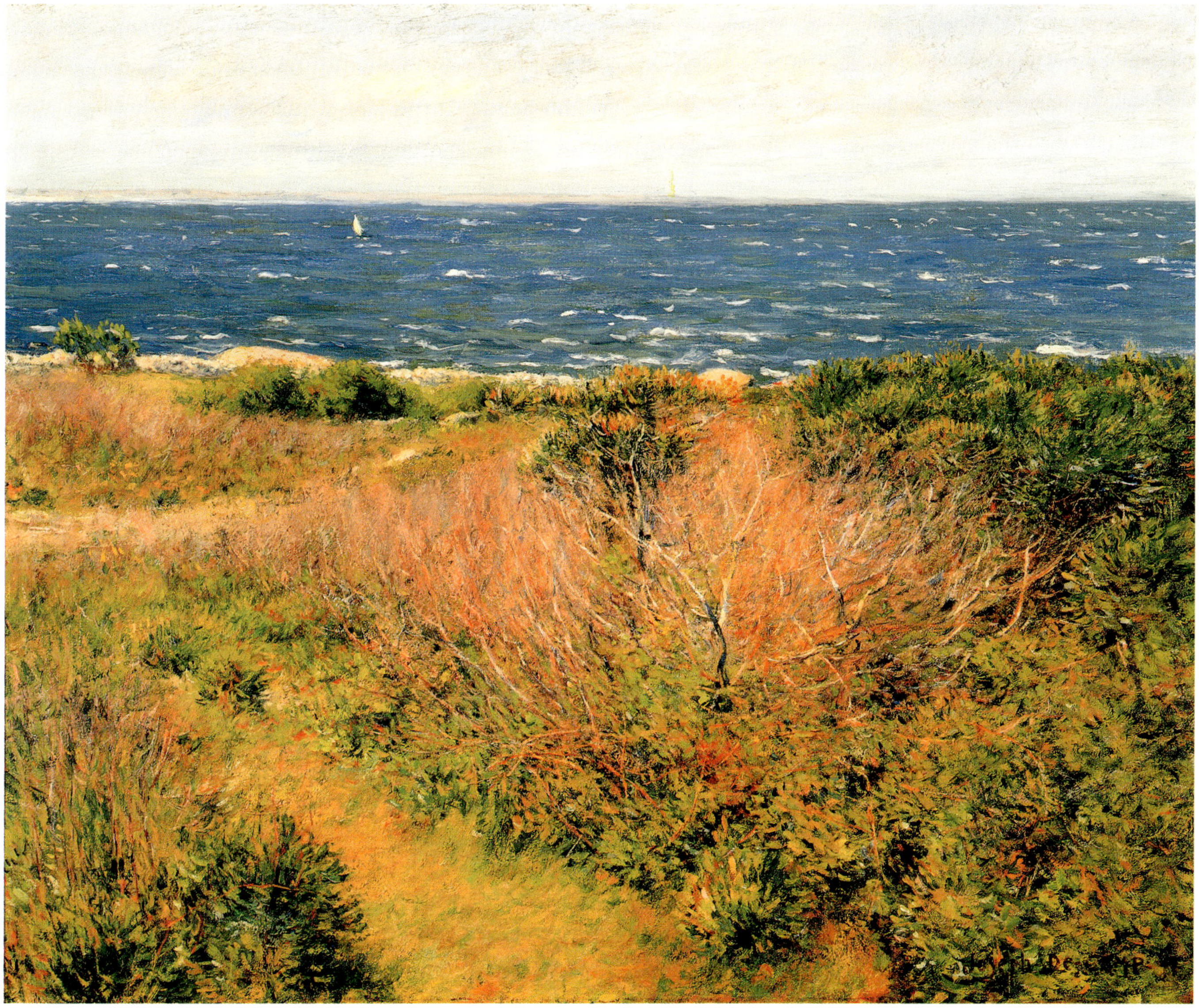

7 *Seascape*, mid-1890s. 25 x 30 in. (63.5 x 76 cm).
Collection of the William A. Farnsworth Library and Art Museum, Rockland, Maine

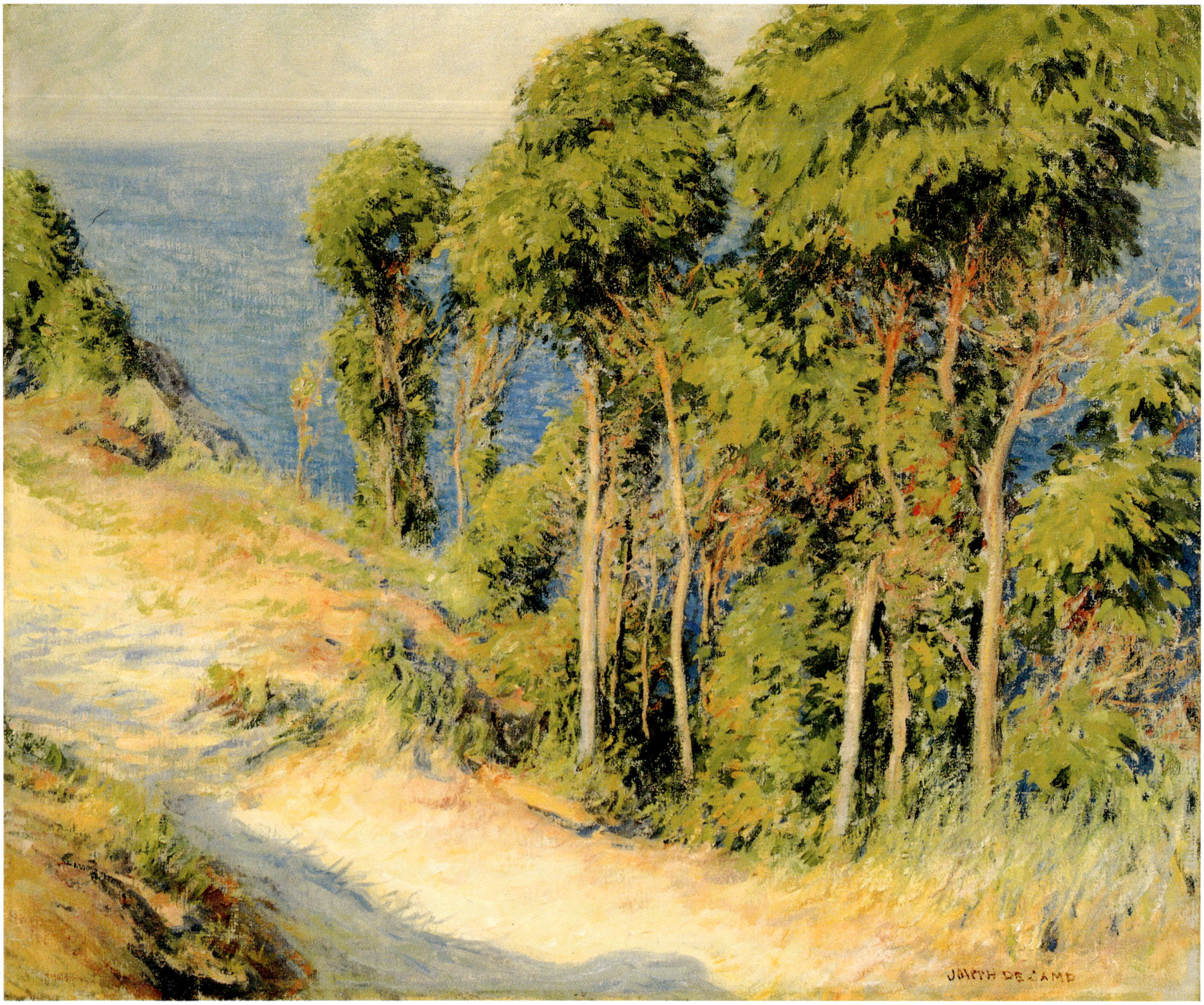

8 *Trees Along the Coast* (*Road to the Sea*), mid-1890s. 25 x 30 in. (63.5 x 76 cm). Private collection

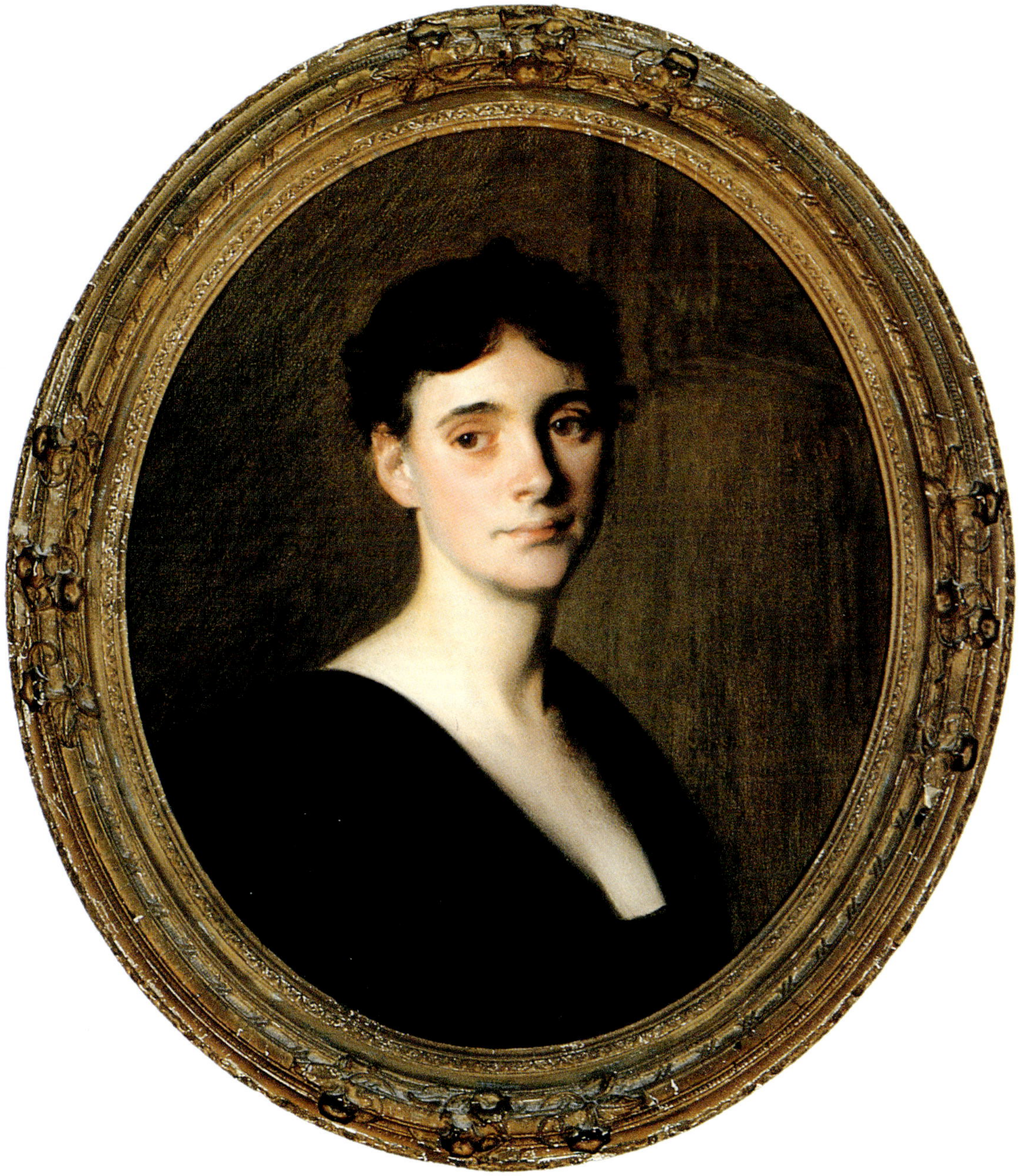

9 *Edith*, ca. 1895. 24 x 18 in. (61 x 45.5 cm). Private collection

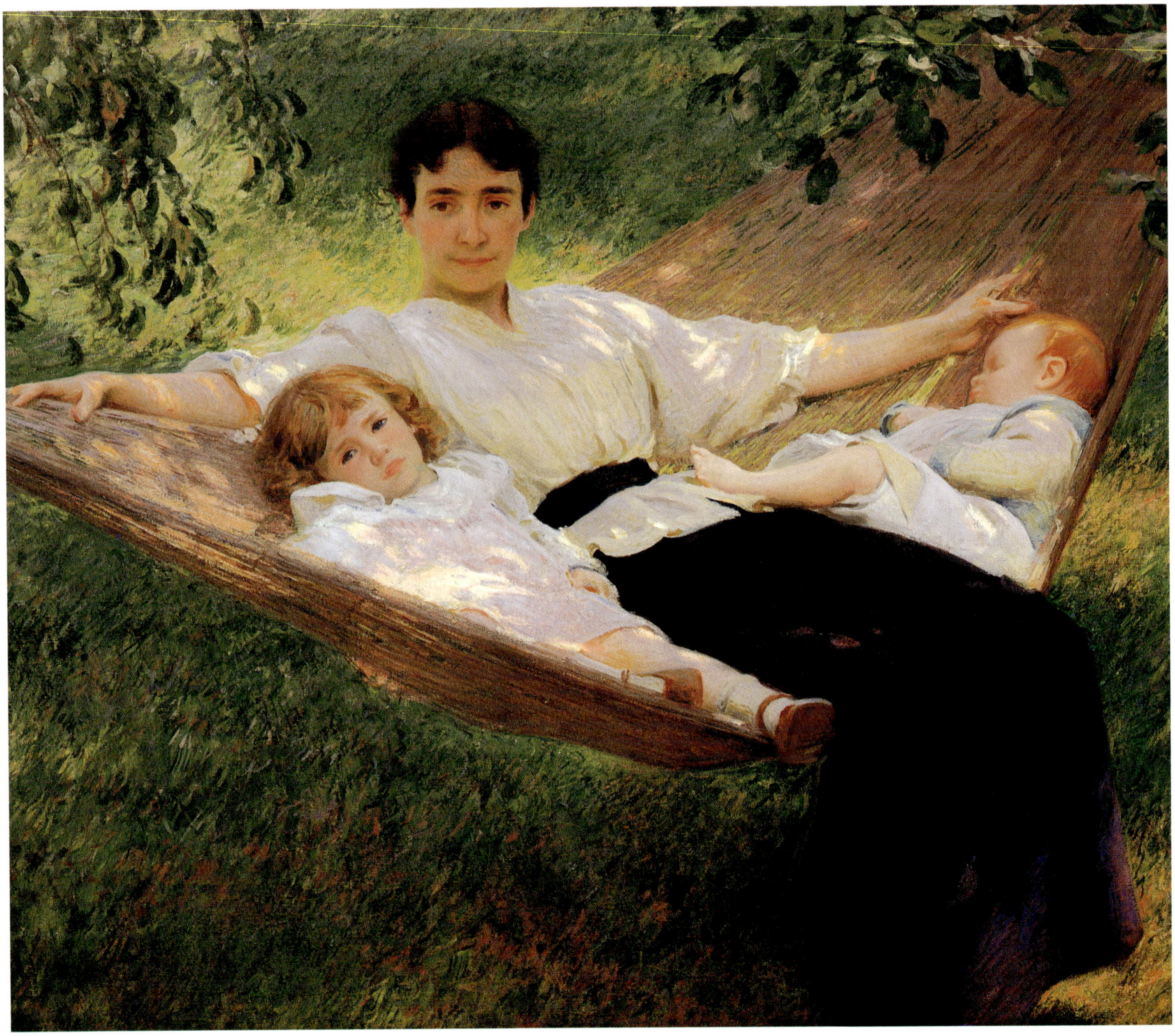

10 *The Hammock*, ca. 1895. 44 x 50 in. (112 x 127 cm). Adelson Galleries, Inc., New York

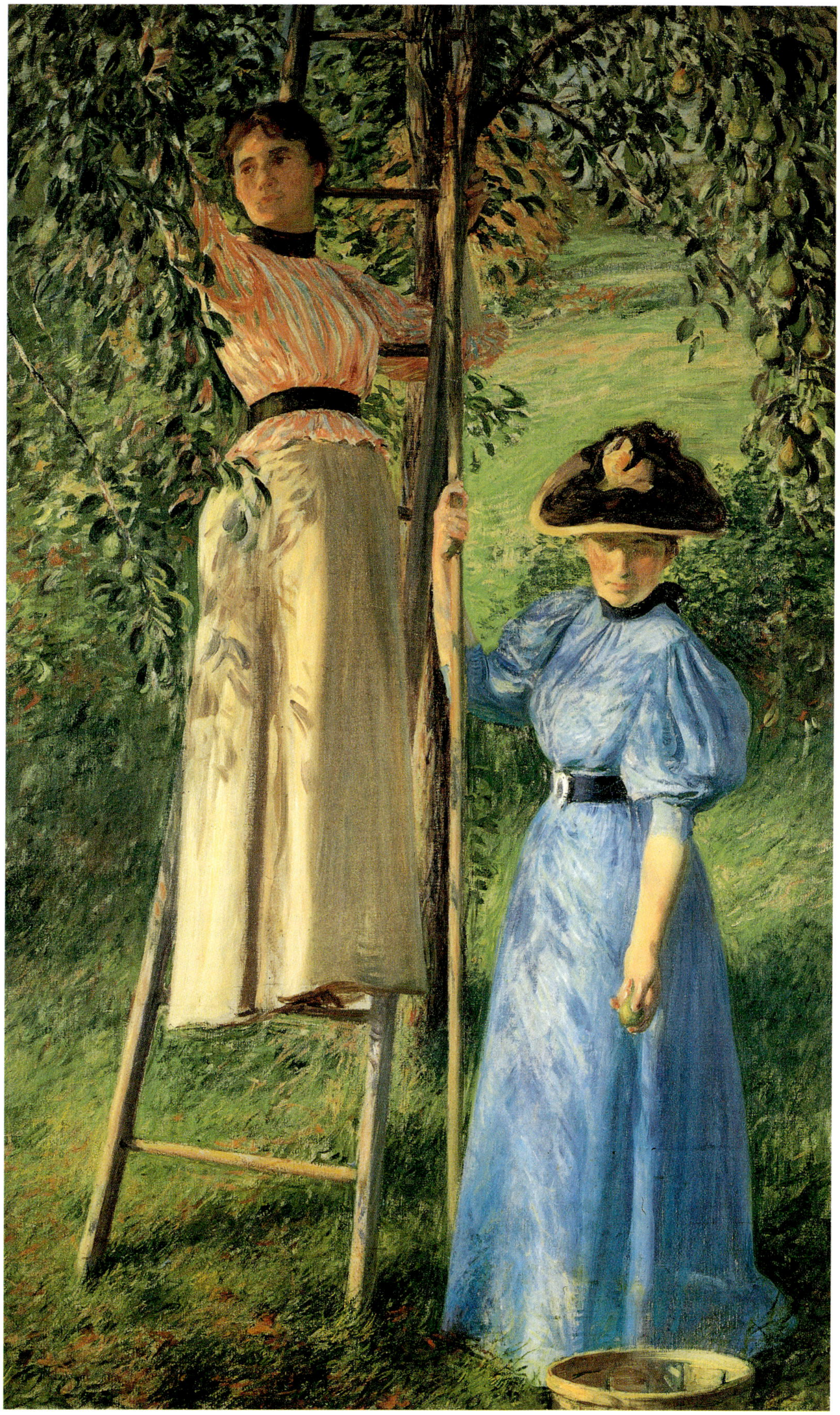

11 *Pear Pickers* (*The Pear Orchard*), mid-1890s. 60 x 35½ in. (152.5 x 90 cm). Private collection

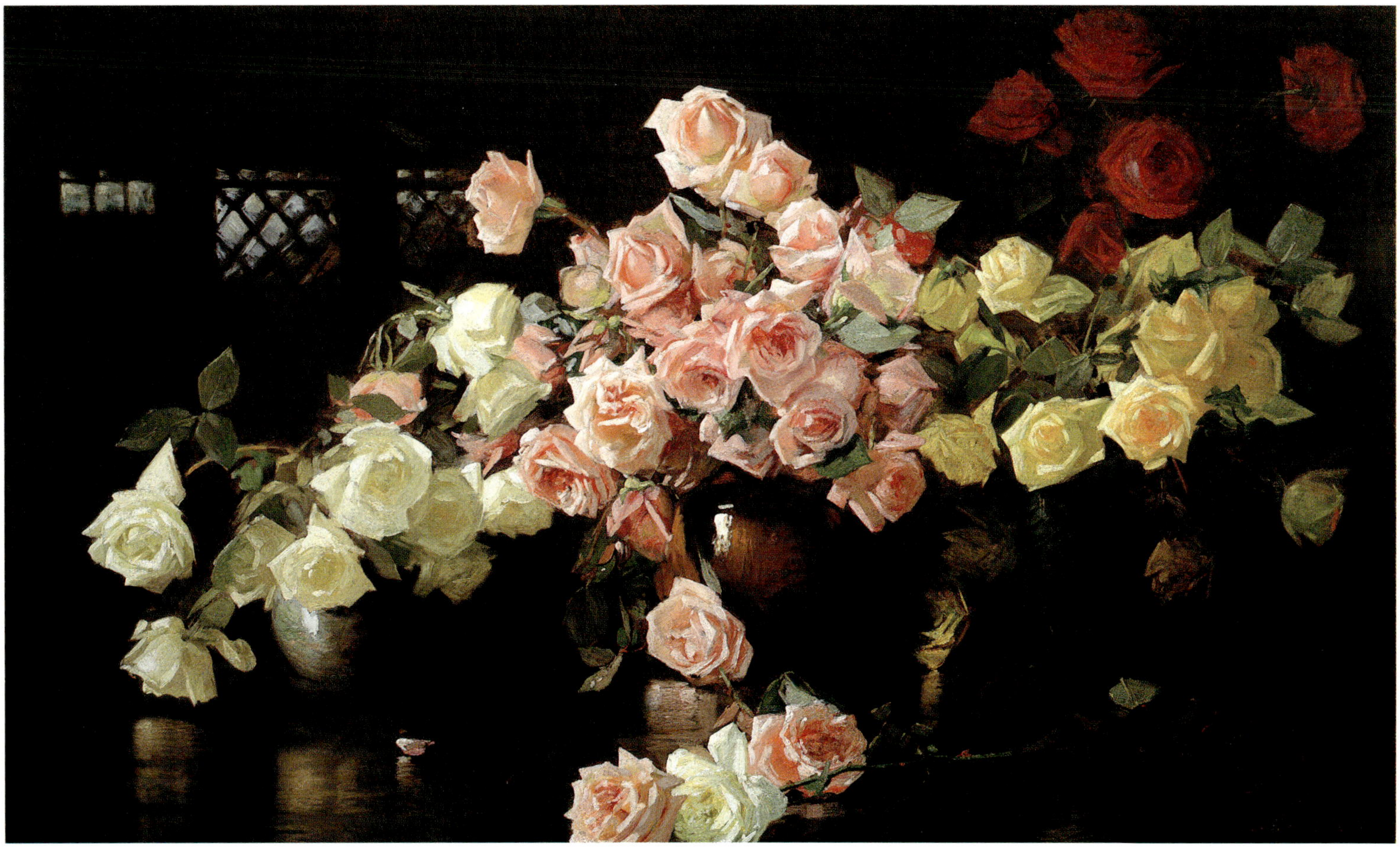

12 *Roses*, 1890s. 37 x 60 in. (94 x 152.5 cm). Private collection

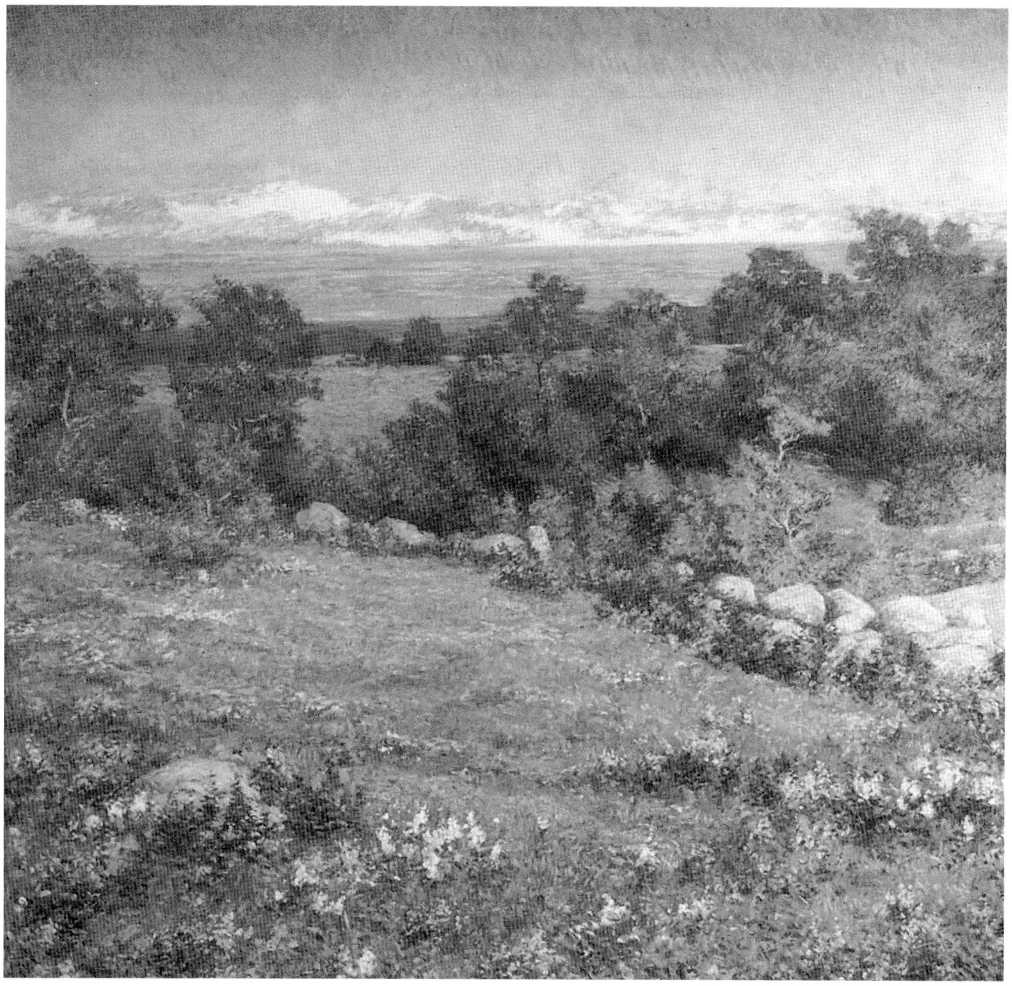

Fig. 24
John Leslie Breck,
Near Annisquam, Autumn, ca. 1894.
45 x 46½ in.
(114.5 x 118 cm).
Private collection

resemblance to Tarbell's *Mother and Child in a Boat* of 1892 (fig. 27), in which the figures are similarly nestled within an encompassing structure and under an overhanging bower of leaves. An earlier work by DeCamp, also titled *The Hammock* (unlocated), was first shown at the Boston Art Club in January 1893 and, according to the *Boston Evening Transcript* critic, depicted "two young women taking the outdoors in the shade of a tree. One of them reclines in a hammock and the other sits in a chair and appears to be reading."[34] Critics of the painting were quick to point to its source in Tarbell's *In the Orchard* of 1891 (fig. 28). "Mr. DeCamp's 'The Hammock' follows too closely Mr. Tarbell's brilliant success of last year, 'In the Orchard,' in subject, manner, color and conception," wrote the reporter for the *Boston Evening Transcript*, "to escape the obvious imputation of being a *pasticcio*, yet the composition is entirely different... and very skillfully done."[35] This latter remark, given the figure style of the extant *Hammock*, may have been a reference to the treatment of the figure, which, in comparison to Tarbell's more painterly technique, appears academic. Here again, the work of Tarbell was the yardstick against which other artists of the Boston School were measured, leading to the designation "Tarbellite" for DeCamp and the

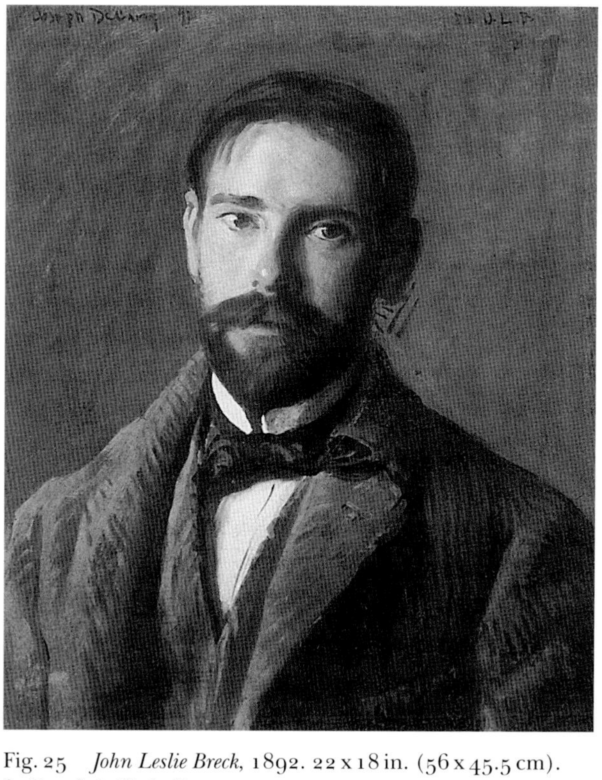

Fig. 25 *John Leslie Breck*, 1892. 22 x 18 in. (56 x 45.5 cm). St. Botolph Club, Boston

others. Nevertheless, DeCamp's *Hammock* brought him his first major award, a bronze medal at Atlanta's International Exposition of the Cotton States in the fall of 1895.

Another outdoor figural work, *Pear Pickers* of the mid-1890s (plate 11), shows Edith and Myra Highley, a family friend, in a fruit orchard (possibly that adjoining the West Medford farmhouse). This, too, displays a more conservative approach to nature when compared to DeCamp's pure landscapes. The figures are carefully composed to follow the path of the plucked fruit from tree to foreground basket, but remain intact against a rich background of interwoven brushstrokes. DeCamp and numerous other Americans who underwent intensive academic training abroad were reluctant to expunge all traces of draftsmanship from their paintings, even from their finest examples of *plein air* Impressionism. *Pear Pickers* owes much to the central figures in Mary Cassatt's mural *Modern Woman* (unlocated, fig. 29), produced for the Woman's Building at the 1893 World's Columbian Exposition in Chicago. There is no evidence that DeCamp attended the exposition, but he may have seen a reproduction of the mural in the September 1893 issue of *Cosmopolitan* or in the handbook of the exposition itself.[36] Although the subject of *Modern Woman* has been clearly identified as relating to women plucking the fruit of the Tree of Knowledge,[37] the mural also belongs to a body of work, by Berthe Morisot, Camille Pissarro, and others, on similar agrarian themes. According to Robert L. Herbert, an international "heyday of books and articles on peasant art, particularly on Barbizon art, occurred between 1875 and 1914."[38] In America the Philadelphia Centennial of 1876 sparked a period of reflection upon the country's colonial roots and, particularly, on the self-sufficiency of the home. DeCamp's *Pear Pickers* celebrates the individual's resourcefulness in utilizing the bounty of his or her own land at a time of increasing mechanization and the concurrent displacement

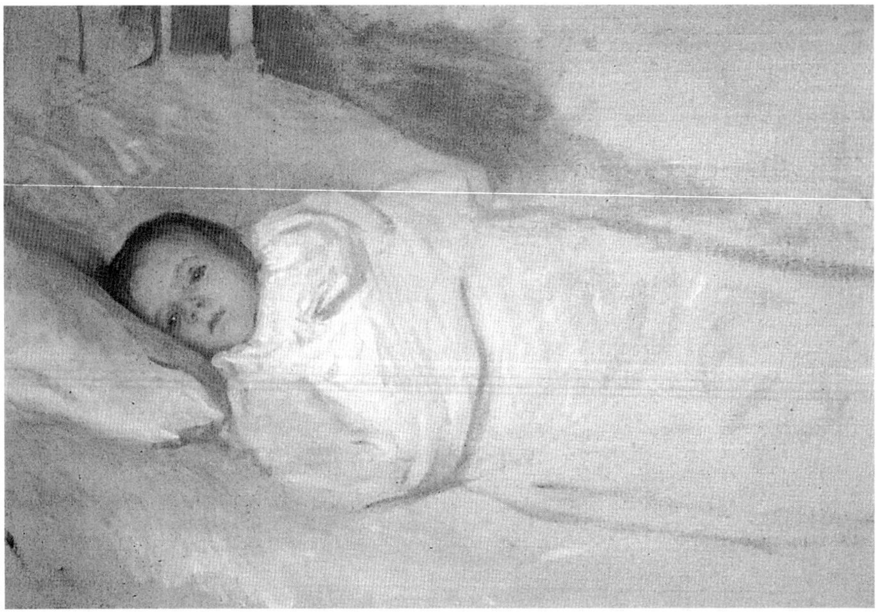

Fig. 26 *Pauline (Polly)*, 1899. 22 x 40 in. (56 x 101.5 cm). Mr. and Mrs. Thomas A. Rosse

Fig. 27 Edmund C. Tarbell, *Mother and Child in a Boat*, 1892. 30 x 35 in. (76 x 89 cm). Museum of Fine Arts, Boston, Bequest of David P. Kimball in memory of his wife, Clara Bertram Kimball

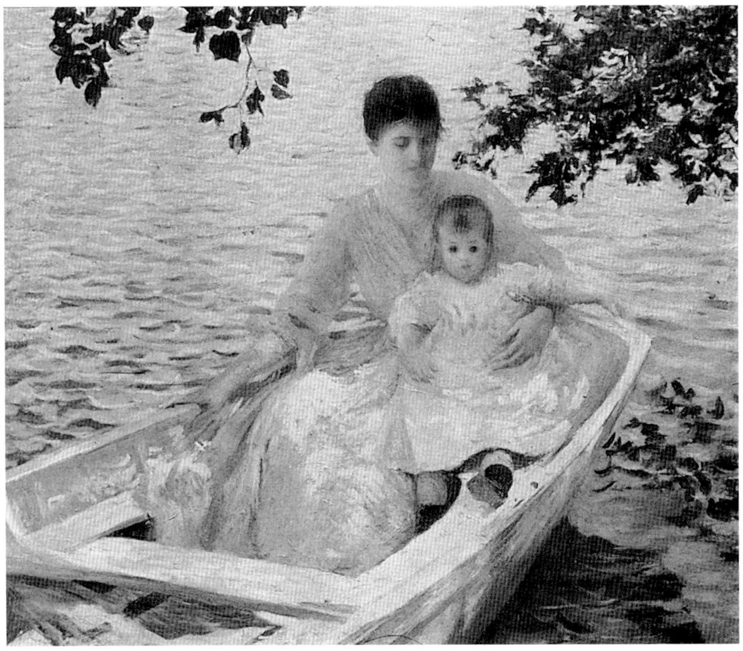

Fig. 28 Edmund C. Tarbell, *In the Orchard*, 1891. 60¼ x 65 in. (153 x 165 cm). Daniel J. Terra Collection, Terra Museum of American Art, Chicago

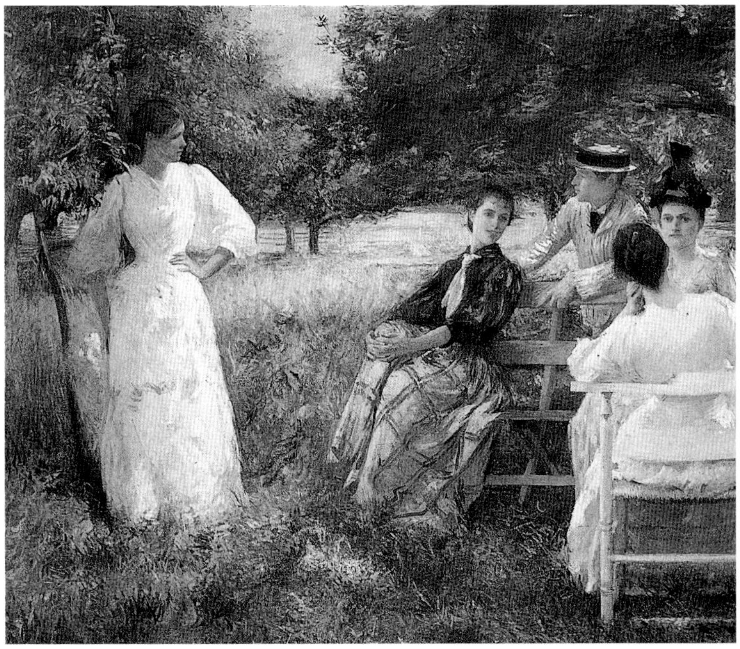

of the rural populace to large urban centers.[39] Ownership of a home and of property, and pride in starting a family, may also have figured in DeCamp's choice of subject in *The Hammock* and *Pear Pickers.* Like Europeans pursuing peasant themes in the 1890s, DeCamp draws on the art historical past, monumentalizing the figures in *Pear Pickers* to the scale used by Jean-François Millet and subtly suggesting Madonna and Child imagery in *The Hammock.*

A glance at DeCamp's exhibition history (see pp. 147–55) reveals that, unlike Tarbell and Benson, who periodically switched from indoor to outdoor subjects in their figural work, he customarily showed paintings on a variety of themes.[40] Another genre that DeCamp explored in the 1890s was the idealized figure in an interior setting. The first such picture by him dates from 1890, the very year that Tarbell turned to the theme with his firelit *After the Ball* (unlocated). Benson's indoor works began a year later, with *Twilight* (private collection), also a fireside painting. Critics encouraged this type of image, in which portraiture *per se* is clearly subordinate to "spirited execution, allied to sweet and delicate color," as Harley Perkins, a *Boston Evening Transcript* reviewer and friend of DeCamp's, put it.[41] *At the Piano* of 1890 (unlocated) was described as "a half-life size of a... young woman in yellow, at her piano."[42] *Arrangement in Black and Red* (unlocated), shown in New York at the Society of American Artists annual of 1892, won a gold medal the following year as *Carnation and Black* at the Massachusetts Charitable Mechanics Association, Boston, a pre-showing of the Massachusetts contingent of artwork for the World's Columbian Exposition. It represented "a lady in a red dress, with a black lace shawl thrown over the shoulders."[43] When exhibited in Boston, the work was called "a bit hard" but, nonetheless, "a bright and agreeable decoration,"[44] and, when it finally reached Chicago, it received mixed reviews, even from Boston critics: "Much as we admire and enjoy brilliant and positive color, there is such a thing as a surfeit and the limit seems to have been more than reached in this case. Color, in the painter's sense, is entirely a matter of contrasts and relations of tones, and is not to be got by extracting the strongest pigments wholesale from tubes, and putting people's eyes out by a blaze of violent hues. There is a golden mean in everything."[45]

Three other indoor figural works of this period deserve mention. *Portrait of Miss X* (unlocated), shown at the seventh Philadelphia Art Club annual of 1895, was described as an "artfully posed lady in Colonial-like costume."[46] *Head of a Young Woman* (unlocated), which DeCamp sent to three different exhibitions, also shows a posed woman in a fancy dress,[47] while *The Looking Glass* (unlocated), of about 1899, was described as "a bust portrait of a girl with her back to the spectator, looking at her own face in a mirror" and "pinning her corsage at the throat."[48]

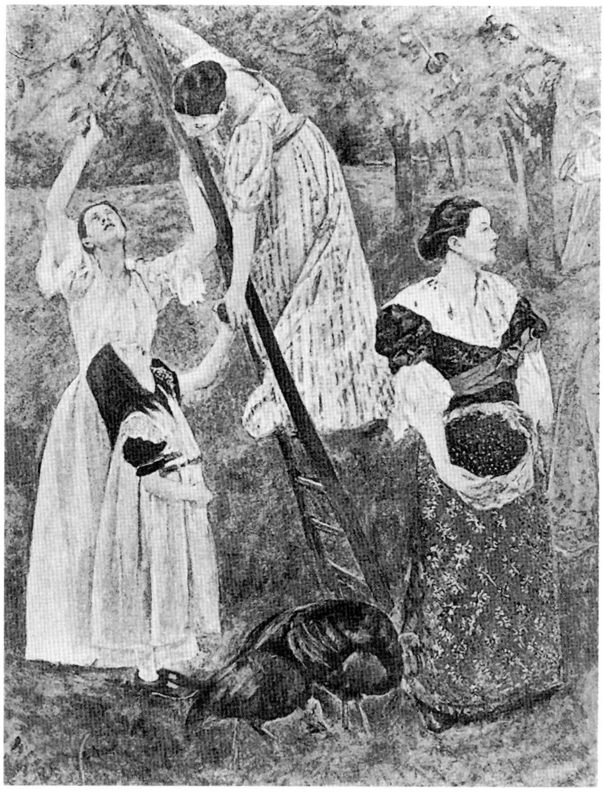

Fig. 29 Mary Cassatt, *Gathering Fruit*, 1893. Detail of the mural *Modern Woman*

DeCamp rarely painted pure still lifes, yet the wonderfully realized florals and decorative objects included in his figural works attest a highly developed skill in the genre. One mature example of a pure still life has survived. *Roses* (plate 12), an enormous display of yellow and pink roses held in ceramic vases or strewn over a glistening tabletop, is said to have been painted for a Chicago collector named Arthur Aldis.[49] In a manner reminiscent of the artist's Munich style, the arrangement fades into a dark background, particularly at upper right; the faint image of a stained-glass window appears at upper left.

According to Kathryn Corbin, Breck had executed comparable large floral pieces in the mid- to late 1880s, "carefully composed against dark backgrounds and incorporating decorative objects the artist had collected in Europe."[50] Abbott Thayer, J. Alden Weir, and Emil Carlsen, a still life specialist who was an instructor at Wellesley College at the same time as DeCamp, had all done the same. Breck was still painting very large florals, albeit in a lighter palette, in the mid-1890s, including *Chrysanthemums* (private collection), which he exhibited at the Newton Club, Boston, in 1896. Unfortunately, since DeCamp's further essays in still life were limited to arrangements in his portraits and figure studies, it is difficult to assess his place within the American still life tradition.

DeCamp's need to make his work more widely known was particularly acute in the 1890s. Not only had he reached artistic maturity, but also the city he had chosen as home was, perhaps, proving to be a less than ideal forum. By 1880 annexation and landfill had tripled Boston's ground area and, over the next fifty years, its population would double.[51] There was an increasing awareness that the city needed to do more to encourage its own artists. Reviewing a show at the Boston Art Club in January 1893, one critic remarked that there were "not less than nine art exhibitions in progress, containing in the aggregate, in round numbers, 1200 works of art.... Today [there are] hundreds of professional artists in and around Boston where there were only a few dozen of them twenty years ago.... The only wonder is how so many painters can make a living, and it is well understood that they could not do so without resorting to teaching, illustrating, decorating, and the like."[52]

Rather than move to New York, as other Boston artists had done—Bunker, Thomas W. Dewing, Childe Hassam, Robert Reid, and Edward Simmons, for example—DeCamp looked to Philadelphia, which was experiencing artistic growing pains of its own, especially at the Pennsylvania Academy of the Fine Arts. "Years ago," a Philadelphia *Public Ledger* reviewer noted in 1894, "when Philadelphia was an art centre, and not a recruiting station for artists, the academy was the foremost institution of its kind in the country. By degrees this proud position was lost, and during the last few years efforts more energetic and more liberal than ever before made by the Academy have been put forth to regain the lost ground."[53] The person most responsible for this energy was the academy's new director, Harrison S. Morris, who had been hired in 1892 after a career "in the treasury of the Philadelphia & Reading Coal and Iron Company."[54] Beginning with a trip to Boston in 1892 to meet Tarbell, DeCamp, and Benson, he immediately set out to entice major living artists to exhibit at the academy's annual.[55]

About this time, Morris was looking for "the best man in the field of teaching" as a successor to Robert Vonnoh. "Undoubtedly, this was Joseph DeCamp," Morris later wrote, "but he was pretty reluctant to make a change. After long hesitation and much persuasion, however, he decided to accept the post.... We arranged that he should travel down from Boston every week and devote two days to the classes in painting [life drawing and still life]."[56] Morris continued:

> With the opening of the Schools this began, and the success of his teaching was marked. His hearty geniality won the students, and his grasp of his art was convincing to even the tyro. Things went on well for the school season, but I began to perceive that Joseph's health was apparently affected by the night travel so constantly kept up, an effect I have observed in others who must use the Pullman too repeatedly. He had to slacken the pace before long, and I have it on my conscience that perhaps I had unwittingly planted an evil seed that injured his very strong frame; for his health gave out at intervals after this.... To me he was one of the finest spirits in the realm of Art.... I can see him come hurrying into the Academy office fresh from Boston, or from the Art Club where he spent his one night in Philadelphia, in his robust, hearty way, full of eagerness to meet his classes, with that urge to expression, and the lifted and inverted thumb of emphasis, with argument and theory on Art and laughter on his broad honest face; and he remains in memory one of the characters I cherish from those rich days of unreflecting good fellowship .... A noble artist, a lasting comrade.[57]

Morris also recalled the unfortunate circumstances surrounding a mural competition that he and the United States attorney for the eastern district of Philadelphia, James M. Beck, had instituted in 1896 in order to brighten "the ugliness of the Philadelphia City Hall."[58] The mural movement in America, initiated in Boston in 1876 with the interior decoration of Henry Richardson's Trinity Church, was in full swing at this time, as evidenced by the extensive wall paintings executed for the World's Columbian Exposition in Chicago in 1893. Thirty-nine entries were received for the Philadelphia competition. Charles Yardley Turner, known for his mural work, received second prize, and Benson, who had been extremely active in the field of wall painting in the mid-1880s, came third; but the jury awarded first prize to DeCamp, who had never done work of this kind. His entry was described as "allegorical of Wise Legislation, Truth, Courage and Moderation under the benign influences of the Sciences and the Arts."[59] An extant proposal sketch (fig. 30), one of three panels, is known as *Plato's Garden* and includes obvious references to Raphael's *The School of Athens* (1500–11; Stanza della Segnatura, Vatican Palace, Rome); a smaller study is in a private collection. As sketchy as the composition and figures are in both paintings, they nevertheless help us to visualize what the mural might have been like and the position it might have accorded DeCamp in the field.

DeCamp's mural was never executed. Edward Simmons was one of the jurors for the competition and later recalled that the funder of the project, George W. Elkins, had predetermined that Edwin Austin Abbey was to win.[60] "Needless to say," Simmons noted, "the young artist never got a chance to carry out his work, although they were obliged to give him his prize money."[61] In addition, contemporary newspaper reports provide some evidence that the city was reluctant to realize DeCamp's designs. The *Evening Bulletin* of May 27, 1896, mentions that they did not meet the "condition of a historic commemoration,"[62] indicating that a Philadelphia historical subject was favored. The *Philadelphia Times* was more supportive: "It is quite probable that the average unprofessional person would not have preferred Mr. DeCamp's sketch to the more elaborately finished and more obvious design of Mr. Turner, or the more immediately imposing composition of Mr. Benson. Yet a little consideration will

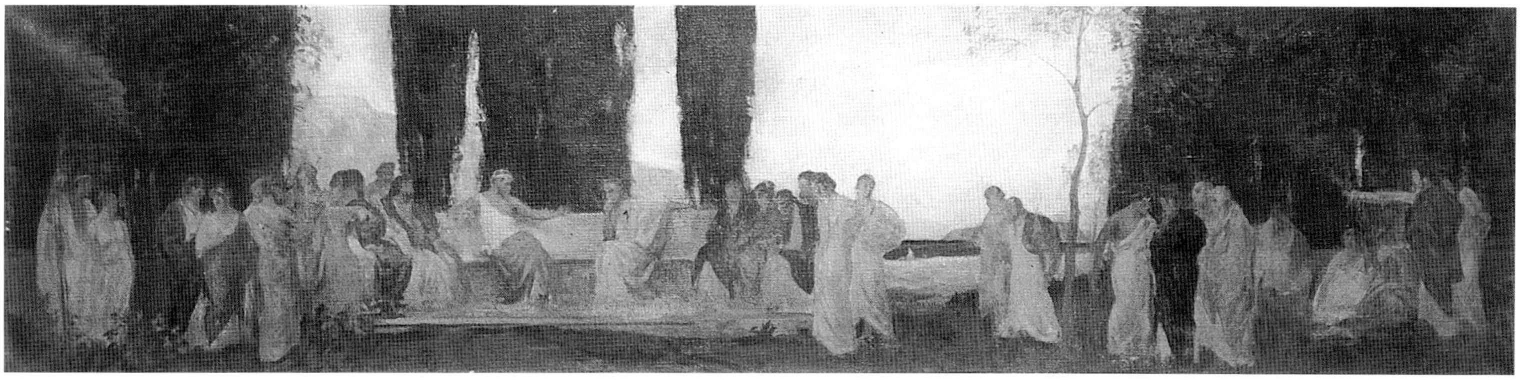

Fig. 30
Plato's Garden, 1896.
32 x 124 in.
(81.5 x 315 cm).
Private collection

show not only the larger dignity of Mr. DeCamp's decorative conception... but also the essential fact that more fully than any of the others he has met the particular conditions imposed by the existing architectural features of the room."[63] Several jury members—Simmons, John J. Boyle, Frank Duveneck, John Lambert, Jr., Emily Sartain, and C. Howard Walker—were moved to write the Commissioners for the Erection of the Public Buildings of Philadelphia asking them to reaffirm their decision, but to no avail.[64]

At least two other mural projects by DeCamp are known. His decorations for Boston's Hotel Touraine, executed between 1898 and 1906, were described by Harley Perkins in his 1923 memorial piece on DeCamp as "a ceiling decoration with cupid musicians who were... drawn from the artist's own children," and, along the stairway, "another panel of Night and Morning."[65] Unfortunately, these murals were destroyed after World War II when, according to Moffat, the hotel was "modernized."[66] In the clipping files of both the Boston Public Library and the New York Public Library are reproductions of another mural project, *Sketch of a Decoration for a Public Room* (unlocated, fig. 31), which, however, may simply be another of the Philadelphia City Hall competition panels. As late as 1909 *American Art News* announced that DeCamp was "busy with a large mural decoration intended for Temple Ardeth Israel in Boston. The work includes a number of figures, many oft hem life-size."[67] Attempts by the present author to trace this mural have been unsuccessful.

Fig. 31
Sketch of a Decoration for a Public Room, ca. 1896.
Dimensions unknown.
Unlocated

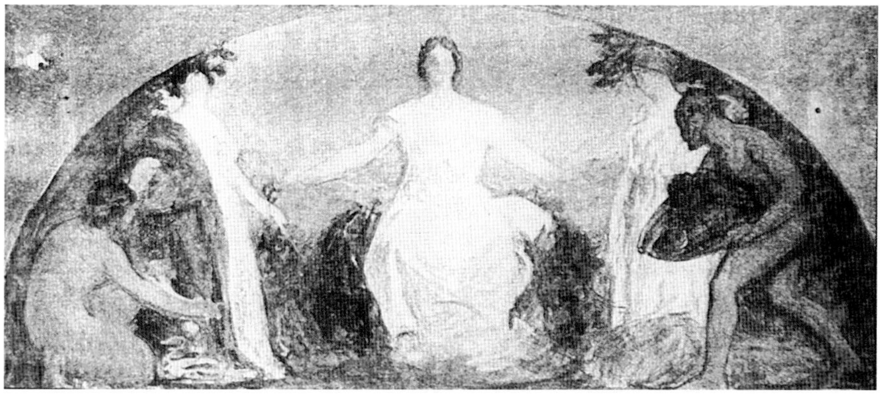

In the mid-1890s DeCamp added yet another subject to his repertoire—the nude. An especially large selection of nudes was shown at the 1893 Society of American Artists exhibition, at which Tarbell was awarded the coveted Shaw Fund prize for his controversial painting of a naked woman in her boudoir, *The Bath* (unlocated). The place of honor, however, was accorded Kenyon Cox's *Sleep* (unlocated), perhaps because of the artist's powerful status within the society. These, along with other nude subjects, by Thayer, Edward Bell, and Charles Courtney Curran, were said both to "attract the most attention" at the show and to have received the greatest public criticism for their portrayal of the nude without a "poetic idea"[68]—a reference to the lack of a mythological or historical theme. Tarbell's *Bath*, clearly derived from Edouard Manet's *Olympia* (1863; Musée d'Orsay, Paris), was considered too coarse a subject[69] and was cited as an example of the French school infecting the art of the Americans.[70] The following year, the artists made an even more determined effort to exhibit nude subjects at the society as a response to the government's outcry over Augustus Saint Gaudens's submission of a nude devoid of historical associations as the official medal for the World's Columbian Exposition in Chicago. A *Washington Post* article announced that the "Great Gothom [*sic*] Art Exhibition" would have as its objective "To Glorify the Nude." The subtitle of the article read: "American Artists Determined to Administer a Public Rebuke to the Senate for Its Absurd Prudery in the Matter of St. Gaudens' World's Fair Medals."[71]

DeCamp joined the 1894 hoopla at the society with the first of a series of nudes, *The Mirror* (unlocated), which the *Boston Sunday Herald* described as a "woman who sits at the end of a couch [and] surveys herself in a mirror in which her form is seen in the mysterious indefiniteness of reflected shadow, her body and side being in full light."[72] The painting was considered "a forward step" for DeCamp by the *Art Amateur* critic, but the same reviewer cautioned: "It would do him no harm to wait until he had made further progress before exhibiting his studies publicly."[73] At the Pennsylvania Academy of the Fine Arts, on the other hand, it was hailed as "the best painting of flesh in the gallery."[74] When it was shown at the Art Club of Detroit, a critic described its technique: "Closer inspection of the work reveals the curious workmanship of it. The brush touches made all one way, the brush having been lifted from the canvas after each stroke, after the manner of an artist working in pen and ink, depending upon strokes successively laid one above the other.... The painting is an oil, with effect of a pastel."[75]

Sleep (unlocated), its title echoing Cox's triumph of 1893 at the society show, pictured "a nude young woman asleep in the light of the early dawn" against a dark red backdrop and with a "greenish blue atmosphere about the figure."[76] The picture was exhibited at the Pennsylvania Academy's annual of 1894 and, in January 1896, at the Boston Art Club, where a reviewer found it "carelessly drawn," but applauded its color.[77]

Gold-Fish, later retitled *Girl with a Globe* (unlocated), caused some concern when shown at the Boston Art Club in 1895 owing to the precariousness of a heavy bowl being held aloft by a woman![78] In New York the critics liked the "dexterous flesh painting"[79] but not the background, with "its curves suggesting that of the fish."[80] In Philadelphia it was applauded: "The tones are warm and rich, and the bright color of the fish contrasts strikingly with the pure flesh tones of the model."[81]

With *Magdalene* (alternatively, *Magdalen*, fig. 32) DeCamp returned to religious subject matter. As mentioned above, a naturalistically painted nude, executed for its own sake, was still a point of controversy, and the artist may have painted the penitent Magdalene—a favorite subject of Baroque painters, Caravaggio and his followers among them—in order to appeal to conservative patrons, who might find the image of a naked woman acceptable if it were placed in an historical or a sacred context. When *Magdalene* was first exhibited, at the Philadelphia Art Club in 1896, one critic was enamored of the "weeping woman, nude, with a mass of warm, red hair falling over her shoulder,"[81] while another found "nothing penitential about this model."[82] The painting was purchased by W. J. Little, undoubtedly one of DeCamp's earliest patrons, who later sold his collection at Leonard's Gallery in New York, where the artist found it again and bought it on the spot.[83] Presumably, it stayed in DeCamp's possession until its acquisition by the Cincinnati Art Museum a year after his death.

Reflections (unlocated) did not fare as well with the critics, the reviewer for an 1898 issue of *Art Amateur* finding the method of hatching used in the flesh areas unappealing.[84] On the other hand, *Woman Drying Her Hair* (plate 13), which owed much to Tarbell's *Venetian Blind* (fig. 33) in pose, technique, and subject, attained the pinnacle of success for DeCamp's nudes, receiving the Temple Gold Medal at the Pennsylvania Academy's annual of 1899.

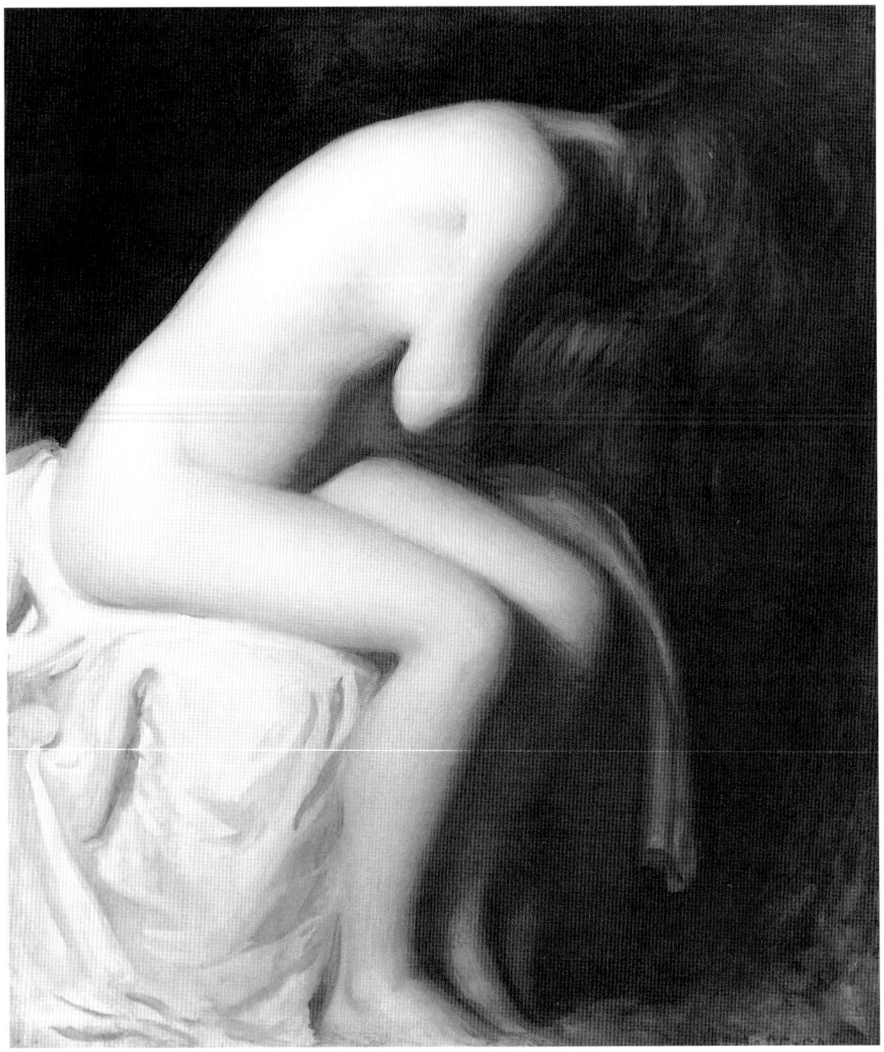

Fig. 32 *Magdalene* (*Magdalen*), ca. 1896.
30 x 25 1/16 in. (76 x 63.5 cm). Cincinnati Art Museum, John J. Emery Endowment

As early as 1895, DeCamp had been called a "superb painter of the nude,"[85] a characterization that stayed with him throughout his career. His academic training, with its intensive focus on figure and portrait studies, surely accounted for this prowess. Even in the prudish world of Boston, the drawing of the nude was considered the supreme artistic challenge, testing the draftsman's sense of proportion and his or her skill in volumetric modeling. A New York *Evening Post* critic put it succinctly: "The handling of the nude figure is, and has been since art began, the criterion of artistic ability in both form and color. It is at once the most difficult and, when well rendered, the most beautiful of all subjects."[86]

With so much critical praise accorded his paintings of nudes, it is no wonder that, having been asked to join the Ten American Painters in 1897—an important association of mostly Impressionist artists (fig. 34)—DeCamp exhibited nudes in the group's first two shows. If his aim was to stand out distinctly from

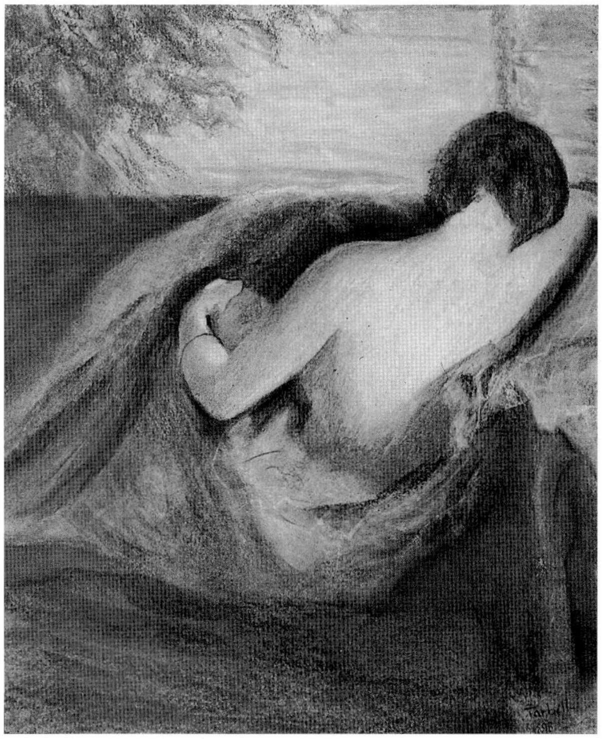

Fig. 33 Edmund C. Tarbell, *Venetian Blind*, 1898.
51⅞ x 38⅛ in. (132 x 97 cm).
Worcester Art Museum, Massachusetts, Museum Purchase

the rest of the Ten, he was most successful, the nudes in the 1898 exhibition—the group's first—being "perhaps the most controversial works in the show."[87] While some critics for both the 1898 and 1899 exhibitions found the draftsmanship and the flesh tones of the nudes of good quality,[88] others felt they were not worthy of the artist.[89] Still others welcomed DeCamp's works as a pleasant relief both from the shrill colors of Robert Reid's paintings[90] and from the "angular creature of shreds and patches, like Mr. Hassam's [*The Bather*, unlocated]."[91]

Other members of the Ten were Benson, Dewing, Simmons, Tarbell, Weir, Willard Metcalf, John Henry Twachtman, and William Merritt Chase, who was asked to join two years after Twachtman's death in 1902. With the possible exception of Twachtman, DeCamp's associations with members other than the Boston contingent scarcely went beyond his serving with them on juries at various national venues, such as the Pennsylvania Academy of the Fine Arts or the Society of American Artists. His ties with Tarbell and Benson, however, were strong: as will be remembered, he had shared a studio space with them at 20 St. Botolph Street in 1894 and 1895 and had exhibited with them. It was in 1897 that the unfortunate term "Tarbellites" was first used in print; referring to the triumvirate Tarbell, Benson, and DeCamp, it implied that the last two were under the Tarbell umbrella.[92] The "umbrella" may have worked to DeCamp's advantage in his selection to the Ten, since an invitation to one of these three Boston painters applied, by extension, to all of them. Once included, they were continually reviewed as a separate grouping of the Ten.

The annual Ten show was clearly DeCamp's favorite exhibition forum. He was a regular contributor to its remarkable twenty-one-year history and generally offered work fresh from the easel.[93] Not one of the key figures in the formation of the group,[94] DeCamp nonetheless was a spokesman when news of the Ten's secession from its parent organization, the Society of American Artists, surfaced in the press. The society had, according to DeCamp, "outlived its usefulness .... There was a time when it was deemed an honor for an artist to be enrolled among the membership ... but that time has passed. The composition, with a few exceptions, of the society, has reached such a state that so-called artists, who would never be admitted to the original society, are admitted openly."[95]

At various times in the history of the Ten exhibitions, DeCamp's work was singled out for recognition. The year 1908 was a particular boon for the artist, the critics outdoing each other in praise of his spectacular advances, as evidenced especially by *The Guitar Player* and *The Cellist* (plates 28, 29).[96] James B. Townsend of *American Art News* pronounced *The Blue Cup* (plate 31) the "star" of the 1909 show, and Arthur Hoeber considered *The Fur Jacket* (plate 32) the best of the 1910 display.[97] DeCamp did not hesitate to include his more conservative formal portraits in the Ten exhibitions, and they received their fair share of recognition. His portrait of Frank Duveneck (fig. 57), presented at the 1913 show at Boston's Copley Gallery, was called "one of the important portraits of this century" and the portrait of composer George Whitefield Chadwick (fig. 61) was hung in the place of honor in the 1917 New York exhibition.[98]

Recognizably different, DeCamp's work was often used by reviewers to characterize the paintings of the other artists in the group, as with the previously mentioned comparison of his nudes with those by Reid[99] or, in 1911, when Benson's entries were considered much closer to nature than DeCamp's.[100] At other times, especially in the periods when DeCamp was exhibiting his *plein air* work and, later, during a phase of Vermeer influence, his work fit comfortably with that of his Boston colleagues, and the critics were quick to draw attention to the trio's common sensibilities.[101] As William H. Gerdts has pointed out, it was the Boston School that set the genteel tone for the group in its later years, especially after the Vermeeresque phase in their work from 1905 to 1910 or 1911.[102] Within the broader scope of criticism devoted to the Ten exhibitions, however, it was DeCamp's academic approach, his ability to capture a certain sophistication in his sitters, and, above all, his sheer expertise in the handling of paint that gave him a special place within the group.

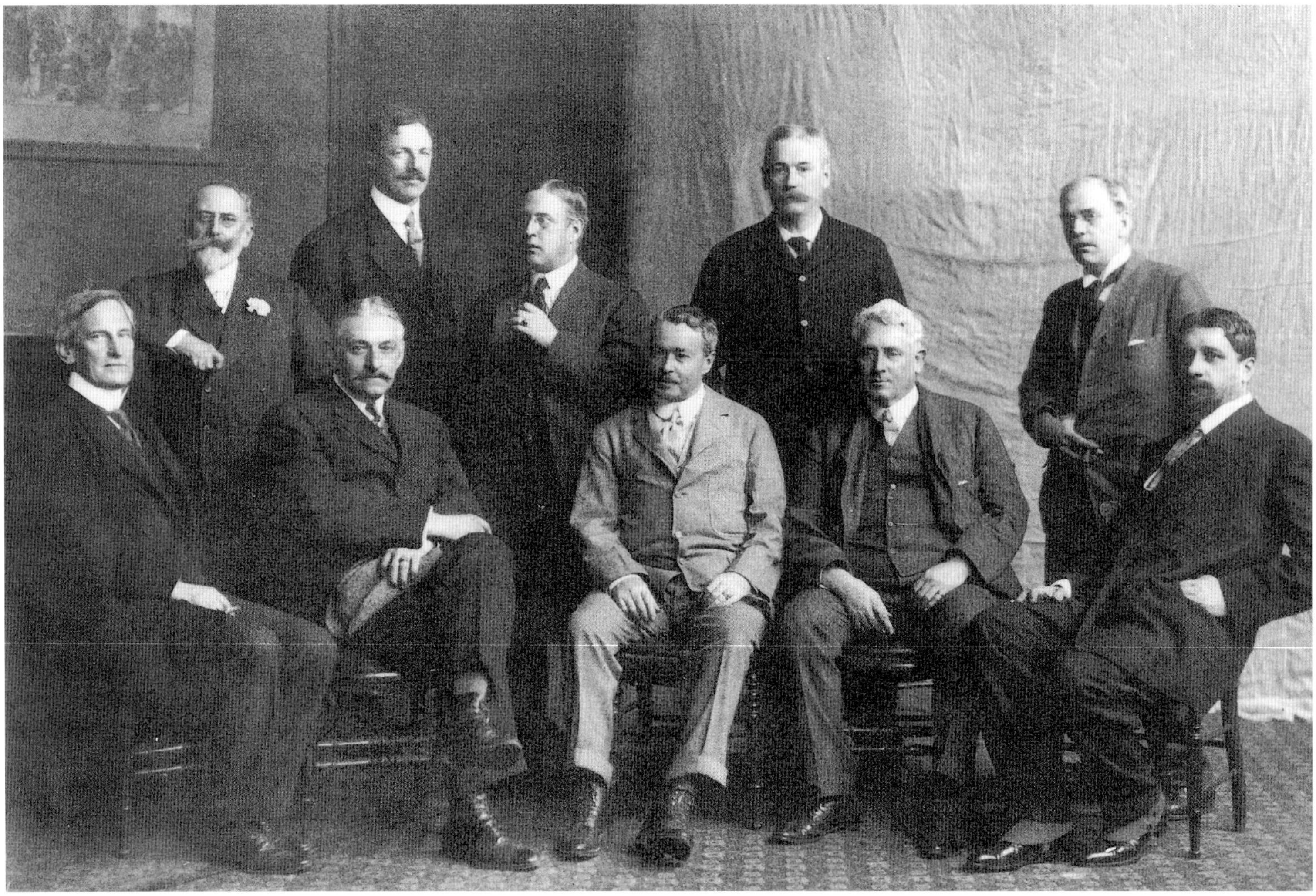

Fig. 34 "Ten American Painters," 1908. Seated, left to right: Edward E. Simmons, Willard L. Metcalf, Childe Hassam, J. Alden Weir, Robert Reid; standing, left to right: William Merritt Chase, Frank W. Benson, Edmund C. Tarbell, Thomas W. Dewing, DeCamp

Notes

1 Donald Moffat, "Joseph Rodefer DeCamp: Biographical Sketch," unpublished typescript, Frick Art Reference Library, New York, 1955–57, p. 25. There are no known extant paintings by Edith DeCamp.

2 City directory, Medford, Massachusetts, 1891.

3 "Squibs from 'Squam," *Cape Ann Breeze*, July 9, 1891, p. 4. The only new member listed for the Lavender Club is Miss Lizzie H. Snowden. Philadelphia was one of three regions represented at Annisquam, according to the *Cape Ann Breeze* of July 18, 1891 ("Squibs from 'Squam," p. 4): "Here come the cultured Bostonians and the scholarly Cambridgettes. Philadelphia sends her Quaker lads and lasses, soft spoken and precise; the wild and wooly west, her wide awake and energetic sons and daughters."

4 "Squibs from 'Squam," *Cape Ann Breeze*, September 15, 1891, p. 6.

5 Joseph Rodefer DeCamp and Edith Franklin Baker Marriage Certificate (private collection).

6 Moffat, "Joseph Rodefer DeCamp: Biographical Sketch," p. 25.

7 *Ibid.*

8 City directories, Medford, Massachusetts (1892 at 14 Water Street; 1893–96 at 107 High Street).

9 "J. R. DeCamp Dies Suddenly: Famous Boston Portrait Painter Passes Away in Florida, Brother-in-Law of Postmaster Baker," *Boston Herald*, February 12, 1923, p. 16.

10 Baker's relationship to Homer is mentioned in William Howe Downes, *The Life and Works of Winslow Homer* (Boston: Houghton Mifflin Co., 1911), p. 18. Homer's later visit to the DeCamps' rental cottage at Prout's Neck, Maine, and his gift of a drawing of himself by Joseph Baker to Mrs. DeCamp that summer is recounted there on pages 241–42.

11 Moffat ("Joseph Rodefer DeCamp: Biographical Sketch," p. 26) dates the purchase of the West Medford home to 1894, but the city directory records their first year there as 1897.

12 *Ibid.*, p. 26.

13 "DeCamp's Roosevelt," *Medford Mercury*, February 19, 1909, p. 4.

14 Moffat, "Joseph Rodefer DeCamp: Biographical Sketch," p. 26. Edith is listed under "communicants" in the Grace Episcopal Church records (p. 236), which do not mention DeCamp.

15 *Ibid.*, p. 32, and city directories, Boston, 1889–93.

16 City directories, Boston, 1894–95.

17 Minutes of the Nominating Committee, School of Drawing and Painting of the Museum of Fine Arts, Boston, April 14, 1893; Library Archives, Museum of Fine Arts, Boston.

18 Minutes of the Annual Meeting of the Permanent Committee, School of Drawing and Painting of the Museum of Fine Arts, Boston, May 10 and November 20, 1893. My thanks go to Benson's biographer, Faith Andrews Bedford, for this information.

19 Trevor J. Fairbrother, *The Bostonians: Painters of An Elegant Age, 1870–1930*, exh. cat. (Boston: Museum of Fine Arts, 1986), p. 50.

20 S. C. de Soissons, *Boston Artists: A Parisian Critic's Notes* (Boston: Carl Schoenhof, 1894), pp. 41–42.

21 [Royal Cortissoz], "A Strong Exhibition," *New-York Daily Tribune*, May 2, 1892, p. 7.

22 "The Fine Arts," *Boston Daily Advertiser*, January 3, 1892, p. 5.

23 H[arley]. T. P[erkins]., "The Fine Arts," *Boston Evening Transcript*, May 6, 1893, p. 13. *September Afternoon* may be identical with *September Afternoon—Milton [sic], Massachusetts* (plate 5). The latter was formerly owned by Harrison S. Morris, who was appointed director of the Pennsylvania Academy of the Fine Arts in 1892.

24 [Royal Cortissoz], "The Society of Artists," *New-York Daily Tribune*, Arpil 24, 1893, p. 4.

25 "The Academy's Display," *Public Ledger—Philadelphia*, December 23, 1895, p. 12.

26 A Paris- and Munich-trained portrait and landscape artist, Vinton became known in Boston as the painter of men, a mantle DeCamp would inherit upon the senior artist's death in 1911.

27 "The Fine Arts," *Boston Daily Advertiser*, January 30, 1894, p. 4.

28 "The Fine Arts," *Boston Evening Transcript*, February 9, 1894, p. 5.

29 "Society of American Artists," *Sun*, March 18, 1894, p. 3.

30 "A Strong Exhibition," *Public Ledger—Philadelphia*, November 19, 1895, p. 7.

31 "Lines from Lanesville," *Cape Ann Evening Breeze*, June 19, 1895, p. 5. DeCamp's pupils that summer, according to this article, were Baily Cross, Louisa Dresel, Grace Hall, Marion Nickerson, and Nellie Thompson. No mention is made of their home towns. I wish to thank Ann Fisk, Director of the Rockport Art Association, Massachusetts, and Carolyn O'Connor, Gloucester, for their help in identifying this and many other local sites shown in DeCamp's paintings.

32 The name "Big Five" was no doubt a reference to the contemporary political scene in Boston, where the leaders in the various districts of the city were known as the "Big Four." My thanks go to Jeffrey Brown and Kathryn Corbin for discovering photographs of DeCamp among those in the Blaney Family Archives.

33 "Art Notes," *Brush and Pencil* 4 (April 1899), p. 62, and Dora M. Morrell, "Boston Notes," *Brush and Pencil* 4 (June 1899), p. 159.

34 "A Good Show of Pictures," *Boston Evening Transcript*, January 20, 1893, p. 10.

35 "The Fine Arts," *Boston Evening Transcript*, January 26, 1893, p. 6.

36 "Outsider's View of the Women's Exhibit," *Cosmopolitan* 15 (September 1893), p. 560. I am grateful to Pamela A. Ivinski, Senior Research Associate of the Mary Cassatt Foundation, New York, for this information.

37 See Judy Sund, "Columbus and Columbia in Chicago, 1893: Man of Genius Meets Generic Woman," *Art Bulletin* 75 (September 1993), pp. 443–46.

38 Robert L. Herbert, "City vs. Country: The Rural Image in French Painting from Millet to Gauguin," *Artforum* 8 (February 1970), p. 50.

39 *Ibid.* See also Françoise Cachin, Anne Distel, Christopher Lloyd *et al.*, *Pissarro*, exh. cat. (London: Arts Council of Great Britain, and Boston: Museum of Fine Arts, 1980).

40 A full examination of DeCamp's work in relation to that of Benson and Tarbell—desirable, but feasible only if and when more of DeCamp's early figure paintings surface—would have an exemplary precedent in the study undertaken by William H. Gerdts to separate Benson from the Tarbellite mantle. See William H. Gerdts, "Frank Benson—His Own Man: A Study of the Artist's Development and Its Critical Reception," in John Wilmerding, Sheila Dugan, and William H. Gerdts, *Frank W. Benson: The Impressionist Years*, exh. cat. (New York: Spanierman Gallery, 1988).

41 Perkins, "The Fine Arts," p. 13.

42 "The Society of American Artists Exhibition," *Art Amateur* 23 (June 1890), p. 3.

43 "Art and Artists," *Boston Sunday Globe*, October 9, 1892, p. 17.

44 "The Fine Arts," *Boston Evening Transcript*, October 8, 1892, p. 8.

45 "The Fine Arts," *Boston Evening Transcript*, January 19, 1893, p. 5.

46 [Cortissoz], "A Strong Exhibition," p. 7.

47 The work was entered in the Society of American Artists show of 1896, the Fifth Annual Exhibition of Works by American Artists at the Cincinnati Museum Association in May 1898, and, in September of that year, the Fifteenth Annual Exhibition of the St. Louis Exposition and Music Hall Association.

48 "The Week in Art," *New York Times* (Sat. supp.), April 8, 1899, p. 240, and Henri Pene Du Bois, "Plays of Light Painted by Nine Men," *New York Journal and Advertiser*, April 4, 1899, p. 10.

49 This information was provided by dealer Irma Rudin of New York. Aldis was a Harvard-educated lawyer who made his fortune in Wyoming real estate. He settled in Lake Forest, Illinois, and actively participated in the Chicago art world as a trustee of the Art Institute of Chicago and a member of the Society of Friends of American Art. For more information on Aldis, see *Who's Who in America, 1906–07* (Chicago: A. N. Marquis & Co., 1907), p. 12.

50 Kathryn Corbin, "John Leslie Breck: American Impressionist," *Antiques* 134 (November 1988), p. 1144.

51 Fairbrother, *Bostonians*, p. 10.

52 "The Fine Arts," *Boston Evening Transcript*, January 26, 1893, p. 6.

53 "An Attractive Display," *Public Ledger—Philadelphia*, December 17, 1894, p. 2.

54 Harrison S. Morris, *Confessions in Art* (New York: Sears Publishing Co., 1930), p. 3.

55 *Ibid.*, p. 5. DeCamp did show at the Pennsylvania Academy of the Fine Arts that year (1892), when Impressionism was announced as the focus of the show. With Benson, Weir, John H. Twachtman, and Theodore Robinson, he was on the Jury of Selection and Hanging Committee for the 1893 annual and, in 1895, he participated in the exhibition as the "new teacher" at the institution. Curiously, he did not show at the academy again until 1899, when he won the Temple Award.

56 *Ibid.*, p. 64.

57 *Ibid.*, pp. 66–68.

58 *Ibid.*, p. 67. Further information on Beck can be gleaned from *Who's Who in America 1906–07*, p. 121.

59 "The City Hall Decoration," *Evening Bulletin*, May 27, 1896, p. 4.

60 Edward Simmons, *From Seven to Seventy: Memories of a Painter and a Yankee* (New York and London: Harper & Bros., 1922), pp. 225–26.

61 *Ibid.*, p. 226. According to Moffat ("Joseph Rodefer DeCamp: Biographical Sketch," p. 28), the prize money was $3,000; Morris (*Confessions in Art*, p. 67) gives the sum of $5,000, the *Evening Bulletin* (May 27, 1896, p. 4) that of $3,500.

62 "The City Hall Decoration," *Evening Bulletin*, p. 4.

63 "The City Hall Decoration," *Philadelphia Times*, May 28, 1896, p. 6.

64 John J. Boyle, Frank Duveneck, John Lambert, Jr., Emily Sartain, Edward Simmons, and C. Howard Walker to Commissioners for the

Erection of Public Buildings, Philadelphia, May 1896; Joseph DeCamp scrapbook, family of the artist.

65 Harley Perkins, "The Fine Arts," *Boston Evening Transcript*, January 8, 1924, p. 13. "Two ceilings with figures" are listed for DeCamp's decoration of the Hotel Touraine in William Walton's "The Field of Art: Mural Painting in This Country Since 1898," *Scribner's Magazine* 40 (November 1906), p. 639.

66 Moffat, "Joseph Rodefer DeCamp: Biographical Sketch," p. 29. It is now a cooperative apartment building.

67 "Boston," *American Art News* 8 (November 27, 1909), p. 2.

68 See [Royal Cortissoz], "American Artists," *New-York Daily Tribune*, April 22, 1893, p. 11.

69 Charles DeKay, "The Society of American Artists," *Harper's Weekly* 37 (April 22, 1893), p. 373.

70 [Royal Cortissoz], "Exhibition of the Society of American Artists," *New-York Daily Tribune*, April 15, 1893, p. 6.

71 "To Glorify the Nude," *Washington Post*, February 25, 1894, p. 15. The following year, two pieces of legislation, known as the Mullin and Ainsworth bills, were introduced in Congress to prevent what were termed "immoral" public exhibitions. The Mullin Bill, said to be "the work of the women," came before the Senate of the State of New York as "an act to better protect public morals, defend the innocence of youth, prevent the degrading of women and girls, protect the honor and preserve the respect due to women." The Ainsworth Bill, before the Assembly, stated the same goals with some different, far-reaching provisions concerning indecent exposure and public distribution of nude images in books, pictures, paintings, drawings, pamphlets, circulars, and the like. See Nym Crinkle, "To Stop Nude Exhibitions," *World*, April 7, 1895, p. 18. In Boston, already known for its prudery, a battle was raging in the press over the design by Marcus Waterman for the entrance to the public library, a shield supported by two nude boys. See "Is the Nude in Art Ever Necessary?" *Boston Sunday Globe*, February 18, 1894, p. 20.

72 "The Fine Arts," *Boston Sunday Herald*, February 4, 1894, p. 13.

73 "The Exhibition of the Society of American Artists," *Art Amateur* 30 (April 1894), p. 128.

74 "An Attractive Display," *Public Ledger—Philadelphia*, December 17, 1894, p. 2.

75 "Detroit Art and Loan Exhibition," *Detroit Free Press*, May 19, 1895, p. 14.

76 "Prizes Awarded," *Boston Daily Advertiser*, January 11, 1896, p. 7.

77 "An Attractive Display," p. 2.

78 "Boston Art Club's Exhibition," *Boston Daily Advertiser*, January 19, 1895, p. 5.

79 "Society of American Artists," *New York Times*, April 5, 1895, p. 4.

80 "American Artists Attractive Show," *New York Herald*, March 23, 1895, p. 9.

81 "Triumphs of Fine Arts," *Philadelphia Record*, December 22, 1895, p. 5.

82 "The Art Club Exhibition," *Philadelphia Press*, November 22, 1896, p. 11.

83 Edith DeCamp to Joseph H. Gest of the Cincinnati Art Museum, October 21, 1924; DeCamp artist file, Library, Cincinnati Art Museum.

84 "Ten American Painters," *Art Amateur* 38 (May 1898), p. 134.

85 Frank T. Robinson, "An American Art School," *Art Interchange* 39 (July 1895), p. 12.

86 "Society of American Artists," *Evening Post*, March 30, 1895, p. 17.

87 William H. Gerdts, "The Ten: A Critical Chronology," in *Ten American Painters*, exh. cat. (New York: Spanierman Gallery, 1990), p. 15.

88 See Orson Lowell, "Three Important New York Exhibitions" *Brush and Pencil* 2 (May 1898), p. 89; Henri Pene du Bois, "First Exhibition of Ten American Painters," *New York Journal and Advertiser*, March 30, 1898, p. 10; and "Ten American Painters," *World*, April 4, 1899, p. 6.

89 See [Royal Cortissoz], "Art Exhibitions," *New-York Daily Tribune*, March 30, 1898, p. 7; "The Art World," *Commercial Advertiser*, March 30, 1898, p. 7; and "The Art World," *Commercial Advertiser*, April 4, 1899, p. 5.

90 "The Note Book," *Art Amateur* 40 (May 1899), p. 114.

91 B. F., "Ten American Painters," *Evening Post*, April 6, 1899, p. 7.

92 See Sadakichi Hartmann, "The Tarbellites," *Art News* 1 (March 1897), pp. 3–4.

93 See Carol Lowrey, "Index to the Exhibitions of the Ten," in *Ten American Painters*, pp. 179–80.

94 For a full summary of the founding of the Ten, see Gerdts, "The Ten: A Critical Chronology," in *Ten American Painters*, pp. 11–13, and Ulrich W. Hiesinger, *Impressionism in America: The Ten American Painters* (Munich: Prestel, 1991), pp. 15–32.

95 "Artists Agree to Disagree," *New York Herald*, January 9, 1898, p. 7.

96 See, for example, "Around the Galleries," *Sun*, March 25, 1908, p. 6; "Annual Exhibit of the Ten," *American Art News* 6 (March 21, 1908), p. 4; and Arthur Hoeber, "Art and Artists," *Globe and Commercial Advertiser*, March 17, 1908, p. 6.

97 James B. Townsend, "Annual Exhibit of the Ten," *American Art News* 7 (March 20, 1909), p. 6, and Arthur Hoeber, "Art and Artists," *Globe and Commercial Advertiser*, March 24, 1910, p. 10.

98 "Art by 'The Ten,'" *Boston Herald*, April 13, 1913, p. 21, and F[rederick]. W. Coburn, "Boston Composer Portrait Marks 'Ten's' 20th Show," *Boston Herald*, March 11, 1917, sect. D, p. 4.

99 "The Note Book," *Art Amateur*, p. 114.

100 William Howe Downes, "The Spontaneous Gaiety of Frank W. Benson's Work," *Arts and Decoration* 1 (March 1911), pp. 195–96.

101 See, for example, "The Fine Arts," *Boston Evening Transcript*, November 4, 1903, p. 16; Bulkeley Cable, "Art Museum Exhibit Exceeds All Former Displays," *St. Louis Republic*, September 12, 1909, p. 6; and "New Remington Depicts West's Wilderness Ways," *Boston Sunday Herald*, May 3, 1914, sect. 5, p. 6.

102 Gerdts, "The Ten: A Critical Chronology," p. 74. For more information on DeCamp's role within the Ten, see Laurene Buckley, "Joseph DeCamp," in *Ten American Painters*, pp. 92–97.

Chapter Six

Maturity: Final Landscapes, Portraits of Men, 1900–1917

DeCamp's mature period is full of surprises. He virtually ceased to paint the nude subjects that had gained him initial notoriety within the Ten American Painters group. His succession of pure landscapes, too, came to an end, but these evolved into a short-lived but highly successful second series of figures outdoors, the last of which coincided with the final summers he spent in Gloucester and with a disastrous studio fire in 1904 that destroyed much of his early work. From that point on, figures placed in interiors—either formally posed portraits of men or full-length female figures in domestic scenes—inhabited the artist's canvases.

DeCamp's circumstances at the beginning of what would be his most fruitful period were not the best. In a letter of June 21, 1899, to Joseph H. Gest, Director of the Cincinnati Art Museum, the artist offered to "modify the scheduled price very considerably" for his *Woman Drying Her Hair.*[1] He gave a "bottom" price of $500 for the work, a picture that had won the Temple Gold Medal at the Pennsylvania Academy's annual the previous year. "I think I ought to have more, but I am so situated that I must take what I can get," he wrote.[2] In a second letter to Gest he speaks of being "dreadfully hard-up" and in a later letter to the museum, when asking for the painting to be lent to the Paris Exposition Universelle of 1900, he deplores his "unusally unproductive" activity in recent years.[3]

If this latter remark refers to his nudes, he did indeed curtail their production. Only one other oil of a nude, entitled *Woman Braiding Her Hair* (unlocated, fig. 35), was exhibited in the artist's lifetime, and it was hardly a success. Despite the prominent display of Japanese prints in the background—a sure sign of sophisticated taste at this time—the painting was considered crude in comparison to Thomas W. Dewing's *Le Jaseur* (ca. 1907, Minneapolis Institute of Arts) when both were shown at the Ten American Painter's exhibition of 1907.[4] The *New York Times* critic found it "ugly about the lower torso," while the *Evening Mail* reviewer bemoaned the "large-armed, thick chested, heavy shouldered" model who lacked "the magic that might have rendered [these features] absorbingly interesting."[5]

In the field of landscape, too, DeCamp had been increasingly "unproductive" (although this was about to change, with a last flourish of outdoor work between 1900 and 1905). His discouragement at this time may have been connected with the lack of patronage in Boston. He was certainly considering a move to New York at a slightly later date: On being asked in 1903 to teach at the Massachusetts Normal Art School, a position he would hold until the end of his life, he stalled in his acceptance because, according to the reminiscenses of the person assigned to recruit him, he was thinking of "packing up and going to New York for good."[6] DeCamp had already developed many ties to that city. Along with being one of the Ten American Painters, who, except in 1906, always started their annual touring exhibition in New York, came pro forma membership in New York's Players Club, where the Ten planned their shows. In addition, the season of 1900–01 found DeCamp teaching painting and drawing at the Art Students League in New York;[7] he entered a portrait (unlocated) in the exhibition held on the occasion of the League's twenty-fifth anniversary in May 1900. Among his fellow instructors were three Cincinnati-born artists: Robert Blum, Kenyon Cox, and John Henry Twachtman, the last two trained in Munich.

Twachtman and DeCamp were especially close at this time, initiating a joint summer school for the New York Art Students League pupils at Gloucester in 1902, the year of Twachtman's sudden death.[8] They had also been together in Gloucester the previous two summers in what can be viewed as a veritable reunion of Cincinnati-born and Duveneck-trained artists. The Hotel Rockaway was the gathering place, in the summer of 1900, for Frank Duveneck and his former pupils, and it served as the salon for an important end-of-season exhibition.[9] Edward Potthast and Charles Corwin were also staying at the hotel, and Twachtman had secured apartments at the Amenity Cottage, a new annex to the Rockaway.[10] The nearby Hawthorne Hotel held a further contingent of art students and artists, providing what the *Gloucester Daily Times* called a renewal of "the artistic atmosphere of bygone seasons."[11] Theodore

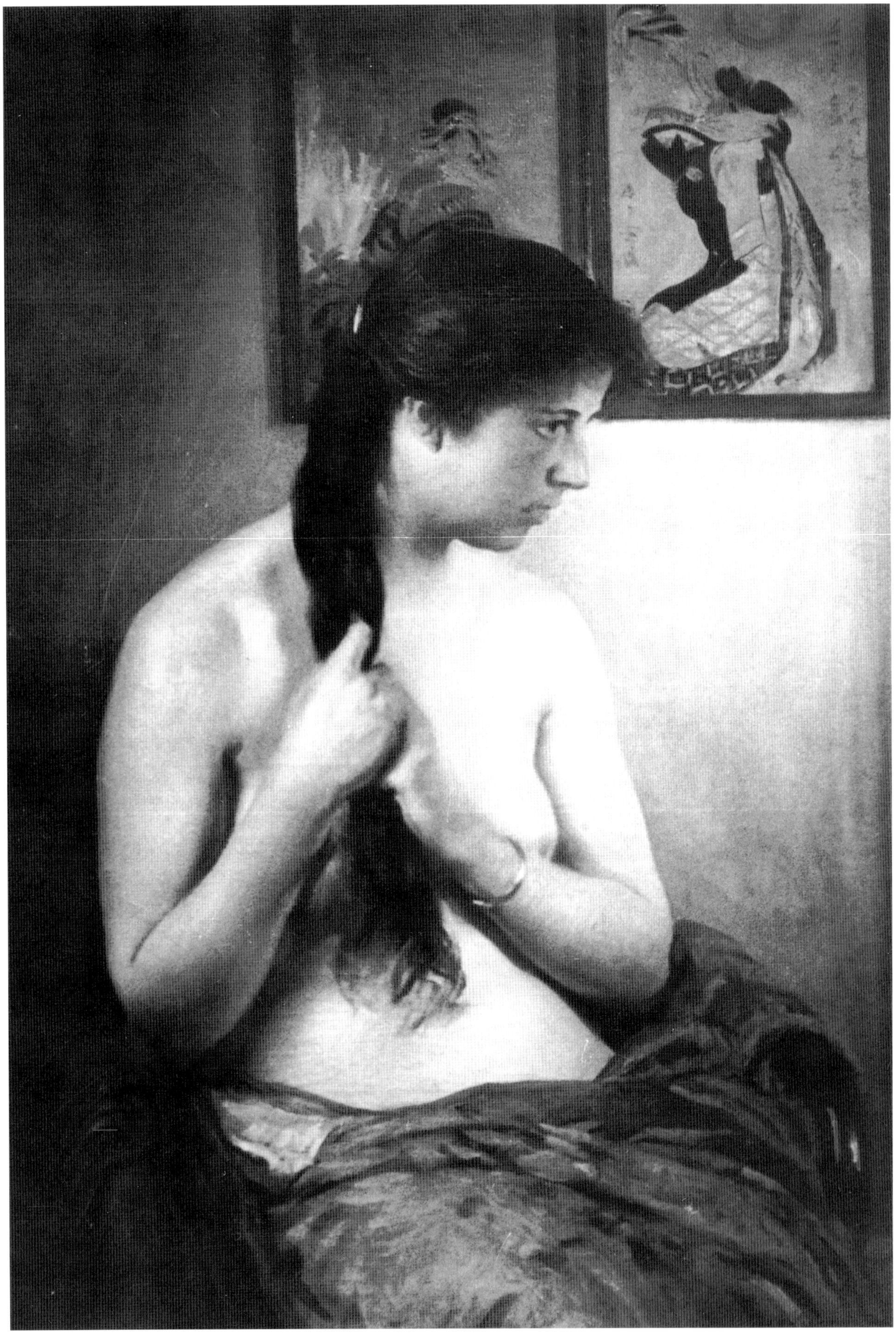

Fig. 35 *Woman Braiding Her Hair*, ca. 1907. 40 x 30 in. (101.5 x 76 cm). Unlocated

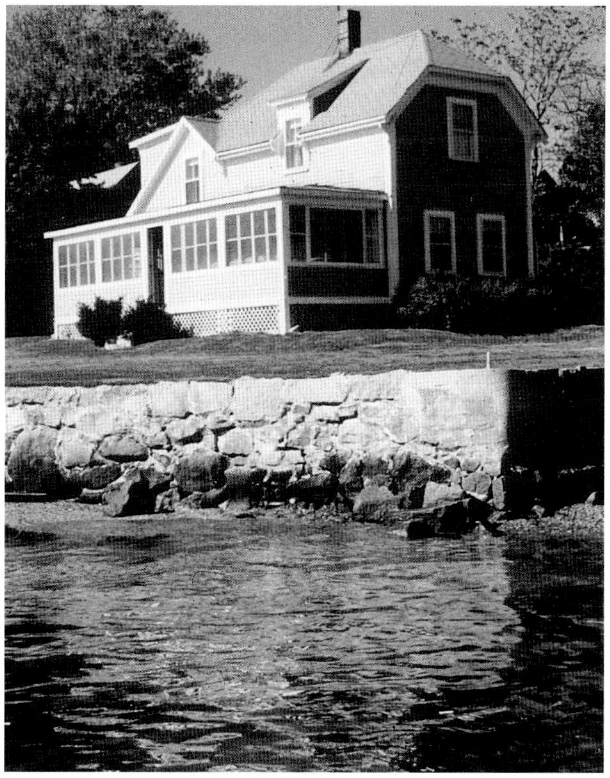

Fig. 36 Edward Mehlman's cottage, Rocky Neck, Gloucester, Massachusetts

Fig. 37 John H. Twachtman, *Fishing Boats at Gloucester*, ca. 1900–02. 25⅛ x 30¼ in. (64 x 77 cm). National Museum of American Art, Smithsonian Institution, Washington, D. C., Gift of William T. Evans

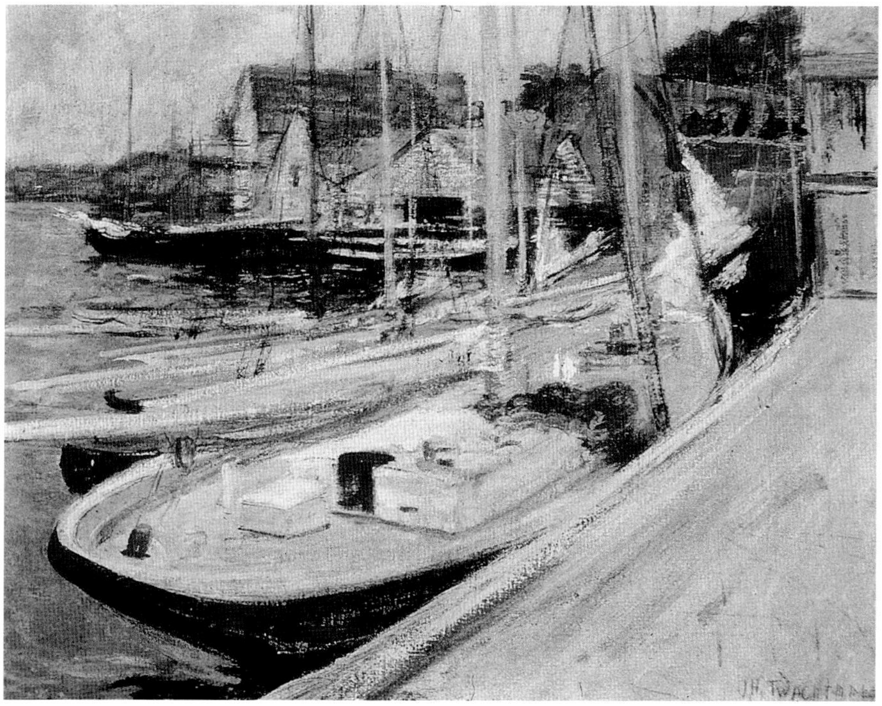

Wendel was at the Rockaway in June at least,[12] and, not far away, DeCamp and his family spent their first summer at Police Officer Edward Mehlman's cottage at Rocky Neck (fig. 36).[13] Next door was George de Forest Brush, whose wife and children befriended the DeCamps.[14]

Two landscapes by DeCamp—*Wharf, Gloucester* and *At Gloucester*—were exhibited after the 1900 summer's stay at Cape Ann; one of them may have been the picture now owned by the Cincinnati Art Museum (plate 14).[15] Executed in subdued grays, browns, and blues and in broad strokes of the brush, the work recalls Twachtman's tonal palette, although at the time the latter was starting to use richer hues, as in *Fishing Boats at Gloucester* (fig. 37). The oblique angle of the wharf in DeCamp's *At Gloucester*, another Twachtman feature, dominates the foreground and directs the eye toward the schooners and the marine railway building at the right, where vessels were hauled in and repaired in the inner harbor of Gloucester.[16] Henceforth, DeCamp would avoid both the harbor and the tonal landscape, concentrating instead on subjects closer to his doorstep, perhaps because of growing tourism in the areas around the harbor.

The following summer, DeCamp and his family were once more at the Mehlman cottage.[17] Situated on the north edge of Wonson Cove, it was a stone's throw from the Hotel Rockaway, where Duveneck, Twachtman, and pupils from the Art Students League of New York were again holding court.[18] No mention of an art show appears in the press this time, but the students were said to be the "prime movers in one of the prettiest and jolliest costume dances ever given in the summer colony at the Rockaway."[19] Years later, Edith DeCamp would recall the blissful evenings when Duveneck, Twachtman, Wendel, and others sat on the porch of their cottage and reminisced about their Munich times.[20] The days were not as idle. Despite the many hours needed to produce his own work, DeCamp still found time to teach. In a review of the colony's activities the *Boston Herald* critic remarked on DeCamp's "numbers of pupils—many of them beyond the rank of amateurs—from all parts of the country."[21]

Other artists in Gloucester that summer were Cecilia Beaux, Walter and Eliot Clark, Walter Dean, Arthur Hazard, Henry H. Kitson, William Paxton, Edmund C. Tarbell, and Everett Warner.[22] DeCamp's friend Charles Grafly, a Philadelphia artist known for his ability in sculpting the male model (as DeCamp would become for his skill in painting the male portrait in oil), was staying at nearby Annisquam,[23] and this may have been the occasion on which Grafly produced his bust of DeCamp. A photograph (fig. 38) shows the two artists during the creation of the work, which was exhibited in 1903, at both the St. Botolph Club, Boston, and the Pennsylvania Academy of the Fine Arts, Philadelphia.[24]

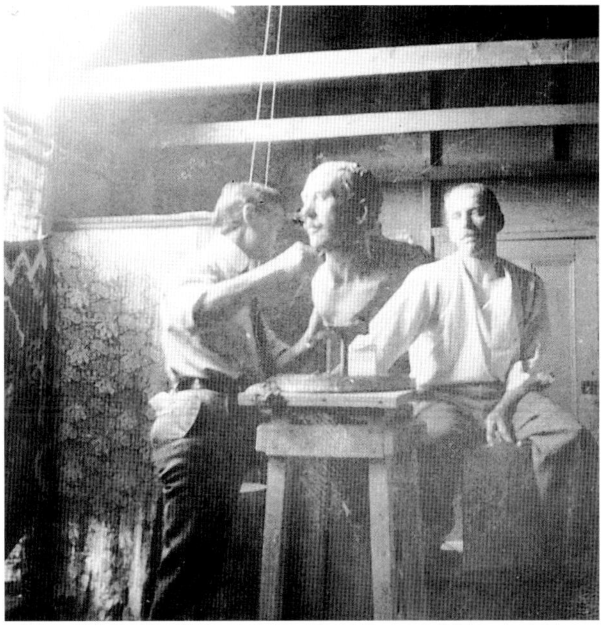

Fig. 38 DeCamp sitting for the portrait bust by Charles Grafly, 1901

A spate of canvases came from DeCamp's brush during the summer of 1901. These included several landscapes, but also important outdoor figural works. One of the former, *Ferry Landing—Low Tide* (unlocated), was considered "technically interesting" with "a very individual and pleasing scheme of color" when shown at the 1902 Ten American Painters exhibition in New York.[25] *Jetty at Low Tide* (formerly *The Water Pier*, plate 15), probably also created in the summer of 1901, is a far cry from the subdued palette of DeCamp's landscapes of the previous summer, its heightened color resembling Duveneck's of this period, especially in the background. The painting also utilizes a favorite motif of Duveneck's—the row of pilings leading diagonally away from shore, as seen in the older artist's *Gloucester Pier* of about 1900 (fig. 39). The scintillating brushwork in *Jetty at Low Tide*, particularly noticeable in the foreground, brings DeCamp closer to the early Impressionism of Monet and Renoir than ever before. The view, across Smith's Cove below Banner Hill, was a favorite with Gloucester artists. A natural flow of fresh water came down from the hill and was carried along the pipeline shown in the painting to waterboats, which then sold the water to bigger vessels. Another pure landscape of 1901, *Silvery Day* (fig. 40), exhibits the same tonalities as *Jetty at Low Tide*, and may have been done at one of the marshy sites on Cape Ann, perhaps at Annisquam or on Eastern Point, the latter a favorite Duveneck haunt.

At the same, 1901 Philadelphia Art Club annual at which *Jetty at Low Tide* was first exhibited, DeCamp showed a large painting, titled *The Pink Settee* (unlocated), "of children playing out of doors in the strong sunlight."[26] It is tempting to speculate how this compared to Tarbell's outdoor family pictures of the period, such as *My Family at Cotuit* (fig. 41) or, even more so, to Frank W. Benson's contemporary portrayals of his children frolicking in the brilliant sunlight, a series begun in the late 1890s. Of all the artists at Gloucester during these summers, very few produced figural work.[27] Two who did—Paxton and DeCamp—were members of the Boston School, which by this time was known for images in this genre. Paxton, who had been DeCamp's student at the Cowles School of Art, would paint his well known *The White Veranda* (fig. 42) in Gloucester during the summer of 1904.[28]

The Pink Settee inaugurated a string of outdoor figural paintings. At least two of these utilized the motif of a mother and child seated at the shore. *June Sunlight* (plate 16), probably the same work as that titled *June* or *June Sunshine*, was said by the New York *Sun* reviewer to "fairly exhale light" when it was shown at the Ten's 1902 exhibition. "The picture brims with fragrance and delight of life," he added.[29] The painting shows the artist's wife, Edith, dressed in her finest summer attire and reading to the couple's first born, Sally, against the backdrop of Wonson's Cove. Visible in the distance is the pier that stretched out into the water from the Harbor View Hotel with a sailboat anchored at its far end. The treatment of the foliage is typical of DeCamp in its feathered strokes and drybrush technique, but the mother and child, instead of remaining firmly intact like the figures in the earlier *Hammock* and *Pear Pickers*, seem to fuse into one shape and even into the pastel tonalities of the watery background. The work was a favorite of the artist's and was exhibited by him in no fewer that twelve shows around the country.

Fig. 39
Frank Duveneck, *Gloucester Pier*, ca. 1900. 20 x 25 in. (51 x 63.5 cm). Private collection

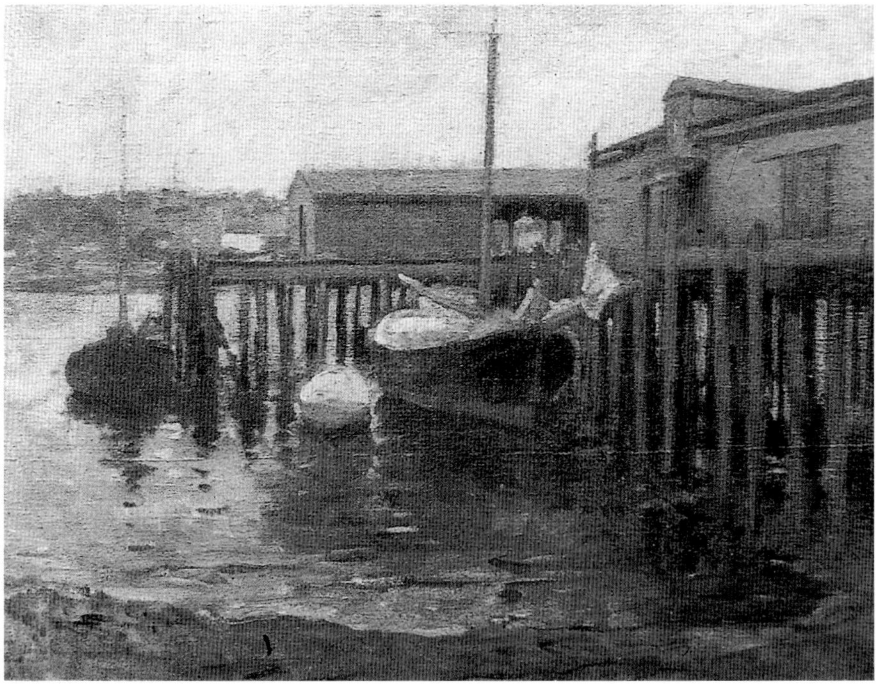

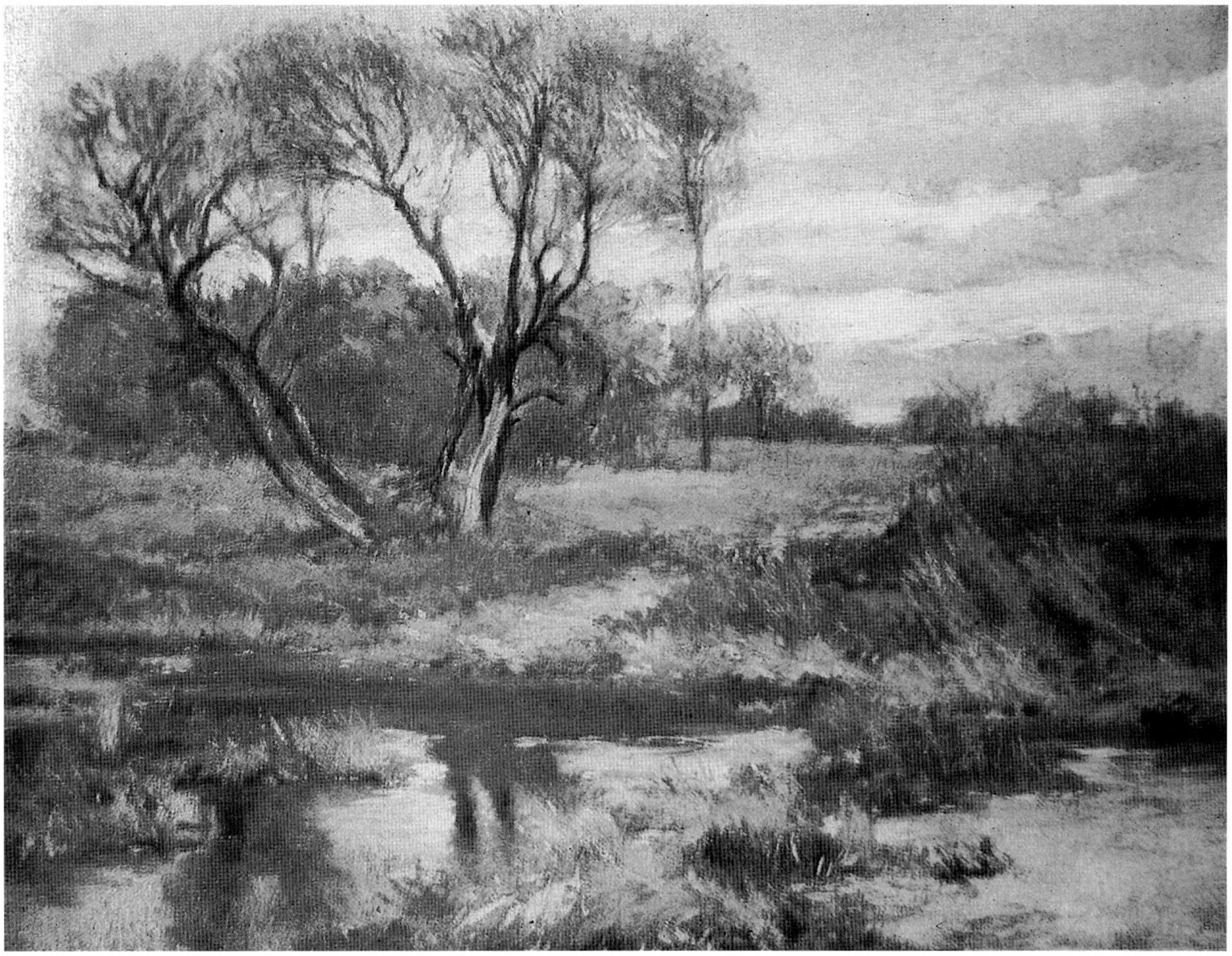

Fig. 40
Silvery Day, 1901.
21 x 27 in.
(53.5 x 68.5 cm).
Private collection,
courtesy of
R. H. Love Galleries,
Chicago

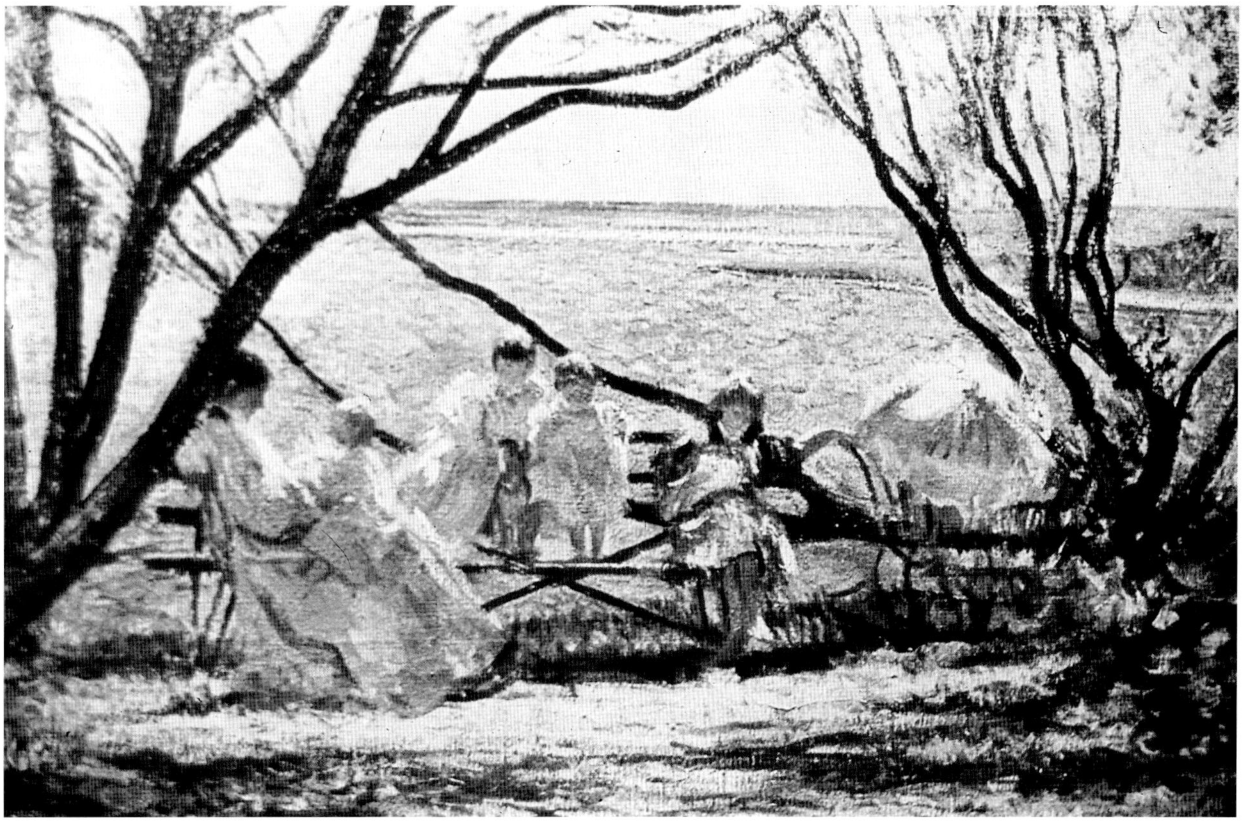

Fig. 41
Edmund C. Tarbell,
My Family at Cotuit, 1900.
24 x 30 in.
(61 x 76 cm).
Private collection

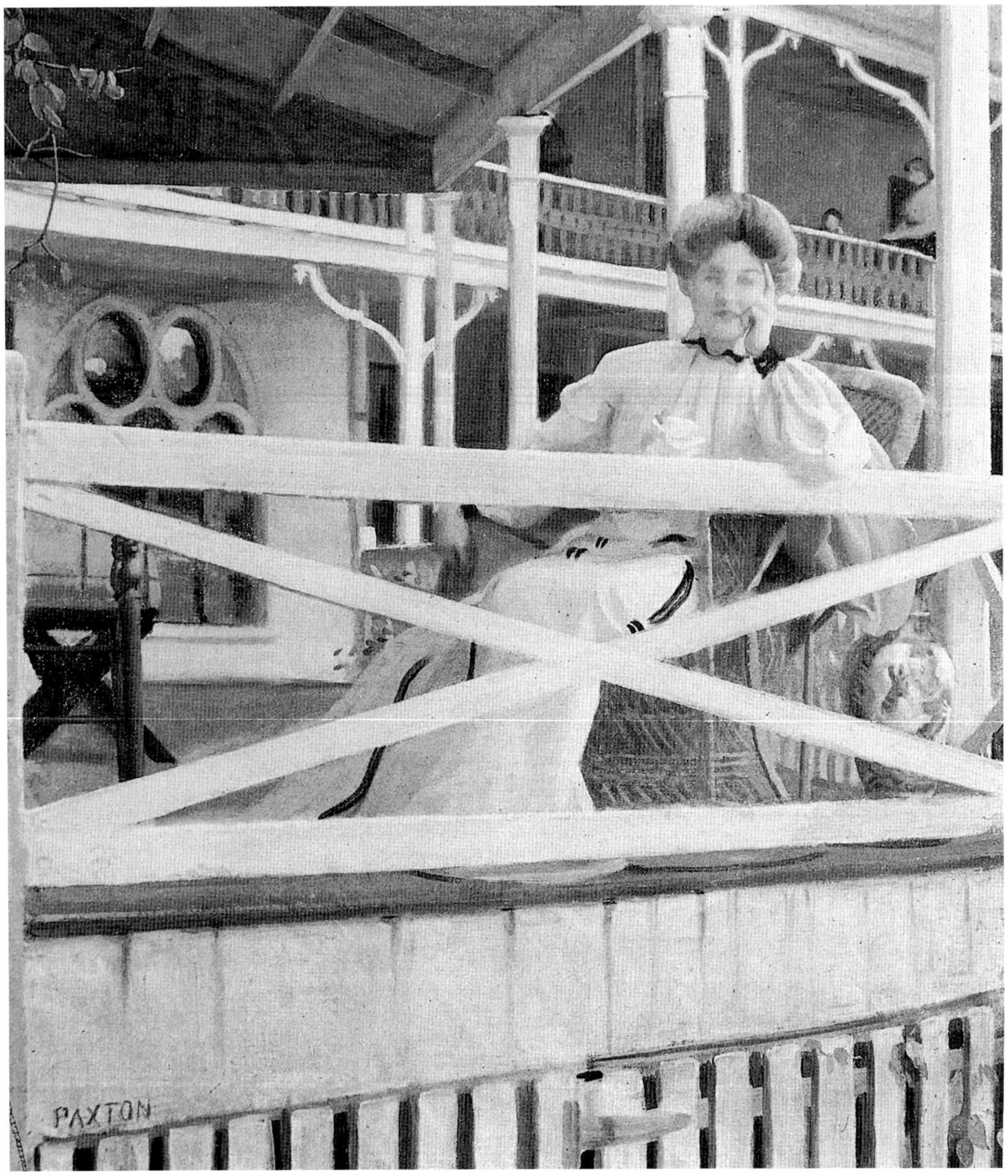

Fig. 42 William Paxton, *The White Veranda*, 1904. 30 x 25 in. (76 x 63.5 cm). Private collection

September Afternoon, probably identical with *On the Sea Wall—September* (unlocated), "is almost but not quite as clever in its analysis of atmosphere," wrote Royal Cortissoz when it appeared with *June Sunlight* in the Ten's show of 1902.[30] "On other accounts," he continued, "the design is poor and the forms are inadequately portrayed."[31] Once again depicting Edith and Sally, this time in profile, the picture concentrates on the figures as part of a large foreground shape; more in line with Benson's and Tarbell's handling of paint, very little attention is paid to the details of facial features or costume. As in *June Sunlight*, a high horizon line serves to flatten the images against a broad, "tipped-up" expanse of water, thereby further emphasizing the element of abstract design in the compositions. With these works DeCamp not only proclaimed his allegiance to the Boston School and consolidated his national reputation—*September Afternoon* received a gold medal at the Saint Louis Exposition of 1905—but also moved closer to the overall diffusion and the formalist tendencies characteristic of French Impressionism. A reviewer for *Booklover's Magazine* recognized this: "[*On the*] *Sea Wall: September* is characteristic of the Boston School, of which he is a prominent member.... Their frequent theme of a woman and child bathed in sunlight is in this instance handled in masterly fashion; Mr. DeCamp's clever brush has admirably expressed what his impressionist eye has rightly seen—the predominance of the color patch, the haziness of outline—where our untrained eye and too well-trained imagination often see only firm outlines."[32]

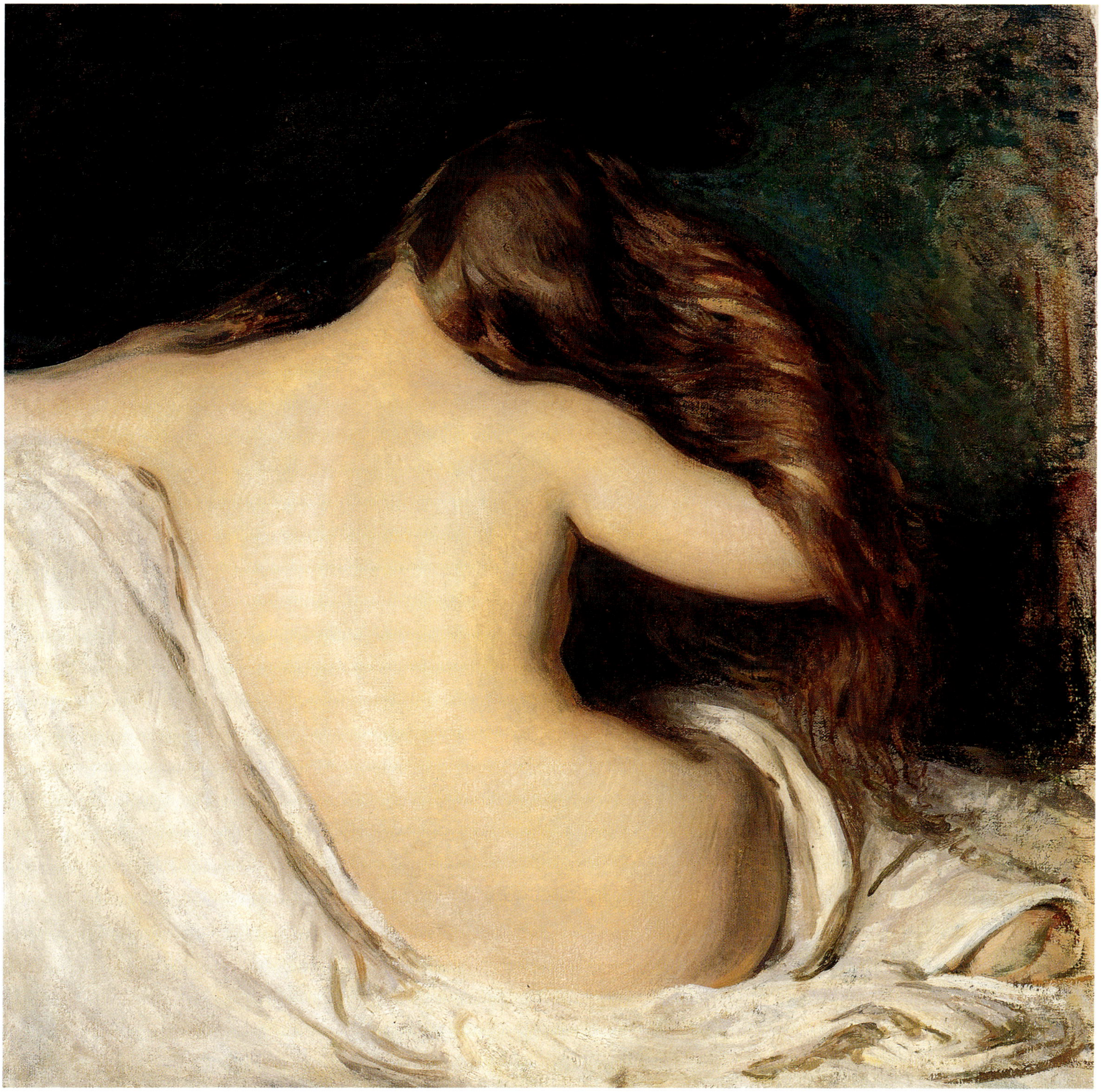

13 *Woman Drying Her Hair*, ca. 1899. 36⅛ x 36⅛ in. (92 x 92 cm).
Cincinnati Art Museum, Mary Dexter Fund

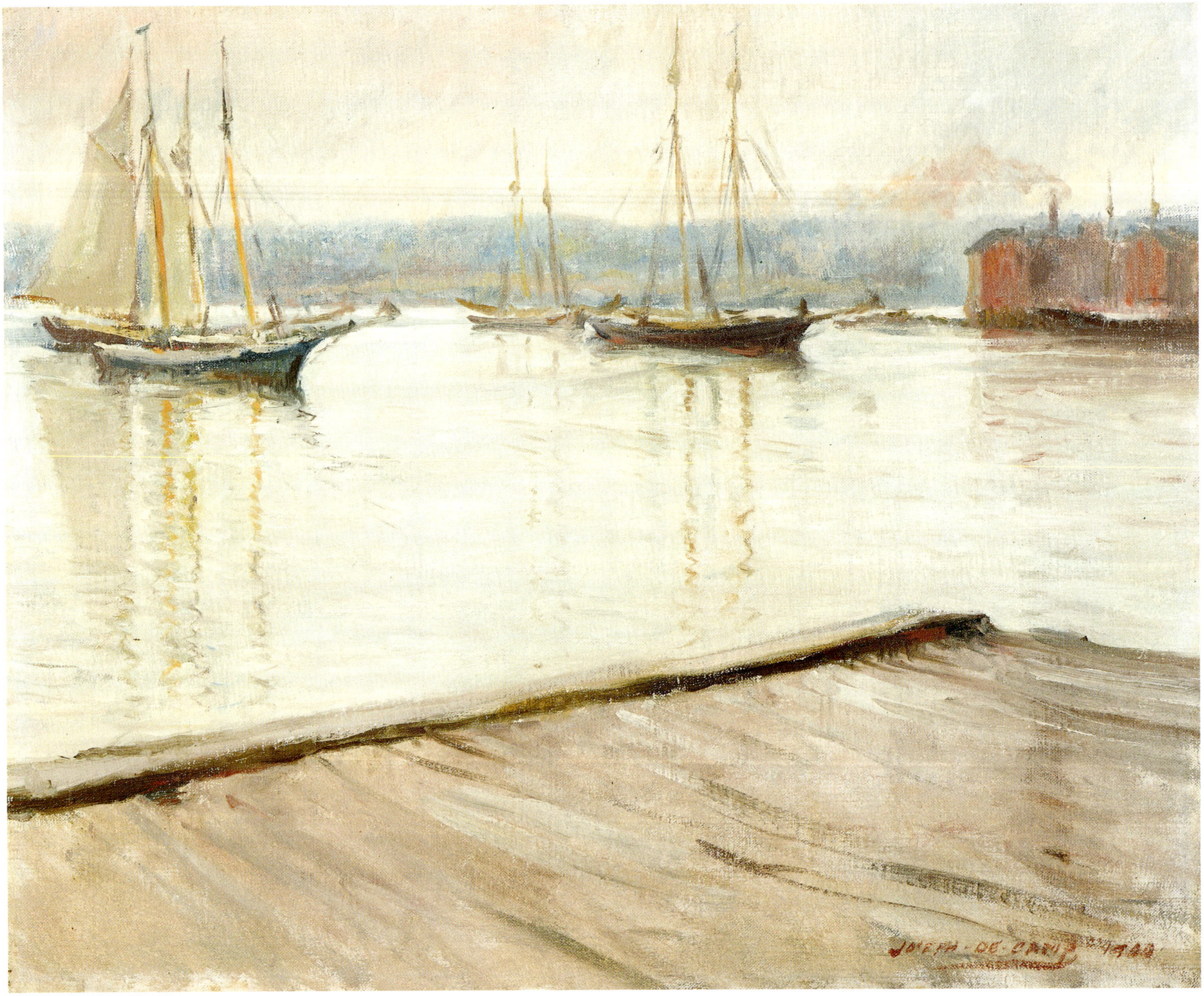

14 *At Gloucester* (*Gloucester Harbor*), 1900. 20 x 24$^{1}/_{16}$ in. (51 x 61 cm).
Cincinnati Art Museum, Gift of Frank Duveneck

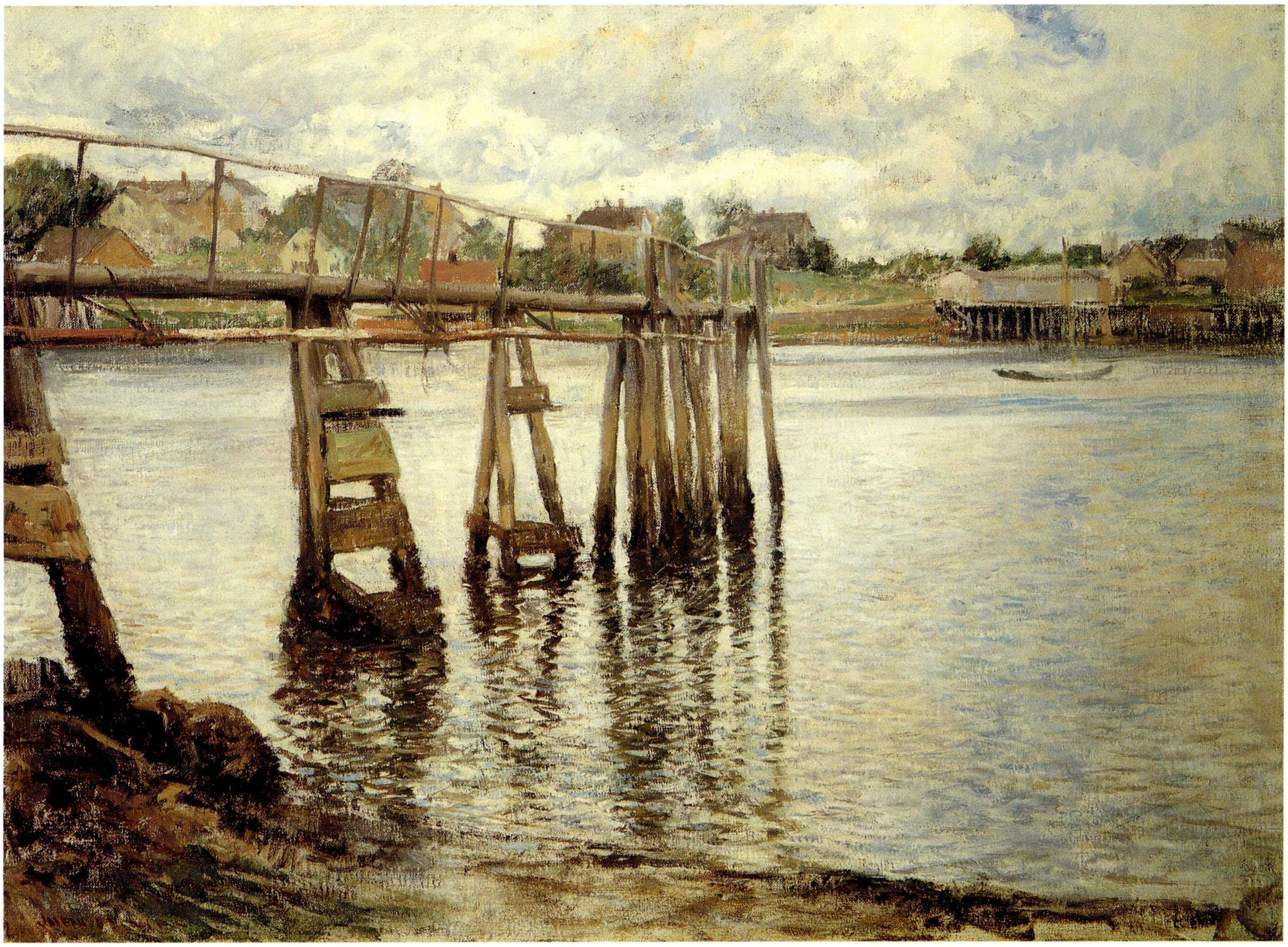

15 *Jetty at Low Tide* (*The Water Pier*), ca. 1901. 22 x 30 1/16 in. (56 x 76.5 cm).
Daniel J. Terra Collection, Terra Museum of American Art, Chicago

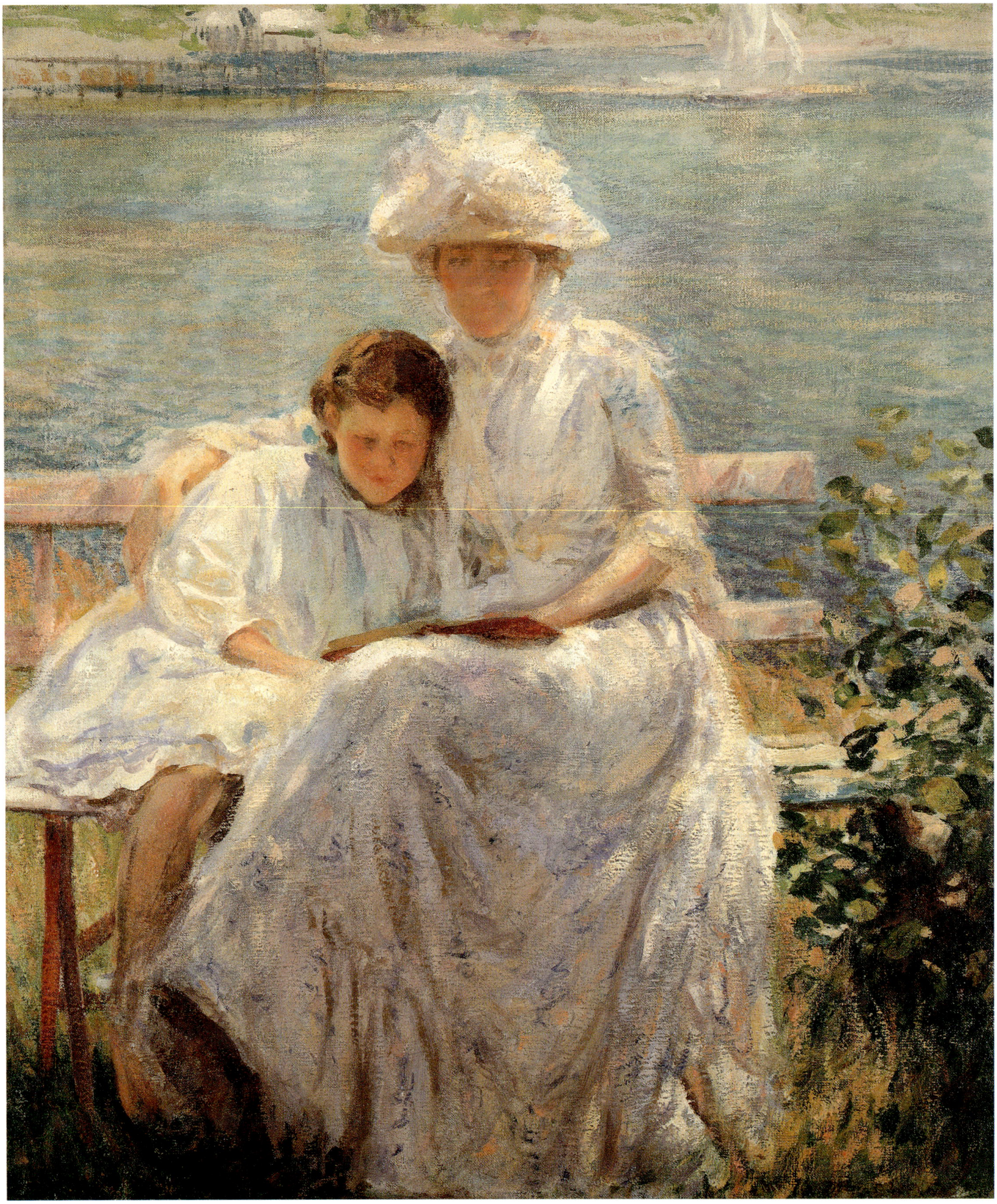

16 *June Sunlight*, ca. 1902. 30 x 25 in. (76 x 63.5 cm). Private collection

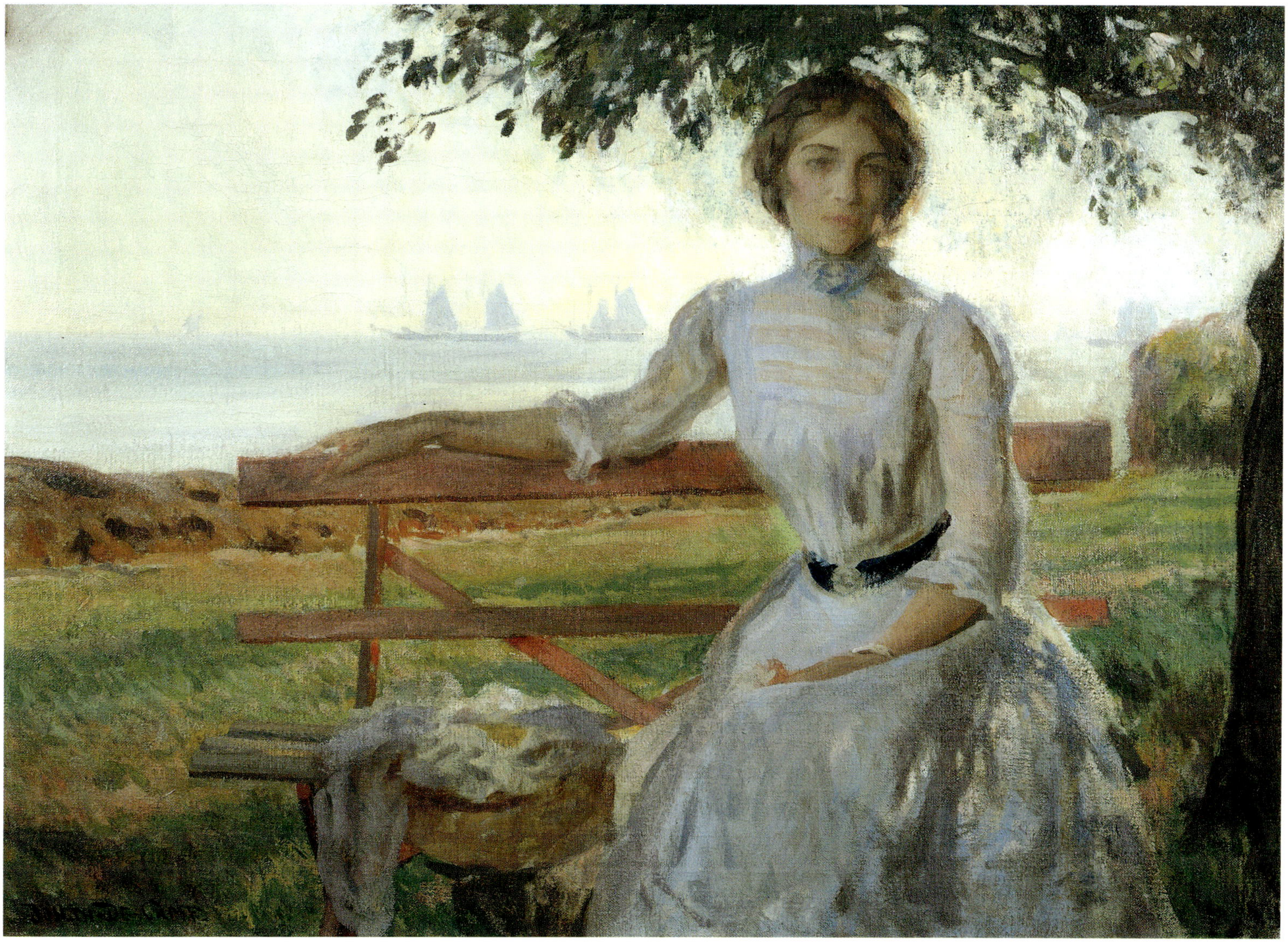

17 *Mrs. Ernest Major*, 1902–03. 22¼ x 30¼ in. (56.5 x 77 cm). The Procter & Gamble Company, Cincinnati

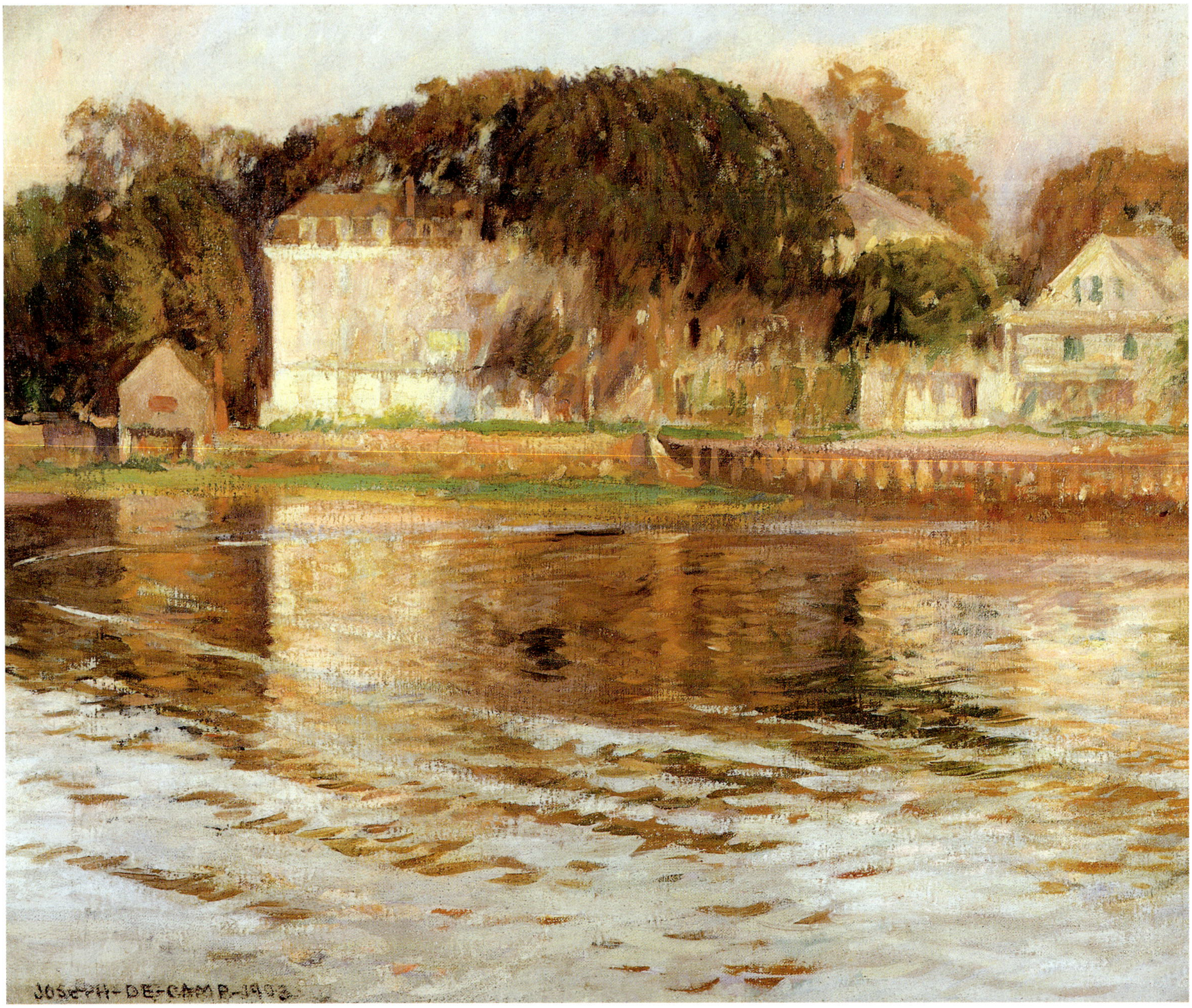

18 *The Little Hotel*, 1903. 20 x 24$\frac{1}{16}$ in. (51 x 61 cm).
Courtesy of the Pennsylvania Academy of the Fine Arts, Philadelphia, Joseph E. Temple Fund

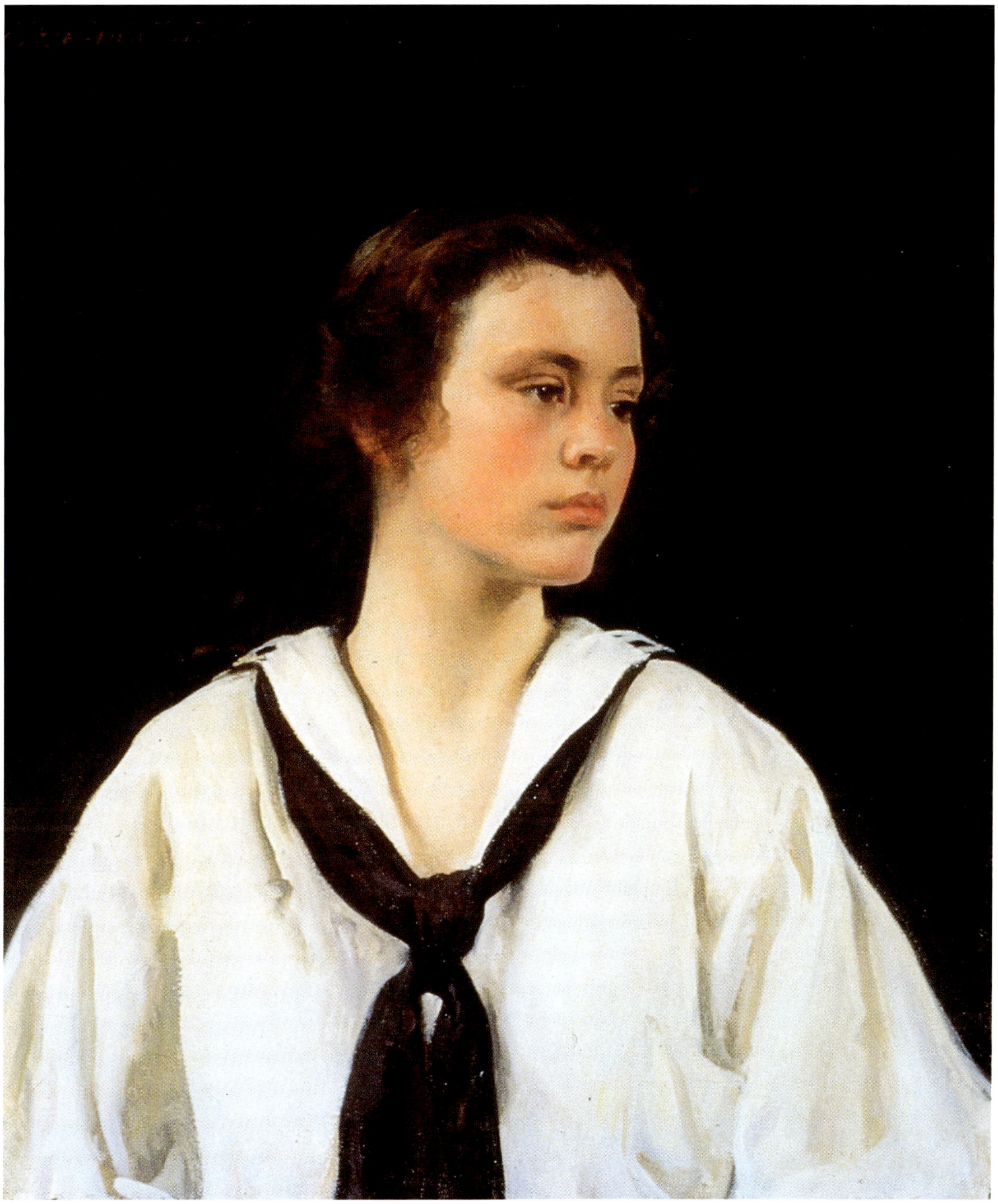

19 *Sally*, ca. 1907. 26½ x 23½ in. (67.5 x 59.5 cm).
Worcester Art Museum, Massachusetts, Museum Purchase

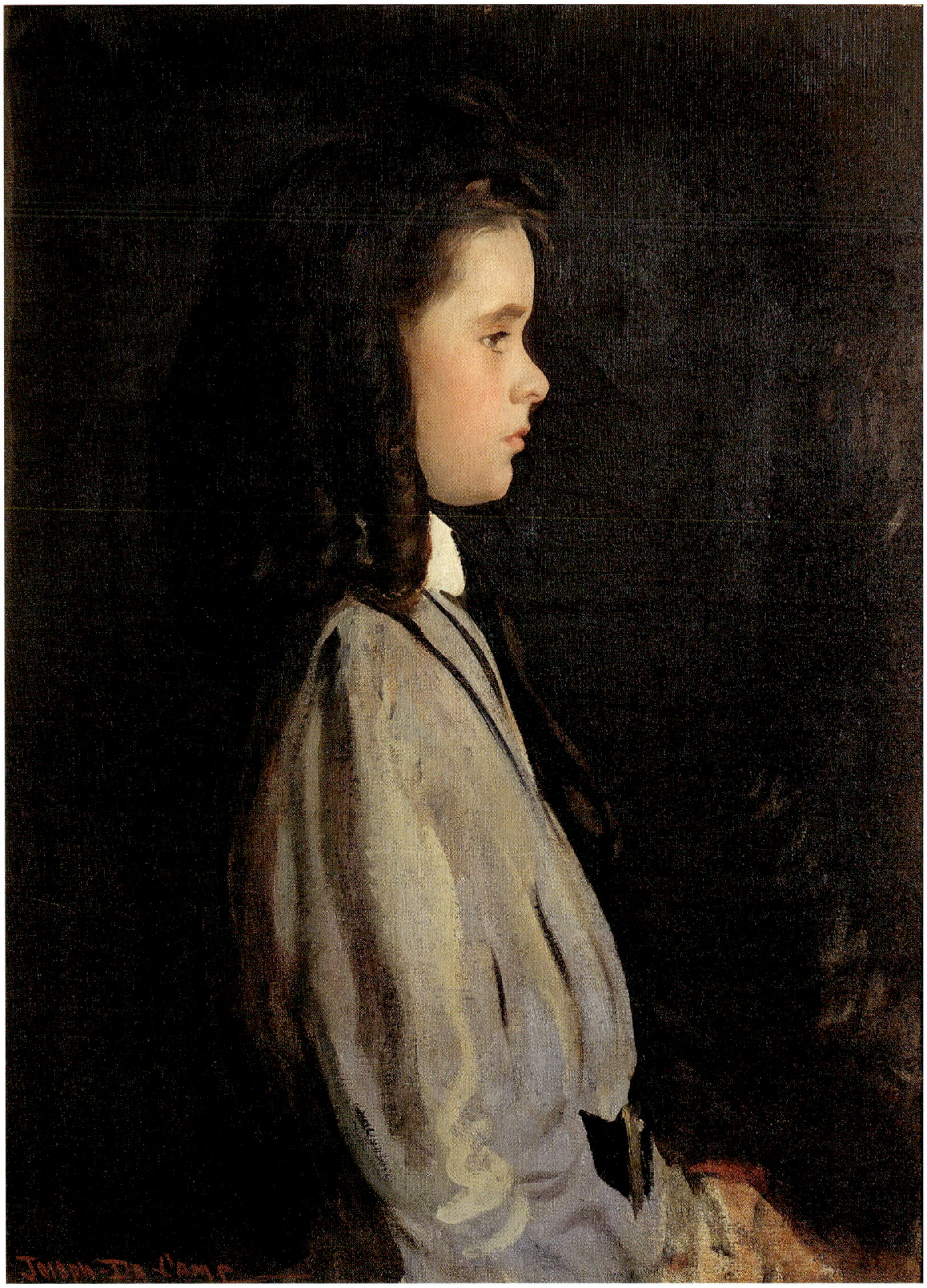

20 *Pauline*, ca. 1907. 24 x 20 in. (61 x 50 cm). Private collection

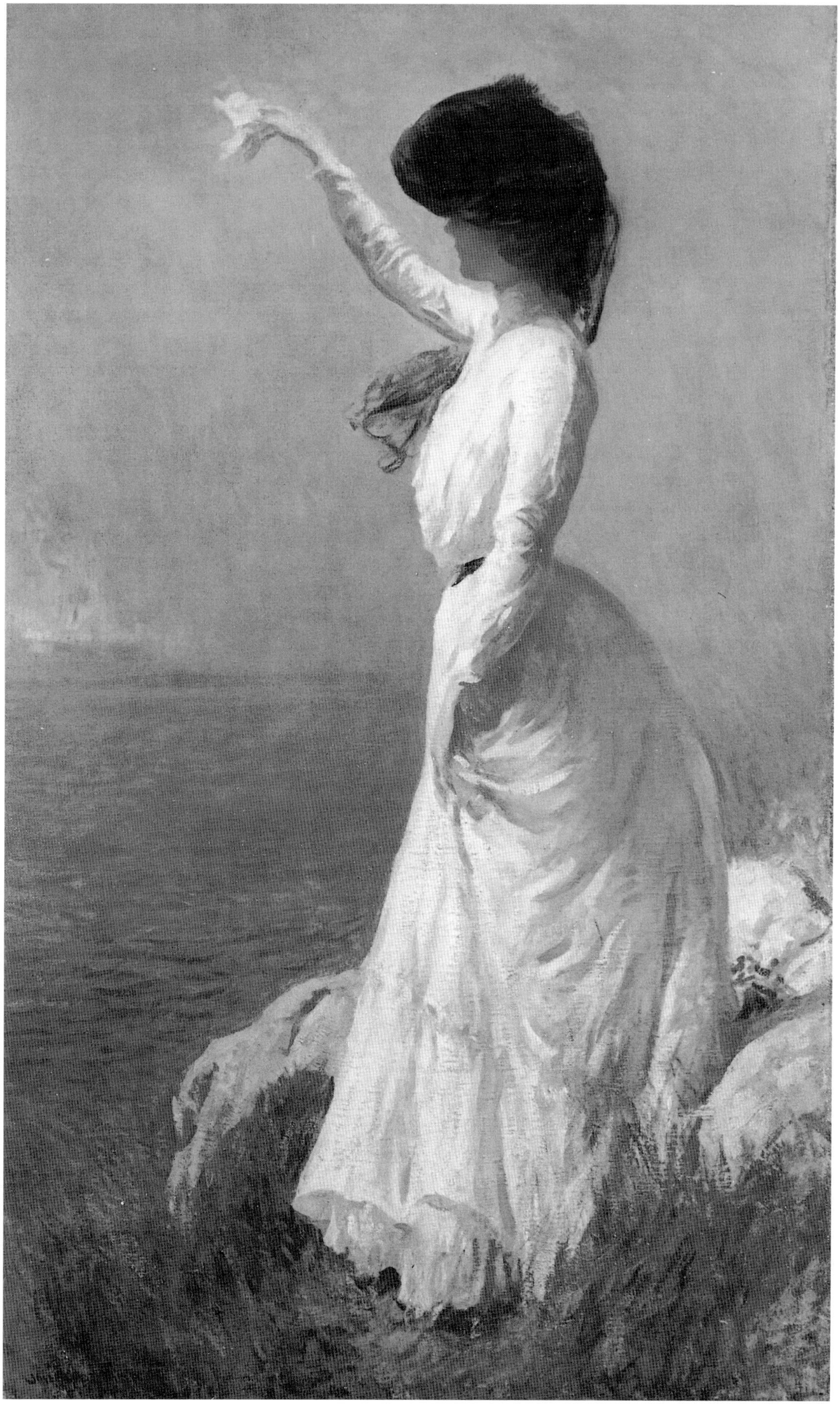

Fig. 43 *Farewell*, ca. 1900–02.
36 x 21¼ in. (91.5 x 54 cm). Unlocated

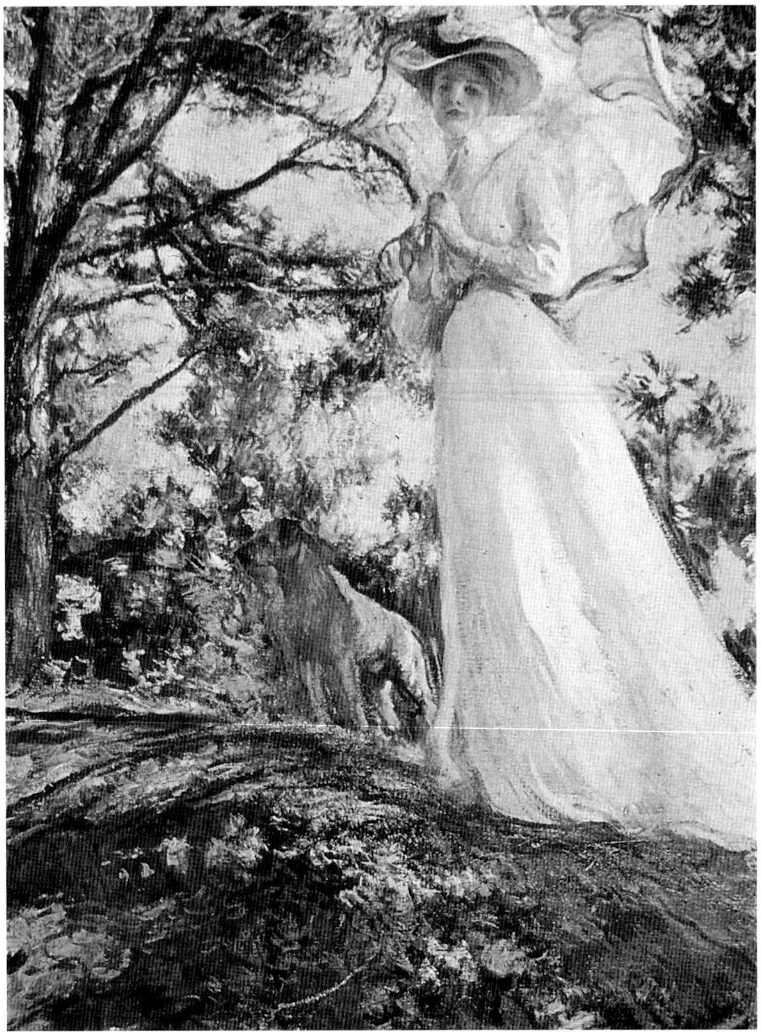

Fig. 44 Edmund C. Tarbell, *On Bos'n's Hill*, 1901.
40 x 30 in. (101.5 x 76 cm). © The Cleveland Museum of Art, Ohio, 1995.
Gift of Mr. and Mrs. Thomas A. Mann and Robert A. Mann, 92.398

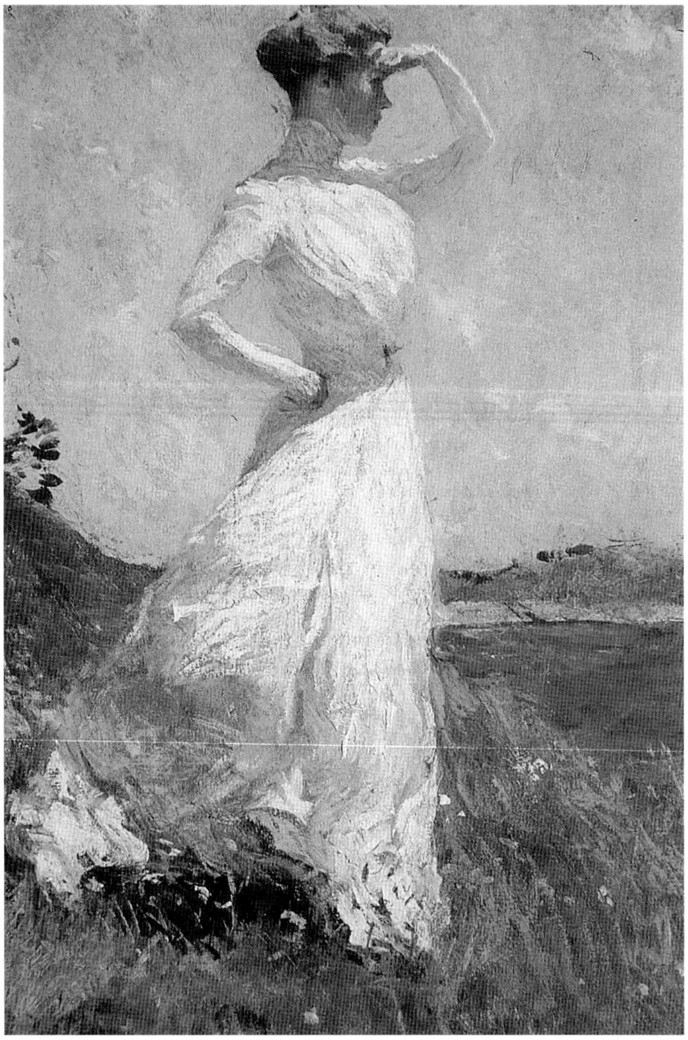

Fig. 45 Frank W. Benson, *Sunlight*, 1909.
32½ x 20 in. (82.5 x 51 cm).
©1995 Indianapolis Museum of Art, John Herron Fund

Judging by the treatment of the figure and the foreground landscape, *Farewell* (fig. 43) was probably created during these summers at Gloucester. More anecdotal than is usual for DeCamp, the painting recalls Tarbell's *On Bos'n's Hill* of 1901 (fig. 44) and may have helped to inspire Benson's series of hilltop images, begun around 1905 with *The Hilltop* (Malden Public Library, Massachusetts) and best exemplified by *Sunlight* of 1909 (fig. 45).

Another artist with strong ties to DeCamp was Ernest Major: They taught together at the Cowles Art School and, from 1900 to 1903, also at the Massachusetts Normal School of Art. A portrait by DeCamp of Major's wife (plate 17) probably dates to 1902–03 and, since the Majors frequently spent their summers in Annisquam, it may have been executed during a visit with DeCamp at Rocky Neck. Mrs. Major sits on the bench occupied by Edith and Sally in *June Sunlight,* but the backdrop is now seen from a different angle and enhanced by distant sailboats. A drawing for the painting (fig. 46) reveals that she originally wore a broad hat with plume.

The summer of 1903 was the last that the DeCamps spent at Gloucester. The local paper reported that Beaux, Dean, Paxton, Potthast, Wendel, William Burpee, and Childe Hassam were also there.[33] Probably owing to the studio fire that destroyed most of the artist's accumulated work the following year, only one landscape has survived from this summer. Titled *The Little Hotel* (plate 18), it was purchased by the Pennsylvania Academy of the Fine Arts in early 1904 and thus escaped the fire. Taken from the front lawn of the Mehlman Cottage looking east across Wonson Cove at half-tide, the view focuses on the Harbor View Hotel, a complex of buildings with two studios for rent, one of which was occupied by Twachtman in the summer of his death. This tiny studio stands out clearly at the left of the mass of architecture, perhaps intended by DeCamp as a memorial to his close friend. The brilliant color scheme of *The Little Hotel* suggests

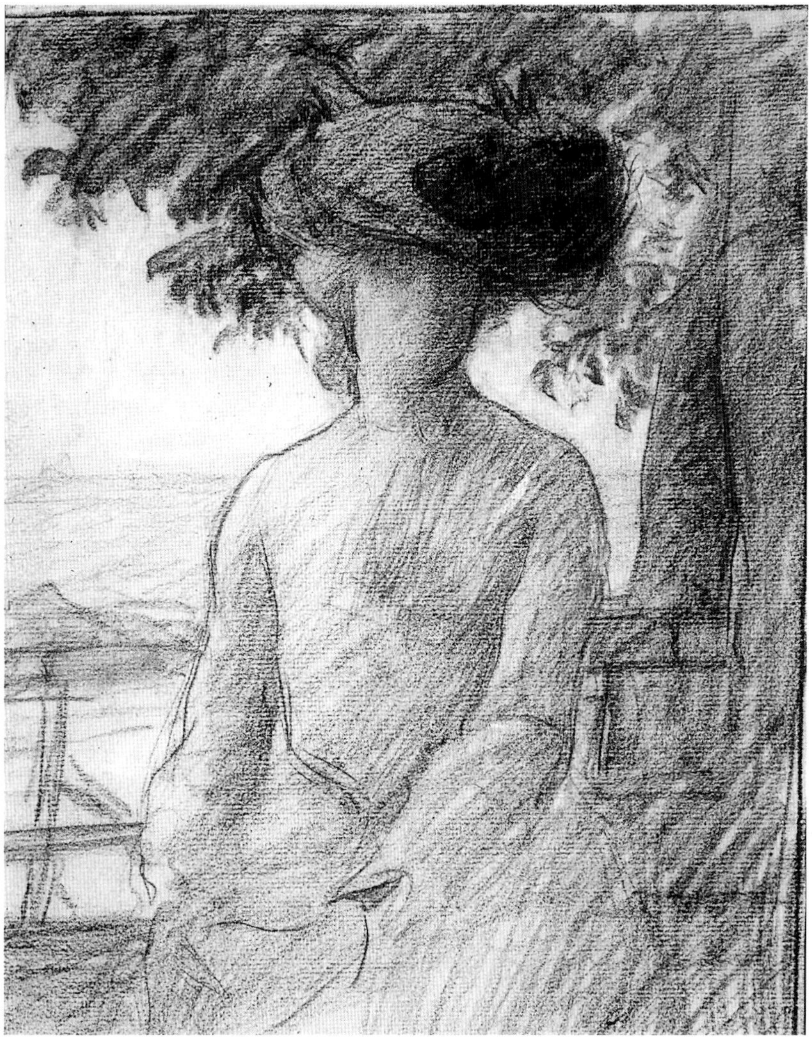

Fig. 46 *Study for "Mrs. Ernest Major"*, 1902–03. Charcoal on paper, 14 x 10 in. (35.5 x 25.5 cm). Private collection

Twachtman's influence, and the shimmering water, reflecting the richly colored buildings and trees along the shore, provides further confirmation of DeCamp's knowledge of French Impressionism.

Extant examples of the very few landscapes created by the artist after *The Little Hotel* are *Seascape, Prout's Neck* of 1904, said to have been painted from the porch of the summer cottage owned by DeCamp's friend Phineas Sprague;[34] *Summer Landscape* of 1905; and *Summer in the Country* of about 1905 (all unlocated). Critics who followed DeCamp's work throughout his life deplored the lack of continued activity in the landscape genre. In a memorial piece of 1923, Rose V.S. Berry noted: "Those who knew him best feel that it was a serious loss to the American landscape lovers that DeCamp left so few of his delighted [*sic*] out-of-door compositions. 'The Little Hotel'... is a fine example of his skill along that line, [if only he had] followed it more frequently."[35] DeCamp's short career in *plein air* work did, however, plant him securely in the American Impressionists' camp: In the first exhibitions of the Ten American Painters he stood apart for his nudes painted in subdued tonalities, but now he was hailed as a member of a subdivision of the group, the "Vibratory Seven," along with Benson, Hassam, Tarbell, Twachtman, Robert Reid, and J. Alden Weir.[36] In addition, DeCamp's outdoor imagery solidly established his key position within the Boston School. A writer for the *Boston Evening Transcript* found that of "all the ten it is the three Boston members, Benson, DeCamp and Tarbell, who have carried the painting of sunshine to the highest level."[37] Another critic, reviewing a 1903 show of paintings and sculpture at Boston's St. Botolph Club, found "the figure pictures by Mr. Benson, Mr. Tarbell, Mr. DeCamp, Mr. Paxton and Mr. [Philip Leslie] Hale... all in the modern manner, in which the chief purpose is to show the figure as it appears in an outdoor light, and as a decorative rather than descriptive object. Allowing for the personal equation which must always exist, and which produces interesting variations of style, these works are nevertheless of a certain similarity. The ruling pre-occupation, that of the sunlight effect, as it affects color, brings about this result of brilliant sameness, so that the dominant note is rainbow-like, and the minor key is conspicuous by its absence."[38]

DeCamp's outdoor figural works, like his landscapes, came to an end with the Gloucester period, except for the occasional portrait of one of his children seen against summer skies. A 1903 portrait of his son Ted (private collection) continues the artist's series of sensitive portrayals of children and was described as a "stoop shouldered boy," a "dark blue-purple figure" with a "white sky" background."[39] Another reviewer found that this juxtaposition of figure and sky gave the painting a "disagreeable coldness,"[40] while yet another noted the "human side of [a] sitter" who was presented in a strikingly "healthy manner."[41]

The image of Ted may have been the last portrait that DeCamp executed in Gloucester. Two years later, in 1905, he and his family spent their first summer in Maine. They rented a house in Camden (now the Ogier Hill Farm), said to be the location for Edna St. Vincent Millay's poem *Renascence*.[42] According to Moffat, "it was not long after [1905], while visiting his friend Frank Benson on an island in Penobscot Bay, that he found the salt water farmhouse [Crockett House] that his children, grand-children and great-grandchildren still happily look upon as their promissory note on heaven [fig. 48]."[43] Faith Bedford, Benson's great-granddaughter, confirms that Benson, who had summered on North Haven since 1901, took DeCamp by boat to see property on Vinalhaven in August 1910.[44] In Edith's name DeCamp purchased two parcels of land—in December 1910 and in May 1917—that, according to one granddaughter, included "three old farmhouses and a couple of out-

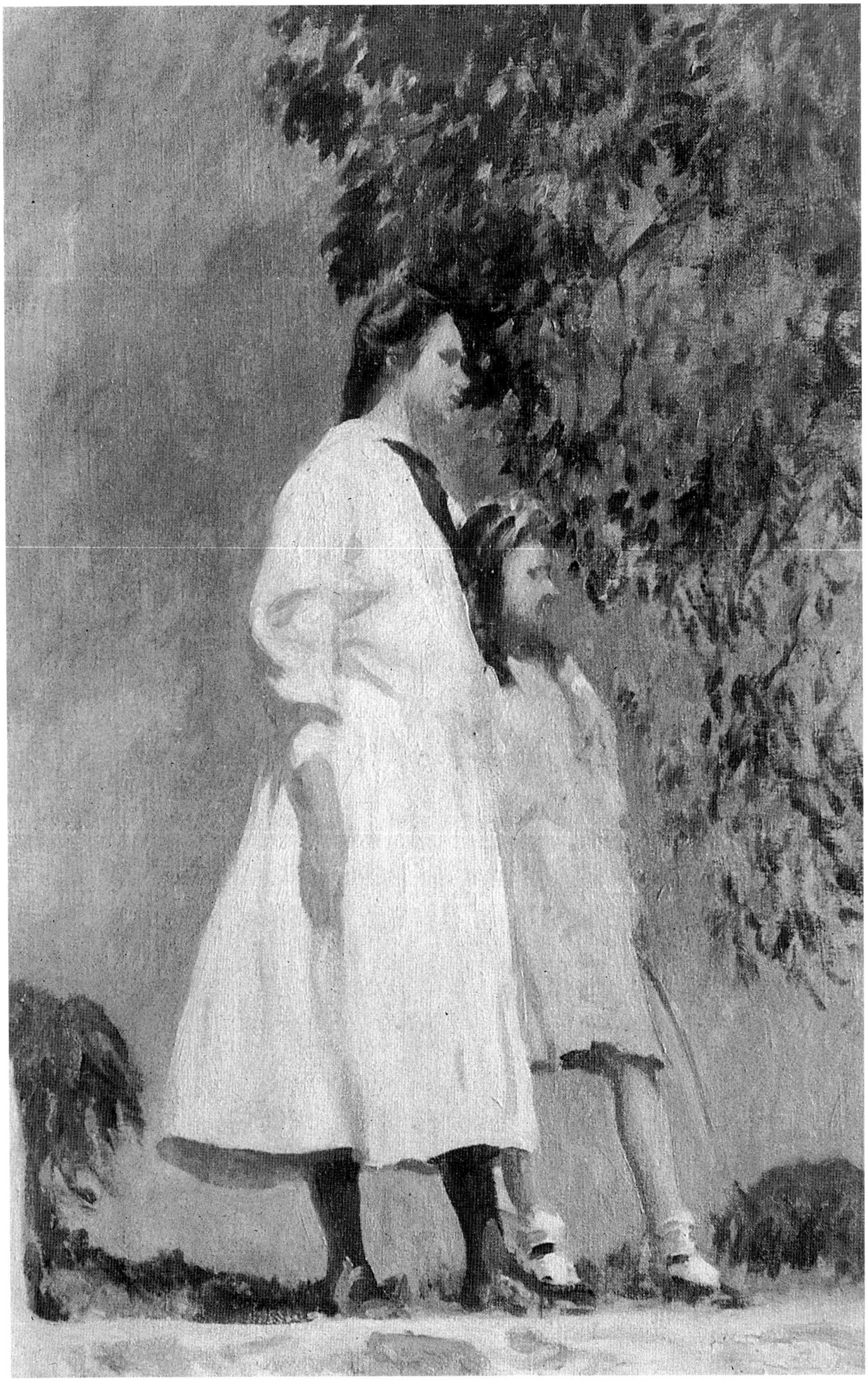

Fig. 47 *Lydia and Pauline,* ca. 1911. 27½ x 17½ in. (70 x 44.5 cm). Private collection

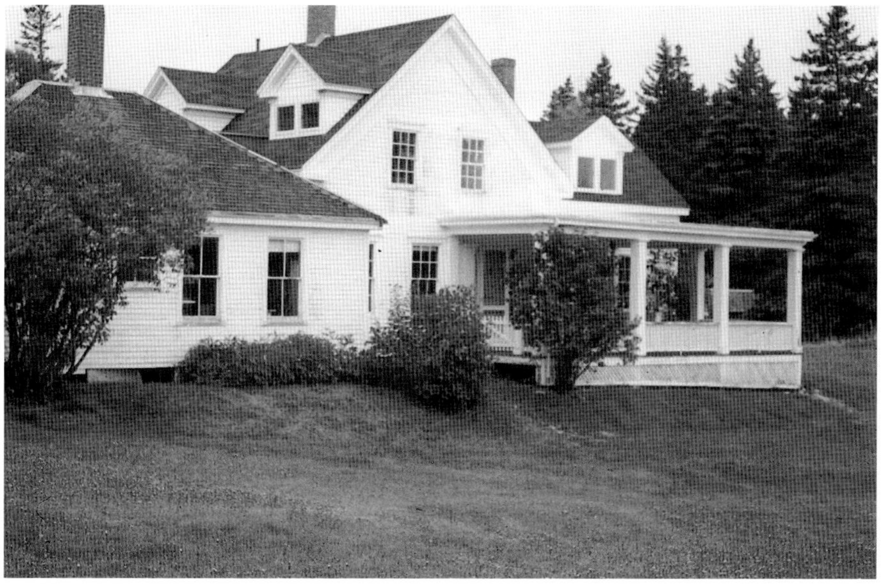

Fig. 48 Crockett House, Vinalhaven, Maine

Fig. 49 *Lydia (Head)*, ca. 1911. 28 x 24 in. (71 x 61 cm). Private collection

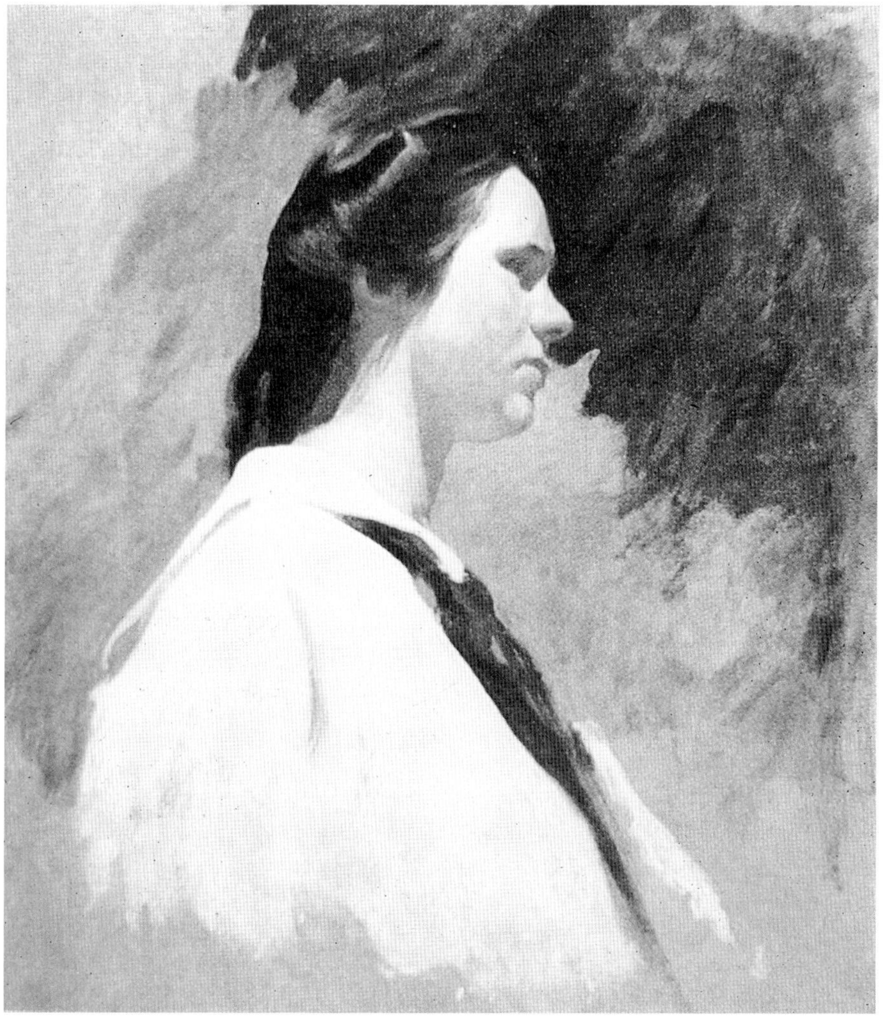

buildings, a boat house and a smaller shack, which his cook lived in.... The barn he converted into a studio and put a big north light into it."[45] With the vistas afforded by the house and its surroundings, it seems peculiar that DeCamp was not interested in continuing his *plein air* work. Moffat states that in Maine the artist carried out only "accumulated painting chores, post mortems or an occasional copying job."[46]

Around 1911, DeCamp created the only known paintings of his that utilize the Maine landscape: a double portrait of Lydia and Pauline (fig. 47), a single portrait of Lydia (fig. 49), and one of Pauline (fig. 50). Images of children never became a specialty of DeCamp's, perhaps because of the sitters' habitual restlessness. Hale addressed this issue in his 1909 book on children's portraits, in which he advised that, in order to capture the "thousand movements of a child... one desires a subtle something in the set of the head, in the movement of the hands, that shall give it the look of life."[47] None of DeCamp's portraits of children exuded this fresh "look of life" more completely for contemporary reviewers than *Sally* of about 1907 (plate 19), an indoor picture of the artist's eldest daughter in a sailor's blouse complete with four-in-hand tie. Called a "straight-from-the-shoulder painting"[48] and a "charming study of earnest, precocious juvenility,"[49] it became something of an icon of American youth. "It presents simply and frankly, a distinct American type," wrote Hale, "quite different from the convention which we have come to know as European. This young girl, although well characterized and of distinct personality, also represents something typical—the fresh, fearless intelligent type so characteristic of our young American."[50] Remarks of this kind may have represented a conservative reaction to the portraits of immigrant children that were beginning to appear in exhibitions of The Eight, a group of radical, realist painters formed in 1907. Benson's blonde-haired, healthy children, shown frolicking in the summer breezes, were reviewed in similar fashion.

An equally endearing portrait of Sally, painted when she was about six years old (fig. 51), shows her wistfully gazing in the other direction. The look of boredom on her face and the unfinished painting of the costume suggest that the patience of both sitter and painter had reached its limit. DeCamp's youngest daughter, Pauline, appears in a strict profile view (plate 20) that recalls the images of children that the artist had painted in Venice and, by extension, the fifteenth-century portraits that had influenced them. Shown in an exhibition of DeCamp's portraits at the St. Botolph Club in 1911, the work was described as a picture of "a little girl in a blue dress and careful curls" that displayed "a certain quaintness of character."[51]

DeCamp's nudes, his landscapes and *plein air* work were ultimately eclipsed in the first decade of the twentieth century by his idealized images of women in

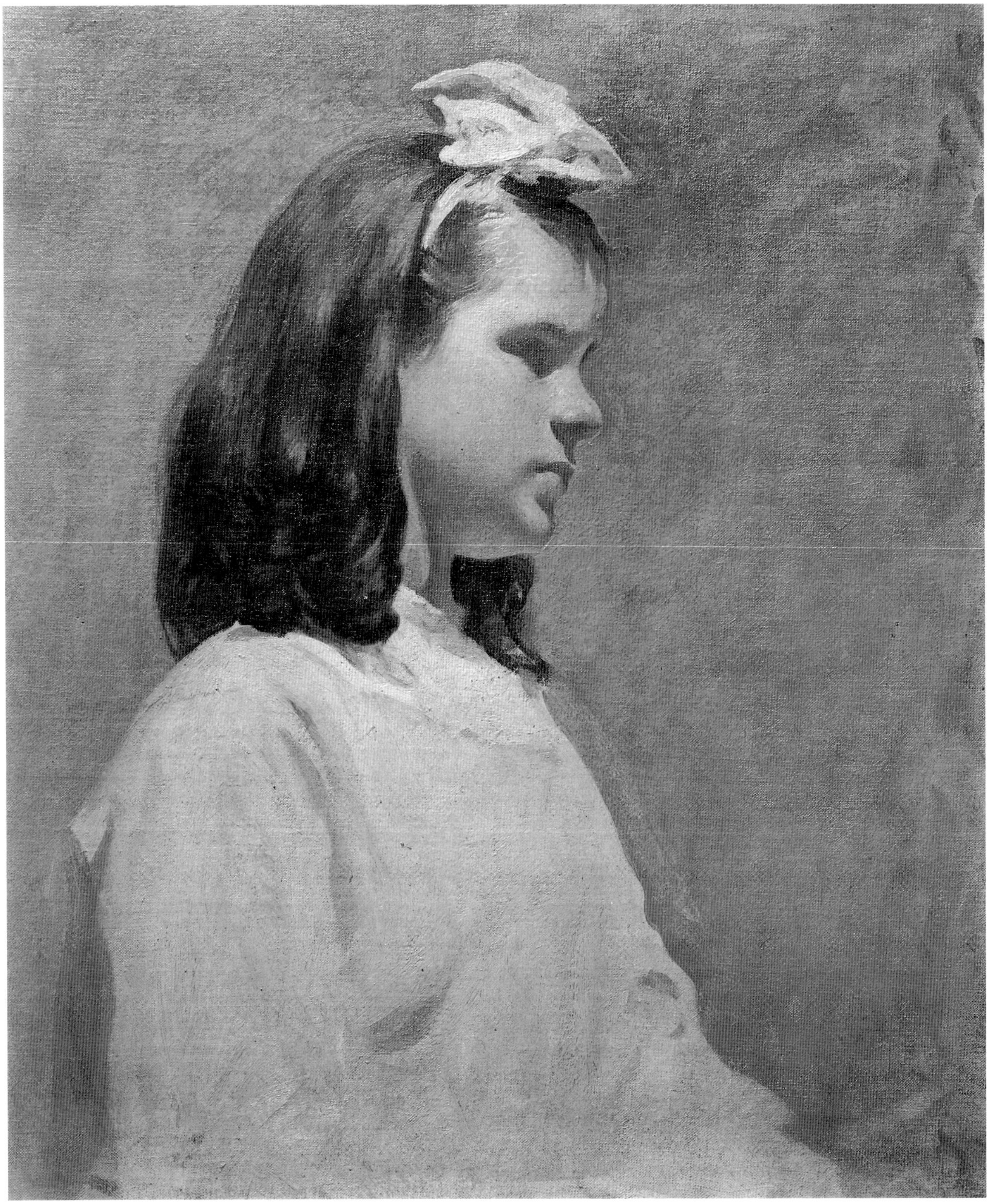

Fig. 50 Pauline (Head), ca. 1911. 23x19¼in. (58.5x49cm). Private collection

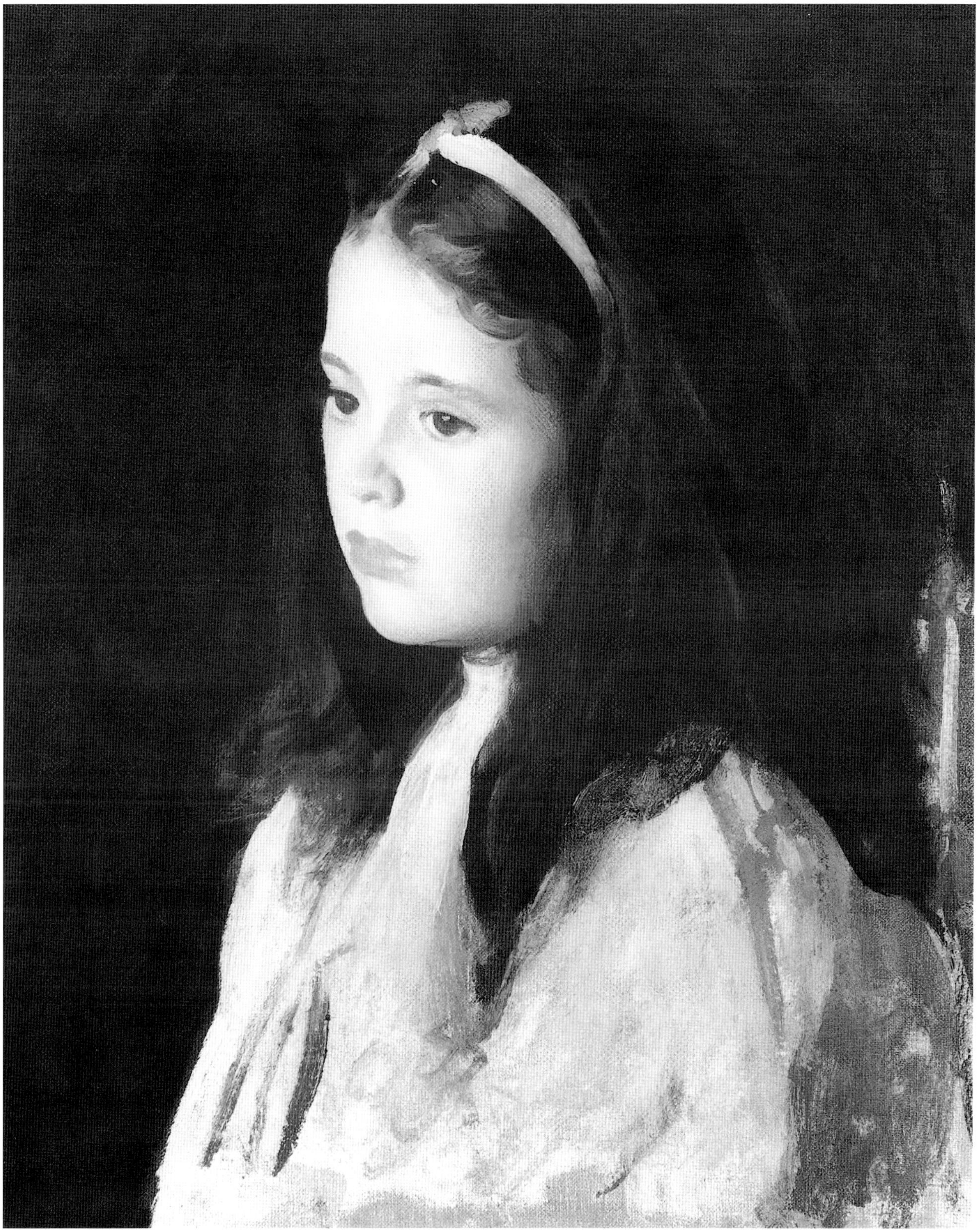

Fig. 51 *Sally (at about Six)*, ca. 1898–99. 20 x 16 in. (51 x 40.5 cm). Private collection

domestic interiors and by his formal, mostly male, portraits.[52] The artist's intensive involvement with the latter subject has been traced by numerous authors to an incident that occurred shortly after a four-alarm blaze gutted DeCamp's Harcourt Street studio on the evening of November 11, 1904. Firemen rushed to rescue the block-long building housing thirty artists' studios only to find the situation hopeless; they could save only the surrounding structures. Many of the occupants narrowly escaped death; they included the painter Mary Danforth, who collapsed over her studio windowsill.[53] Among the artists who suffered great losses were Burpee, Hazard, Paxton, Tarbell, and William W. Churchill. Paxton and Tarbell were fortunate in that much of their work was away on exhibition at the time, but the losses suffered by DeCamp and the others were total. The fire raged for nearly twenty hours, but the following day the artists were still trying to save what little was left. *Hearst's Boston American* reported: "A number of the artists gathered around the ruins today, while the firemen were still playing streams of water on the smouldering lumber stored in the basement. Some of them ventured into the ruins in the hope of recovering property, and a few emerged with withered articles that would serve only as mementoes of the fire."[54] Family tradition has it that DeCamp burned his hands trying to rescue his paintings.[55] The next morning, he is said to have marched into the St. Botolph Club, a haven for the Boston elite, and announced that he would paint anyone's portrait at a vastly reduced price.[56] Several members of the club took him up on the offer, initiating a series of lucrative portrait commissions that would continue until the artist's death nearly twenty years later.

DeCamp's flourishing career in portraiture went hand in hand with his growing national reputation. In the early years of the century he was asked to be a juror for numerous exhibitions outside of Boston; as already mentioned, he won a gold medal at the St. Louis Exposition of 1904 and the important Temple Award at the Pennsylvania Academy of the Fine Arts, Philadelphia, the following year; the Boston Art Club purchased his *Arrangement in Pink, Black and Gold* (unlocated) in 1901; and the Boston Museum of Fine Arts bought his masterpiece, *The Guitar Player*, in 1908. The artist's shift to portraiture matched the demands of the period. Michael Quick has called the years 1895 to 1915 the "great age of the society portrait"[57] and the first decade of the new century appears to have constituted a special peak in the production of portraits. Numerous critics commented on the predominance of portraiture in major exhibitions held in New York, Boston, and Philadelphia.[58] DeCamp was in the right place at the right time.

There were two leading portraitists admired by Boston patrons when DeCamp began working intensively in the genre. One was John Singer Sargent, who set the standard for portrayals of women with his soft, fluid handling of paint and opulent settings. Highly sought after for this specialty, Sargent frequently had to contend with the whims of moneyed individuals, a burden he eventually found too wearisome. Sargent admired DeCamp's work and he would later pass on the important Versailles commission to the younger painter. Possessing the more solid style, DeCamp apparently appealed to conservative, masculine tastes; Sargent's painterly and consciously stylish imagery was considered a more feminine ideal.

The other portrait specialist well known in Boston and throughout the country was Frederic Porter Vinton, who was often cited for his austere, realistic renderings of men. Trained in Paris under Léon Bonnat (also a painter of men), and later in Munich, where the emphasis was on the portrait head, Vinton established the tone of male portraiture in Boston with his dark backdrops, strong lighting, and sitters who confront the viewer head-on. Following Bonnat's propensity for harsh realism, Vinton may not have been particularly interested in portraying the status of his male sitters. DeCamp's men, on the other hand—and this is confirmed by contemporary criticism—proclaimed to the viewer that they possessed a certain social standing. When compared with those of the two older artists, DeCamp's portraits are more in line with Vinton's, especially in their plain, somber backgrounds, their emphasis on modeling, and their strong sense of draftsmanship underlying the forms. Both painters met their sitters "eyeball to eyeball," which indicates that they moved with considerable ease in Boston society.

DeCamp's portraits of Philadelphia notables invite comparison with those by Thomas Eakins, with whom he apparently had very little contact. Also a student of Bonnat, Eakins—like Vinton—portrayed his sitters with the intense naturalism characteristic of the Frenchman's style. Yet Eakins's men (and his women) are bathed in atmosphere; DeCamp's, in contrast, bask in a spotlight of what almost seems like "virtual reality." They confront the viewer directly, whereas Eakins's figures are often lost in their own private world. DeCamp's sitters—wealthy middle-class professionals—sought him out, while Eakins selected his own subjects, who, though also accomplished individuals, were not necessarily members of a specific class.

In particular, DeCamp's portrayals of Boston men—their postures, their rapport with the viewer (and, by extension, with the artist), their austere attire—seemed to contemporaries to accord his sitters a stature above that of ordinary mortals. A portrait by DeCamp, then, conferred a certain class status on the subject if he did not actually belong to that social stratum, and, if he did, set the seal of approval on his place in society. Largely denying his artistic personality, DeCamp allowed the individuality of his sitters to emerge; and forsaking the accoutrements that had

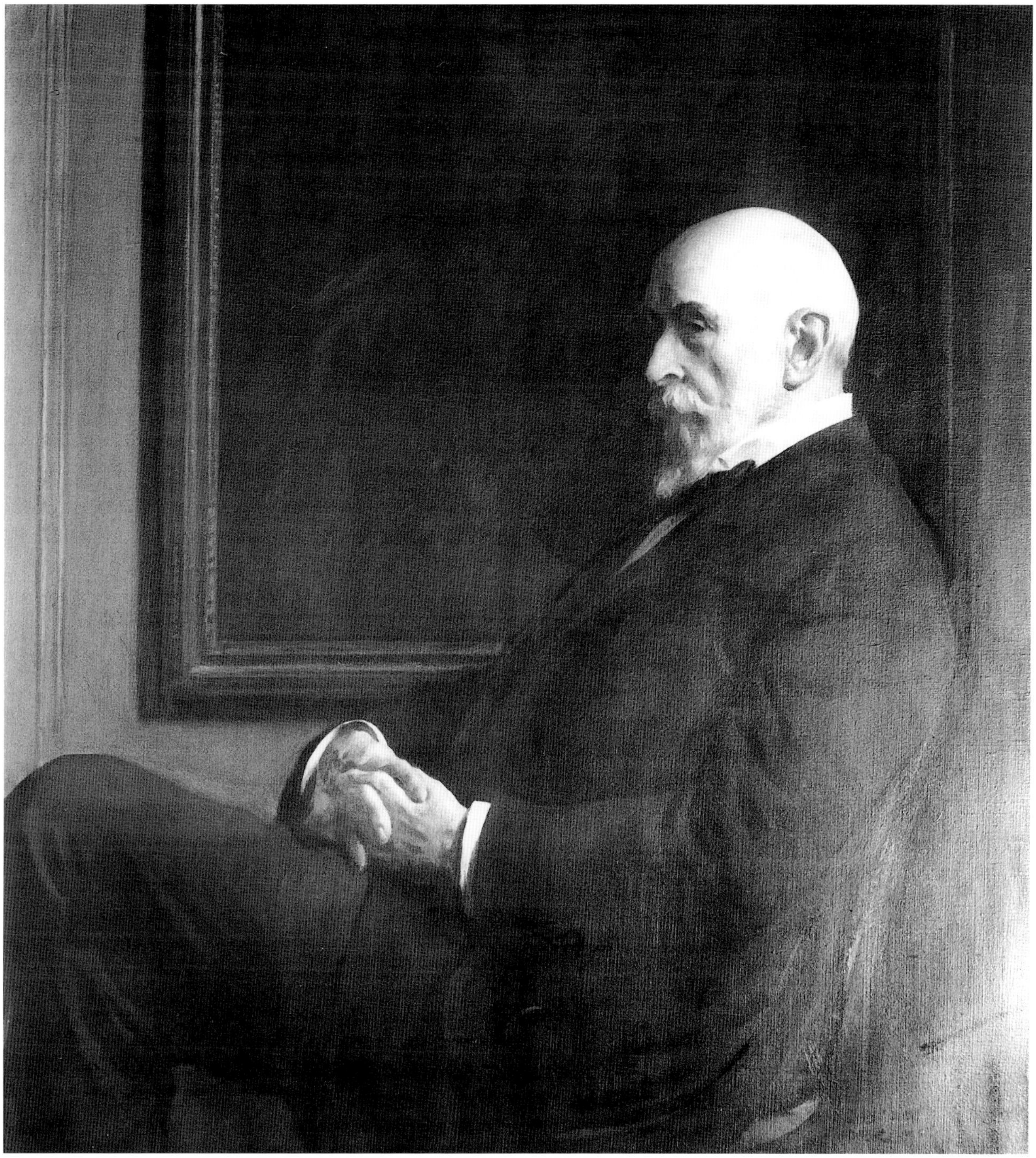

Fig. 52 *Benjamin Ames Kimball*, ca. 1905. 44½ x 39½ in. (113 x 100 cm). Hood Museum of Art, Dartmouth College, Hanover, New Hampshire, Gift of Benjamin A. Kimball, Class of 1854

appeared in American portraits since the Colonial period—books for men, flowers for women, and so forth—he created status symbols by means of his subjects' faces alone.

The artist's first critical successes with formal portraiture came with his renderings of, among others: J. Eastman Chase, the Boston art dealer, of about 1900 (unlocated); Joseph Baker, the artist's father-in-law and a well-known lithographer, of about 1903 (private collection); Frederick Forchheimer, a Cincinnati physician and teacher, of 1905 (Cincinnati Medical Heritage Center, University of Cincinnati); Benjamin Ames Kimball, a prominant business and political figure in New Hampshire, of about 1905; Horace Howard Furness, a Philadelphia scholar, of 1906; and Albert Hayden Chatfield, a Cincinnati businessman, of 1905. It will be noted that the subjects of all these portraits are male; most are seated against a plain backdrop with their faces turned slightly to the side. A review of the material collected by Moffat reveals that these were characteristic features of DeCamp's portraiture in general: Of the seventy-seven portraits of which Moffat secured photographs, sixty-six were of men and only eleven of women; sixty-nine of the sitters were seated and all but eight, who were shown in profile, faced forward.[59] DeCamp's commissioned portraits of women were painted in lighter tones and, by and large, included more evidence of home furnishings—a clear reference to the association of women with domesticity.

Reviews of the Chase portrait, which was shown at the Ten American Painters exhibition of 1900 and at the Boston Art Students Association the same year, set the tone for the critical reception of the entire series. Described as a "bust portrait of a middle-aged man with white hair and beard [and] thoughtful blue eyes framed in gold rimmed spectacles,"[60] it was said to be a "very triumph of likeness."[61] The other prime requisite of portraiture at this time—to capture the inner character of the subject—was met with the depiction of the "calm forcefulness of the sitter."[62] A *Harper's Weekly* writer found this intensity "one of the hardest qualities to reproduce in art, for it needs corresponding intensity and concentration on the part of the artist."[63]

In the Baker portrait critics noted DeCamp's ability to capture the sitter's "alert action."[64] Drafting pen in hand, the veteran lithographer was said to exhibit a "wonderful resemblance, painted throughout in a 'big' manner, and with a subtle appreciation of character."[65] The atypical, strict profile view of Kimball (fig. 52), his bald head starkly outlined against an indeterminate background, also was thought to be revealing of character. At its debut in the Ten American Painters exhibition of 1905, the *New York Times* found it "firmly, intelligently painted" and expressive of "an earnest, intelligent nature, although the look from the eyes is a trifle guerulous."[66] Kimball could afford to be a trifle forbidding, since he was a member of the House of Representatives of New Hampshire, President of the Concord and Montreal Railroad, a partner in the Ford and Kimball Foundry, President of the Cushman Electric Company, the Light and Power Company of Concord, and the Mechanics National Bank of Concord, as well as an incorporator and director of the Manufacturers and Merchants Mutual Fire Insurance Company. The work was commissioned by Dartmouth College, of which Kimball was a trustee.[67]

Equally distinguished is the portrait of Forchheimer, a Cincinnati professor of physiology and dean of the Ohio Medical College.[68] Entered in the Ten show of 1906, it was called one of the strongest paintings in the exhibition and was noted for the "quality of the flesh color, especially in the shadows."[69] A close friend of Forchheimer's, Albert Hayden Chatfield, was painted by DeCamp in 1905 (plate 21). A strong supporter of the arts in Cincinnati, Chatfield had a studio built

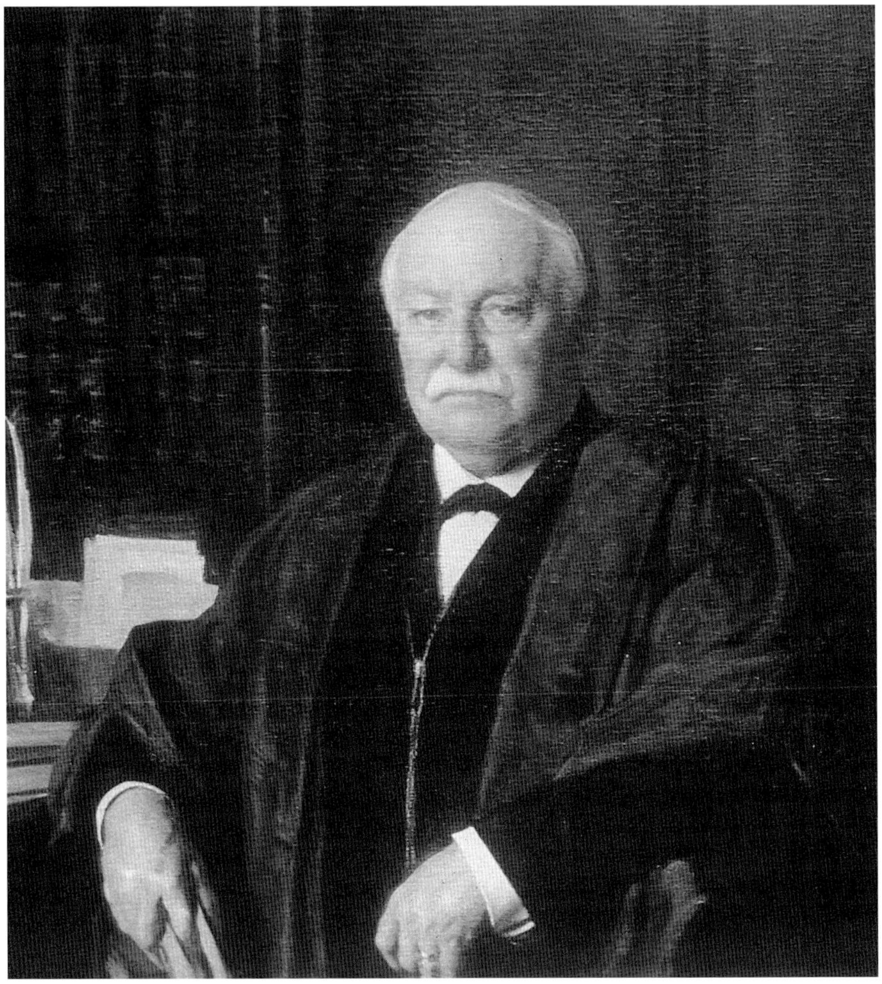

Fig. 53 *Horace Howard Furness*, 1906. 36½ x 33½ in. (92.5 x 86 cm). Pennsylvania Academy of the Fine Arts, Philadelphia

in about 1905 near his summer house in Camden, Maine, for the use of DeCamp and another Ohio artist, Lewis Meakin.[70] A contemporary photograph shows DeCamp, Meakin, and Chatfield, whose portrait appears at the left, relaxing in the studio (fig. 54). A letter written by the artist to John E. D. Trask of the Pennsylvania Academy of the Fine Arts confirms DeCamp's presence at Camden that summer. "My dear Trask," he wrote, "I am at Camden, Maine, and can give you a bed... any time you appear."[71] The letter included a bill of $300 for expenses relating to the portrait of Horace Furness (fig. 53), which had been commissioned by the academy. Adding this sum to the honorarium of $500, one can see that DeCamp's portrait prices had escalated quickly since his offer of $100 to members of the St. Botolph Club the previous year. The prestige of the artist's sitters kept pace with his rising reputation. Furness, a noted Philadelphia Shakespearian scholar, trustee of the University of Pennsylvania, and President of the Philadelphia Theatre Association, stares out at the viewer in his bright red academic robes. Exhibited at the Pennsylvania Academy's annual of 1907, the painting was called the "strongest portrait of the show" by the reviewer for the *Philadelphia Inquirer.* "The color is very rich," he continued, "since the doctor is wearing his scarlet gown, seated in his study against a background of brown bound books. The portrait has immensely the man's character; the hands are powerfully drawn and modeled; the head is done most carefully and is the best possible criticism upon the chic of Miss [Cecilia] Beaux's portrait or those of [Robert] Henri."[72] DeCamp's work obviously answered the demand for a middle-ground approach to portraiture, somewhere between the flamboyant Sargentesque style typical of Beaux and the dark, spontaneous work of Henri.

DeCamp's methods in approaching his sitters are well documented. Rose V. S. Berry noted in 1923: "DeCamp seldom required a fixed, rigid pose of his model. He walked around the sitter, he felt of the head, discovered the texture of the ear, examined its placement upon the head, and proceeded in general with much the line of attack which a sculptor takes."[73] Before he began to paint, however, he would take time to contemplate the person before him. "Put your canvas up near your sitter," he was quoted as saying, "sit down in the most comfortable chair you have, put your watch on the table, and sit for ten solid minutes just looking and deciding things. Then get on your feet and go to work."[74] Having progressed a long way from the fussy 1880s portrait of his elderly father, DeCamp now approached his subject with assurance, in both technique and style. He detested "niggling," according to his friend the writer Harley Perkins, who defined the term as the "attempt to get character by overemphasis of the individual features of the face."[75] DeCamp's knowledge of pigments and their preparation was legendary;[76] the final hues of a painting mattered less to him than its tones, which he considered of prime importance.[77]

Fig. 54 DeCamp, Lewis Meakin, and Albert Hayden Chatfield, ca. 1905, in the studio built for the artists by Chatfield at Camden, Maine

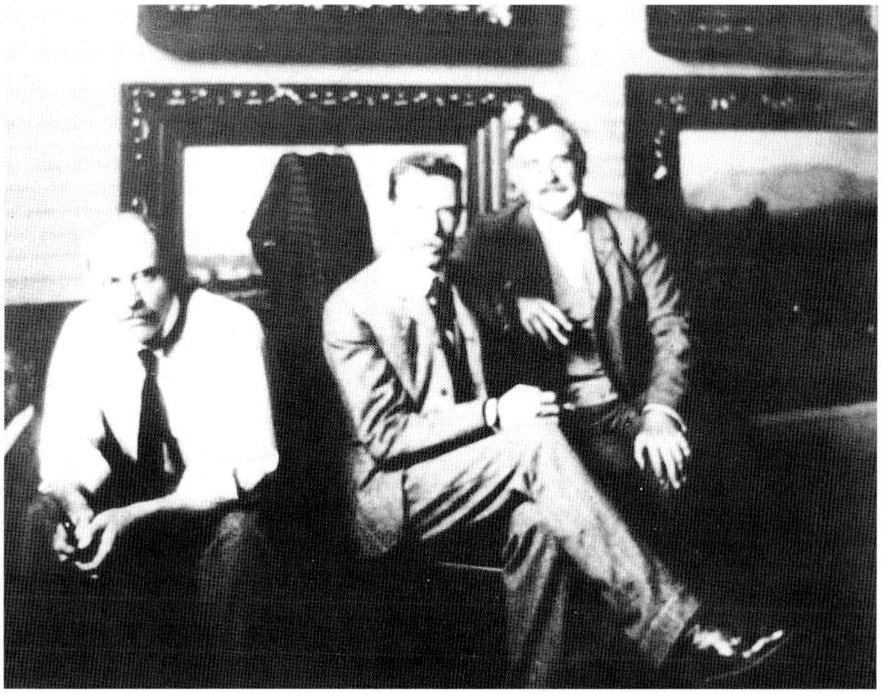

The most salient feature of the artist's portraits is the superb rendering of the flesh tones, for which his nudes were also praised. The faces come alive, especially when they gaze at the viewer in what Quick has called "confrontational immediacy"—according to him, an essential characteristic of French and American realist portraiture of the period.[78] It is perhaps also the most outstanding feature in the work of Diego Velázquez, the Spanish seventeenth-century painter whom DeCamp was known to idolize. Throughout his long teaching career, DeCamp used reproductions of Velázquez's work for demonstration purposes. "I can still picture DeCamp reaching into a portfolio for some photographs of paintings by Velasquez [*sic*]," wrote Gammell. "First he selected the celebrated bodegone representing an old woman cooking eggs [National Gallery of Scotland, Edinburgh], and pointed to the rigorous insistence with which each detail had been worked out. Then he took up the *Rokeby Venus* [National Gallery, London] and said with a characteristic sweep of his long fingers across the broadly modelled forms, 'But before he got through he made them like this!'"[79] When DeCamp finally visited Spain in the summer of 1909, his profound awe in the presence of the master's work was recalled by the noted Boston critic William Howe Downes, who apologized to his readers for not being able to repeat the artist's "vivid and picturesque words": "Speaking of the marvelous freshness and perfection of conditions which distinguished the pictures there [DeCamp] said they looked, some of them, as if they were 'painted last Tuesday.'"[80]

Other male portraits by DeCamp, not exhibited, from the early years of the twentieth century reinforce the clientele profile of those attracted to the artist's work: wealthy middle-class professionals. These portraits include: Joseph W. Symonds, an associate justice in the Supreme Judicial Court of Maine (1901); Frederick Robie, a former governor of Maine (1901; both Maine State Museum, Augusta); Arthur Elisha Mann, a Boston manufacturer (ca. 1902; unlocated); Royal Elisha Robbins, treasurer of the Waltham Watch Company (ca. 1902; private collection);[81] and Fairman Rogers, a posthumous image of the Philadelphia engineer and patron of Thomas Eakins (ca. 1907; Pennsylvania Academy of the Fine Arts, Philadelphia).

As early as 1900, Hale was singing DeCamp's praises as a portraitist: "It is a wonder that Mr. DeCamp does not favor us with more portraits of men, for I know of no one who paints a better or more convincing likeness."[82] Four years later, Charles Caffin also hailed DeCamp as a major painter of men: "While another Boston artist, Joseph R. DeCamp, has done some charming pictures of women and children, his most notable works have been occasional portraits of men. These are of unusual merit, revealing that searching analysis, here applied to character, which has made him one of the best painters of the nude in America."[83] No wonder, then, that in 1908, when the Harvard class of 1880 wished to commission a portrait of its greatest alumnus, Theodore Roosevelt, DeCamp was the artist chosen. The difficult sittings are well documented. "Mr. DeCamp has been to Washington to see the President and has talked over the proposed sittings," announced the *Boston Evening Transcript* on October 16, 1908. "The work is to be begun at once, and there are to be daily sittings of an hour and a half until the portrait is completed.... The President is not an easy subject for a portrait painter."[84] The artist himself gave a fuller account to his wife: "This is just to say that I have had two sittings and am still alive. He is the most restless thing I have ever seen—not still a minute. However, I have rubbed in a lot and he has sort of promised to do better in a day or two, when he has finished some dictation.... I mean to tame him if I can, but he is a hard proposition, though better natured than I had expected."[85] In a second letter to Edith, DeCamp continued: "The President has finally become quite interested and has given me a sitting this morning all alone and has promised others. The head is almost finished and certainly looks like him.... When I have made that and one hand I will... do the rest at home, with several sittings later if I need them. If all goes well, I will surely throw out my chest and fear no sitter; as no one could be worse than his Presidential highness."[86]

DeCamp later expanded on his role in the "taming" of the President: "My reputation is at stake," he reportedly said to Roosevelt, "and if you cannot give me proper sittings, I'm man enough to shut up my box and give up the whole matter."[87] The full-length, authoritative figure represented in the painting (fig. 55) surely is one of DeCamp's finest achievements. In a less than formal stance, the President, dressed in gray, stands between two elegant pieces of White House furniture, his left leg forward, his left hand thrust into his pocket. Roosevelt peers out from behind the familiar spectacles, his demeanor bespeaking leadership. A large expanse of background space adds to the august importance of the sitter, yet the bouquet of pink roses helps to soften that effect. The artist responded to complaints about this juxtaposition of roses with a President of action by remarking: "Would you prefer a bunch of rifles?... The President is fond of flowers, and has them always around him. Besides, I wanted a pink note there."[88] Critics noted the work's superiority to other portraits of Roosevelt, especially those by foreign artists. In an article of 1908, Hale observed: "Various portrait painters of other nationalities have had a crack at him. Mr. Chartran painted him as a Frenchman, Mr. Benziger as a Swiss, Mr. Laszlo as a Hungarian and Mr. Sargent as a cosmopolite. Now it will be interesting to see him painted as an American."[89] DeCamp may have studied the "Landsdowne" portrait of President George Washington by Gilbert Stuart with regard both to the stance of the figure and, more especially, to the arrangement of table and chair within a cramped foreground.

The Roosevelt portrait occupied the place of honor in the artist's first one-man show devoted to portraits, which was held at Boston's St. Botolph Club in 1911, the year that Vinton, DeCamp's rival in male portrayals, died. Some reviewers called the work a statement of mere external truth,[90] but others, particularly the critic for the *Boston Traveller*, felt that DeCamp had captured the true character of the man: "A more 'strenuous' subject is not to be found, and Mr. DeCamp's portrait has completely mastered the 'strenuosity.' The personality which has moved two continents has moved the artist's brush and caused him to paint in lineaments of the face, the searching glimpse of the eye—as if it caught sight of a trust fraud in the distance or saw it creeping stealthily in at the door—in the hand thrust into his pocket or the foot that rests, but not inactively, on the floor, the toe of the boot slightly elevated, the Roosevelt whom all the world knows."[91]

Other commissioned portraits in the 1911 exhibition included those of Daniel Merriman, President of the Worcester Art Museum (1910); Francis I. Amory (ca. 1911; private collection) and Frank Duveneck (ca. 1911–12). A.J. Philpott of the *Boston Globe* called the show an "event of importance and one in which Bostonians can take some pride. For Mr. DeCamp is a Boston artist and one of the leading painters of this country today."[92] Edith Burnham of the *Boston Traveller* particularly praised the male figures: "Mr. DeCamp's portraits have a vitality and vigor which seems to make it difficult for them to hang on the wall .... Especially is this true of his portraits of men of affairs, whose mental acumen shows with such force in their faces.... His work has nicety without precocity, naturalness without mannerism, individuality and penetration without cutting incision, and distinction without glaring distinctiveness."[93]

Francis I. Amory, a member of the St. Botolph Club, was called "a Bostonese of the Bostonese"[94] when DeCamp's painting of him was hung in the 1912 Pennsylvania Academy of the Fine Arts annual, at which it won the Carol H. Beck Gold Medal for best portrait. The artist had apparently captured the quintessence of Boston Brahminism: "'I'm from Boston' is said as plainly in the fingers over the edge of the closed book as in a certain patrician hauteur of pose and countenance and Harvard education," wrote a reviewer for the Philadelphia *Public Ledger*.[95] When shown in the

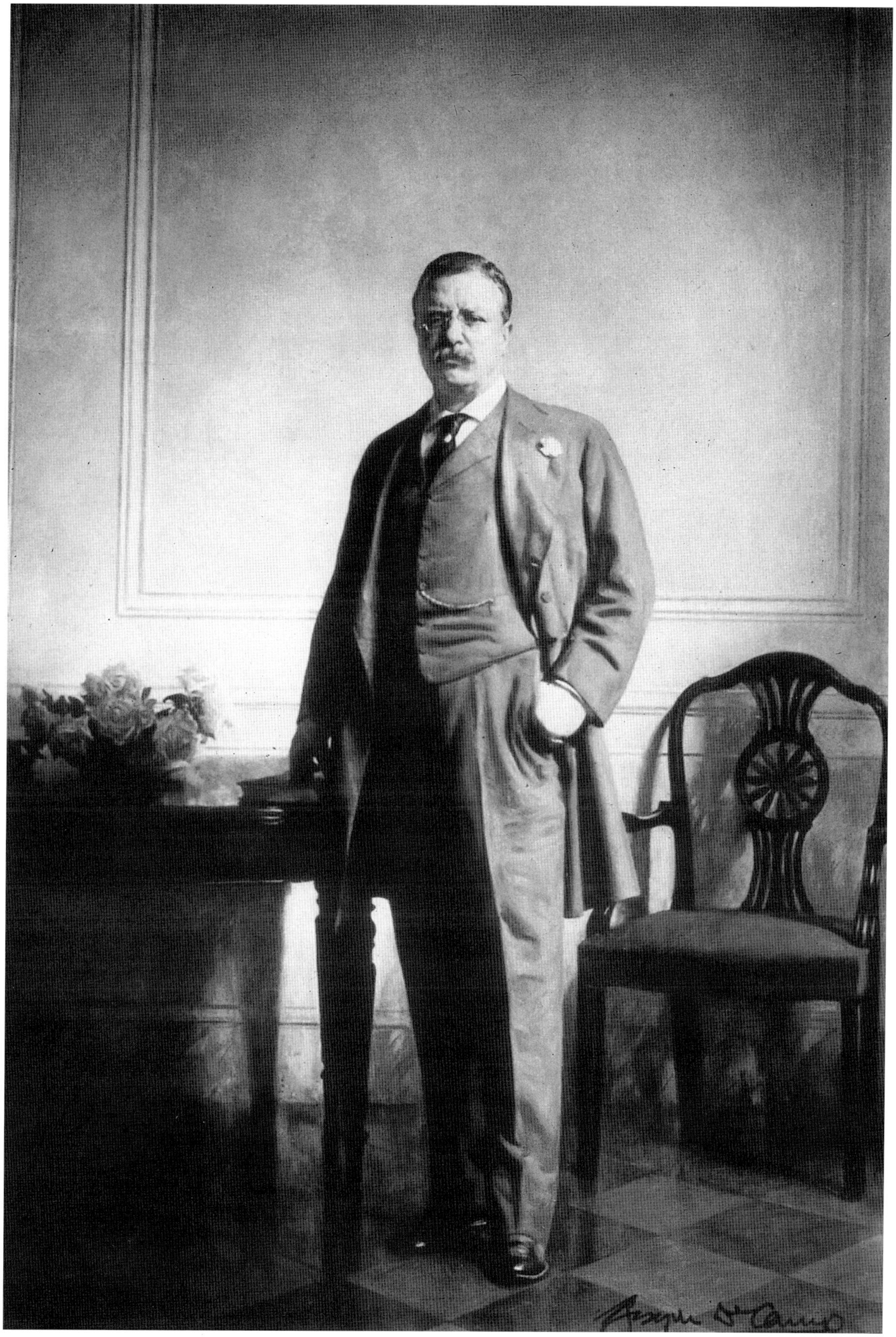

Fig. 55 *President Theodore Roosevelt,* 1908. 96 x 66 in. (244 x 167.5 cm).
Courtesy of the Harvard University Portrait Collection, Cambridge, Massachusetts, Gift of class of 1880

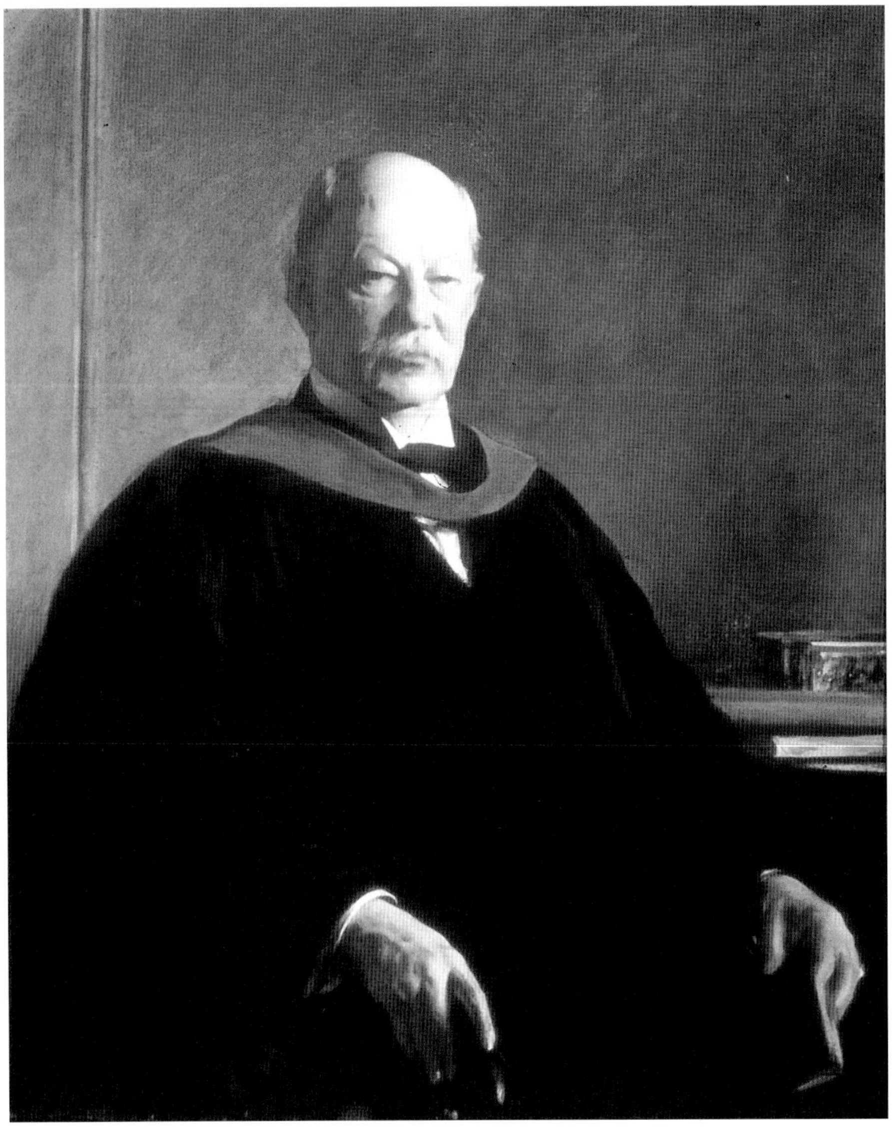

Fig.56
Reverend Daniel Merriman,
1910. 41x34in. (104x86.5cm).
Worcester Art Museum,
Massachusetts,
Gift of Mrs. Daniel Merriman

Ten American Painters exhibition of 1911 in New York, the painting was said to display "all the precise, definite notations and accents... eloquent both of the personality of the sitter and of the conscience and intelligence of the painter."[96] References to portraits as reflecting the intelligence of both the subject and the painter were rare in DeCamp's time; here again, one is reminded of the work of Velázquez, who treated his sitters, royalty and servants alike, as equals.

DeCamp also succeeded in portraying the essence of clergyman Merriman's personality (fig. 56), according to a *Boston Globe* reviewer: "Running through all the linear detail of that seamed face is the character of the man—evidently a reserved, cautious, calculating man, and ponderous."[97] It was the Duveneck portrait (fig. 57), however, that received the most plaudits at the 1911 exhibition, not only owing to the reputation of the sitter, but also because of DeCamp's ability to depict the crucial features of his lifelong mentor. "The big human bulk of the man, the head in semi-profile with its shaggy mane of hair, the big capable hands, all in their way synchronize in giving generous expression to a dominant mentality that has been an important factor in shaping the art of our times," noted Harley Perkins.[98] When DeCamp donated the portrait to the Cincinnati Art Museum in 1912, the director passed on what, to the artist, was perhaps the supreme compliment: "The Old Man [Duveneck] is evidently much pleased with it. You know how he looks and does not talk when particularly well satisfied with anything."[99]

Other portraits created in the years immediately prior to the 1911 one-man show were those of James Tyson, author of medical literature and dean of the University of Pennsylvania Medical School (1910; fig. 58), and Louis Starr, a noted Philadelphia physician (1910; School of Medicine, University of Pennsylvania, Philadelphia). These elicited some negative response when shown at the Pennsylvania Academy of the Fine Arts annual in 1910. "DeCamp carried his madness one peg too far," noted the reviewer for the

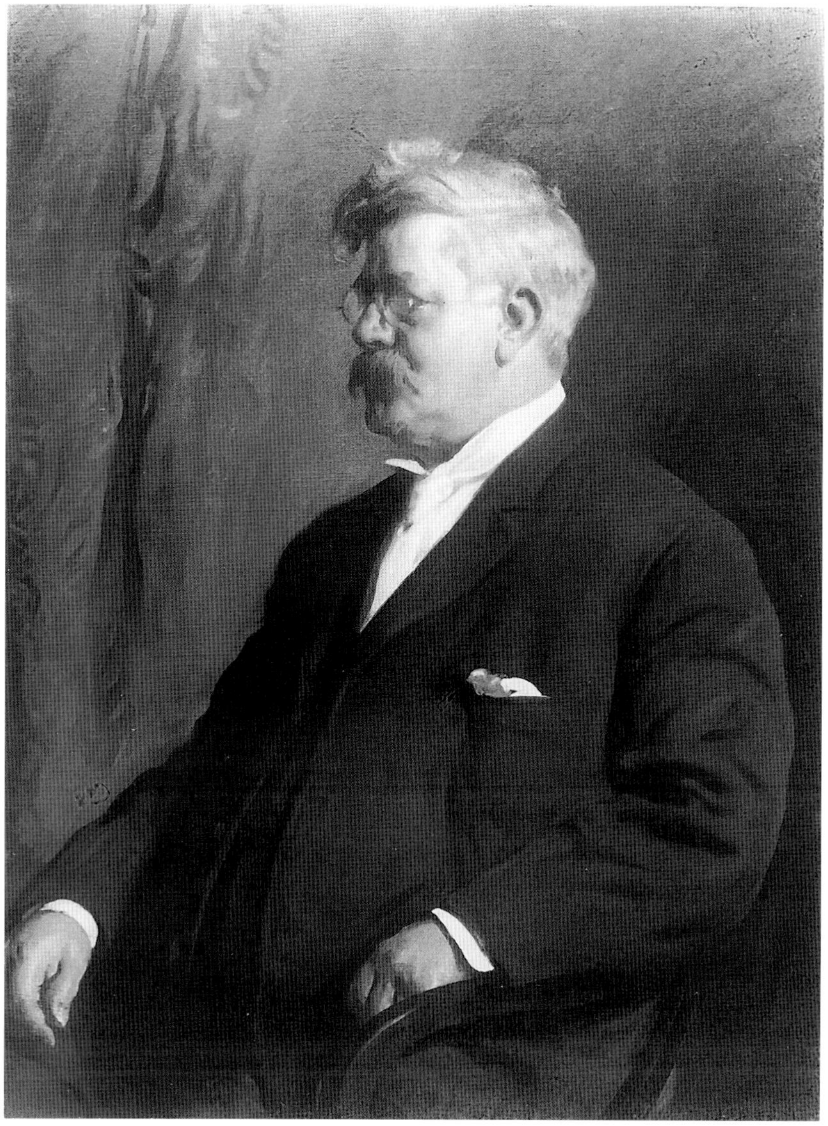

Fig. 57 Frank Duveneck, ca. 1911–12. 43⅛x32⅛ in. (109.5x81.5cm). Cincinnati Art Museum, Gift of Joseph R. DeCamp

Philadelphia Inquirer. "His portraits are so honest and so strong in construction that they verge sensibly toward the mission furniture sort of thing. He needs more romance, more imagination and a cooler palette."[100] Similar criticisms would be leveled at DeCamp in the future.

An unusual portrait, of 1912, is that of the Clothiers: Isaac H., Isaac H. C., Jr., and Isaac H. C., III, members of three generations of the well-known Philadelphia mercantile family (fig. 59). Carefully composing the heads within rectilinear backdrops, as in most of these works, DeCamp breaks the formality of his typical male portraits in allowing the warmth of the relationship between grandfather and grandson to come to the fore. Appropriately, the painting is also called *Three Friends.*

"Informality" is perhaps the best word to describe the direction that DeCamp's portraits take from this point on. In general, his sitters exhibit increasingly relaxed facial features and postures, matching the contemporary turn to comfort in menswear. "In 1900 durability, wearableness, was the prized quality," according to Mark Sullivan in *Our Times*, a social history of the period. "Between 1900 and 1925 man adventured into grays, light shades of brown, powder blues; [they] wore soft felt hats, soft collars and cuffs, and socks of silk or lisle or other light-weight material."[101]

Only four years after the 1911 portrait show at the St. Botolph Club, DeCamp mounted another, this time at the Guild of Boston Artists, an organization founded in 1914 to foster sales and encourage the reputations of its member artists in a series of traveling exhibitions. Based on the painters' guilds of seventeenth-century Holland, the group included active as well as associate members, the latter drawn from leaders of the Boston community.[102] DeCamp's 1915 exhibition at the Guild included portraits of Frederick Cheever Shattuck, a physician and instructor at Harvard Medical School (1912, Harvard University Medical School, Cambridge); Augustus George Bullock, a noted business man of Worcester, Massachusetts (1913, State Mutual

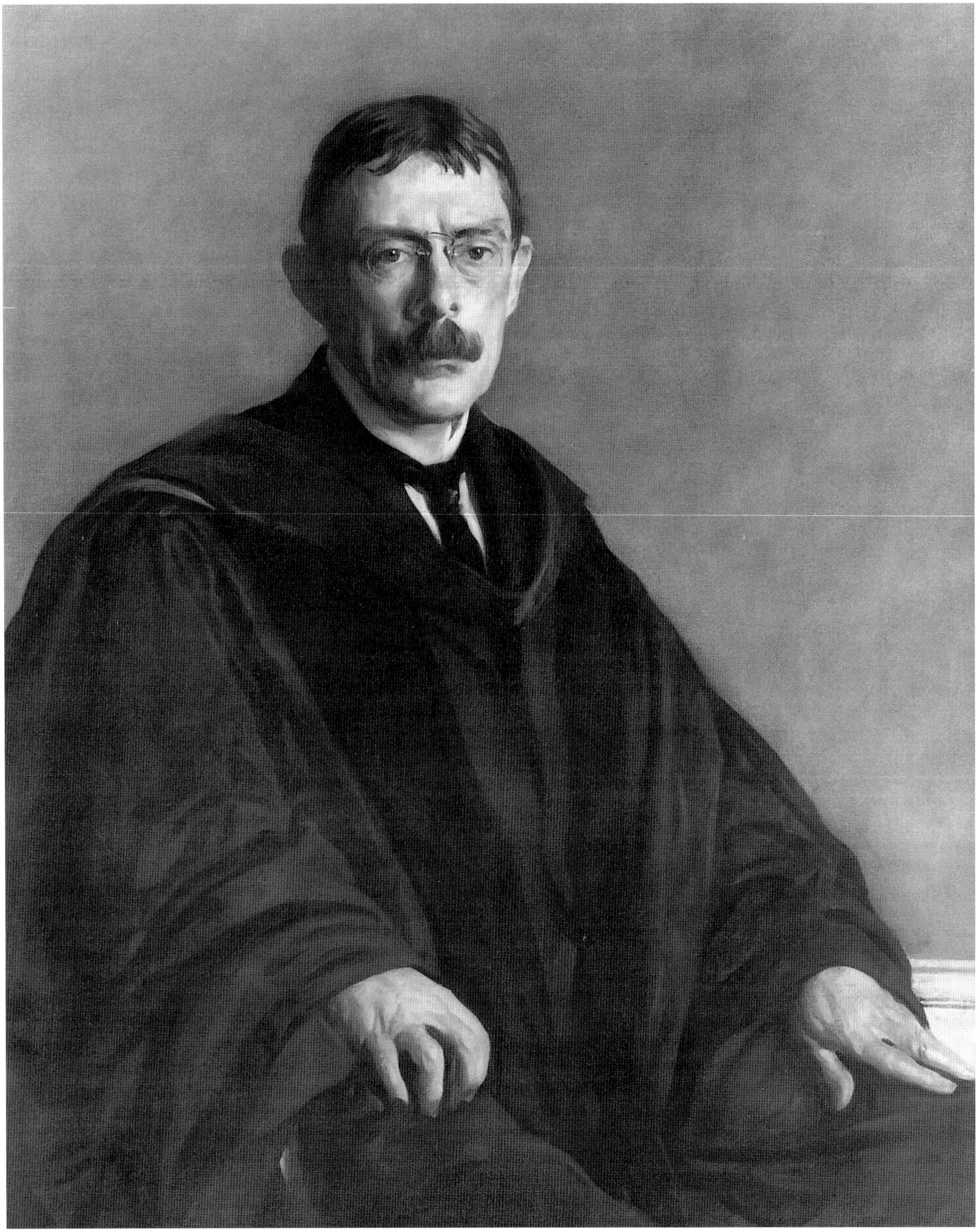

Fig. 58 *James Tyson*, 1910. 41¼ x 33¼ in. (105 x 84.5 cm). Mütter Museum, The College of Physicians of Philadelphia

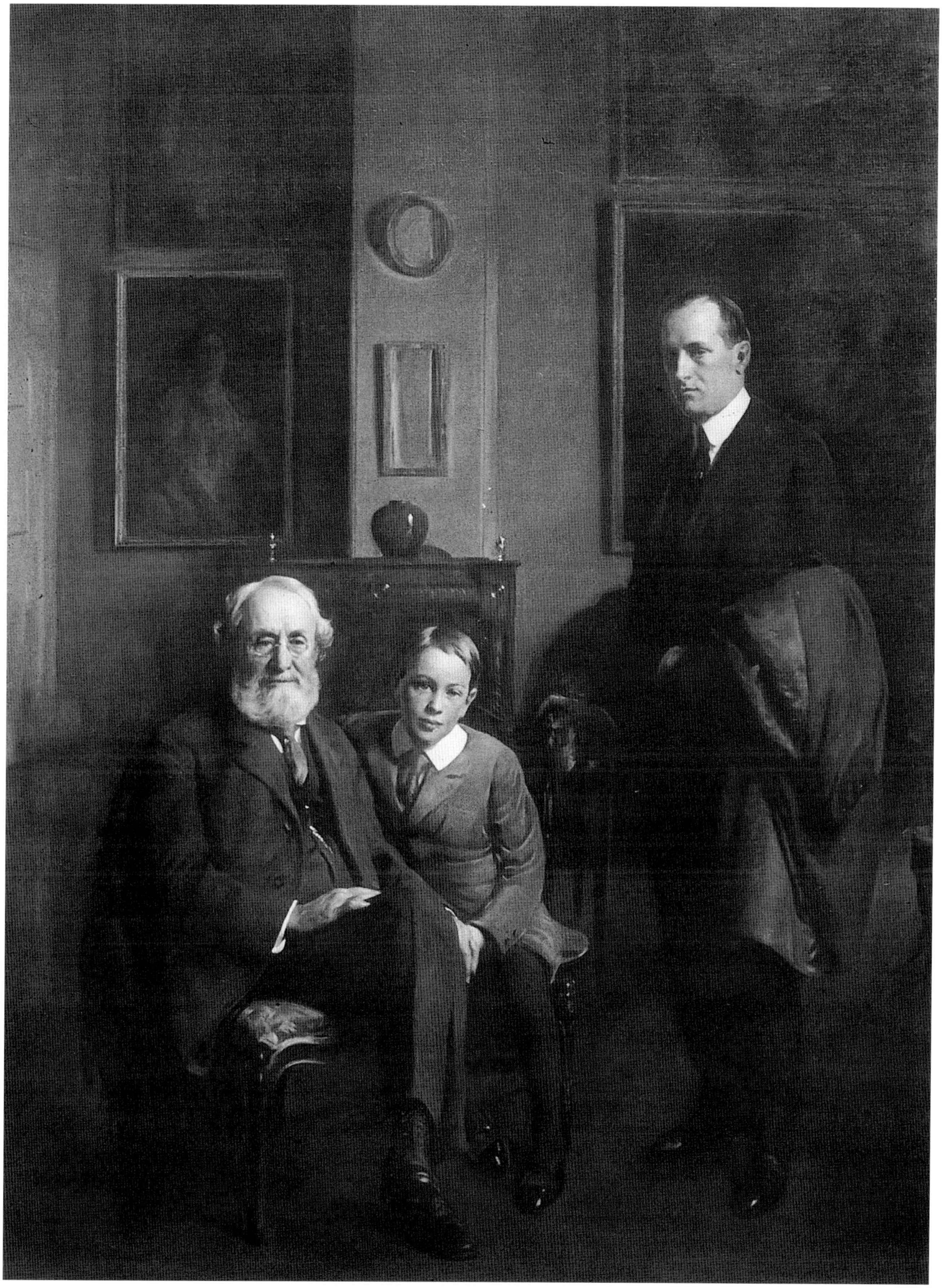

Fig. 59 *The Clothier Group (Three Friends)*, 1912. 94 x 67¼ in. (239 x 171 cm). Swarthmore College Art Collection, Pennsylvania

Life Assurance Company, Worcester);[103] Frank G. Webster (1913); Amy Morris Homans, a dean of Wellesley College, Massachusetts (ca. 1914; Wellesley College);[104] Edmund Clark Sanford, a psychologist and president of Clark University, Worcester, Massachusetts (ca. 1914, Clark University);[105] and Charles Sprague, a friend of the DeCamps in Maine (1915, private collection). Also shown in the exhibition was a double portrait of Robert Saltonstall and his son William (ca. 1915; Milton Academy, Massachusetts), which displays the same rapport between male members of a family as the Clothier group.

Once again, critics applauded DeCamp's ability to capture the specific character of his sitters, who were now also recognized as belonging to a particular stratum of society. Of the Shattuck portrait, the *Boston Sunday Herald* reviewer wrote that the artist had "succeeded in giving to this physician and teacher an uplifting rectitude of aspect. Instinctively, you straighten up in his presence. A light gray background of rectilinear divisions helps to impress this sensation of physical and mental uprightness. Here, as elsewhere, Mr. DeCamp is interpreter in extraordinary of our neo-Puritans. The man he paints is far from being austere or unlikeable, but in the etymological sense of the word he is quite Puritanical—he is 'putus et purus.'"[106] The *Boston Globe* critic felt that the Webster portrayal (fig. 60) took "no apparent effort in the doing of it. It is closely drawn and freely painted. The character is in the pose, the lighting, the look, and the lives are as perfect in harmony as the color." The same writer thought the Saltonstall portrait showed considerable skill in the portrayal of two figures, "finely contrasted and showing the relationship at a glance."[107]

The reviews were especially favorable, naturally, when their authors were from Boston. One of them even compared DeCamp's work to that of Frans Hals: "It is doubtful if there could be brought together 13 portraits by one American painter of such superlative excellence as these which Mr. DeCamp exhibits. This is not a collection of fads and fancies. Every one is a genuine work of art—big, honest, sincere and superb in workmanship. This man is surely the Hals of our time, with the difference that he is more searching in his analysis of character and a little more careful in his work. There is the bigness and the buoyancy of Hals in these paintings and that feeling for the structure of the head in its details, as well as its pose, which characterizes the best of Hals' portraiture."[108] The *American Art News* reviewer repeated the sentiments of the *Boston Sunday Herald* critic: "In Joseph DeCamp's admirable portrait show at the Guild may be seen the apogee of Boston Puritanism," he noted. "For, if there is any Puritanism left in America, it is certainly to be found in a certain type of cultivated Boston 'gentlemen.' It is austere, rather than a genial, type, impressing one with its unswerving rectitude, not to say smug hypocrisy. In it

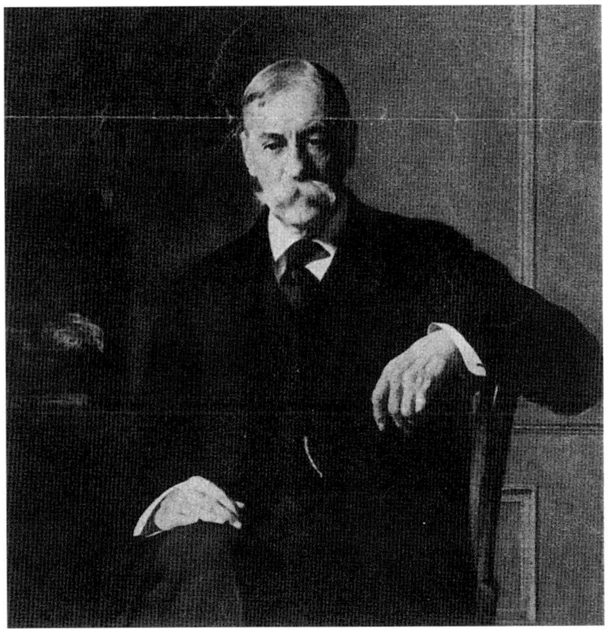

Fig. 60 *Frank G. Webster*, 1913. 41½ x 36½ in. (105.5 x 92.5 cm). Unlocated

the artist has found inspiration for some of his best work, which seems to be not so much painting as incisive and masterly character analysis."[109] Downes accorded DeCamp a measured compliment: "Other portrait painters perhaps might set down all that they could see, with a similar measure of skill in the descriptive part of their métier, but few of them have the eyes to see as much as Mr. DeCamp; he is perhaps more wonderful in his seeing than in the painting of what he sees."[110] In light of the startling discoveries seen two years previously at the famous New York Armory Show, which introduced European Modernism to the American public, laudatory statements such as this, even if they were uttered by conservative critics, seem *retardataire*. As at the 1911 exhibition, DeCamp's work did receive negative comment, the most forthright being that of the reviewer for the *Christian Science Monitor*: "All but two of the works are portraits of men, and practically all are in the artist's most subdued color mood. The effect is somewhat depressing in view of this painter's tendency to present each of his subjects in a manner irreproachably dignified... a room full of unruffled best behavior is somehow not just what gives the most joy to a visitor.... One inevitably feels a reaction in favor of something less cold... something colorful... something joyous."[111]

DeCamp would never again put together a show of portraits, but the flow of commissions for such work continued uninterrupted until his death in 1923. Among those he portrayed in the years immediately following the 1915 exhibition were Robert Treat Paine, a Boston lawyer and entrepreneur (1916, unlocated); George Whitefield Chadwick, a noted composer (ca. 1917); businessman William M. Wood (ca.

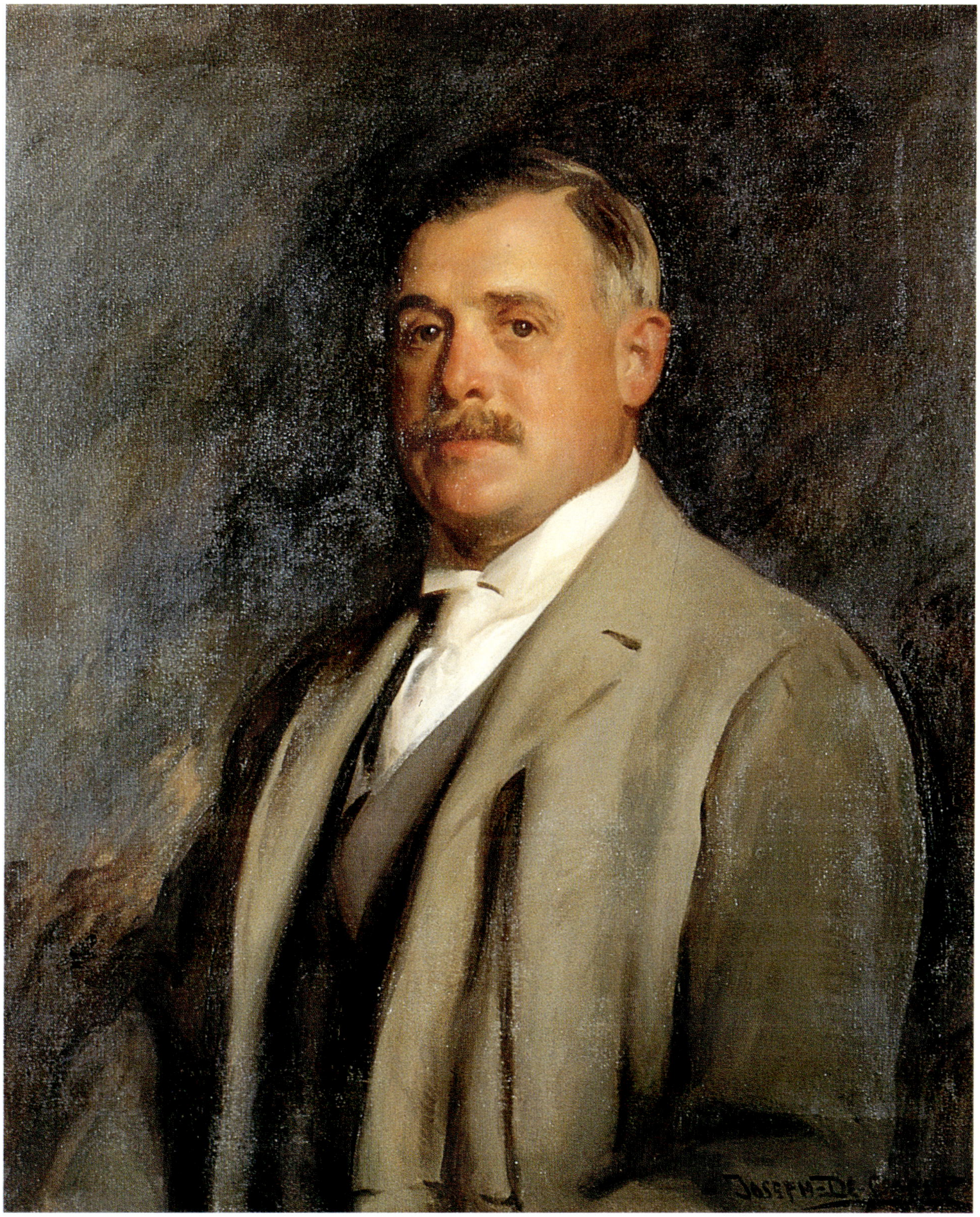

21 *Albert Hayden Chatfield,* 1905. 29⅞ x 24¾ in. (76 x 63 cm).
Collection of the William A. Farnsworth Library and Art Museum, Rockland, Maine

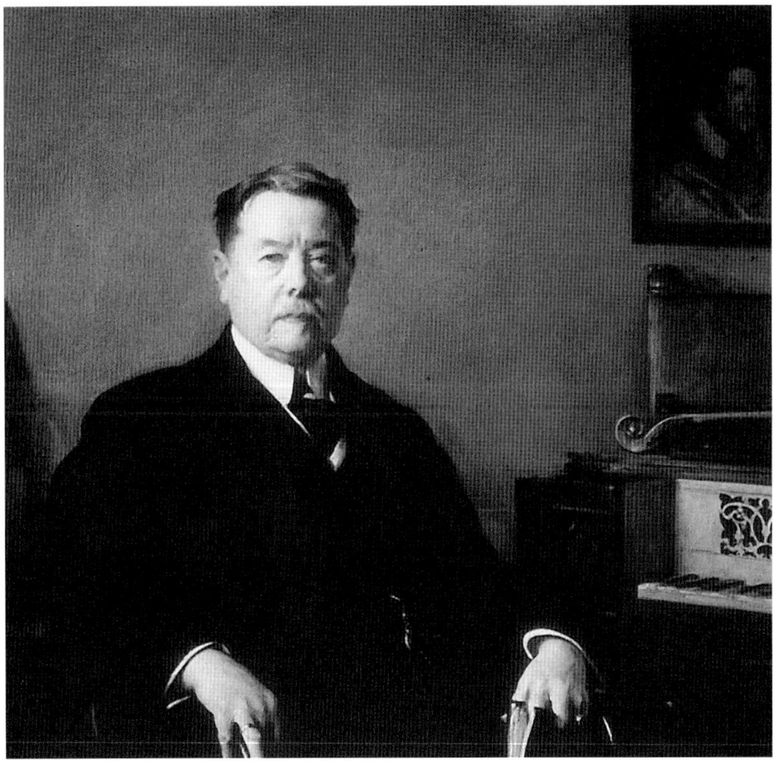

Fig. 61 *George Whitefield Chadwick*, ca. 1917. 37 x 41½ in. (94 x 105.5 x cm). Unlocated

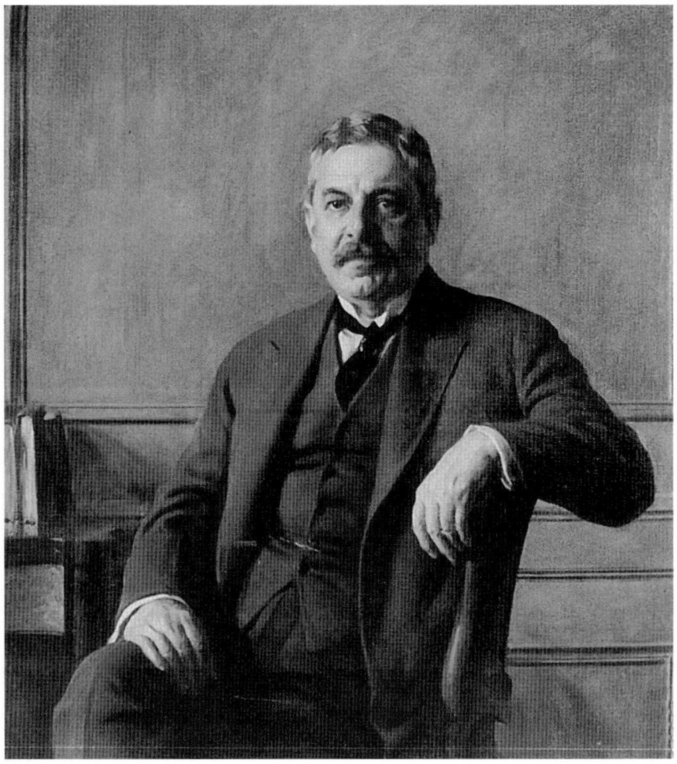

Fig. 62 *William M. Wood*, ca. 1917. 40 x 36¾ in. (101 x 93.5 cm). Unlocated

1917); and Mrs. Frank G. Webster, whom the artist depicted twice—seated, in a formal portrait of 1916, and in her wedding dress in 1917 (both unlocated).

The Paine portrait was called "heavy as lead and hard as hickory," while the same critic felt that the "musical accessories" in the picture of Chadwick (fig. 61) matched the "conscientious performance" of the artist, without having the "air of being dragged into the setting."[112] A fascinating glimpse of DeCamp's personality is afforded by an incident that occurred during his work on the portrait of Wood (fig. 62). While putting the finishing touches to the picture, the artist was interrupted by an elderly visitor who proclaimed it a "perfect likeness," advising the artist not to "touch another brush to that canvas." DeCamp, irritated, scraped the entire face clean of pigment, asked the sitter to turn his head at a different angle, and proceeded to repaint the portrait completely. Approaching the visitor, "their faces inches apart," the artist reprimanded him: "Don't let me ever hear you speak to a painter about 'catching a likeness.' You can either paint what you see, or you don't see straight, or you can't paint." The visitor "evaporated without a word," and DeCamp scraped and repainted Wood in the original pose.[113]

Notes

1 Joseph DeCamp to Joseph H. Gest, June 21, 1899; DeCamp artist file, Library, Cincinnati Art Museum.

2 *Ibid.*

3 Joseph DeCamp to Joseph H. Gest, June 22, 1899, and Joseph DeCamp to A. T. Goshorn, October 30, 1900; DeCamp artist file, Library, Cincinnati Art Museum. The painting won an honorable mention for the artist at the Exposition Universelle.

4 David Lloyd, "The Exhibition of the Ten American Painters," *International Studio* 31 (April 1907), p. 94.

5 "Ten American Painters," *New York Times*, March 25, 1907, p. 6, and "Art Proficiency in the Ten's Show," *Evening Mail*, March 21, 1907, p. 5.

6 Lee W. Court, ed., *Joseph DeCamp: An Appreciation* (Boston: Student Association of the Massachusetts Art School, 1924), unpaginated.

7 [Royal Cortissoz], "The Art Students League," *New-York Daily Tribune*, May 6, 1900, supp., p. 8. This is confirmed by the records at the League.

8 "East Gloucester," *Gloucester Daily Times*, June 24, 1902, p. 5: "Mr. J. H. Twachtman, an annual artist guest and a prominent instructor at the New York Art Students League, will have a summer class here in conjunction with Mr. Joseph DeCamp, his colaborer in New York."

9 "East Gloucester," *Gloucester Daily Times*, August 10, 1900, p. 6.

10 "East Gloucester," *Gloucester Daily Times*, June 6, 1900, p. 3.

11 "East Gloucester," *Gloucester Daily Times*, September 1, 1900, p. 5.

12 "East Gloucester," *Gloucester Daily Times*, June 26, 1900, p. 5.

13 "East Gloucester," *Gloucester Daily Times*, July 5, 1901, p. 7: "Mr. DeCamp, the well-known New York artist, and family are occu-

pying Police Officer Edward Mehlman's Rocky Neck cottage again this season."

14 Nancy Douglas Bowditch, *George de Forest Brush: Recollections of a Joyous Painter* (Peterborough, N.Y.: William L. Bauhan, 1970), p. 60.

15 *Wharf, Gloucester* is listed among the works shown at the Twenty-Fifth Anniversary Exhibition of the School of the Museum of Fine Arts, Boston (April 6–28, 1901), and a painting titled *At Gloucester* appeared in the Eighth Annual Exhibition of American Art at the Cincinnati Art Museum (May 18–July 8, 1901), probably loaned by Frank Duveneck, to whom DeCamp had given it. This work was purchased by the Cincinnati Art Museum in 1915 and was included in the memorial exhibition, "The Work of Joseph DeCamp," held at the museum in October 1924, when it bore the title *At Gloucester.*

16 My thanks again go to Carolyn O'Connor of Gloucester who owns and rents the former cottages that Brush and DeCamp occupied.

17 "East Gloucester," July 5, 1901, p. 7.

18 See "East Gloucester," *Gloucester Daily Times*, June 24, 1902, p. 5; "East Gloucester," *Gloucester Daily Times*, July 1, 1901, p. 5; and "East Gloucester," *Gloucester Daily Times*, August 20, 1901, p. 8.

19 "East Gloucester," *Gloucester Daily Times*, August 20, 1901, p. 8.

20 Edith DeCamp, as quoted in a letter from Donald Moffat to Mrs. Eiseley, March 27, 1955; correspondence files, Pennsylvania Academy of the Fine Arts, Philadelphia.

21 Untitled, unpaginated *Boston Herald* clipping; William Paxton Papers, Archives of American Art, Smithsonian Institution, Washington, D.C.

22 "Artist Colony at Gloucester is Picturesque," *Boston Sunday Herald*, August 10, 1902, magazine sect. p. 5.

23 Pamela H. Simpson, "The Sculpture of Charles Grafly," Ph.D. diss., University of Delaware, 1974, p. 265.

24 My thanks go to Mike Kelly, Curator, Wichita State University Museum, Kansas, for providing this photograph.

25 [Royal Cortissoz], "Art Exhibitions," *New-York Daily Tribune*, April 2, 1902, p. 9.

26 Untitled, unpaginated *Boston Herald* clipping; William Paxton Papers, Archives of American Art, Smithsonian Institution, Washington, D.C.

27 See William H. Gerdts, "John Twachtman and the Artistic Colony in Gloucester at the Turn of the Century," in *Twachtman in Gloucester: His Last Years, 1900–1902*, exh. cat. (New York: Spanierman Gallery, 1987), pp. 41–42.

28 Patricia P. Petraglia, "William McGregor Paxton (1869–1941): Artist Biography and Formal Analysis of *The White Veranda*," unpublished MS., Sotheby's American Arts Program, New York, 1989, unpaginated.

29 "Exhibition of Ten American Painters," *Sun*, April 1, 1902, p. 6.

30 [Royal Cortissoz], "Art Exhibitions," *New-York Daily Tribune*, April 2, 1902, p. 9.

31 *Ibid.*

32 "American Art at Pittsburgh," *Booklover's Magazine* 3 (April 1904), p. 464.

33 "East Gloucester," *Gloucester Daily Times*, June 10, 1903, p. 6, and "East Gloucester," *Gloucester Daily Times*, June 20, 1905, p. 5.

34 Donald Moffat, "A Partial List of the Paintings of Joseph Rodefer DeCamp, 1858–1923," unpublished typescript, Frick Art Reference Library, New York, 1955–57, p. 7.

35 Rose V. S. Berry, "Joseph DeCamp: Painter and Man," *American Magazine of Art* 14 (April 1923), p. 184.

36 "The Ten Bolters," *New York Times*, March 19, 1901, p. 9.

37 "The Ten American Painters," *Boston Evening Transcript*, April 2, 1902, p. 8.

38 "The Fine Arts," *Boston Evening Transcript*, November 4, 1903, p. 16.

39 *Ibid.*

40 "The Ten American Painters," *Mail and Express*, April 20, 1903, p. 6.

41 "Art and the Artists," *Commercial Advertiser*, April 21, 1903, p. 7.

42 My thanks go to Charles Packard, Archivist, Old Conway Homestead Complex and Museum, Camden, Maine, for this information. The first four lines of Millay's poem describe the site: "All I could see from where I stood/ Was three long mountains and a wood;/ I turned and looked the other way,/ And saw three islands in a bay."

43 Donald Moffat, "Joseph Rodefer DeCamp: Biographical Sketch," unpublished typescript, Frick Art Reference Library, New York, 1955–57, p. 30.

44 Faith Andrews Bedford, in *Frank W. Benson: A Retrospective*, exh. cat. (New York: Berry-Hill Galleries, 1989), p. 70.

45 Frances Welch, quoted *ibid.*

46 Moffat, "Joseph Rodefer DeCamp: Biographical Sketch," p. 30.

47 Philip L. Hale, *Great Portraits: Children* (Boston: Bates & Guild Co., 1909), p. 64.

48 W[illiam]. H[owe]. D[ownes]., "Mr. DeCamp's Portraits," *Boston Evening Transcript*, December 29, 1915, p. 25.

49 William R. Lester, "Figure Paintings and Portraits at Art Academy Exhibition Overshadow Landscape Pictures in Public Interest," *North American, Philadelphia*, January 26, 1908, sect. 3, p. 9.

50 Philip L. Hale, "The Best Pictures of the Year," *Boston Sunday Herald*, February 23, 1908, p. 5.

51 "Art Studios and Galleries," *Boston Sunday Herald*, February 26, 1911, p. 17, and William Howe Downes, "Joseph DeCamp and His Work," *Art and Progress* 4 (April 1913), p. 922.

52 In a letter of March 24, 1923, to Joseph H. Gest, Director of the Cincinnati Art Museum, Edith DeCamp attributed this development to the loss of so many landscapes and nudes in the Harcourt Street studio fire: "I wonder if you know that about eighteen years ago he [DeCamp] was completely burned out—not even a paint brush left—and of course it meant a hundred or more canvases and drawings from the time he was twenty years of age.... As he was getting ready for an exhibition it meant all of the things he had painted of the children which was a terrible personal loss. At that time he painted nudes a great deal and landscapes and as he never sold more than one a year, they accumulated!" Correspondence files, Cincinnati Art Museum.

53 "Four Alarms in the Back Bay," *Boston Post*, November 12, 1904, p. 8. I am thankful to Karen Zukowski for drawing my attention to this article and others on the Harcourt fire.

54 "All the Harcourt Studio Fire Missing Are Now Accounted For," *Hearst's Boston American*, November 12, 1904, p. 4. Other sources of information on the fire are: "Fire Loss $ 200,000 in Harcourt Studios," *Boston Herald*, November 12, 1904, pp. 1, 5; "Narrow Escapes; Several Injuries," *Boston Daily Globe*, November 12, 1904, pp. 1, 4; "Harcourt Building Ruined," *Boston Evening Transcript*, November 12, 1904, p. 5; "Artists' Big Loss," *Boston Sunday Globe*, November 13, 1904, p. 5; and "Fire Loss Now Half a Million, *Boston Sunday Herald*, November 13, 1904, p. 6.

55 I am grateful to Mrs. Ignatius Sargent for this information.

56 R.H. Ives Gammell, *The Boston Painters: 1900–1930* (Orleans, Mass.: Parnassus Imprints, 1986), p. 59. Gammell gives the price as $ 100.

57 Michael Quick, "Achieving the Nation's Imperial Destiny: 1870–1920," in *American Portraiture in the Grand Manner: 1720–1920*, exh. cat. (Los Angeles: Los Angeles County Museum of Art, 1981), p. 69.

58 See, for example, [Royal Cortissoz], "Art Exhibitions," *New-York Daily Tribune*, March 21, 1901, p. 6; "Pictures at the Academy," *Philadelphia Inquirer*, January 19, 1903, p. 8; "Pennsylvania Academy of the Fine Arts," *Public Ledger—Philadelphia*, January 24, 1904, sect. 2, p. 9; "The Pennsylvania Academy Exhibition," *Evening Telegraph*, January 19, 1907, p. 4; and "Centenary of the Pennsylvania Academy of the Fine Arts," *Public Ledger—Philadelphia*, January 22, 1905, sect. 1, p. 5.

59 Moffat, "Joseph Rodefer DeCamp: Biographical Sketch," p. 7. Much credit is due Moffat for his extraordinarily painstaking compi-

lation of information on, and photographs of, DeCamp's formal portraits.

60 "Art Notes," *Mail and Express*, March 21, 1900, p. 9.

61 Henri Penc Du Bois, "Du Bois Says: The Show of the Ten American Painters is Intensely Modern," *New York Journal*, March 19, 1900, p. 6.

62 Philip L.Hale, "About the Pictures," *Boston Daily Advertiser*, November 21, 1900, p. 8.

63 Charles H. Caffin, "Third Exhibition of the 'Ten American Painters,'" *Harper's Weekly* 44 (April 14, 1900), p. 338.

64 "Ten American Painters," *Evening Post*, April 24, 1903, p. 7.

65 "Art Schools of Shore and Hills," *Boston Sunday Herald*, June 25, 1905, p. 3.

66 "Ten American Painters," *New York Times*, April 1, 1905, p. 11.

67 Harlan C. Pearson, "Benjamin Ames Kimball '54," *Dartmouth Alumni Magazine* 13 (November 1920), p. 9.

68 See Julien E. Benjamin, "Frederick Forchheimer, M. D., 1853–1913," in Cecil Striker, ed., *Medical Portraits* (Cincinnati: Academy of Medicine of Cincinnati, 1963), pp. 95–97.

69 "Opening of the Art Year in Boston," *Boston Daily Advertiser*, November 5, 1906, p. 4.

70 My sincere thanks go to Albert Chatfield, Jr., now in his 90s, who directed me to the studio and the house that the DeCamps rented in Camden in the summer of 1905. Chatfield remembers visiting the DeCamp family at Camden and he also recalls excursions to the Crockett House on Vinalhaven.

71 Joseph DeCamp to John E. D. Trask, undated; Pennsylvania Academy of the Fine Arts Papers, Archives of American Art, Smithsonian Institution, Washington, D. C.

72 "102nd Annual Exhibition of the Pennsylvania Academy of the Fine Arts," *Philadelphia Inquirer*, January 20, 1907, editorial sect., p. 1.

73 Berry, "Joseph DeCamp: Painter and Man," pp. 183–84.

74 Moffat, "Joseph Rodefer DeCamp: Biographical Sketch," p. 9.

75 Harley Perkins, "Joseph DeCamp: Painter and Teacher," *Boston Evening Transcript*, February 13, 1923, sect. 1, p. 6.

76 A pigment was even named "DeCamp Brown." My thanks go to DeCamp's granddaughter, Edith Harding, who is a painter herself, for providing this information. It is not known how or when the pigment was produced.

77 R. H. Ives Gammell, diary entry for June 26, 1919; private collection.

78 Quick, "Achieving the Nation's Imperial Destiny," p. 66.

79 Gammell, *The Boston Painters*, p. 53.

80 Downes, "Joseph DeCamp and His Work," pp. 923–24.

81 See Henry G. Abbott, *History of the American Waltham Watch Company* (Chicago: American Jeweler Print, 1905), *passim*.

82 Hale, "About the Pictures," p. 8.

83 Charles H. Caffin, "Some American Portrait Painters," *Critic* 44 (January 4, 1904), p. 40.

84 "The Fine Arts," *Boston Evening Transcript*, October 16, 1908, p. 11.

85 Joseph DeCamp to Edith DeCamp, date unknown; quoted in Moffat, "Joseph Rodefer DeCamp: Biographical Sketch," p. 35.

86 *Ibid.*

87 *Ibid.*, p. 37.

88 *Ibid.*, p. 38.

89 Philip L. Hale, "Big Sculptures at Art Museum," *Boston Sunday Herald*, October 25, 1908, real estate sect., p. 1. Other Americans who painted Roosevelt at about this time were Orlando Rowland (ca. 1907, unlocated) and Gari Melchers (ca. 1909, unlocated).

90 See W. E. B., "The Fine Arts," *Boston Evening Transcript*, February 21, 1911, p. 20, and "Old Argument Begun by 'Blue Boy,'" *Christian Science Monitor*, February 25, 1911, p. 7.

91 Edith Burnham, "Portraits by DeCamp Here," *Boston Traveller*, February 21, 1911, p. 8.

92 A. J. Philpott, "Portraits of Charm," *Boston Globe*, March 4, 1911, p. 5.

93 Burnham, "Portraits of DeCamp Here," p. 8.

94 James B. Townsend, "Pennsylvania Academy Display," *American Art News* 10 (February 10, 1912), p. 7.

95 "Prize Winners and Critique of 107th Annual Exhibition, Pennsylvania Academy of the Fine Arts," *Public Ledger—Philadelphia*, February 4, 1912, p. 9.

96 "Fourteenth Annual Exhibition of the Ten American Painters at the Montross Galleries," *New York Times*, March 26, 1911, sect. 5, p. 15.

97 A. J. Philpott, "Portraits by DeCamp," *Boston Globe*, January 3, 1916, p. 2.

98 Perkins, "Joseph DeCamp: Painter and Teacher," p. 6.

99 Joseph H. Gest to Joseph DeCamp, June 2, 1912.

100 "Academy of the Fine Arts' Exhibition Cleverly Arranged," *Philadelphia Inquirer*, February 5, 1911, sect. 1, p. 7.

101 Mark Sullivan, *Our Time*, vol. 1: *The Turn of the Century* (New York: Charles Scribner's Sons, 1927), pp. 404, 405.

102 For a good summary of the formation of the Guild of Boston Artists, see "The New Artist's Society," *Boston Evening Transcript*, February 6, 1914, p. 11.

103 See *In Memoriam: Augustus George Bullock* (Worcester: privately printed, 1926).

104 See biographical files, Wellesley College Archives, for a full history of Homans's achievements in education for women.

105 See Martha L. Sanford, "Biographical Sketch," *Publication of the Clark University Library* 8 (June 1925), p. 3–10.

106 "Likenesses DeLuxe at the Artists' Guild by Joseph DeCamp," *Boston Sunday Herald*, January 2, 1916, p. 4.

107 Philpott, "Portraits by DeCamp," p. 2.

108 *Ibid.*

109 John Doe, "Boston," *American Art News* 14 (January 8, 1916), p. 5.

110 W[illiam]. H[owe]. D[ownes]., "Mr. DeCamp's Portraits," *Boston Evening Transcript*, December 29, 1915, p. 25.

111 "Joseph DeCamp Shows at Guild," *Christian Science Monitor*, December 29, 1915, p. 7.

112 "New York Art Exhibitions and Gallery Notes," *Christian Science Monitor*, March 16, 1917, p. 10.

113 A[lexander]. W[hite]. M[offat]., unpublished note, dated January 19, 1956; Joseph DeCamp scrapbook, family of the artist. Alexander Moffat was Donald's brother and DeCamp's other son-in-law, having married the artist's third daughter, Pauline.

CHAPTER SEVEN

Maturity: Images of Women, 1900–1917

In his portrait exhibitions of 1911 and 1915 DeCamp included paintings not strictly of the formal type—posed works for which he used favorite women models, often dressed in evening attire, and to which he gave such titles as *The Violinist*, *The Pink Feather*, and *La Penserosa*. Critics struggled to give this type of portrait a name. One reviewer's solution was simple: "Most of the works in this exhibition are portraits and those that are not strictly such may be classed as 'portrait pictures.'"[1] Noting the preponderance of figure paintings in the Pennsylvania Academy of the Fine Arts annual of 1908, critic William R. Lester distinguished them from "examples of honest and more or less skillful portraiture," applauding a new trend toward idealism. "When Joseph DeCamp has a model before him, instead of a sitter," he observed, "there is likely to result something out of the common run."[2] Lester had realized, most perceptively, that the artist's images of women, particularly in the "portrait pictures," belong to a world fundamentally different from that of his male portraits. As a rule, DeCamp does not personalize his female models; these women exist as ethereal creatures in a silent, idealized realm.

In terms of his artistic development it is not surprising that the artist chose to depict these female subjects in interiors—after years of creating *plein air* imagery he had retreated to the studio. In this, he followed a turn-of-the-century trend. As Julie Anne Springer has pointed out, "for the artist disenchanted with the materialistic, empirical, and rational forces operative in society, the interior became the vehicle for expressing spiritual and aesthetic withdrawal."[3] DeCamp's women joined their sisters of the genteel persuasion in numerous exhibitions throughout the country. Paul D. Schweizer has described this type of woman as she appeared in National Academy of Design shows in New York between 1891 and 1910: "She could frequently be seen in various costumes and in various states of activity ranging from the decorative and symbolic, to the maternal and domestic. In addition to the natural beauty and formal possibilities that such a motif provided, there was a tendency among American artists to use the genteel American female as the visual embodiment of many of the values and morals of the age."[4] Women were generally associated with fashion and with the arts, and DeCamp's first essays in depicting idealized figural subjects in domestic interiors indicate that he was aware of, and probably accepted, such notions.

The sequence of these images reveals great versatility in design, in controlled lighting, and in the rendering of textures. DeCamp's penchant for costumes and/or mirrors in these paintings no doubt arose from the special technical effects that they enabled him to achieve. Early examples of this fascination are *Girl with a Red Shawl* and *Girl with a Green Shawl*. When on display at the Seventh Annual Exhibition of the Cincinnati Museum Association in 1900, the former (unlocated) was described as having "a red note repeated in a mirror [that] plays pleasantly into a scheme of grays."[5] *Girl with a Green Shawl* (plate 23), obviously a favorite of the artist's, was shown in eleven exhibitions, starting in 1900. A *Boston Herald* critic noted that it was "one of the few pictures not burned in the Harcourt fire" when it was exhibited at the Rowlands Gallery in Boston in 1905.[6] With her back to the viewer, the full-length figure comes alive in the reflected mirrored image. In fact, one writer felt that, instead of looking at herself in a mirror, "what she really is doing is looking at a painted portrait of herself."[7] Clearly evincing an awareness of Whistler's figural compositions, of the still influential concerns of the Aesthetic Movement of the 1860s and 1870s, other reviewers admired the color harmonies: "The soft apple green of the shawl with its border of dull blue and crimson is made the prominent note in a quiet harmony of color," wrote a New York *Sun* critic, while a *Commercial Advertiser* writer applauded the painting's "tonal arrangement" as "very harmonious and ably carried out."[8] Executed a few years before DeCamp embarked on his important series of Vermeeresque paintings, these pictures may have prepared the artist for an appreciation of the quiet, tonal domestic scenes in the Old Master's work.

Mirrors and fashionable gowns appear also in *Arrangement in Pink and Blue* (ca. 1901), *The New Gown* (ca. 1903), and *The Heliotrope Gown* (ca. 1905). The

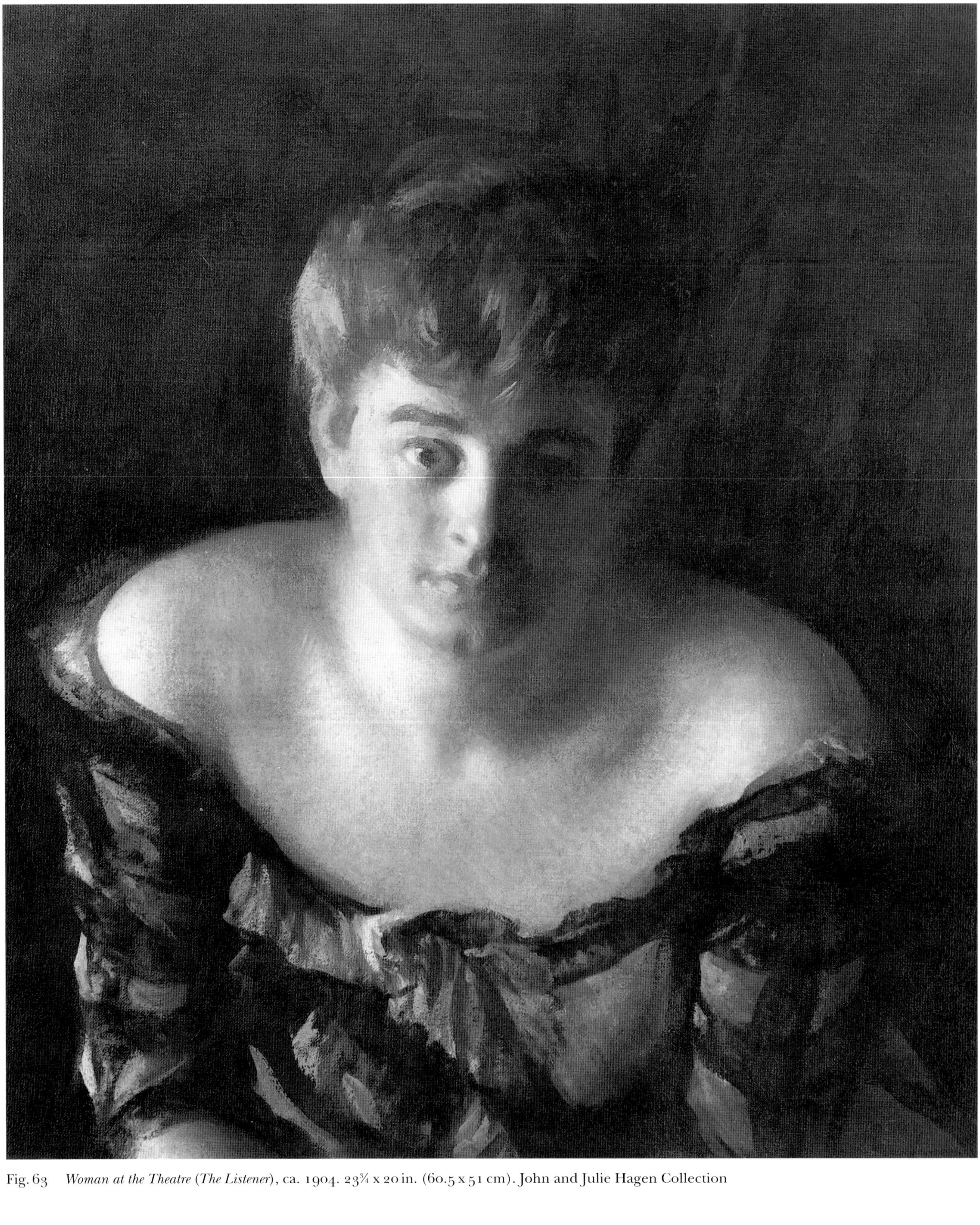

Fig. 63 *Woman at the Theatre* (*The Listener*), ca. 1904. 23¾ x 20 in. (60.5 x 51 cm). John and Julie Hagen Collection

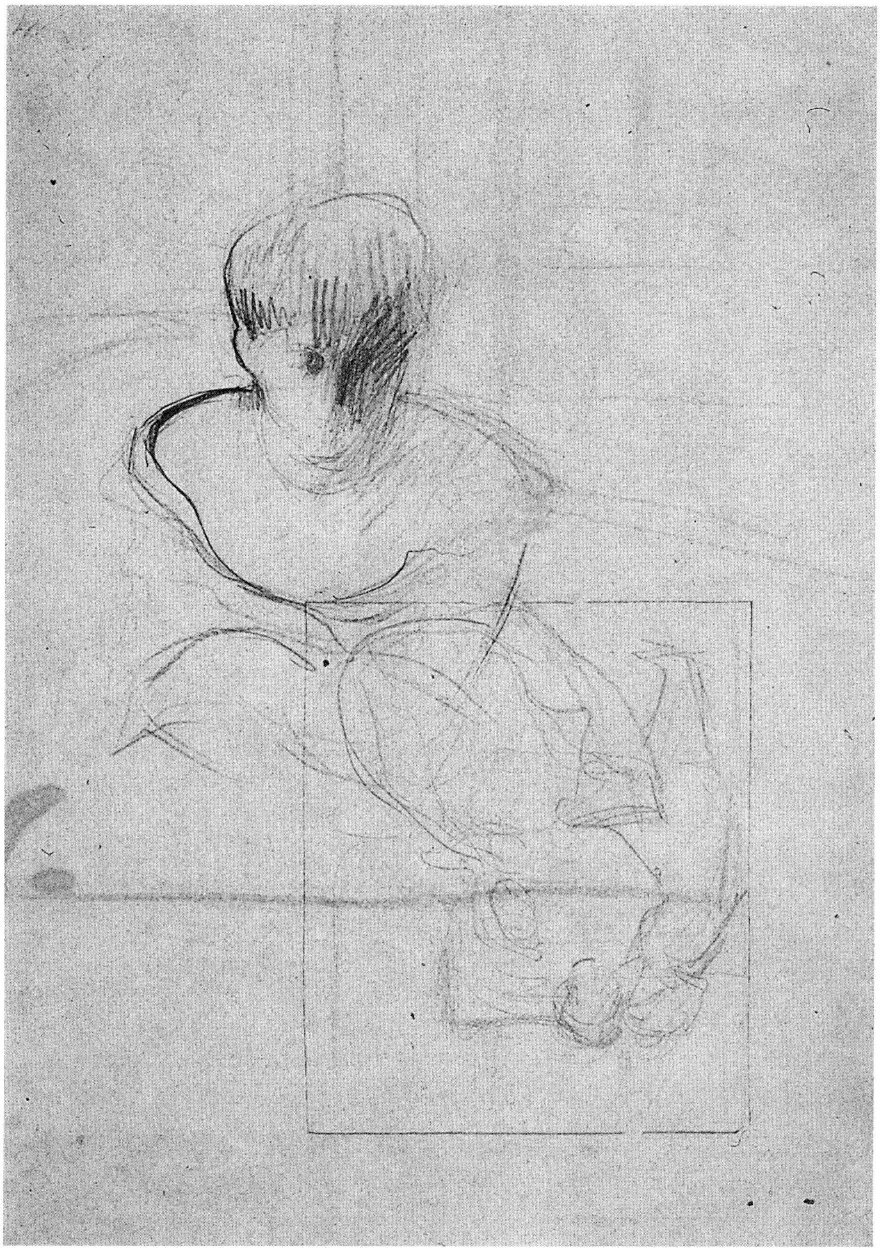

Fig. 64 *Study for "Woman at the Theatre"*, ca. 1904. Pencil on paper, 13⅝ x 10⅝ in. (34.5 x 27 cm). Private collection

first of these (now known as *Reflections*; plate 22), when shown in the 1901 Ten American Painters exhibition in New York, was described as a "study of a young girl, reclining in a mahogany chair, the light falling upon her blonde hair.... The lower part of the gown is in quiet shadows and her head and shoulders are reflected in a mirror. Whether portrait or genre subject, it involves a pleasant scheme of cool, fresh color, craftily lit and well painted, the head and figure being charmingly enveloped in atmosphere."[9] As for the hues pink and blue, "the spectator discovers [al]most any tint but these, and only at the end of his search, does he make them out vaguely."[10]

In *The New Gown* (unlocated) DeCamp reversed the imagery of *Girl with a Green Shawl*, rendering the figure itself, rather than its reflection in the mirror, in detail. The concentration on accessories—the juxtaposition of the woman's elaborate costume with an equally elaborate side chair and background drapery—is rare in DeCamp's work, his interest usually being directed toward formalist experimentation. Shown at the Pennsylvania Academy's 1903 annual, the painting was purchased for the Wilstach Collection at Memorial Hall, Philadelphia, but has since disappeared.[11] *The Heliotrope Gown* (plate 24), another image of a full-length, gowned figure, whose reflection vies for the viewer's attention with the details of an interior arched column, was also praised for its range of hues. "He [DeCamp] runs the entire gamut of this color [heliotrope] from the palest tint to the bunch of deep violets, while the mirror gives an opportunity for repetition of the effects," wrote a reviewer for the *New York Times*.[12] The woman shown with her "other" self in a mirror was a popular subject at the turn of the century: "There is scarcely a figure painter of the period who did not undertake to paint 'woman before the mirror' themes and many, indeed, returned to the theme over and over again," as Bram Dijkstra has written.[13] He sees the subject as representing feminine withdrawal from submission to male dominance and thus as a reinforcement of selfhood. "Before long," Dijkstra explains, "the theme of the mirror as the symbol of self-sufficiency came to be linked inextricably with its traditional use as a symbol of women's vanity."[14] DeCamp's paintings with mirrors undoubtedly belong in this context, though in them he is unlikely to have consciously addressed such broad issues. That he depicted his models in the most fashionable attire does indicate a desire to portray the mistress of a well-appointed household as someone with ample time on her hands. Given the care with which he delineates the fabrics and details of the costumes, the woman becomes essentially another decorative object in a wealthy home.

The woman wearing the heliotrope gown appears in another work of circa 1905, *In the Studio* (plate 26), in which the artist himself is shown at his easel in the background. The self-portrait acts almost as a calling card attached to DeCamp's standard fare—the elegantly attired woman at leisure. Perhaps, too, he wished to show that his idealized woman belonged to the world of the artist's studio. He also subtly connects his work to that of Velázquez by positioning himself in the same attitude as the Spaniard had in his *Las Meninas* (Prado, Madrid). Shown in seventeen different exhibitions, the painting garnered mixed reviews. "The easy pose of the artist in the background and the wonderful textures of the model in the light are worthy of study. The girl's shoulder, her hair, the shiny folds of her satin gown, the flesh of her arm as it is suggested beneath the transparent chiffon falling over it, are skillfully handled," wrote the critic for the *Detroit News Tribune*.[15] John Nutting of the *Boston Daily Advertiser* saw the artist's "attitude of deep study far back in the room" as an "amusing innovation in the way of composition,"[16] but an earlier reviewer had found "the attitude of the artist in the middle distance... not too convincing to the every day person who is not familiar with studios."[17] The latter statement hints at a certain uneasiness at the idealized woman inhabiting the same space as the artist, much as royalty seems out of place in *Las Meninas*. Finally, another writer admired the craftsmanship of the work, but found lacking that "indefinable element, the note of style, which would superimpose charm upon realism."[18]

The same critic described *The Blue Locket* of about 1904 (unlocated) as a "woman in black, well placed in the panel, and in... relation to the screen in the background."[19] This comment suggests, once again, that Whistler's "arrangements" influenced DeCamp. No doubt the artist had seen the major exhibition of Whistler's nocturnes and figural pieces at Copley Hall in Boston in 1904.

That year, of course, saw the fire in DeCamp's Harcourt Street studio. Two paintings, in particular, have been mentioned in the family as having been salvaged from the disaster: *The Music Lesson* and *Woman at the Theatre*. Both pictures have remained in the family and have never been exhibited. *Woman at the Theatre* (fig. 63) is said to have originally contained many more figures; a drawing for it (fig. 64) gives some evidence of more background activity, if not additional figures. Musical themes like these begin to figure prominently in DeCamp's oeuvre in the first decade of the twentieth century. This may have been a result of the artist's contact with Albert Hayden Chatfield, the Cincinnati paper manufacturer whose portrait DeCamp would paint in 1905 (plate 21). Chatfield, it will be recalled, established a studio for DeCamp and Lewis Meakin at this time in Camden, Maine. He was deeply involved in the cultural life of Cincinnati, having served on the board of the Cincinnati Art Museum and having arranged for noted European conductors to appear with the city's symphony orchestra. Mrs. Chatfield had been one of the founders of the orchestra. It is thus more than likely that music was played, perhaps at soirees, during the summers at Camden and this may have inspired DeCamp to paint scenes with musical content.

In *The Music Lesson* (plate 25) Edith DeCamp sits patiently listening to her daughter Sally practicing the piano.[20] The play of light on the backs of the figures, casting their faces in shadow, reinforces the notion that, in his "portrait pictures," DeCamp was more interested in dissolution of form and generalization of figures than in the greater degree of modeling characteristic of his male portraits. "I am painting a girl in a beautiful dress," he once noted, "but I have to keep remembering that it is not a dress I am concerned with but a piece of light."[21] A drawing for the picture (private collection), though it includes only Sally, seems to confirm that the painting as preserved was originally part of a much larger composition.

An earlier work on a musical theme was entered in the 1902 Fourth Annual Exhibition of Oil Paintings at the Worcester Art Museum, Massachusetts, under the title *The Violin*. It may be the painting now known as *The Violinist* (plate 27), which represents a full-length standing figure playing a violin, her back to the viewer. Instead of mirrors, DeCamp here employed a closed Venetian blind to the left and a sunlit curtained window to the right to enlarge the depicted space and to frame the figure. The light reflected on the evening dress gives it an iridescent glow, somewhat akin to that of the glazed Chinese porcelain jar standing on the windowsill. An unfinished oil study for the painting (private collection) shows the woman in a slightly different pose and reveals the vertical element at the right to be a folding screen.

Another subject explored by the artist at this time was that of women reading. A painting entitled *Reading* was exhibited in 1904 at the St. Louis Exposition. It may be the work shown in an installation photograph; though difficult to make out, the composition appears to include a window similar to that in *The Violinist*. *A Girl with a Book* (unlocated) went on display two years later, in the 1906 Ten show at Montross Galleries in New York. Hardly concerned with the small book she holds in both hands, the figure again seems to be primarily a study of light. A former owner called the painting *Firelight*, because "the lighting gives the effect of that kind of a light source." "The tone of the canvas, as a whole, is dark," she wrote, "with rich colors of a type suitable to the effect of blazing logs."[22] One immediately thinks of Frank W. Benson's series of the early 1890s of women seated near fireplaces as a precedent for this work. DeCamp's *La Penserosa* (fig. 65) was viewed as a companion to *A Girl with a Book* when the two paintings, contrasting introverted and extraverted personalities, were shown together in 1906, 1907, and in the 1911 exhibition of the artist's portraits. Reviewers commented on the lighting effects, but more especially on the shadowed areas, which they felt gave a mysterious note, even a suggestion of sensuality, to the sitters.[23] A drawing for *La Penserosa* (private collection) reveals DeCamp's method of conceiving a work in black and white tones before adding color. The colors in both works, however, were considered by at least two critics to be too severe, particularly in the flesh tones.[24] Edith Burnham found the woman in *Girl with a Book* "pensive," but "in a far different way" than the figure in *La Penserosa*, her thoughts "mingling in a happy concourse" with her persona. The women in the 1911 show were the "ones which dream dreams," she continued, *La Penserosa* being "a woman painted in dreams and thoughts. Loose soft strands of hair cloud the

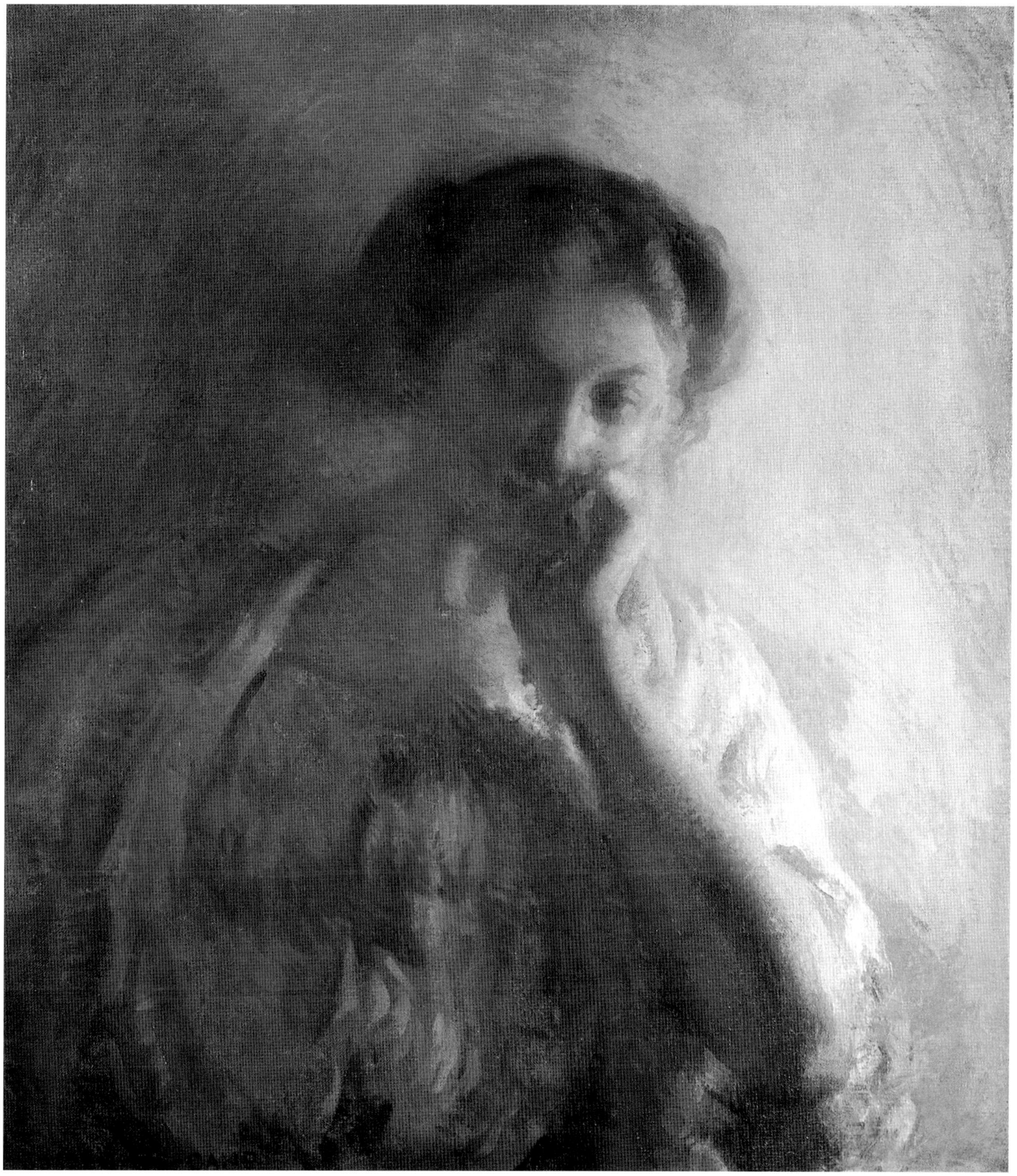

Fig. 65
La Penserosa, ca. 1906.
27 x 24 in. (68.5 x 61 cm).
Private collection

dreamer's eyes, the light falls on her in an enveloping cloud, full of light and mystery; she is warm and human, but her thoughts are wisps of ideals, silken threads that she longs to weave into her life."[25] Our hindsight vision of a woman's life in the early years of the twentieth century, closed off from the world of business, politics, and other "substantial" endeavors, may induce us to interpret this statement as one perceptive critic's recognition of the fact that the woman in *La Penserosa* felt a decided need to make better use of her mental gifts. In truth, the life of a woman in Boston at this time was certainly more active outside the home. On the other hand, the argument of Bernice Leader, that artists deliberately posed their models in quiet domestic interiors to foster the notion that women should be relegated to the home and its activities, has little basis in the writings of these artists (some of whom were female) or of their contemporaries.[26]

The concern with lighting and the soft haze that envelopes the figures in these and other works of

DeCamp's from the first decade of the twentieth century owe much to Jan Vermeer. A reappraisal of Vermeer's oeuvre had established his reputation in France in the mid-nineteenth century, but it was DeCamp's friend Philip Leslie Hale who, in a 1904 volume in the "Masters in Art" series, made Americans fully aware of the seventeenth-century Dutch master's stature.[27] Drawing on Vermeer's structured interiors, his light-filled settings, and his images of women—often playing musical instruments—in domestic surroundings, artists of the Boston School created many paintings in the Vermeer tradition, a superlative example being Edmund C. Tarbell's innovative *A Girl Crocheting* of 1904 (fig. 66). From DeCamp's brush there followed an extensive series of Vermeeresque interior figural works. It is worth looking at these paintings, and the reviews they elicited, in detail, since the artist was associated especially closely with subjects of this kind. As M. Elizabeth Boone has pointed out, the qualities seen in the Old Master's work—elegance and quietude—perfectly matched the genteel image that Bostonians were anxious to grant their own subjects.[28] Other aspects of Vermeer that Americans admired were his wizardry with light and his careful rendering, which they held to be grounded in the principle of "art for art's sake." These are outstanding features of DeCamp's works as well, and indeed, it was only after incorporating the characteristics of Vermeer's art in his canvases that he began to devise his own experiments with interior light and texture. DeCamp's two masterpieces in the Vermeer genre, with which he continued his depictions of musical themes, are *The Guitar Player* and *The Cellist*; both figured prominently in his breakthrough year of 1908. These paintings, along with *The Pink Feather* (or *The Brown Veil*), were shown at the 1908 exhibition of the Ten American Painters. DeCamp was proclaimed the star of the show by Arthur Hoeber: "Surely not before this has he sent so many admirable canvases, each one of which is in its way masterly, and though the word is abused too frequently, we use it in its full significance."[29] Joseph Edgar Chamberlin of the New York *Mail* characterized the work of what he called the "Boston giants": "Tarbell, Benson and Decamp [*sic*]... alone hold unweariedly aloft the banner of exclusive devotion to the gospel of light... and particularly in the female figure.... Mr. DeCamp has changed more since 1898 than any other member of the group, if these three canvases are an example of the way he paints 'for himself' now.... They are romantic-classic in sentiment."[30]

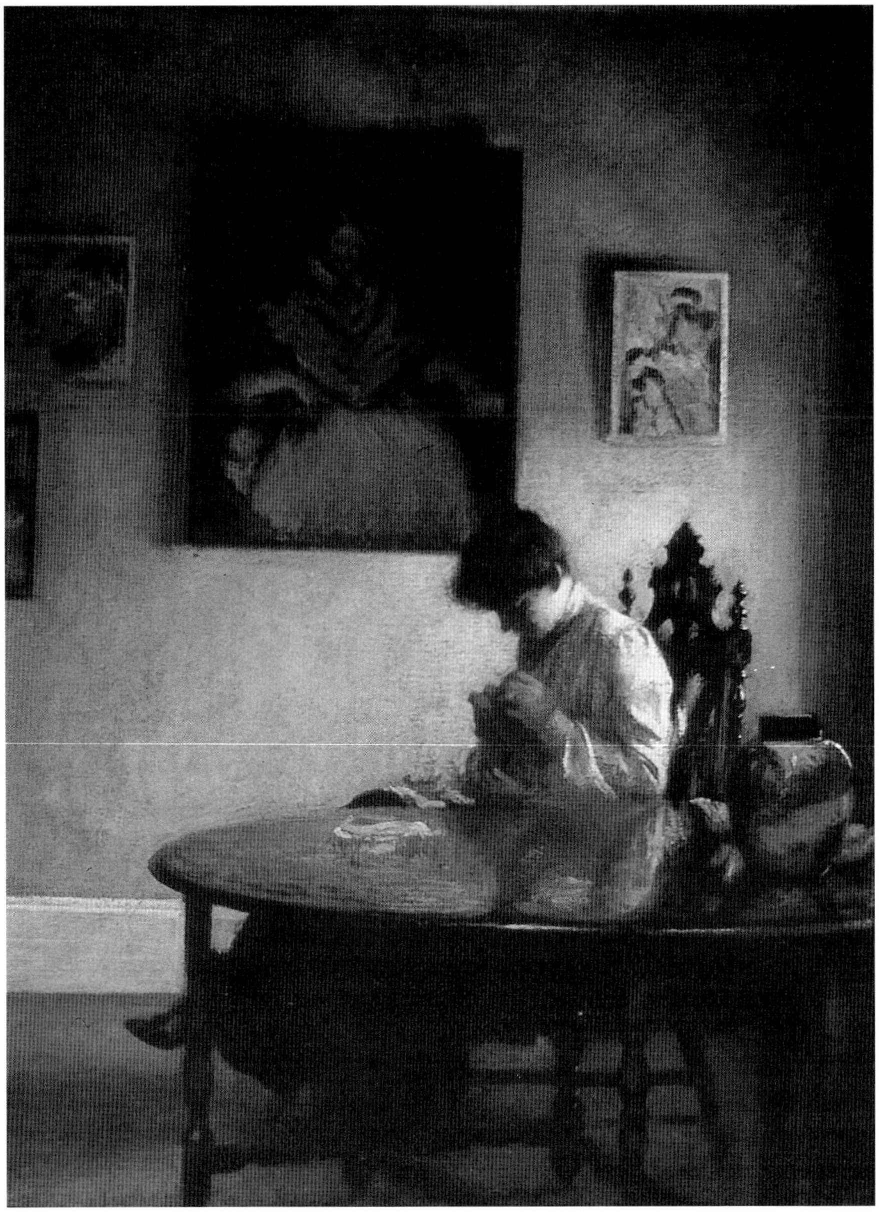

Fig. 66 Edmund C. Tarbell, *A Girl Crocheting*, 1904. 30 x 25 in. (76 x 63.5 cm). Canajoharie Library and Art Gallery, N.Y.

Of the three paintings, *The Guitar Player* (plate 28) clearly interested critics the most. A woman in sparkling evening attire is seated on a plain, upholstered bench, her concentration devoted totally to the instrument held in her lap. A rolled Japanese scroll is propped on the bench to her left, as if in reference to the *japonisme* craze then sweeping Boston.[31] Purchased almost immediately by the city's Museum of Fine Arts, an institution not known for acquiring work by contemporary artists, it was called a "very remarkable example of modern art, and by far the best thing that the artist has ever done.... In all its details the work not only stands the test of the most searching critical analysis, but it invites and rewards the closest scrutiny. The design is original; the expression is lifelike, individual and vivid; the movement of the figure is extraordinary for its vitality and reality.... Technically, it is one of the most perfect examples of painting that we have seen by an American artist for many years.... If a Dutch 'Little Master' of the calibre of Vermeer or Metsu could be

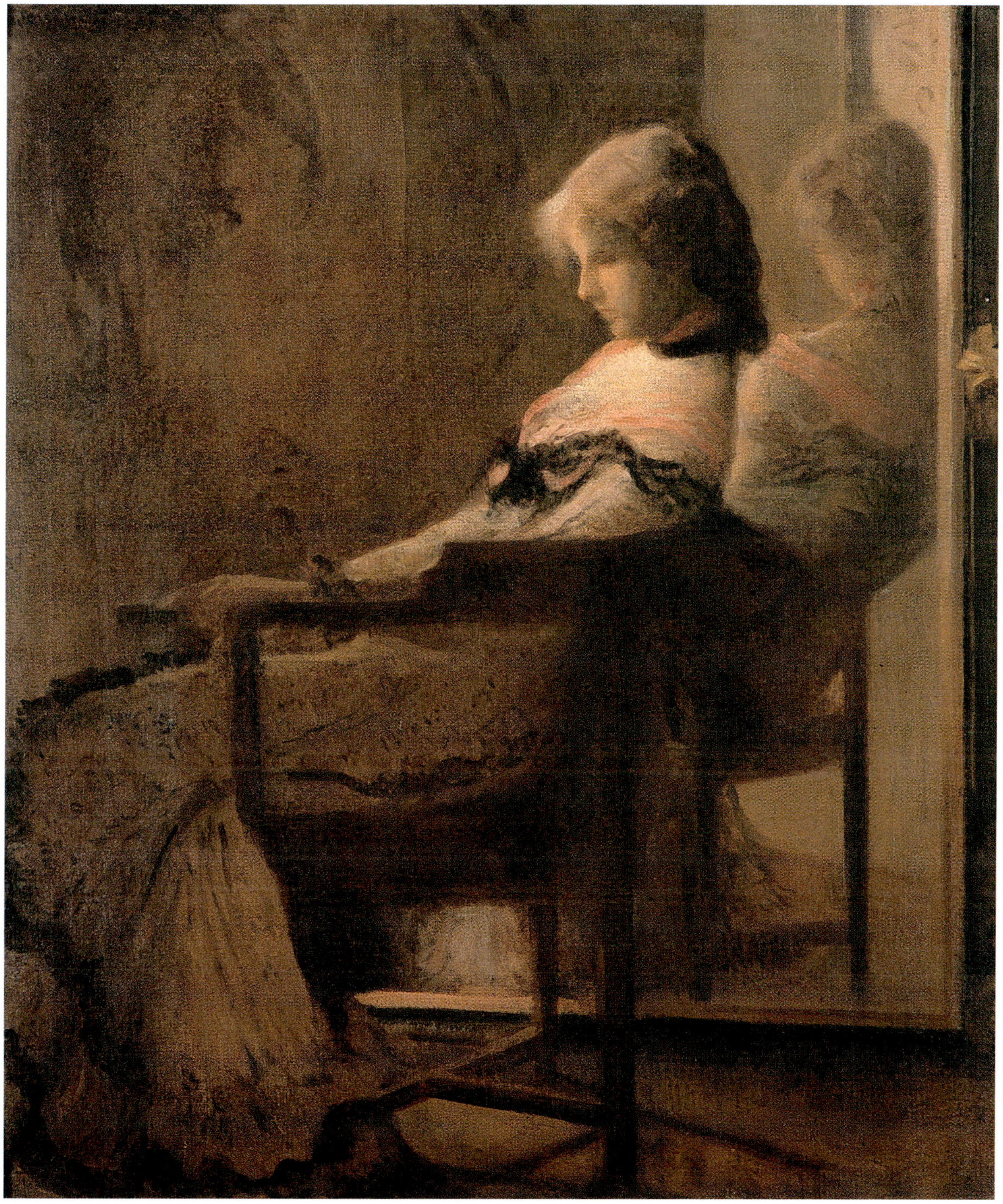

22 *Reflections (Arrangement in Pink and Blue)*, ca. 1901. 30 x 25 in. (76 x 63.5 cm).
Maryhill Museum of Art, Goldendale, Washington

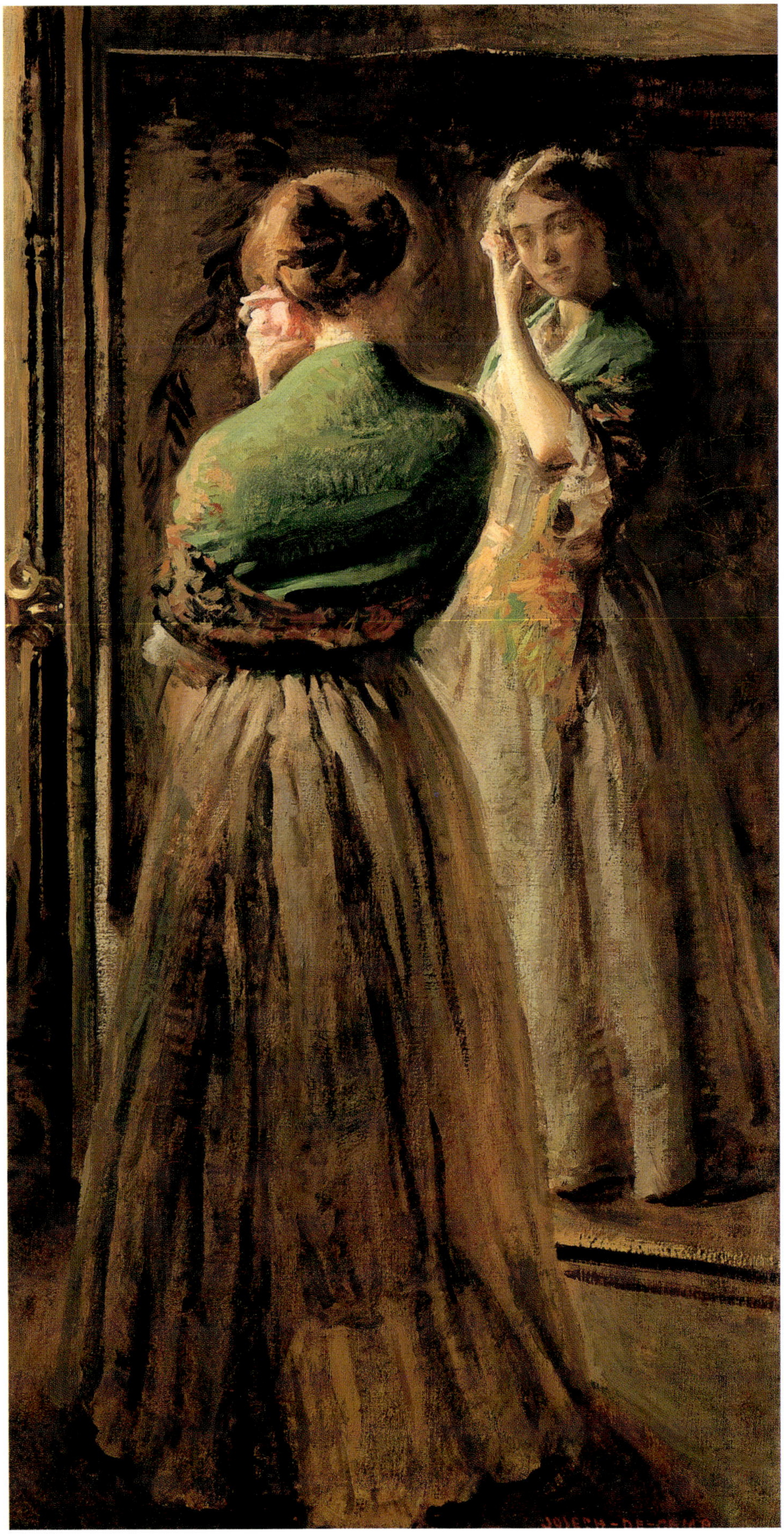

23
Girl with a Green Shawl
(*The Green Shawl*), ca. 1900.
39½ x 21 in. (100.5 x 53.5 cm).
Private collection

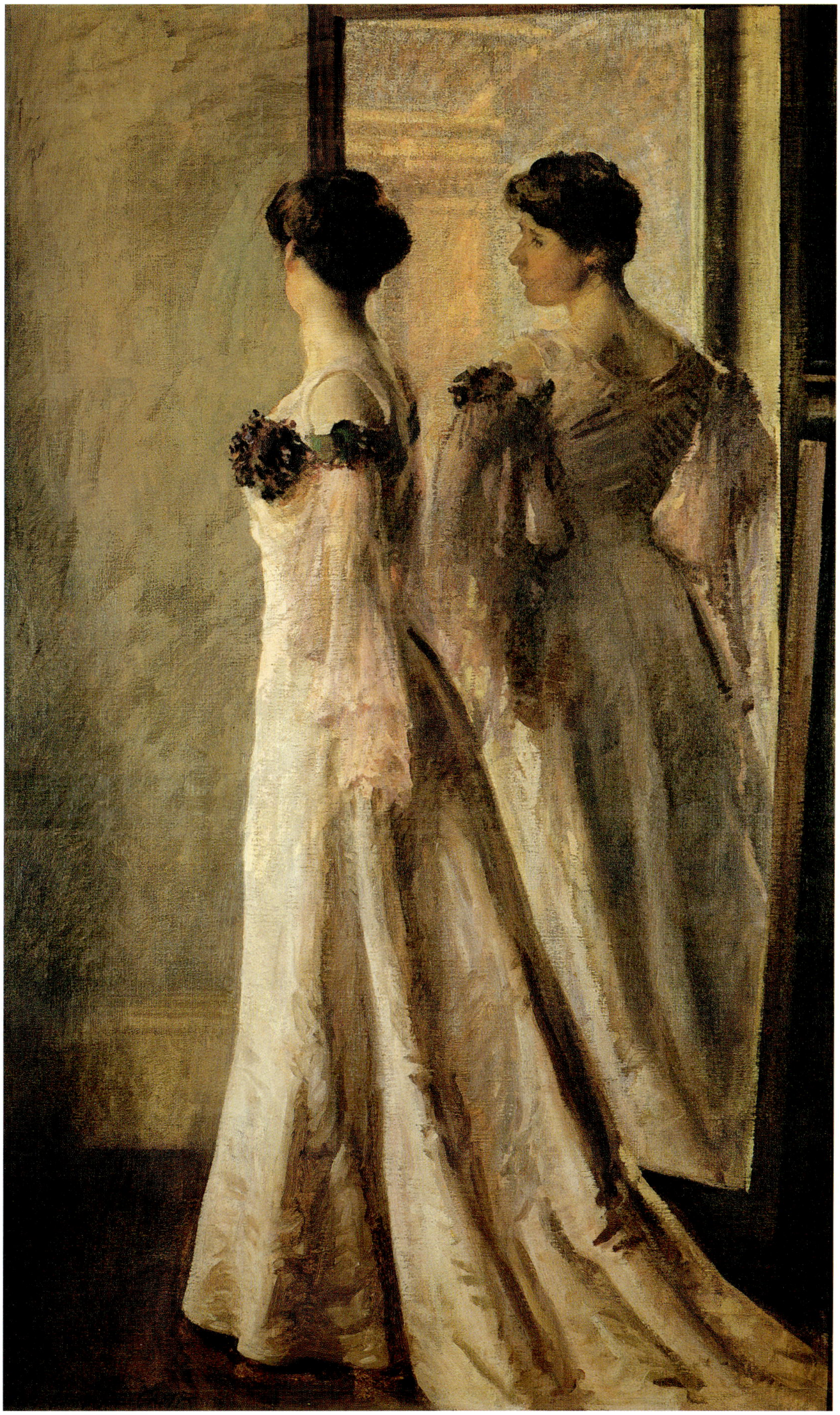

24
The Heliotrope Gown,
ca. 1905.
52 x 32 in. (132 x 81 cm).
Private collection

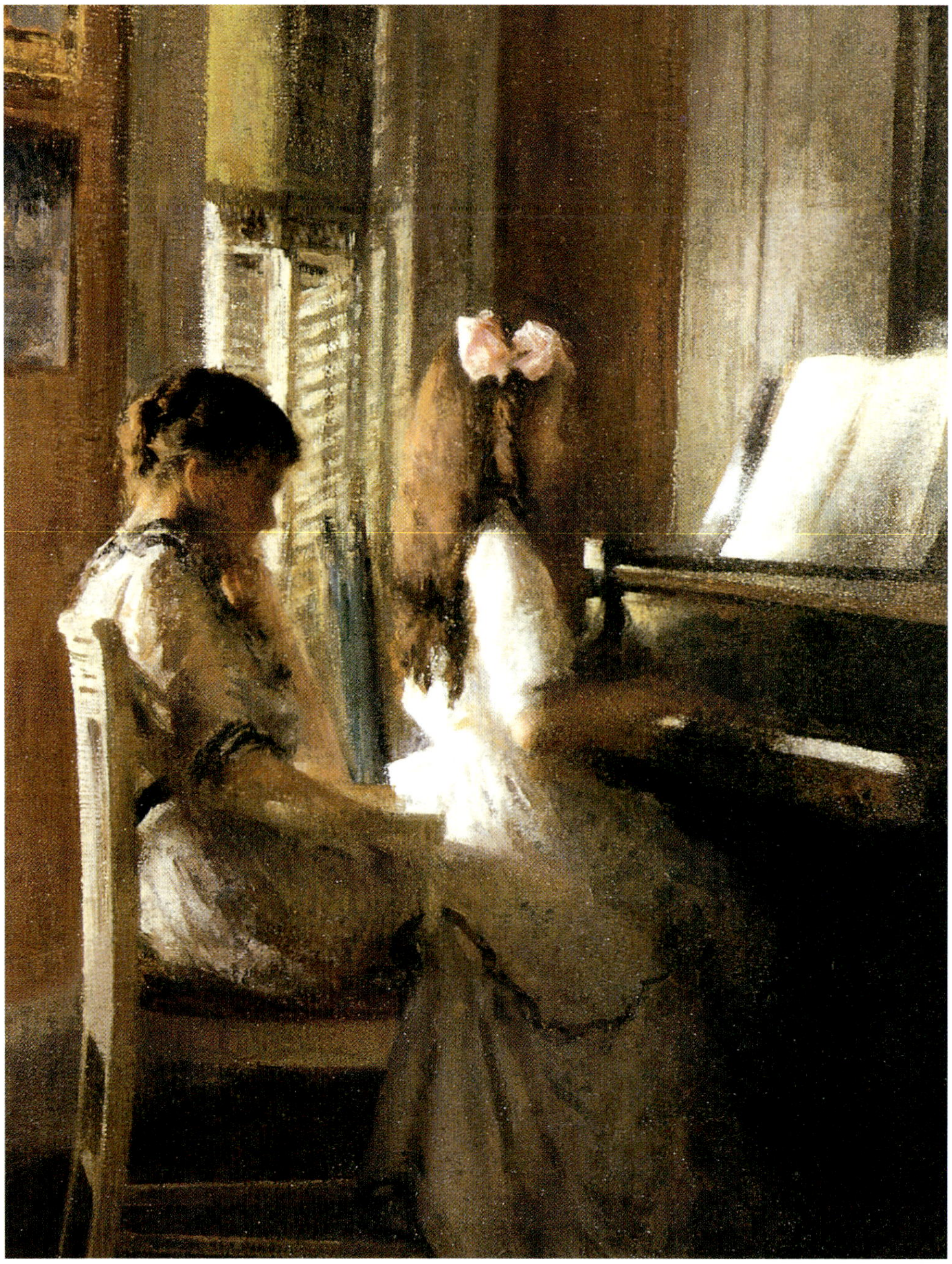

25 *The Music Lesson*, ca. 1904.
21 x 16 in. (53.5 x 40.5 cm). Private collection

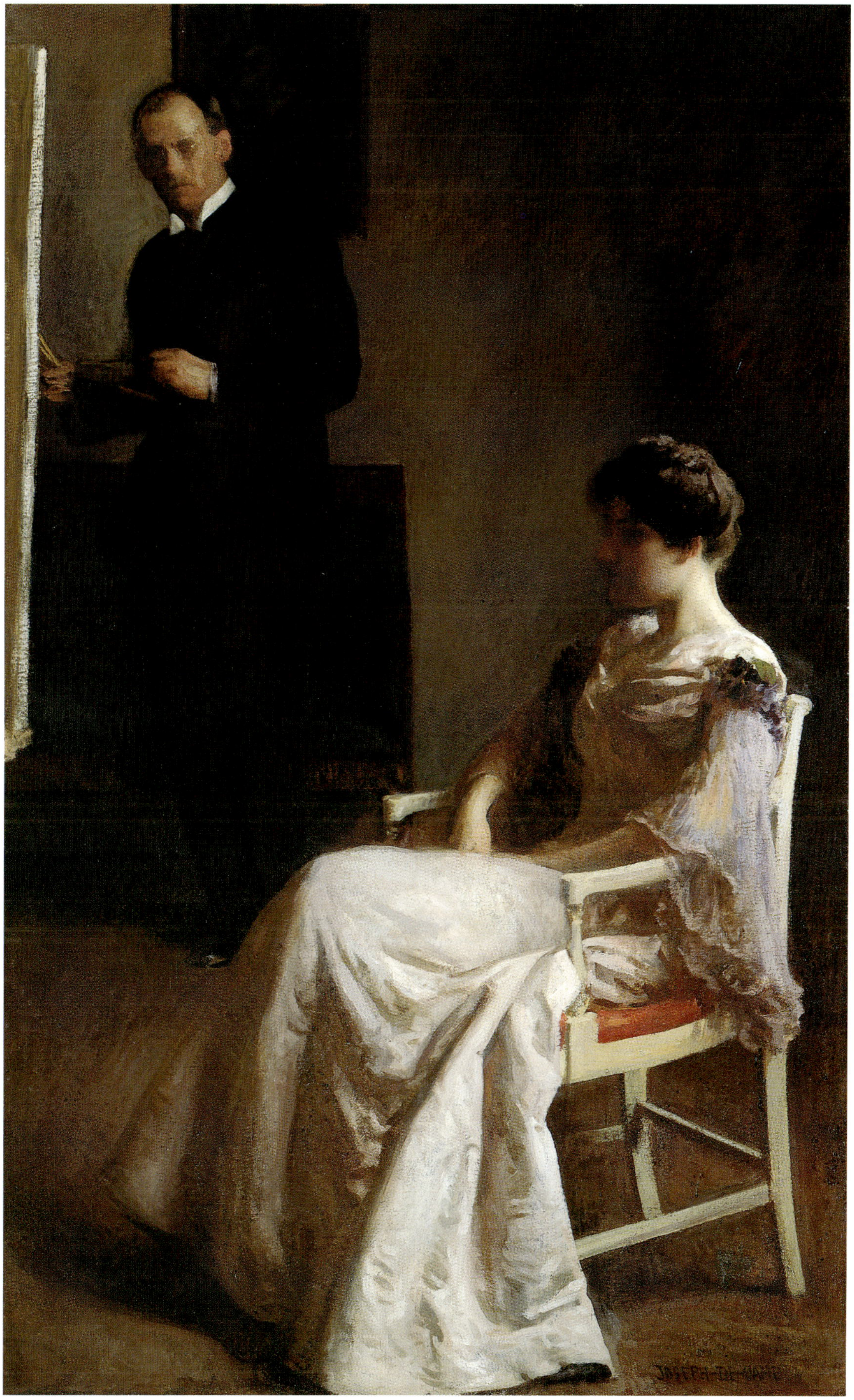

26
In the Studio, ca. 1905.
41 x 25 in. (104 x 63.5 cm).
Mr. and Mrs. Thomas A. Rosse

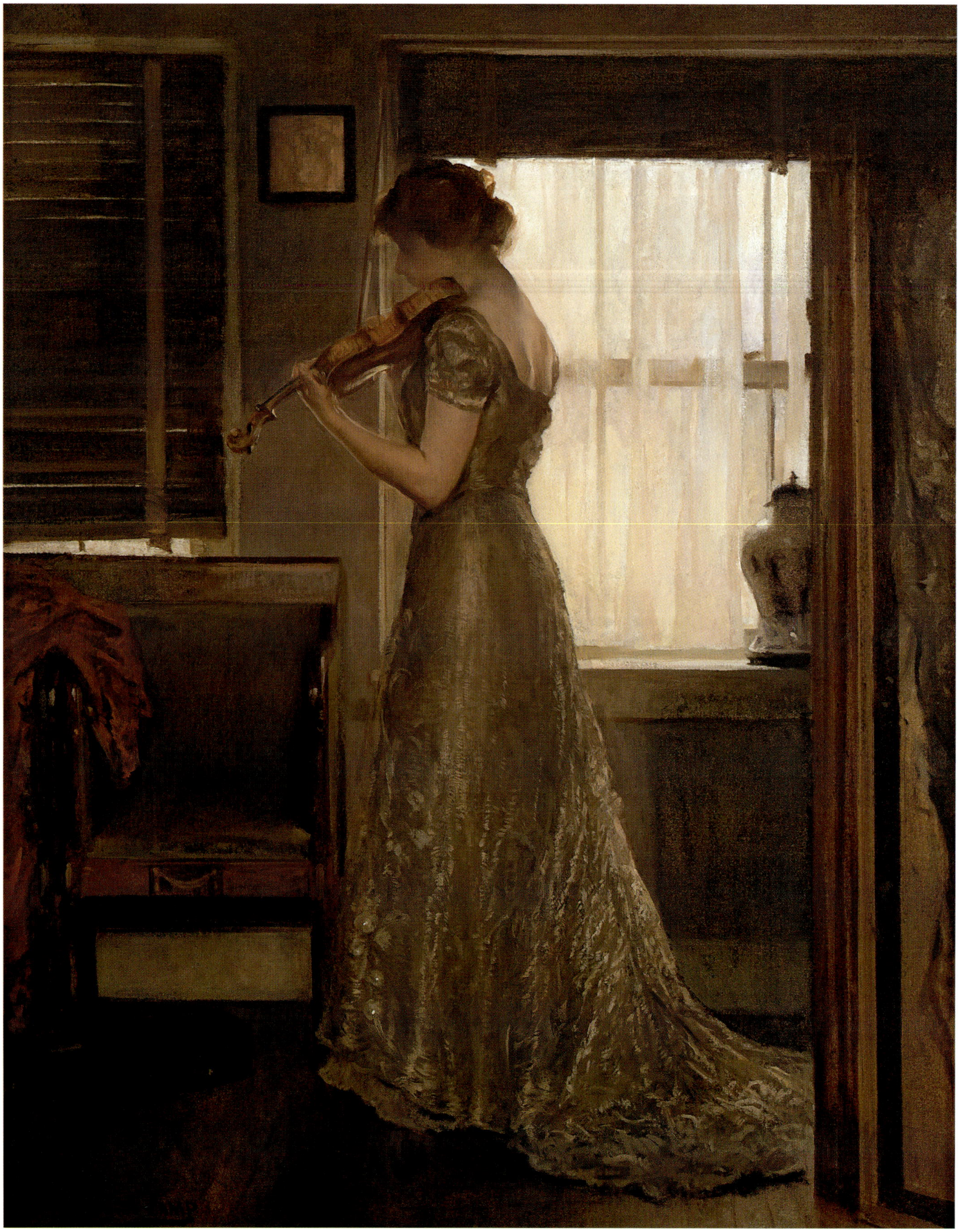

27 *The Violinist* (*The Violin; Girl with Violin III*), ca. 1902. 36¼ x 28¼ in. (92 x 71.5 cm). Private collection

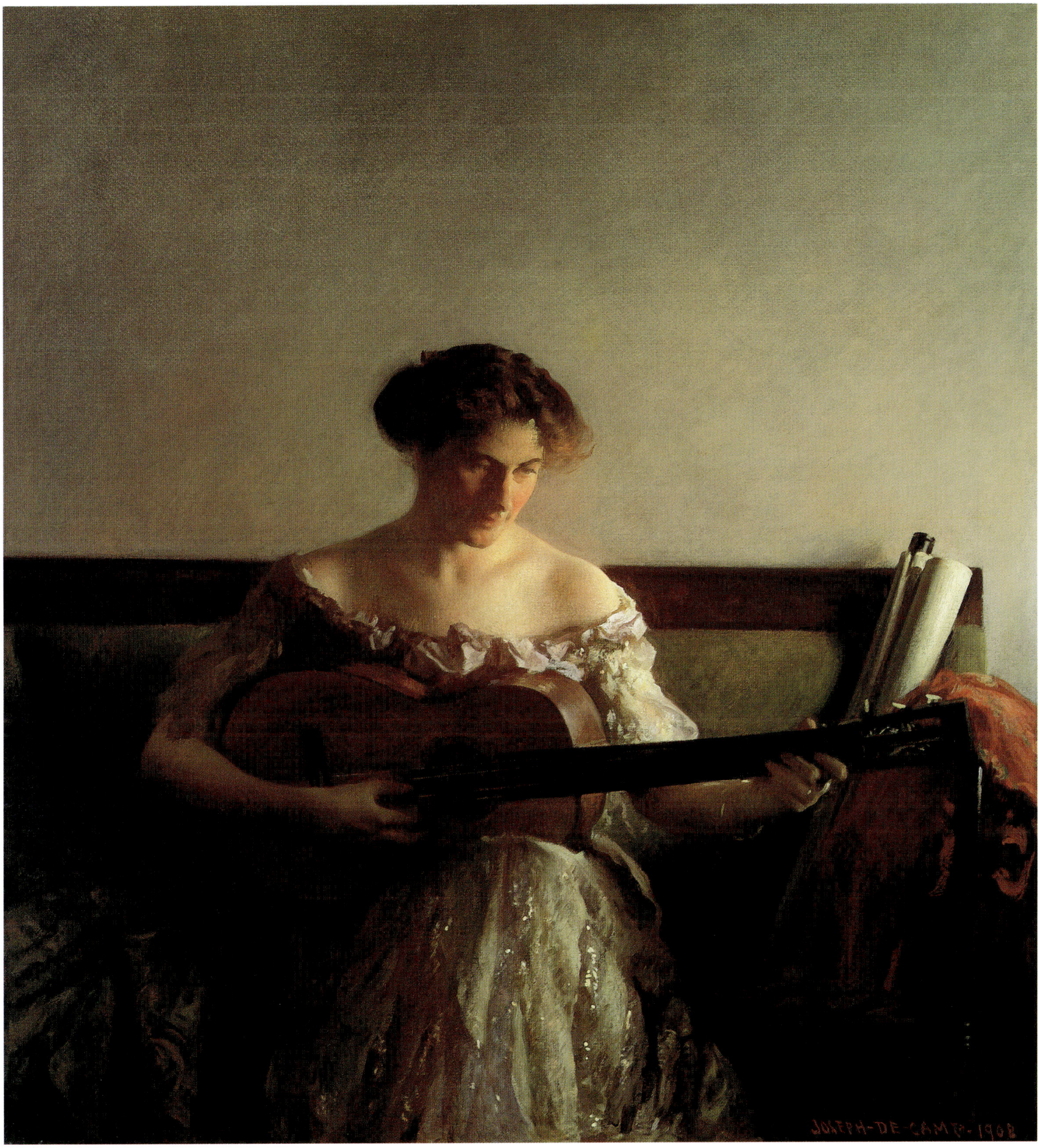

28 *The Guitar Player,* 1908. 50$\frac{3}{8}$ x 46$\frac{1}{2}$ in. (128 x 118 cm). The Hayden Collection. Courtesy, Museum of Fine Arts, Boston

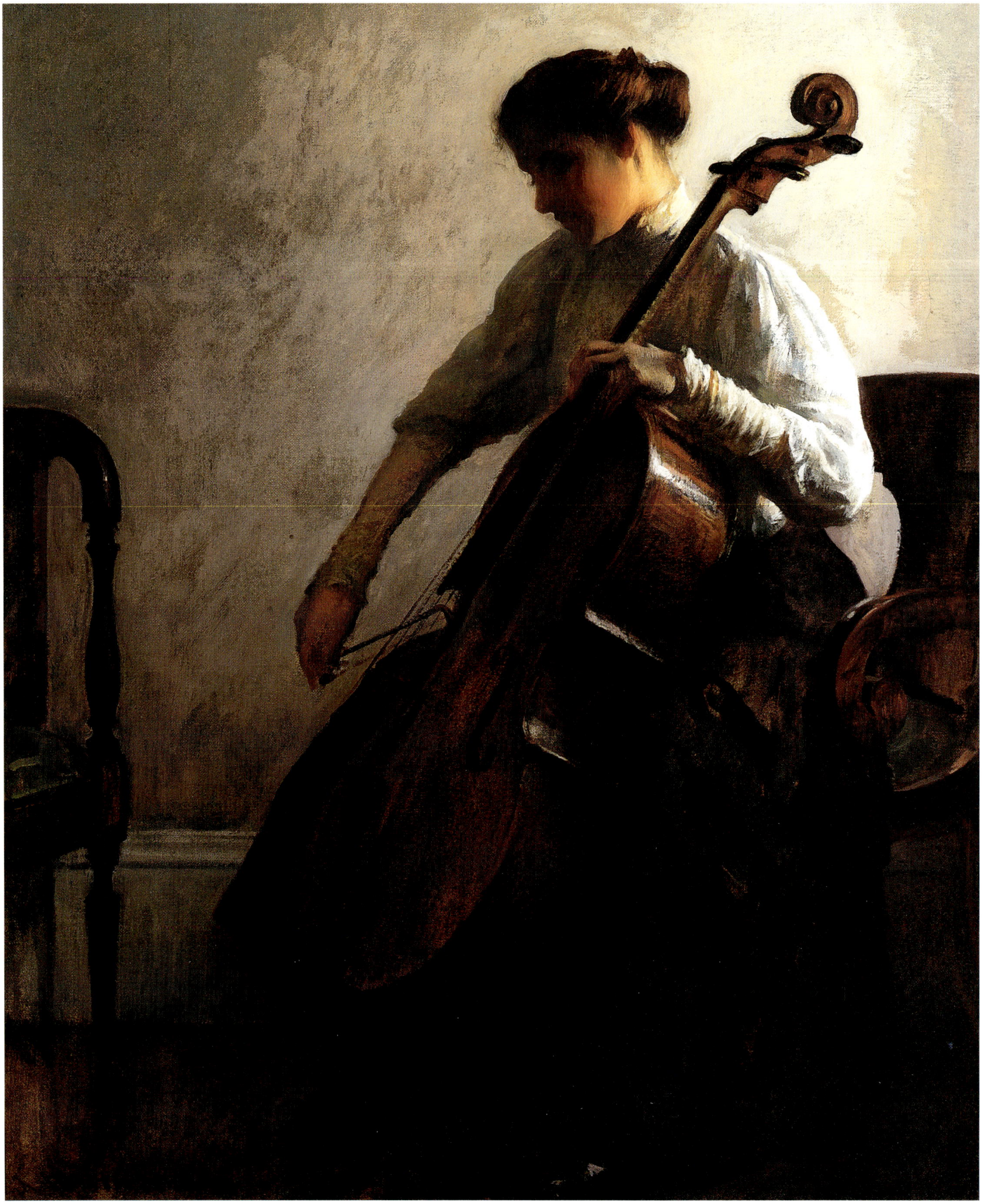

29 *The Cellist*, 1908. 28 x 23 1/16 in. (71 x 23 cm). Cincinnati Art Museum, John J. Emery Fund

imagined enlarged to the lifesize scale, it would look not unlike this modern master work."[32] One need only think of Vermeer's *Playing the Guitar* (Kenwood House, London), then owned by a Philadelphia collector, to recognize the validity of this statement. In his canvas DeCamp has assimilated the essentials of Vermeer's work: the dreamy atmosphere, the light effects surrounding the figure (but not including the actual source of illumination), the quiet domesticity, and a touch of coquetry that he must have perceived in the earlier artist's imagery.

The musical instruments incorporated by DeCamp in his pictures—violin, guitar, cello—were ones often played by women in his day (and usually in evening gowns), but they may also have been selected because of their similarity in shape to the female body. The depiction of a single figure immersed in music bespoke an interiorization of life and experience that had begun to be apparent in the late nineteenth century. According to Celia Betsky, "music in late nineteenth-century American painting seemed intent on a form of expression closely bound up with changing ways of life that were gradually carrying [music in art] indoors and toward an increasing emphasis on the inner self... in an era that homed in on the unspoken, the emotional, the cerebral, and the psychic."[33]

The Cellist (plate 29) was also related to Dutch prototypes by the critics, especially in its treatment of light.[34] Back illumination of the woman, who again appears wholly absorbed in her art, results in the silhouetting of the figure and instrument. This was among the features of the work that Charles DeKay of the New York *Evening Post* noted as untypical: "Warm tones and powerful chiaroscuro characterize an unwonted style in which the former Mr. DeCamp is hard to recognize."[35] Evidently a favorite with the artist, who showed it at sixteen exhibitions between 1908 and 1916, the painting was not sold until after DeCamp's death in 1923, when it was purchased, along with his *Magdalene*, by the Cincinnati Art Museum.

The Pink Feather (plate 30) was also sent to a large number of exhibitions—thirteen in all. DeCamp's health was beginning to fail and perhaps this is why he showed favorite paintings at many venues. According to Rose V. S. Berry, an attack of appendicitis in December 1907 initiated "sixteen years of what would have been total invalidism in the case of the majority of mankind." "Yet, in the face of suffering which was torment, he worked and toiled, producing his best during this period."[36] Critics viewed *The Pink Feather*, too, chiefly in terms of composition and coloration. "The subject is a lovely girl in dark street clothes with a smallish hat on which is a feather that matches her cheeks for color," wrote the reviewer for *Christian Science Monitor*. "A black chiffon veil is drawn over face and hat in such a way as to make a most interesting shape of her head outlined against a luminous gray background."[37] A drawing for the work (fig. 67) indicates that this is exactly what DeCamp had in mind—to create an interesting shape of head and veil. More fascinating to him, however, was probably the challenge of capturing the flesh tones of the face beneath a darkened veil and the possibility of adding a touch of mystery. Hoeber, for one, thought DeCamp had succeeded: "Looking coquettish enough in a brown veil, her lovely face [is] aglow with health, with animation, with joie de vivre. It does not often happen in this vale of tears that it is given to mere man to have so charming a representation of femininity."[38]

Year after year, until his final illness, DeCamp produced portrayals of single, large-scale figures absorbed in various activities related to the home: mending, arranging flowers, reading, playing an instrument, or, as in *The Blue Cup* of 1909 (plate 31), cleaning. Unlike Tarbell and William Paxton, DeCamp rarely portrayed his models as domestics. When he did so—in *The Blue Cup*, for example—his intentions were quite different from those underlying the standard Boston School depictions. As Elizabeth O'Leary has written, the general tenor of Tarbell's and Paxton's imagery was to present "things hoped for"—perfectly attired, impeccably behaved servants, far removed from the real world of growing tensions between mistress and maid.[39] DeCamp disguises the drudgery of household chores in *The Blue Cup*—the highly polished furniture and still life objects in the pristine setting match the decorativeness of the woman herself, who has the hourglass figure so familiar to readers of popular magazines of the day—yet his maid has more on her mind than the latest cleansing agent for the home. A critic for the *Globe and Commercial Advertiser*, in reviewing the Ten's exhibition of 1909, remarked on the woman's intellectual curiosity as she examines the mark on the bottom of the fragile china cup held in her hands.[40] As O'Leary points out, many employers felt it to be their social responsibility to "educate" the worker, especially with the rising tide of immigrants at the end of the nineteenth century: "By trying to elevate their servants' standards and behavior, employers imagined they were bringing benefit to both the workers and society. Until the flow of immigration could be stemmed, efforts had to be made to transform the newcomers with their un-American characteristics into—at the very least—good, law-abiding citizens."[41] No doubt DeCamp was aware of this concern. It is interesting to note that, at the time, he was teaching at the Massachusetts Normal Art School, an institution designed for public education, and that it was suggested that *The Blue Cup* be given to the school in memory of its founder, the noted reformer Kate Gannett Wells.[42] The sitter for the painting was Agnes Woodbury, who appears as a woman of leisure in *The Guitar Player*, *The Fur Jacket*, and *The Blue Veil*. Family tradition maintains that there were servants in the DeCamp household,[43] but there is no indication that the artist's models were maids. A later model, the

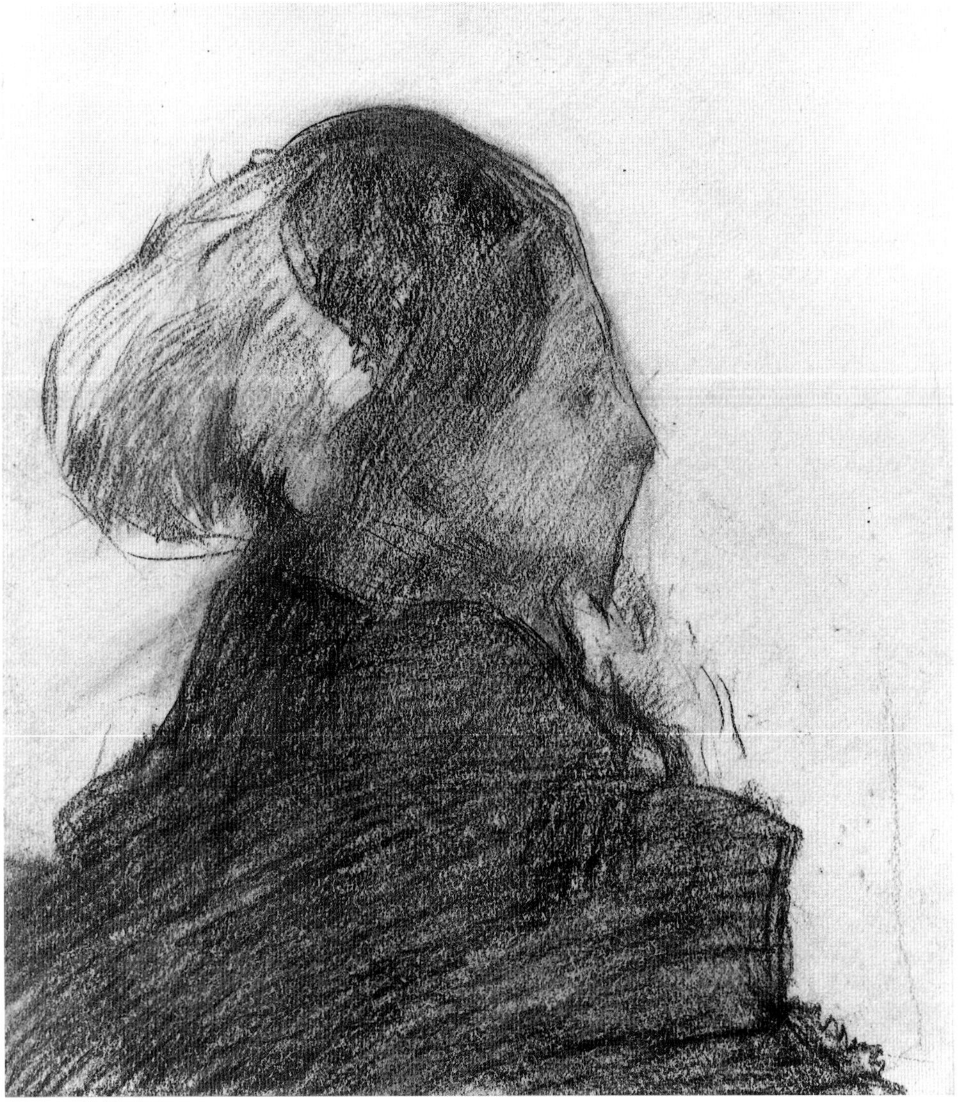

Fig. 67
Study for "The Pink Feather", ca. 1908.
Charcoal on paper, dimensions unknown.
Private collection

Irishwoman "Reddy" Pearson, acted as DeCamp's secretary in the last years of his life.[44]

The Fur Jacket (plate 32), showing a woman in fashionable furs and enormous, broad-rimmed hat, was first exhibited in 1910 at the Pennsylvania Academy's tenth annual exhibition, at which it was called a "peculiarly reserved, toneful work."[45] In this painting DeCamp was obviously challenged by the play of textures within an essentially black and brown image, a strategy he used again in *The Gray Turban* of about 1911 (unlocated).[46] Whistler had explored the same hues in his 1877 *Fur Jacket* (Worcester Art Museum, Massachusetts), a work DeCamp is likely to have seen at the Whistler memorial exhibition held at Boston's Copley Hall in 1904.

Agnes Woodbury also posed for *Roses* (fig. 68), a painting once owned by the St. Louis Museum of Art. She is shown seated, in profile, as she prepares to place a long-stemmed rose among the others in a beautifully painted oriental vase. Although wearing a dress and an apron similar to those in *The Blue Cup*, here she probably represents the mistress of the house, since domestics were rarely allowed the luxury of sitting.[47] A seated maid would have alienated the very patrons whom DeCamp no doubt wished to please with his interior scenes. Apparently, it was acceptable for the woman of the house to perform the task of arranging flowers.

The still life begins to appear as an accessory in these figural works around the time of the Roosevelt portrait (1908) and *The Blue Cup* (1909). When *Roses* was shown at the Ten exhibition of 1910, one critic found that the "dewiness of the flowers" contrasted well "with the dry, shiny browns of that violoncello back of the girl."[48] Another admired the "simplicity, almost naïveté of the rendering." "Its very straightforwardness is alluring in these days of many experimentings"[49]—no doubt a reference to the innovations of The Eight and the early Modernists.

A series of paintings focusing on women sewing, mending, or embroidering followed. This theme of

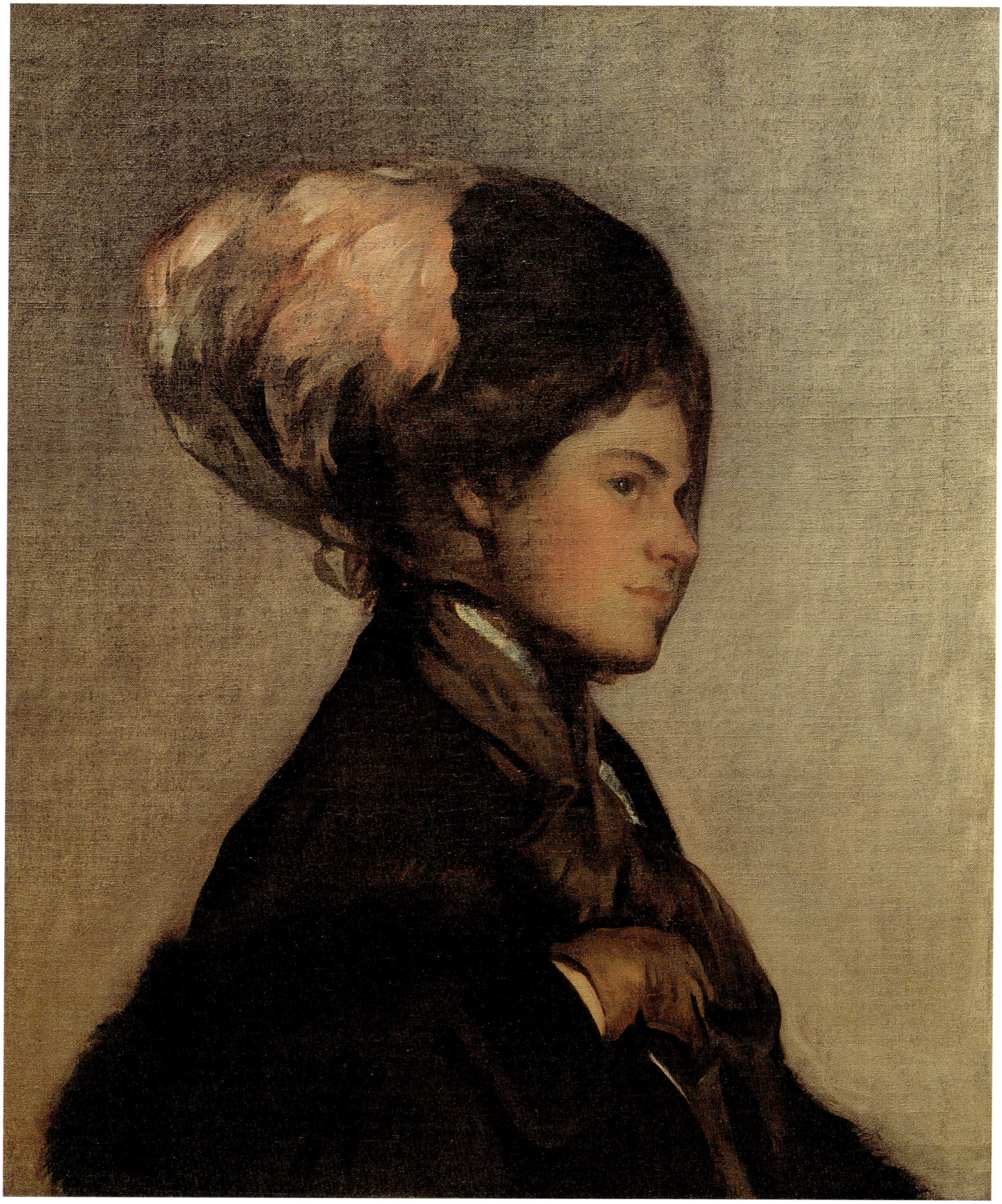

30 *The Pink Feather* (*The Brown Veil*), 1908. 30 x 25 in. (76 x 63.5 cm). Private collection

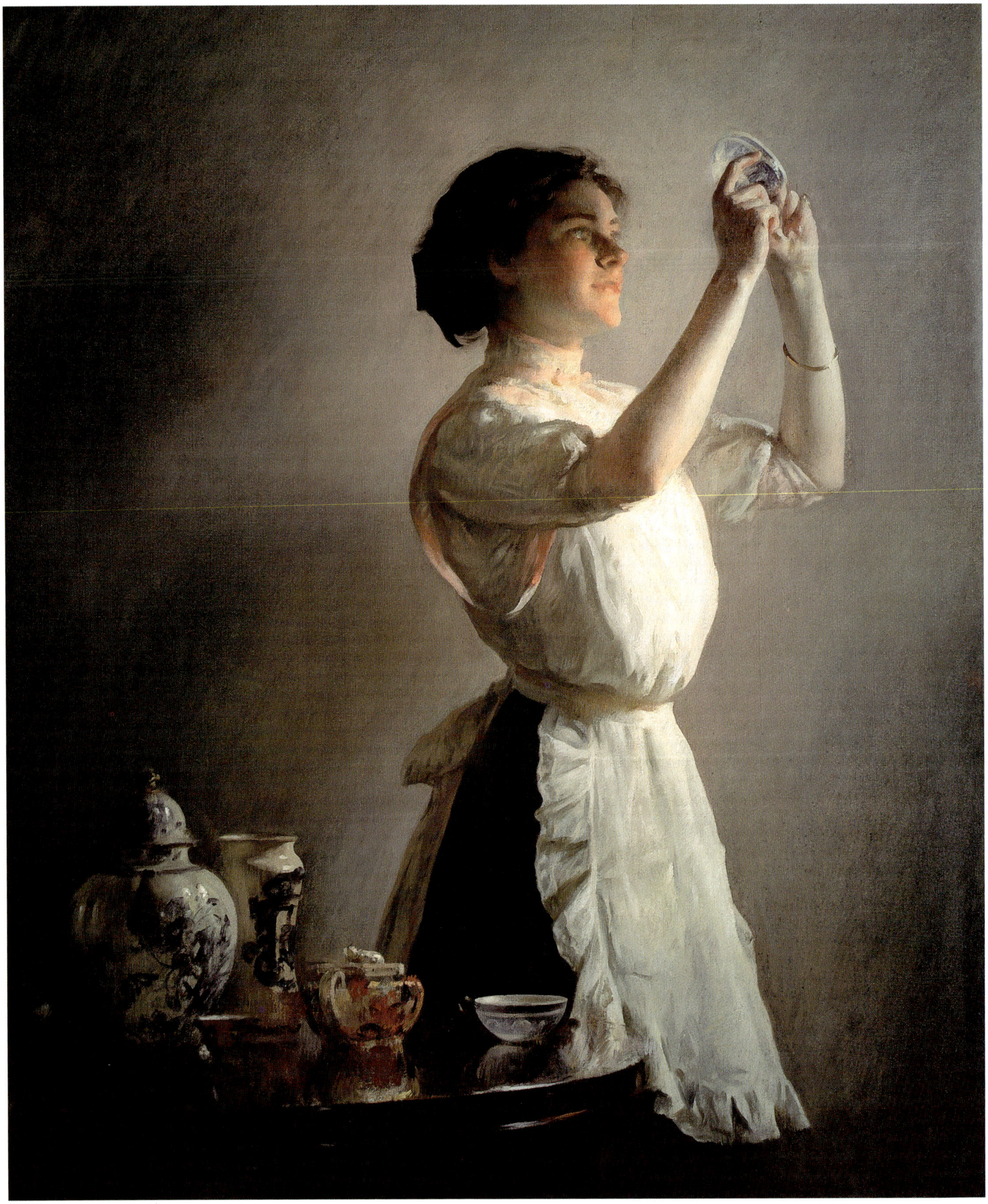

31 *The Blue Cup*, 1909. 50⅛ x 41¼ in. (127.5 x 105 cm). Museum of Fine Arts, Boston, Gift of Edwin S. Webster, Laurence T. Webster, and Mary M. Sampson in memory of their father, Frank G. Webster

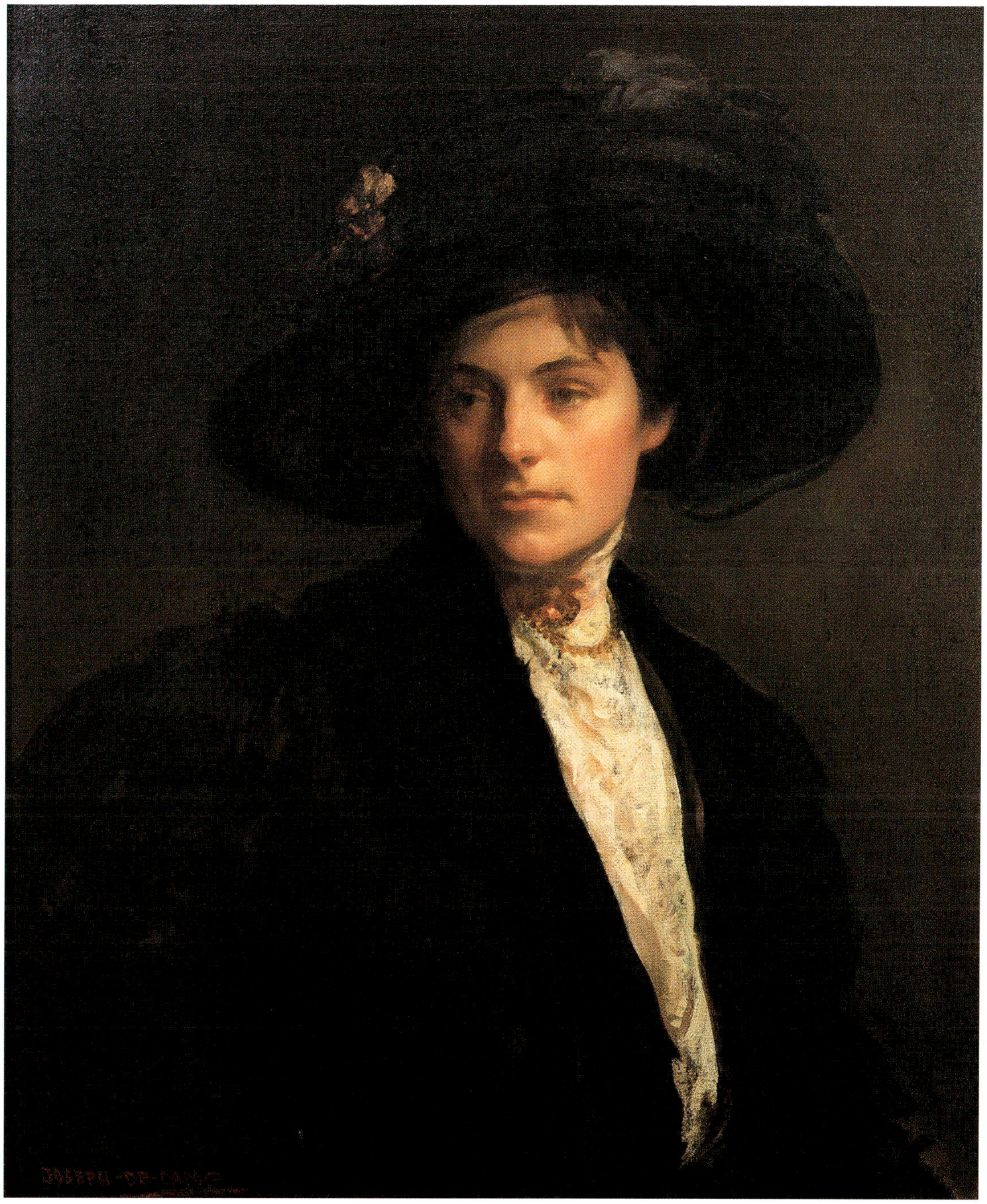

32 *The Fur Jacket*, 1910. 30 x 25 in. (76 x 63.5 cm). Private collection

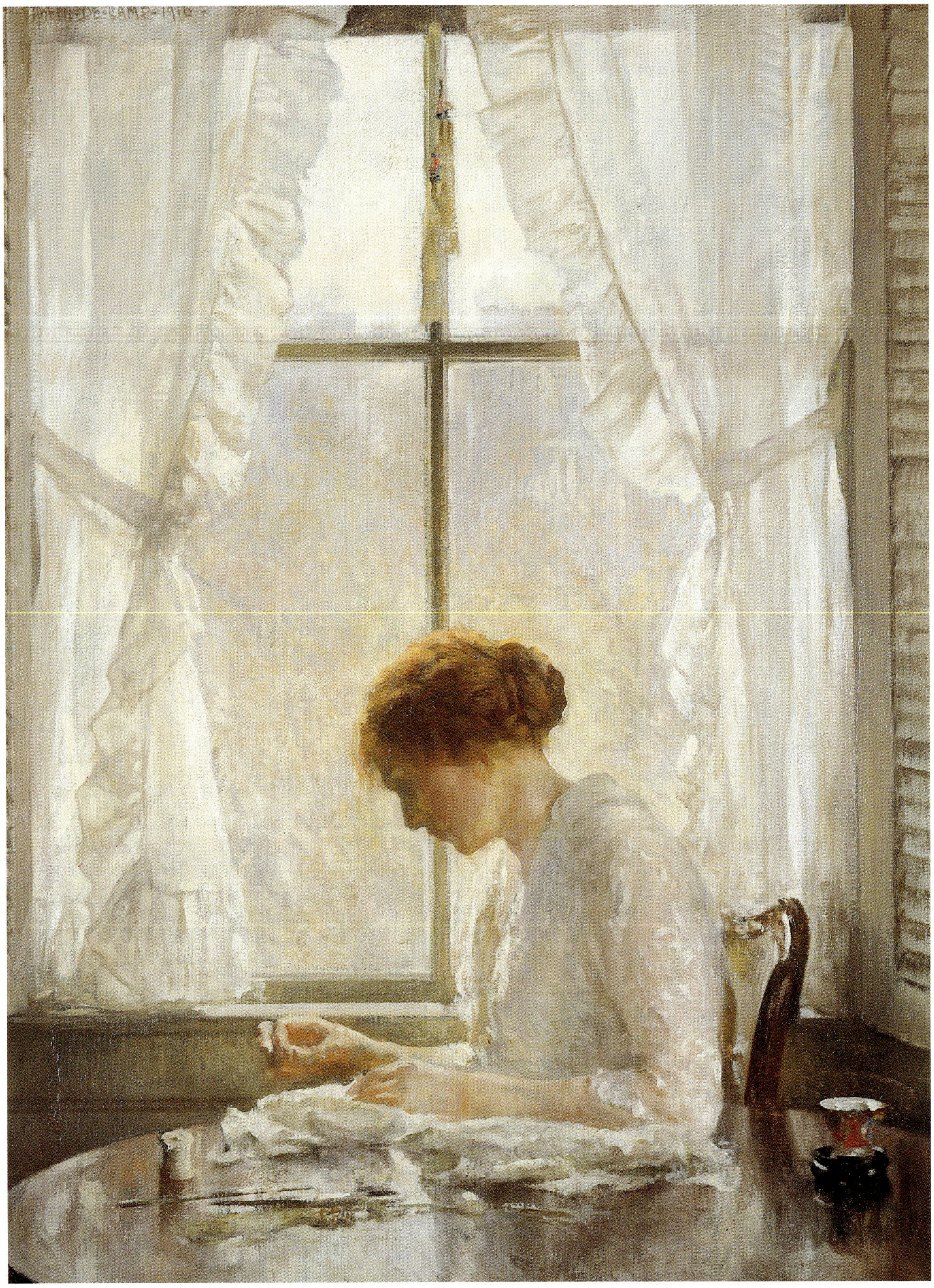

33 *The Seamstress*, 1916. 36¼ x 28 in. (92 x 71 cm).
Collection of the Corcoran Gallery of Art, Washington, D.C.,
Museum Purchase, Gallery Fund

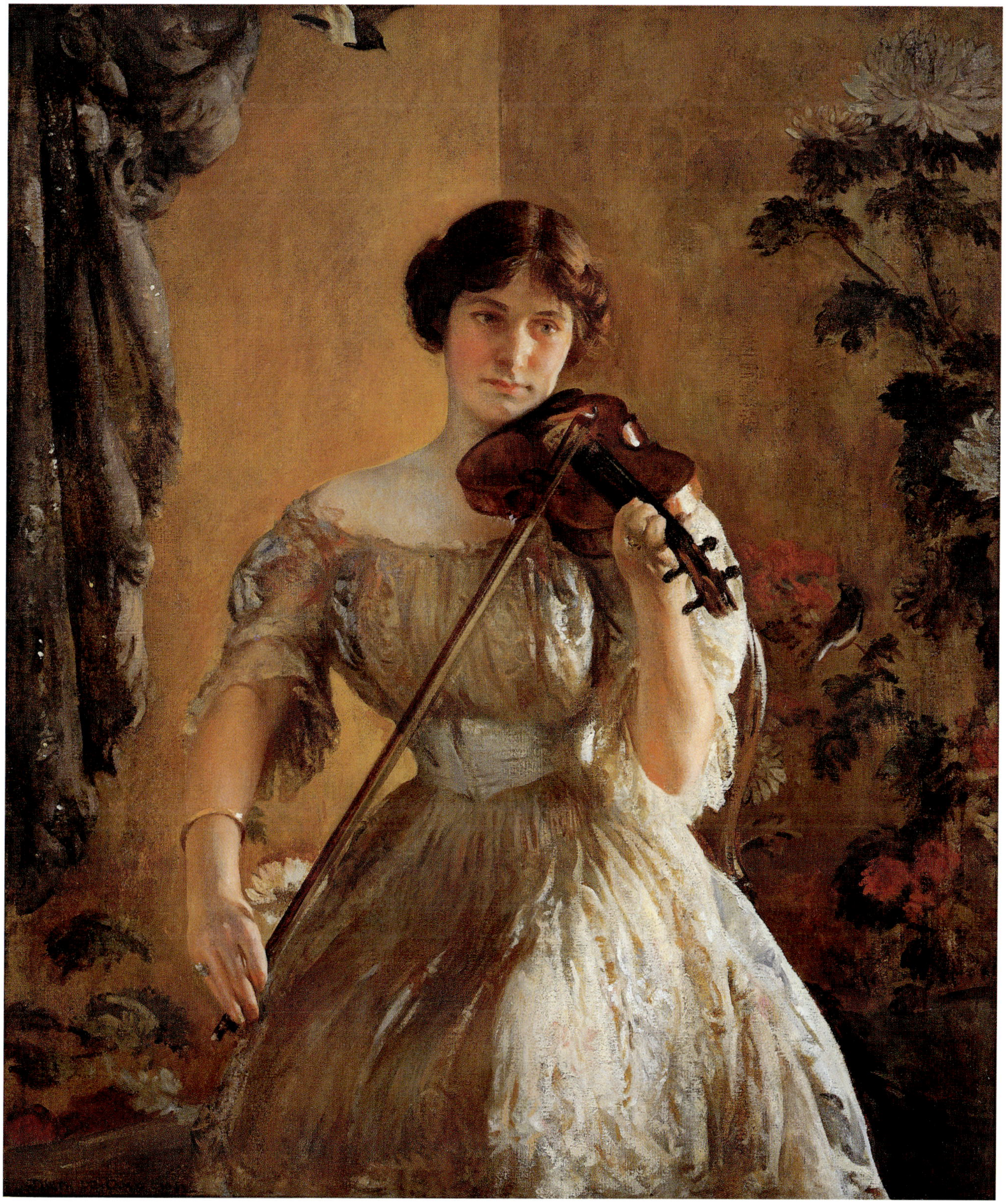

34 *The Kreutzer Sonata* (*Violinist II*), ca. 1912. 48 x 40 in. (122 x 101 cm).
Adelson Galleries, Inc., New York

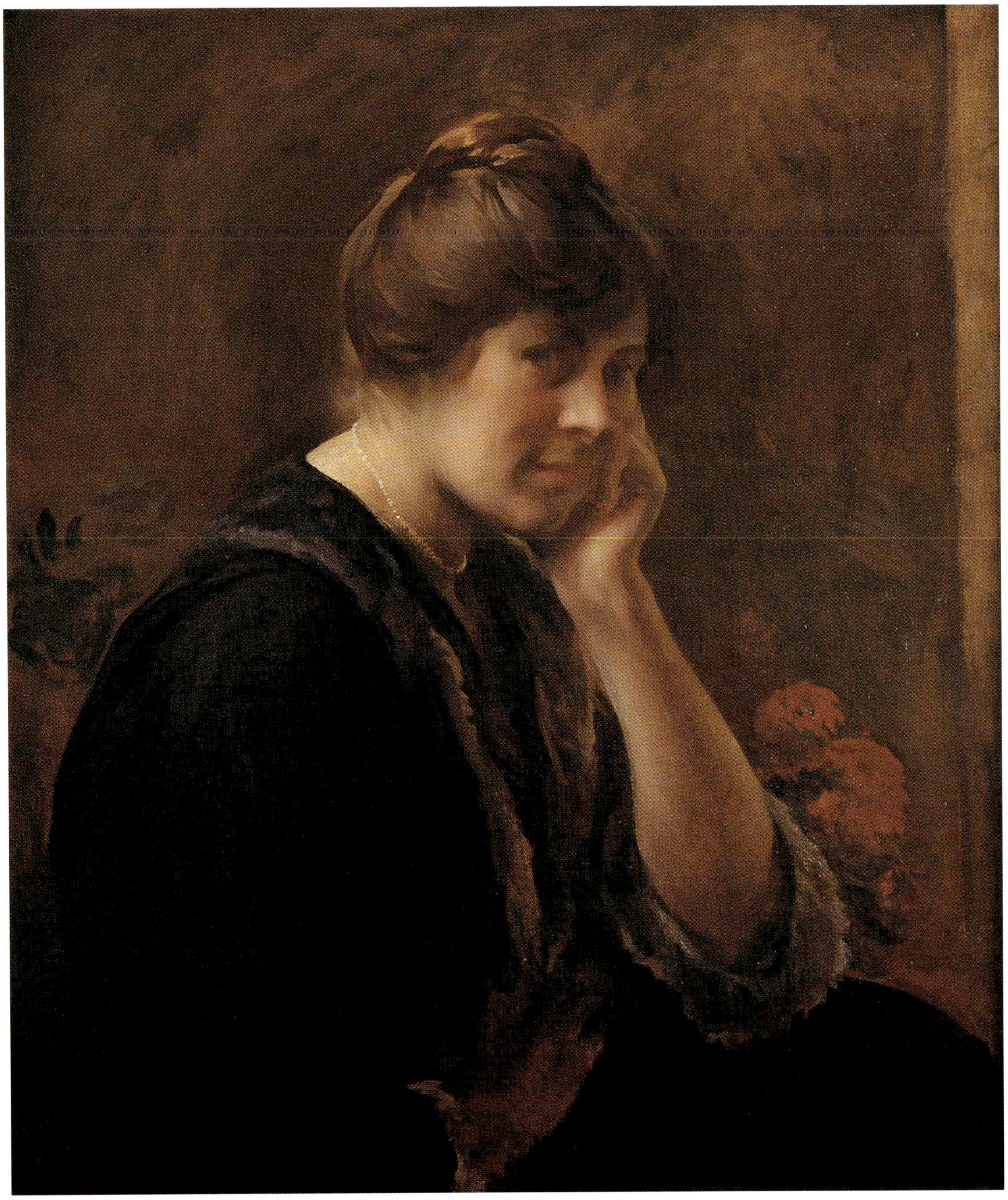

35 *The Flirt*, ca. 1913. 30 x 25 in. (76 x 63.5 cm). Private collection

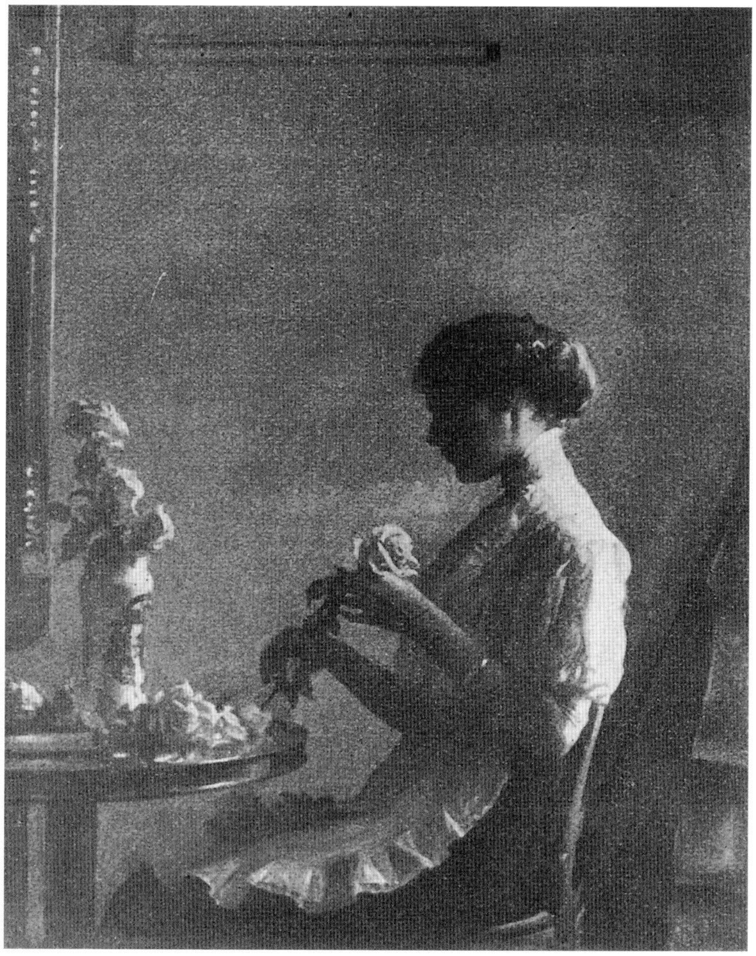

Fig. 68 *Roses*, ca. 1910. Dimensions unknown. Private collection

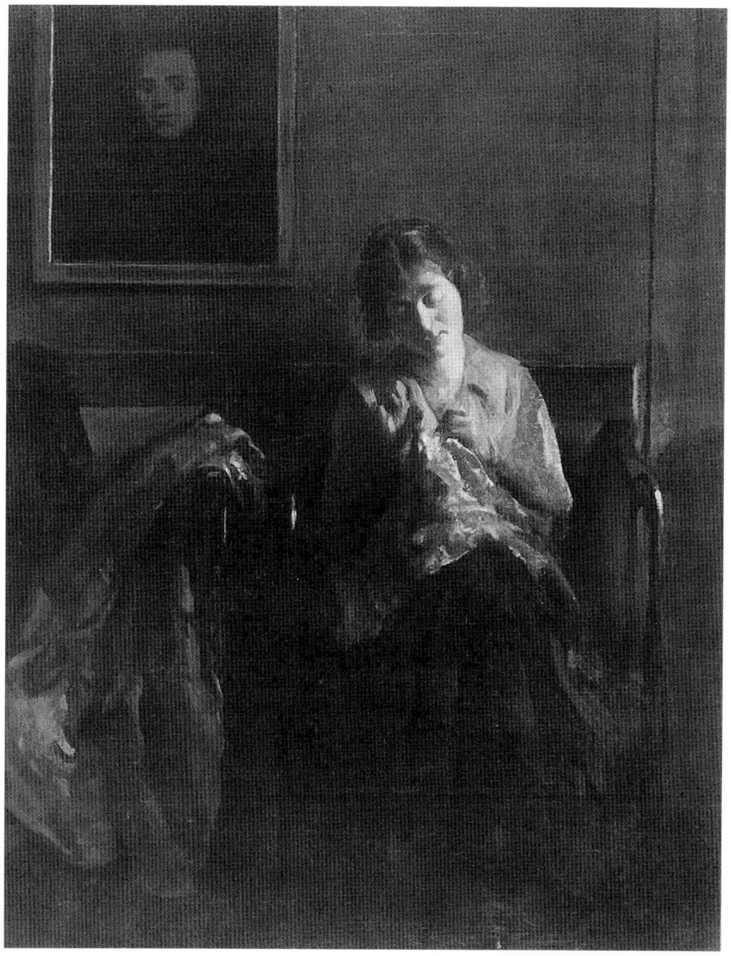

Fig. 69 *Girl Sewing*, ca. 1910. 26½ x 19½ in. (67.5 x 49.5 cm). Private collection

women engaged in needlework proved an abundant source of imagery for other artists as well, especially Tarbell, as evidenced by his *A Girl Crocheting* of 1904 (fig. 66) and *A Girl Mending* of 1905. DeCamp's *Girl Sewing*, shown in the Thirteenth Annual Exhibition of Oil Paintings at the Worcester Art Museum, Massachusetts, may be the painting now in a Vermont collection depicting a woman engrossed in her mending (fig. 69). The small scale of both the canvas itself and the figure within the scene are untypical of DeCamp; the inclusion of a large number of ancillary objects is also unusual and brings the work closer to Benson's and Tarbell's standard versions of the Vermeeresque formula.

The Window (fig. 71), depicting a woman embroidering in front of a sunlit window, was first shown in DeCamp's one-man exhibition of 1911. Here again, critics described the painting in terms of its technical challenges and related it to the color harmonies made popular by the Aesthetic Movement of a decade earlier. "A veritable pearl of a picture . . . a refreshing study in white," noted the *Boston Sunday Herald* reviewer. "A woman stands in charming profile, with a piece of white embroidery in her hands, before a window, draped in thin white curtains, while through the decorative design of the window panes is seen indistinctly a foggy, white landscape. The only note of color is the blue of a Canton jar on a mahogany table, the polished surface of which reflects the white light. It is a study, not of glaring white, but of light seen through various degrees of white transparencies, shading from oyster gray to pearl."[50] J. Nilsen Laurvik called the work "one of the most exquisitely rendered harmonies of delicate gray tonalities" that he had had the "pleasure to see in a long time."[51]

DeCamp would repeat the subject of *The Window* later, in *The Seamstress* of 1916 (plate 33). Here the woman is seated behind a highly polished table, her figure centered within a windowed rectangle of white light. The picture was first shown in the Sixth Exhibition of Contemporary Oil Paintings at the Corcoran Gallery of Art, Washington, D.C., which purchased it immediately. The artist's letter to the director of the gallery, C. Powell Minnigerode, explains his dilemma

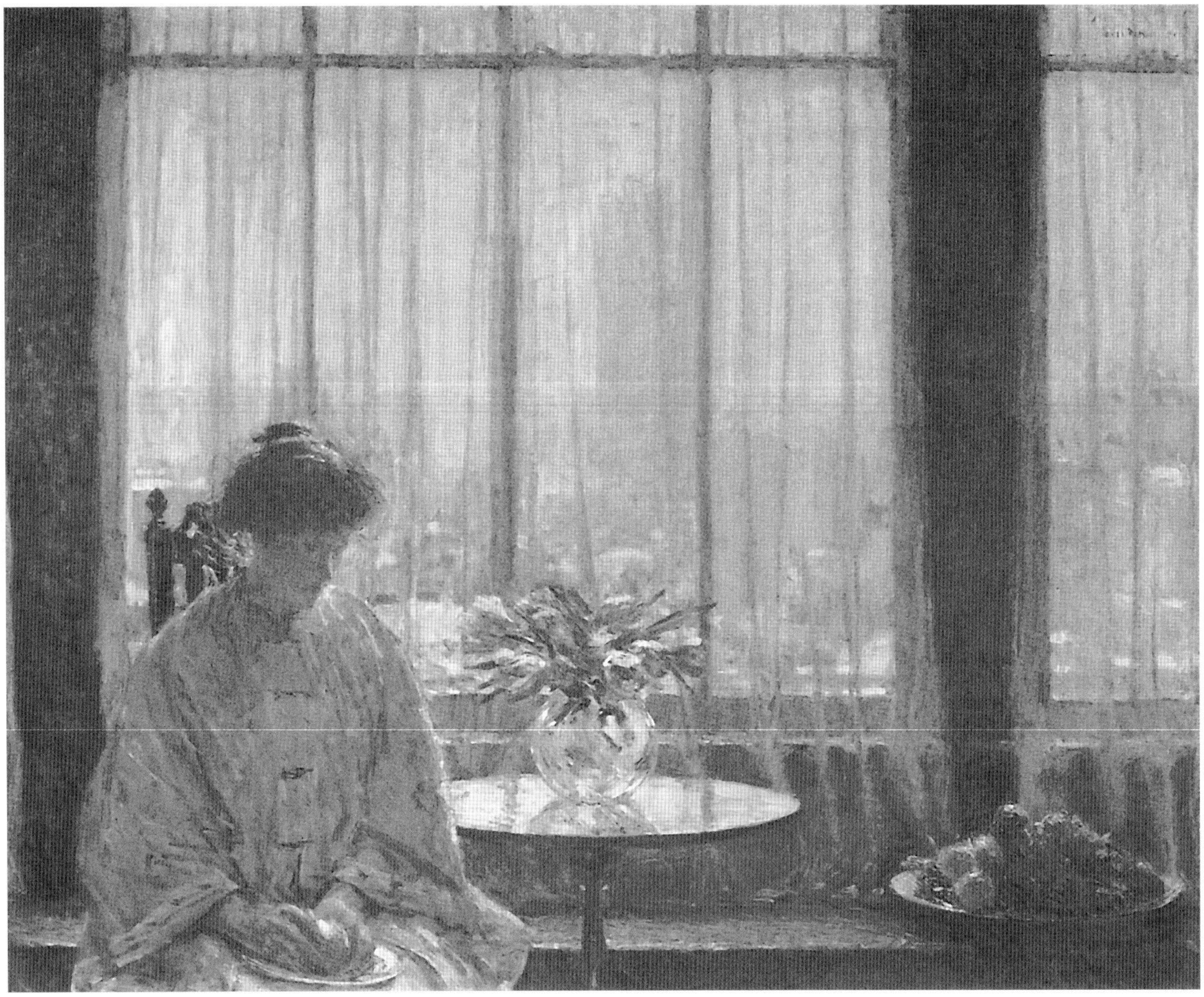

Fig. 70
Childe Hassam,
The Breakfast Room, Winter Morning, 1911.
25⅛ x 30⅛ in.
(64 x 76.5 cm).
Worcester Art Museum, Massachusetts, Museum Purchase

in trying to make the deadline for the exhibition: "I am sending two [entry] cards in the belief that 'The Seamstress' will be finished—a couple of grey days will turn the trick."[52] DeCamp apparently relied on tonal light rather than clear sunny days for the execution of these windowed pictures.

Again, window themes were not limited to DeCamp's oeuvre. Benson, too, began producing paintings of such subjects in 1911, with *Maid in Waiting* (alternatively, *Woman Near Window*, Georgia Museum of Art, University of Georgia, Atlanta), while Childe Hassam's famous Window series, though initiated as early as 1907, was a strong presence in the Ten exhibitions around 1911 (see fig. 70).

In several paintings created toward the end of his mature period, in the years 1912 to 1917, DeCamp returned to some subjects of his earlier work, producing a pair of "violinist" pictures, another image of a veiled woman, a seductive female in the manner of *La Penserosa*, a woman admiring a precious object as in *The Blue Cup*, and a woman reading. He may have wished to repeat previous successes, perhaps because the health problems that had been plaguing him since 1907 deterred him from exploring new territory. At any rate, this latest series of works lacked the freshness of new ideas and was not well received by the critics. Two very similar views of a female violinist date to about 1912. One of them, *Girl with Violin*, exists only in the form of a photograph (fig. 72) and shows the woman against a plain background; the other, *The Kreutzer Sonata* (*Violinist II*, plate 34), depicts the same woman in the same costume against a flowered screen. Both figures differ from that in the earlier *Violinist* in being three-quarter-length, seated, large-bodied, and posed looking straight out at the viewer. Comparing *The Kreutzer Sonata* to the artist's *The Guitar Player* and *The Window*, Laurvik found it "far less successful pictorially."[53] Another writer noted that "the figure is not perfectly related to the background, is heavy yellow in color and without air."[54] Royal Cortissoz also was disappointed with DeCamp's latest effort: "To go over this large and handsome portrait inch by inch is to come upon one passage after another of painting lovingly thought out and executed with a knowledge and skill. But to exam-

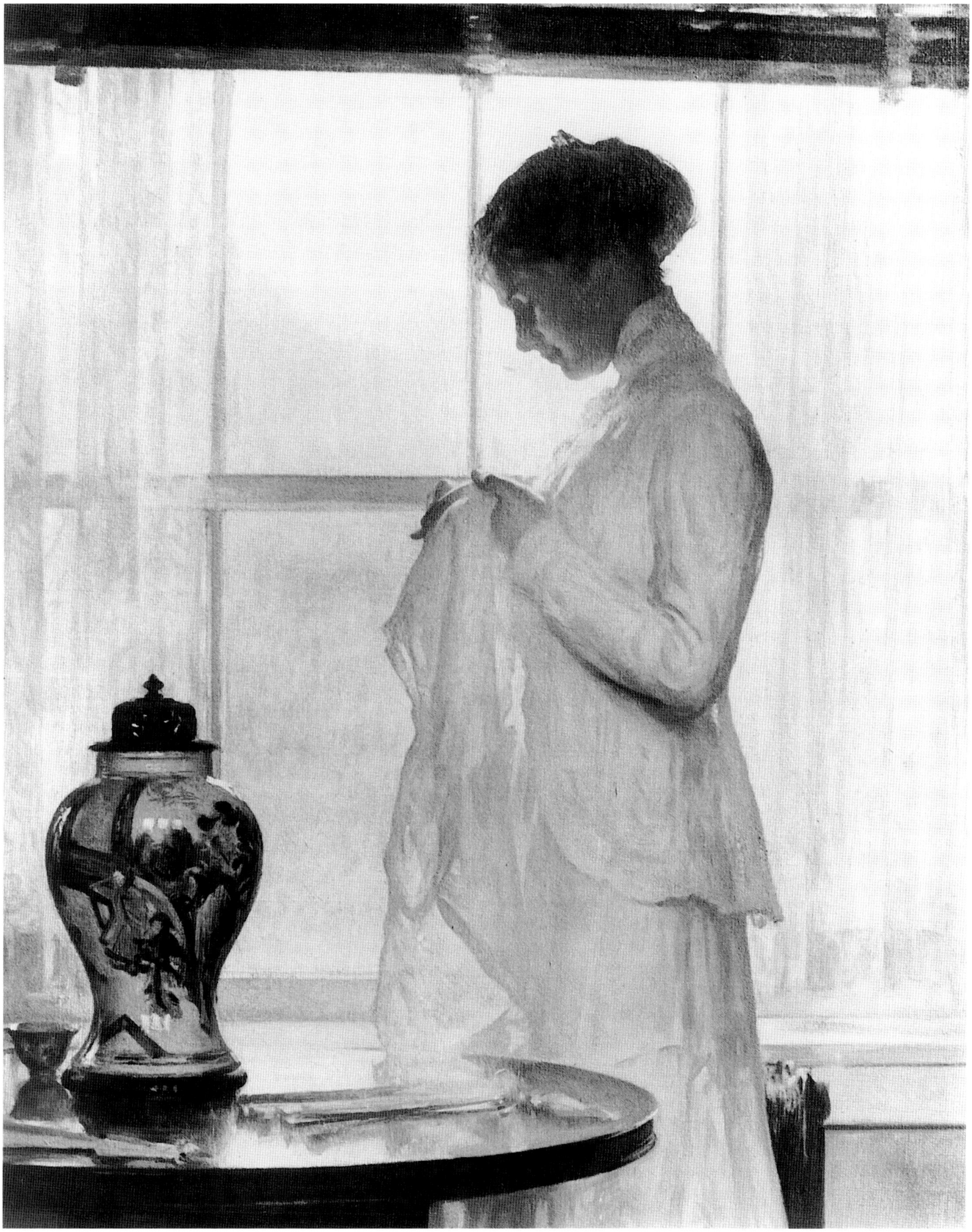

Fig. 71 *The Window*, ca. 1910. Dimensions unknown. Unlocated

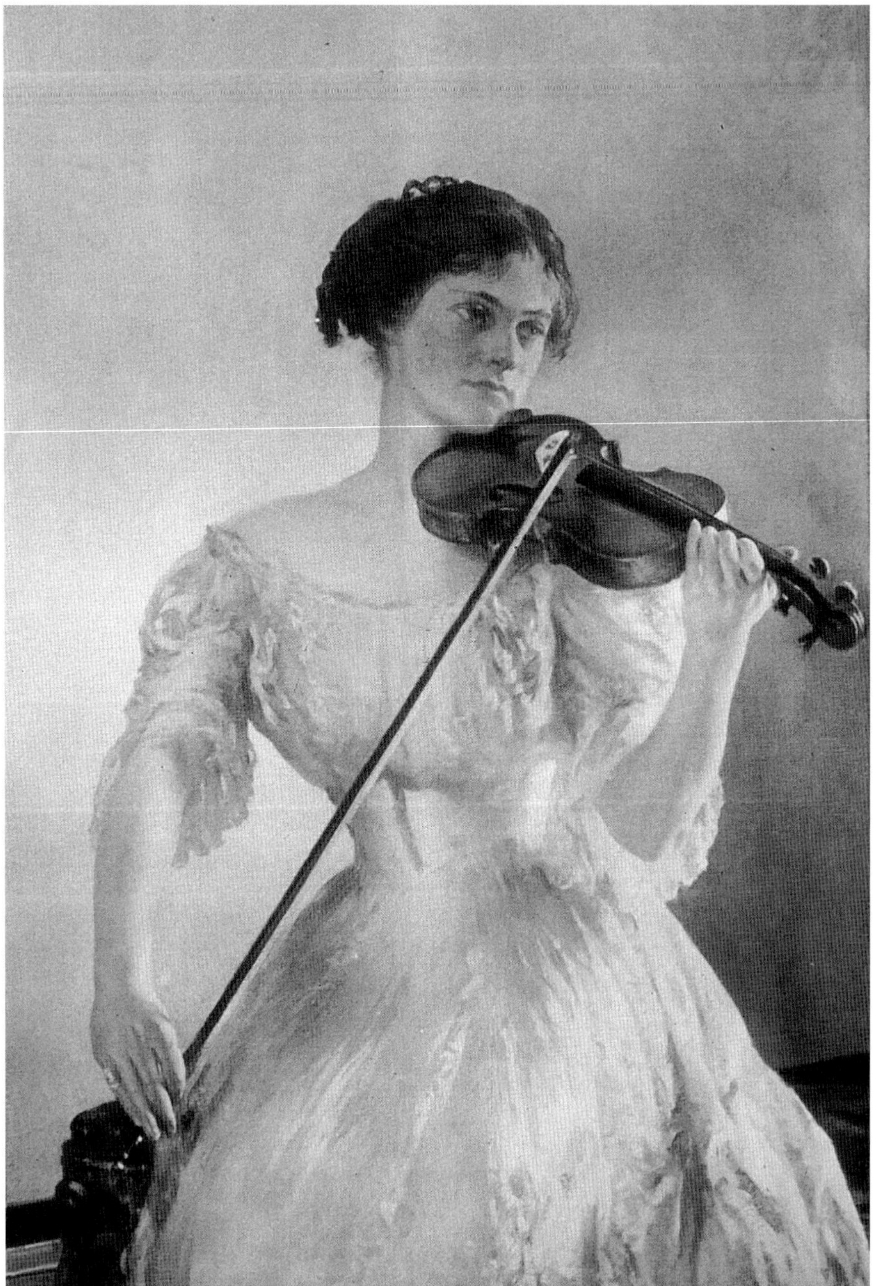

Fig. 72 *Girl with Violin (Violinist I)*, ca. 1912. Dimensions unknown. Unlocated

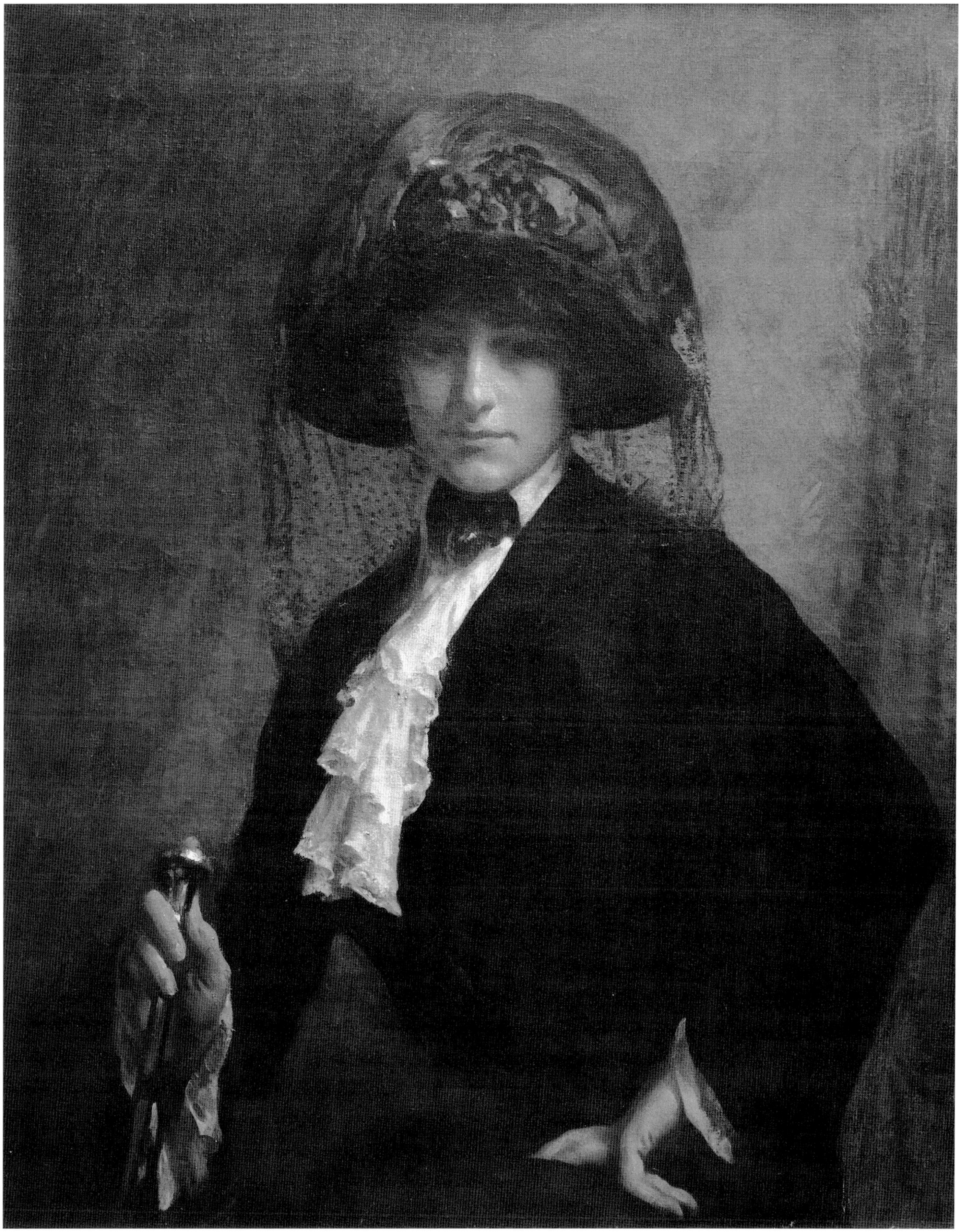

Fig. 73 *The Blue Veil (The Blue Lady)*, ca. 1913. 36 x 28 in. (91.5 x 71 cm). Walske-Longtine Collection

ine the portrait in its unity is to find that that unity has been too laboriously built up.... It is hot and hard where it ought to be suave and flexible. And the heat of the color, like the hardness of the artist's style, is the more distressing because of a sort of nerveless immobility marking the whole canvas.... It seems absurd that a picture so good as the 'Violinist' should not have been made infinitely better."[55]

The Blue Veil of around 1913 (fig. 73), a waist-length portrayal of a woman dressed to go out, is the closest DeCamp ever came to an image of a woman engaging in society at large. With one hand on hip, she grasps the handle of a parasol with the other. As in *The Pink Feather*, but with less success, the artist explores the difficulty of portraying a presence beneath the gauze-like covering. Veils, especially of the type worn by the woman here, were very much in fashion at the time. "Invariably the veil should harmonize with the color of the hat," pontificated a Philadelphia society writer. "If the hat is black, the veil is of the same color. For a brown hat it is a brown veil. But for a green hat it is not a green veil—remember that... it has no witchery; it is too significant of unripe apples and its attendant misery."[56] Presumably, a blue veil matched a blue hat, especially if it added a touch of "witchery" of the kind that one critic noted in connection with the sitter's blue eyes, which seemed to him "as if they might be dangerous to the peace of mind of the masculine part of the community."[57]

A note of sensuality appears in a number of DeCamp's works of 1911 to 1915; indeed, one picture executed around 1913 was actually titled *The Flirt* (plate 35). Again, reviews were not as favorable as they had been at the beginning of the artist's mature period, one writer even calling *The Flirt* "only superficially different" from the work of J. G. Brown,[58] whose highly finished paintings would, by this time, have been considered too "photographic." Most critics concentrated on the flush to the woman's face: The New York *Evening Post* reporter found it to be of a "peculiarly hot color," while his colleague on the *New York Times* saw the woman as a "little, red-faced, impudent lady."[59]

The Silver Waist (fig. 74), a profile view of a seated woman carefully examining a small blue and white vase, was awarded a gold medal when it was first put on display, in February 1915 at the Philadelphia Art Club's annual members' exhibition. Reviewing the eighteenth show of the Ten American Painters in New York the following month, Charles Caffin observed that the "rather unpleasantly brusque treatment of the costume" is forgotten in view of the "real expressiveness of the fingers": "They echo a certain serious feeling in the face, that one had been disposed to overlook in its general suggestion of merely wholesome comeliness. The impression, in fact, that remains with one is of more lasting pleasureableness than a first glance of the picture conveyed."[60] Clearly, Caffin saw the woman as the mistress of the house and he was impressed by her genteel manners. A charcoal sketch for *The Silver Waist* (private collection), in its emphasis on atmosphere and silhouetting, shows that DeCamp thought of the work initially as a study of light.

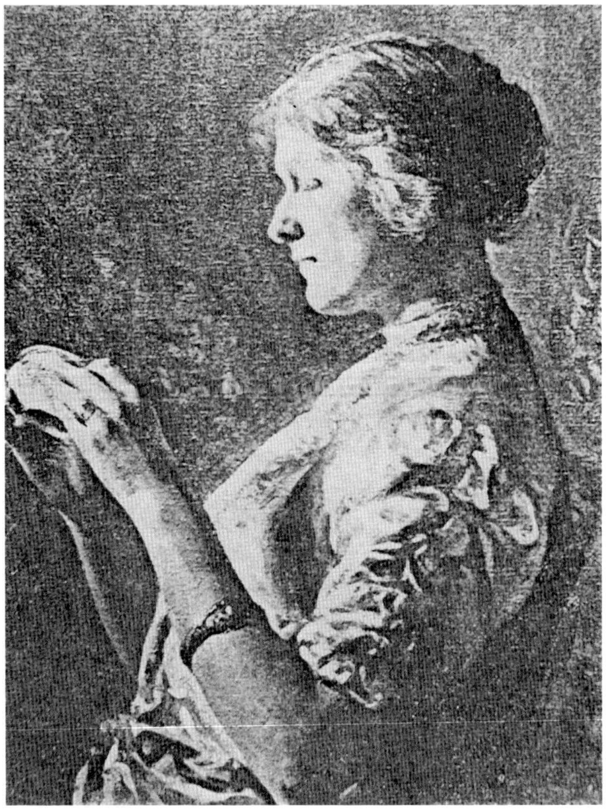

Fig. 74 *The Silver Waist*, ca. 1915. 30 x 25 in. (76 x 63.5 cm). Unlocated

The Reader (unlocated, fig. 75), first exhibited in 1917, is a far cry from DeCamp's earlier *A Girl with a Book*, in which the book is merely an accessory. Here the woman is as engrossed in her reading as the women had been in their musical activities in *The Guitar Player* and *The Cellist*. Set against a blank wall, she leans forward, one arm propped on the shiny table, apparently oblivious to the artist's keen gaze. This may be the first work by DeCamp for which "Reddy" Pearson sat; her flaming red hair would become a keynote in much of the artist's late work.

In nearly all these "portrait pictures" there is more than meets the eye. As noted by the critics of the day, DeCamp chose clothing, lighting, and postures carefully in order to experiment with ever new challenges to his finely tuned skills. The works are deceptively simple, each entailing a study in some element of pictorial representation—the delineation of fur, the depiction of flesh tones behind veils, the differentiation of various white textures, and so forth—that was calculated to enlarge the scope of his art.

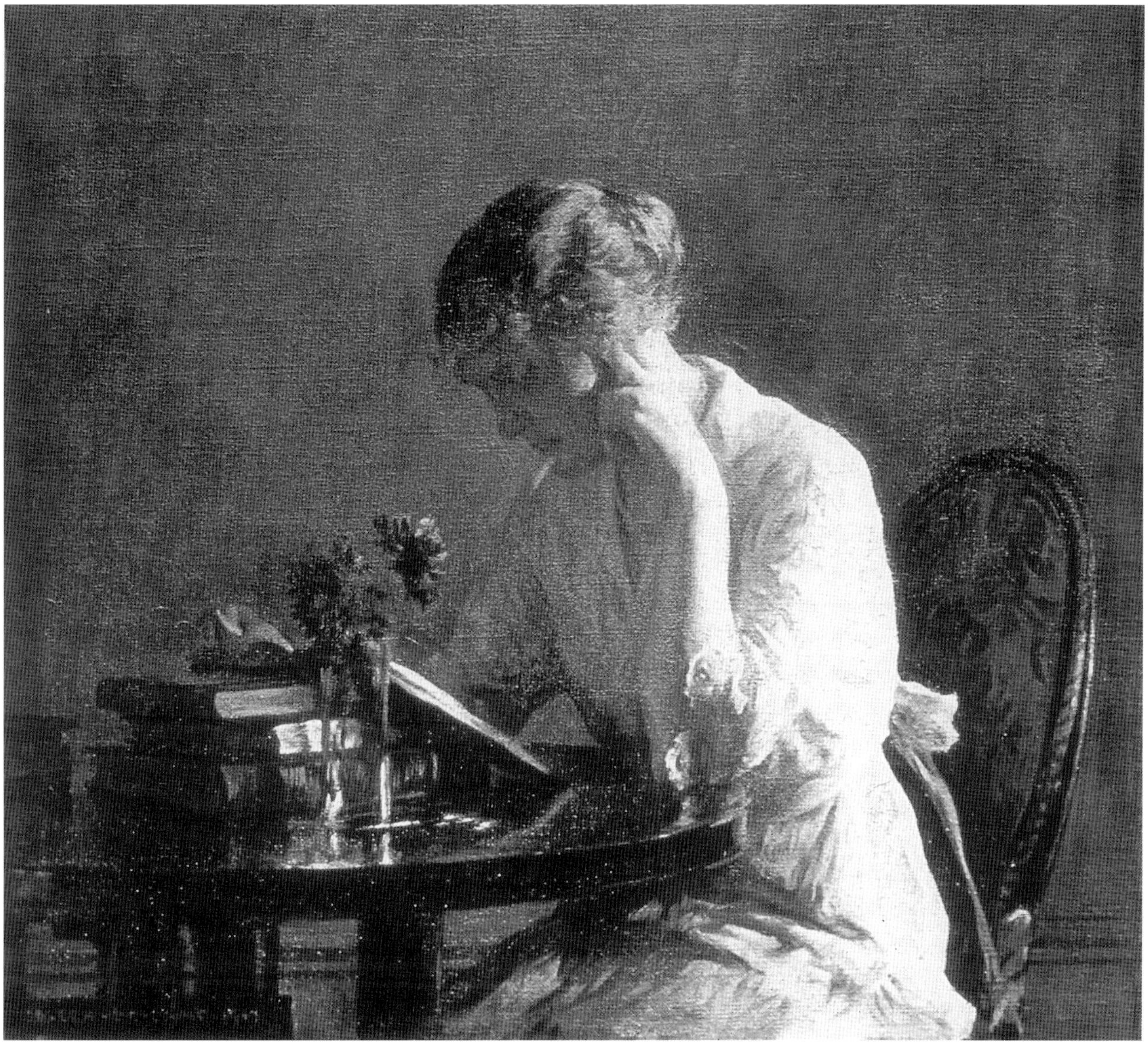

Fig. 75 *The Reader*, ca. 1917. 33 x 36 in. (84 x 91.5 cm). Unlocated

Notes

1 A.J. Philpott, "Portraits of Charm," *Boston Globe*, March 4, 1911, p. 5.

2 William R. Lester, "Figure Paintings and Portraits at Art Academy Exhibition Overshadow Landscape Pictures in Public Interest," *North American, Philadelphia*, January 26, 1908, sect. 3, p. 9.

3 Julie Anne Springer, "Art and the Feminine Muse: Women in Interiors by John White Alexander," *Woman's Art Journal* 6 (Fall 1985/Winter 1986), p. 1.

4 Paul D. Schweizer, "Genteel Taste at the National Academy of Design's Annual Exhibitions, 1891–1910," *American Art Review* 2 (July/August 1975), p. 77.

5 "The Seventh Annual Exhibit of American Art at Cincinnati," *Brush and Pencil* 6 (July 1900), p. 183.

6 "Art Notes," *Boston Herald*, January 29, 1905, women's sect., p. 2.

7 "Pictures of 'The Ten,'" *Evening Post*, March 20, 1901, p. 4.

8 "Around the Galleries," *Sun*, March 20, 1901, p. 6, and "The Art World," *Commercial Advertiser*, March 19, 1901, p. 6.

9 "Around the Galleries," p. 6.

10 "The Art World," p. 6.

11 "With Artists of Two Cities," *Philadelphia Inquirer*, February 22, 1903, sect. 1, p. 11.

12 "Ten American Painters," *New York Times*, April 1, 1905, p. 11.

13 Bram Dijkstra, *Idols of Perversity: Fantasies of Feminine Evil in Fin-de-Siècle Culture* (New York and Oxford: Oxford University Press, 1986), p. 139.

14 *Ibid.*, p. 135.

15 "Pictures Worth Hours of Study," *Detroit News Tribune*, December 16, 1906, sect. 2, p. 9.

16 John Nutting, "Ipsen's Pictures at Twentieth Century Club," *Boston Daily Advertiser*, January 20, 1908, p. 4.

17 "Opening of the Art Year in Boston," *Boston Daily Advertiser*, November 5, 1906, p. 4.

18 [Royal Cortissoz], "The Ten American Painters," *New-York Daily Tribune*, March 26, 1905, p. 7.

19 [Royal Cortissoz], "Art Exhibition," *New-York Daily Tribune*, March 19, 1904, p. 9.

20 My thanks go to Mrs. Ignatius Sargent, Sally's daughter, for this information. Although not a musician herself, Edith would often sit by the piano while her daughter played and did the same for her grandchildren.

21 Quoted in Harley Perkins, "Joseph DeCamp: Painter and Teacher," *Boston Evening Transcript*, February 13, 1923, sect. 1, p. 6.

22 A. Carson Simpson, Santa Fe, New Mexico, to Donald Moffat, March 6, 1956; Joseph DeCamp scrapbook, family of the artist.

23 "Ten American Painters," *New York Times*, March 15, 1906, p. 9; "In the World of Art," *Boston Daily Advertiser*, April 12, 1906, p. 4; and "Seven Paintings by Bostonians," *Boston Sunday Herald*, April 15, 1906, p. 4.

24 See "The Ten American Painters," *Independent* 60 (March 29, 1906), p. 7, and James B. Townsend, "Ten American Painters," *American Art News* 4 (March 17, 1906), p. 2.

25 Edith Burnham, "Portraits by DeCamp Here," *Boston Traveller*, February 21, 1911, p. 8.

26 Bernice Kramer Leader, "Antifeminism in the Paintings of the Boston School," *Arts Magazine* 56 (January 1982), pp. 112–19.

27 See [Philip L. Hale], *Vermeer*, Masters in Art: A Series of Illustrated Monographs 5 (Boston: Bates & Guild Co., 1904).

28 M. Elizabeth Boone, "Gilded Age Values and a Golden Age Painter: American Perceptions of Jan Vermeer," *Rutgers Art Review* 12/13 (1991–92), pp. 47–67.

29 Arthur Hoeber, "Ten American Painters," *Boston Evening Transcript*, March 20, 1908, p. 15.

30 Joseph Edgar Chamberlin, "The Tenth Year of the 'Ten,'" *Mail*, March 19, 1908, p. 6.

31 Spurred on by the Russo-Japanese War of 1904–05, many Bostonians, including the colorful Mrs. Jack Gardner, were in the thrall of *japonisme*. In 1906 Denman Ross gave to the Museum of Fine Arts, Boston, his collection of Japanese pottery, textiles, and prints (1,800 in all), which had previously been on loan to that institution.

32 "The Fine Arts," *Boston Evening Transcript*, January 30, 1908, p. 11.

33 Celia Betsky, "American Musical Paintings, 1865–1910," in *The Art of Music: American Paintings & Musical Instruments, 1770–1910*, exh. cat. (Clinton, N.Y.: Fred L. Emerson Gallery, Hamilton College, 1984), p. 52.

34 Arthur Hoeber, "Art and Artists," *Globe and Commercial Advertiser*, March 17, 1908, p. 6, and *idem*, "The Ten Americans," *International Studio* 35 (July 1908), p. xxv.

35 C[harles]. de K[ay]., "The Ten American Painters," *Evening Post*, March 20, 1908, p. 7.

36 Rose V. S. Berry, "Joseph DeCamp: Painter and Man," *American Magazine of Art* 14 (April 1923), p. 182.

37 "Old Argument Begun by 'Blue Boy,'" *Christian Science Monitor*, February 25, 1911, p. 7.

38 Hoeber, "Ten American Painters," p. 15.

39 Mary Elizabeth Lokay O'Leary, "'Bridget' In Service to the Boston School—1892–1921," in "At Beck and Call: The Representation of Domestic Servants in Nineteenth-Century American Painting," Ph. D. dissertation, University of Virginia, 1993, pp. 504–605.

40 "Art and Artists," *Globe and Commercial Advertiser*, March 18, 1909, p. 6. For other critiques of the painting, see Laurene Buckley, "Joseph DeCamp," in *Ten American Painters*, exh. cat. (New York: Spanierman Gallery, 1990), pp. 146–49.

41 O'Leary, "'Bridget' In Service," p. 579.

42 Harley Perkins, "Joseph DeCamp: The Man and the Artist, as Shown by His Works," *Boston Evening Transcript*, January 5, 1924, p. 8.

43 My thanks again to Mrs. Ignatius Sargent for this information.

44 I am grateful to Edith Harding for sharing this information with me, which has been confirmed by Tom Dunlay, a pupil of Ives Gammell and a member of a present-day group of realist painters centered around Boston that clearly has DeCamp as its source of influence. "Reddy" Pearson continued to serve Mrs. DeCamp after the artist's death, according to two letters from Edith to Joseph H. Gest, Director of the Cincinnati Art Museum (March 14 and 24, 1923; correspondence files, Cincinnati Art Museum).

45 L[eila]. M[echlin]., "The Paintings in the Pennsylvania Academy Exhibition," *Art and Progress* 1 (March 1910), p. 132.

46 Agnes Woodbury apparently sat for this picture, too (its alternative title is *Miss Agnes Woodbury*), in which a landscape—rare in these "portrait pictures"—appears in the background.

47 O'Leary, "'Bridget' In Service," p. 537.

48 "Seen in the World of Art," *Sun*, March 17, 1910, sect. 3, p. 4.

49 Arthur Hoeber, "Art and Artists," *Globe and Commercial Advertiser*, March 24, 1910, p. 10.

50 "Art Studios and Galleries," *Boston Sunday Herald*, February 26, 1911, p. 7.

51 J. Nilsen Laurvik, "The Ten American Painters," *Boston Evening Transcript*, March 23, 1911, p. 16.

52 Joseph DeCamp to C. Powell Minnigerode, Director, Corcoran Gallery of Art, Washington, D. C., November 1916; DeCamp files, Corcoran Gallery of Art.

53 J. N[ilsen]. L[aurvik]., "Ten Americans Going Stale," *Boston Evening Transcript*, March 23, 1912, p. 8.

54 "News and Notes of the Art World," *New York Times*, March 24, 1912, sect. 6, p. 15.

55 Royal Cortissoz, "Art Exhibitions," *New-York Daily Tribune*, March 20, 1912, p. 7.

56 "Veils," *North American, Philadelphia*, November 24, 1907, sect. 5, p. 7.

57 "Ten American Painters," *Boston Evening Transcript*, April 12, 1913, sect. 2, p. 3.

58 "'The Ten' Paintings of Usual Quality," *Sun*, March 22, 1914, p. 12.

59 "Art Notes," *Evening Post*, March 21, 1914, p. 14, and "Art Notes," *New York Times*, March 18, 1914, p. 10.

60 Charles H. Caffin, "'Ten American Painters' at the Knoedler Gallery," *New York American*, March 22, 1915, p. 9.

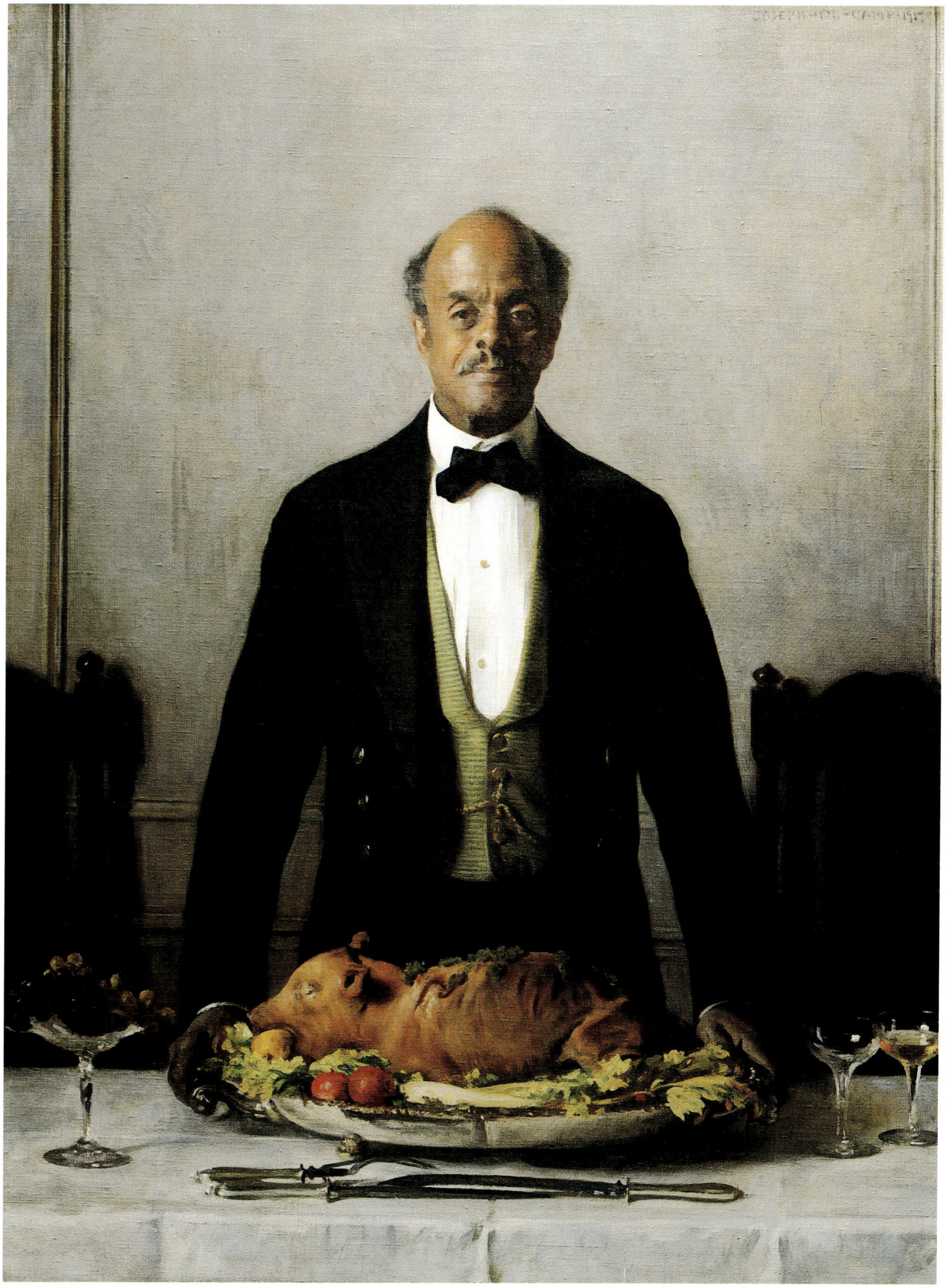

36 *The Steward (Lewis of the Porcellian)*, ca. 1919. 54 x 40 in. (137 x 101 cm). Private collection

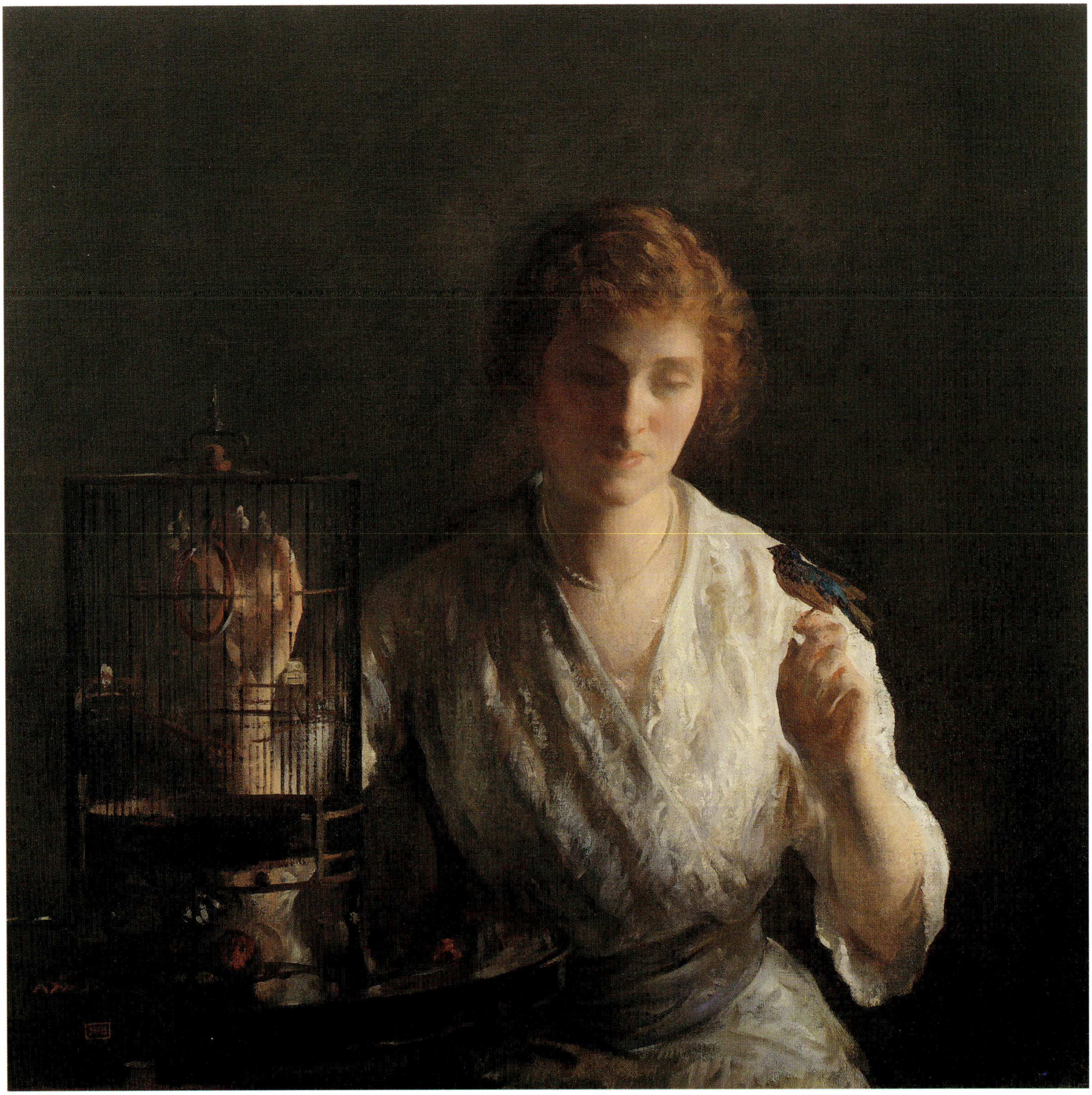

37 *Blue Bird*, ca. 1918. 32 x 32 in. (81.5 x 81.5 cm). Adelson Galleries, Inc., New York

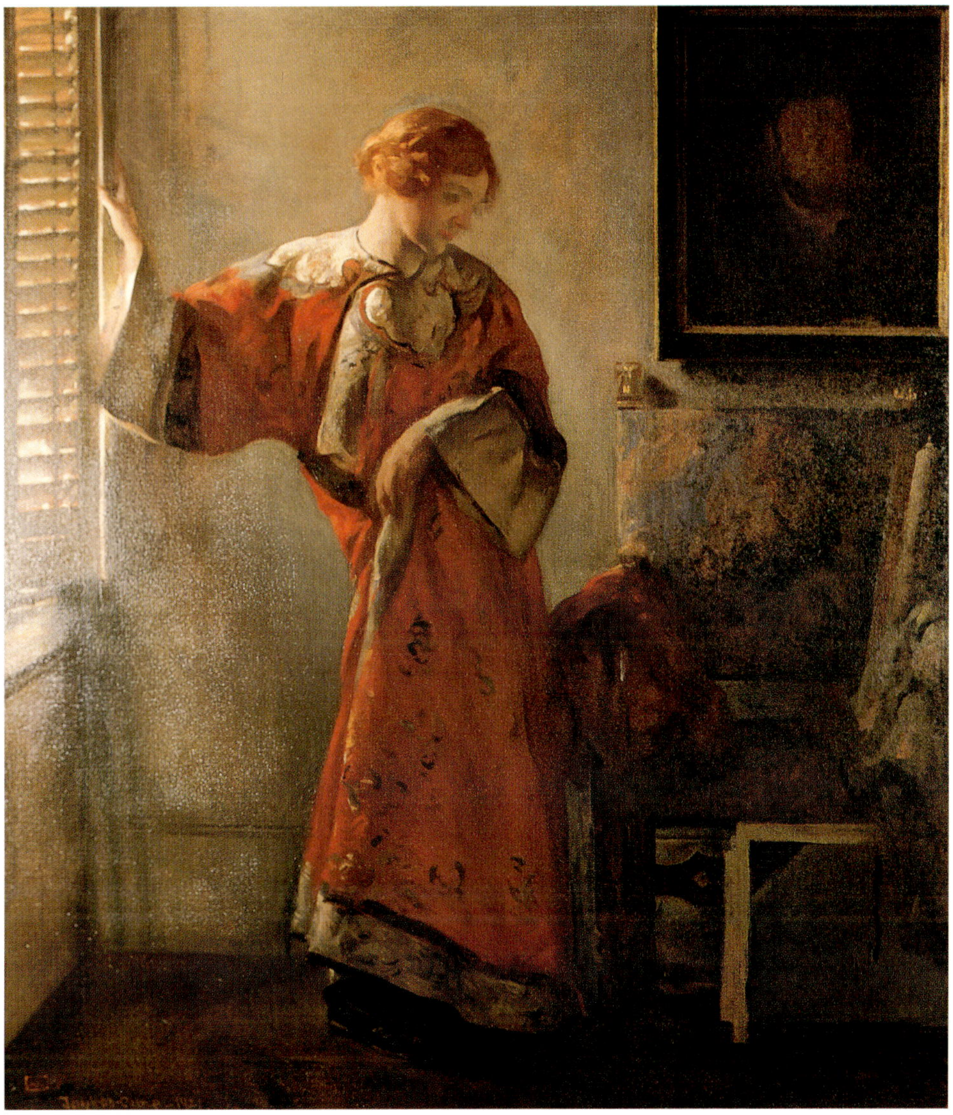

38 *The Window Blind*, 1921. 37½ x 32¾ in. (95 x 83 cm). Private collection

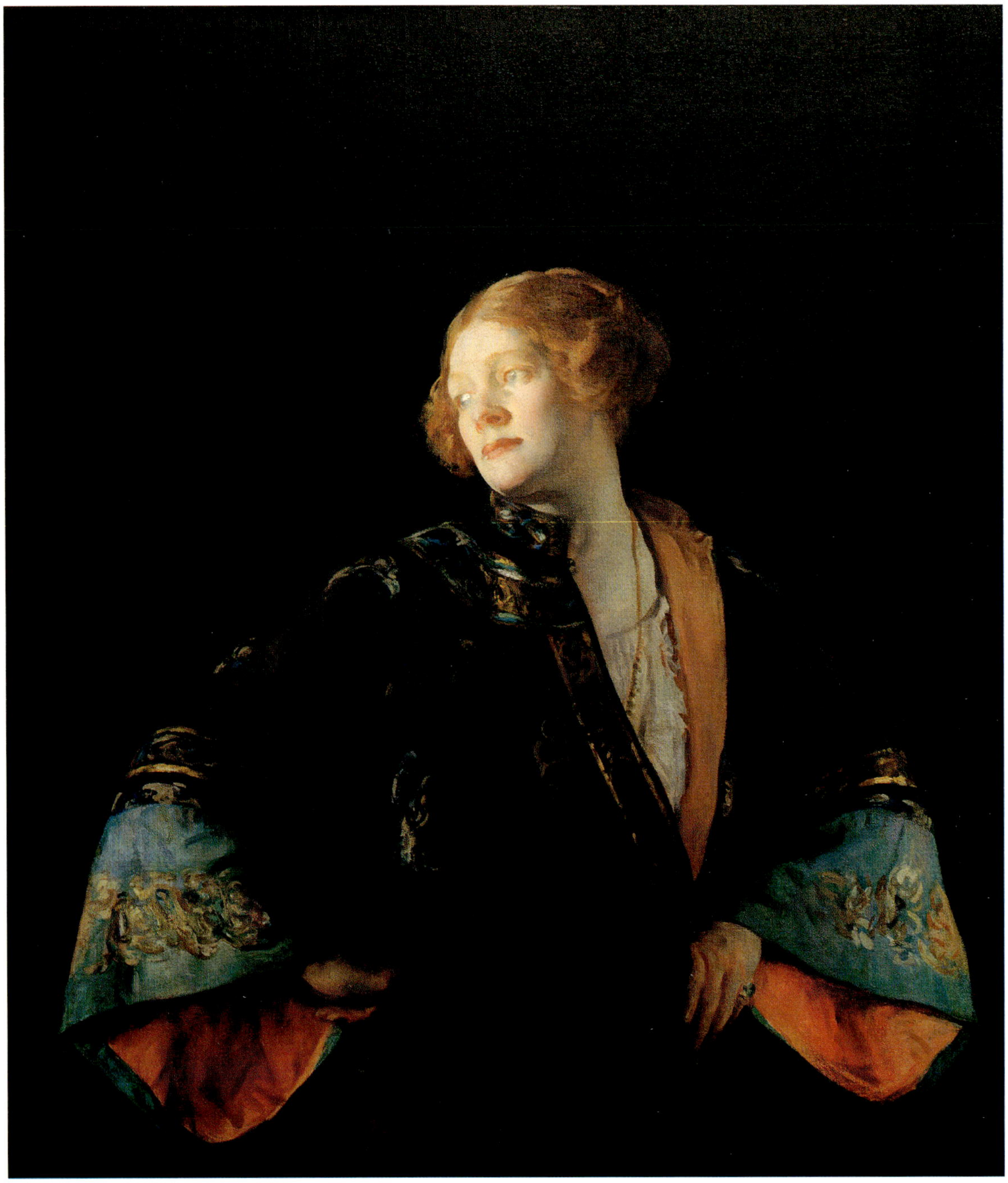

39 *The Blue Mandarin Coat* (*The Blue Kimono*), 1922. 43 x 37¼ in. (109 x 94.5 cm). Private collection

CHAPTER EIGHT

Last Years, 1918–1923

DeCamp's final years saw the culmination of his endeavors in his two main subjects—the formal portrait and the "portrait picture." His women, after being seen for many years through a veil of tonalism and diffused light, now emerged in crisp daylight and were attired in brilliantly colored oriental costumes.

The year 1918 was a key one in DeCamp's career. For the first time in twenty years, there was no showing of the Ten American Painters, no doubt because of the disruptions caused by World War I, which America had entered the previous year, but also perhaps because of the less than laudatory reviews that the artists had received for their 1917 exhibition. According to William Howe Downes, the Ten had "long since ceased to count for anything especial,"[1] and the reviewer for *Arts and Decoration* went even further: "We are back again amid painters like those of the Academy, whose brains or hearts have tired in the years. . . . The flame is flickering or going out. They have left for their personal enjoyment only the game of art, a set of rules and regulations, mechanical manners. The literature of life has never been of very wide scope to them. Tarbell and Benson and DeCamp were early in youth enchanted by Boston drawing rooms and have proved the possession of consistency by never straying far from this first love. We shall not quarrel with them about that."[2]

In spite of such criticism, one last show of the Ten was held, at the Corcoran Gallery of Art in Washington, D. C., in February 1919. Edmund C. Tarbell had moved to that city a year earlier in order to become the principal of the art school, and his associations with C. Powell Minnigerode, Director of the Corcoran, led to the exhibition at that gallery. Minnigerode wrote to DeCamp in early January, telling him that he was the only member still to consent to the show.[3] DeCamp wired back that he would "gladly do what the others think right"[4] and followed up with a letter stating that he had hoped to hear from the others before responding. He expressed agreement with "Mr. Metcalf's contention that it would be better to let the old cat die." "However," he continued, "I have always stood for the majority opinion of the group and mean to continue. If, as you say, the others think it wise, I shall gladly do what I can."[5] To this, Minnigerode responded: "We felt that the very active cat, at its prime and at the height of its power, should live, and continue to show the kittens how to paint."[6]

Nineteen eighteen was also the year of what should have been a crowning achievement for portrait artists in this country. Some of the finest—DeCamp, Tarbell, Cecilia Beaux, John C. Johansen, Douglas Volk, Irving Wiles, and others—were sent to Paris by members of a National Art Committee to record the faces of the signers of the Versailles Peace Treaty.[7] The expenses of this venture were covered by subscriptions from various art patrons in those cities where a traveling display of the works was eventually to be presented: New York City, at the Metropolitan Museum of Art; Providence, at the Rhode Island School of Design; Philadelphia, at the Pennsylvania Academy of the Fine Arts; Washington, D.C., at the National Gallery of Art; Boston, at the Museum of Fine Arts; Cleveland, at the Cleveland Museum of Art; Buffalo, at the Albright (now Albright-Knox) Art Gallery; and Detroit, at the Detroit Institute of Arts. The final repository for the portraits was to be a national portrait gallery in Washington, D. C.

In April 1919 DeCamp received a letter from the secretary and treasurer of the committee, Herbert L. Pratt, a Standard Oil magnate, asking for the artist's immediate assistance:

> In a cablegram just received from Hon. Henry White [United States Ambassador to France], who has been talking the matter over with John Sargent in Paris, he has suggested that you are the man to do the work of the group figures of the Peace Delegates as they sit at the Peace Conference at Versailles . . . . Our plan is to have such American portrait painters as Sargent, Cecilia Beaux, Johansen, Douglas Volk, Tarbell, Jane McLane, Irving Wiles, and yourself, do this work. . . . As but seven or eight people know of this National Art Committee, yourself being the only other artist beside Sargent who has any knowledge of the movement on foot, may I ask you to consider the contents of this letter strictly confidential and private?[8]

Soon after, the *Boston Evening Transcript* leaked news of DeCamp's departure: "Joseph DeCamp sailed at short notice for the other side of the Atlantic last Satur-

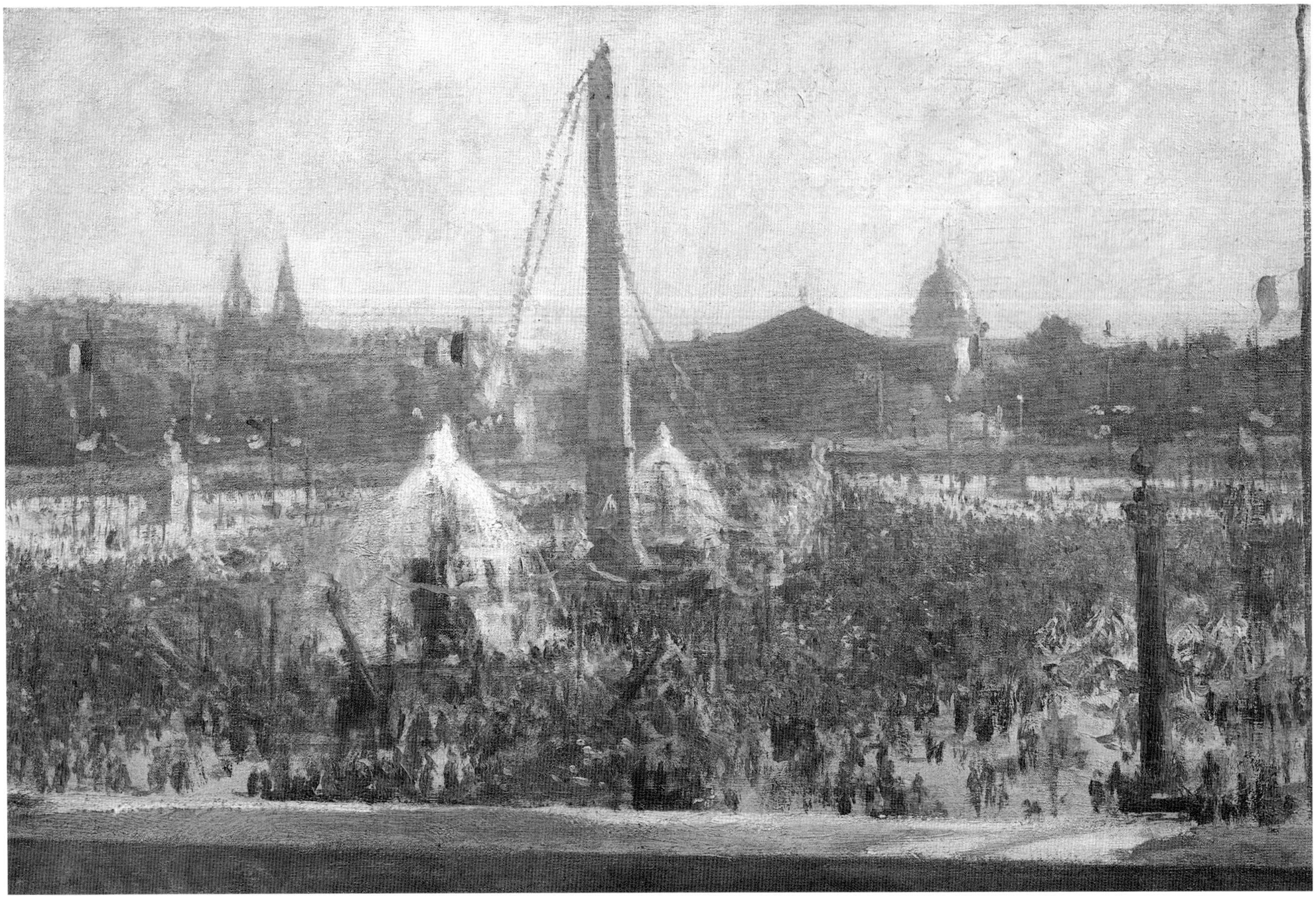

Fig. 76 *Paris, Place de la Concorde,* 1919. 16 x 23½ in. (40.5 x 59.5 cm). Private collection

day, in response to a 'hurry-up call,' the nature of which is not divulged—but one is at liberty to guess what it is. Somebody is to be portrayed, and it must be Somebody of great importance."[9]

In Paris was DeCamp's devoted follower Ives Gammell, who later described the visit: "DeCamp reached Paris in April. I happened to be on duty there myself at the moment and he naturally appreciated my familiarity with the resplendent capital he had only known as a transient visitor. The war was over and my military duties were nominal. I was therefore able to spend a good deal of time piloting my former mentor through the gradually reopening museums while he waited for the overworked statesmen to give him sittings."[10]

DeCamp was in Paris for Bastille Day, July 14, 1919, as evidenced by a view of the celebration at the Place de la Concorde, painted from his hotel window (fig. 76). The painting recalls the long, sweeping boulevard scenes executed by Claude Monet and Camille Pissarro decades earlier. DeCamp's inclusion of the window ledge of the Hotel de Crillon at the lower edge of the canvas may indicate that he intended this as a souvenir picture to document his presence at the festivities.

The artist never executed the mammoth painting that was to have been his most ambitious work in portraiture. Two unfinished studies and numerous drawings are all that remain of the undertaking. Both oil studies reveal the elaborate setting planned for the backdrop of the group, as well as the composition as a whole. Conceived in gradations of tones from white to black, the studies also serve to demonstrate DeCamp's method of laying in a composition in monochrome before applying color. Titled *The Council of Ten*, the more highly finished study (fig. 77) was not part of the national tour of the Versailles portraits, but was sent by DeCamp to four exhibitions, including one at the Pennsylvania Academy of the Fine Arts in 1922, where it was called "simply a valuable pictorial record of a great event, and not at all what the painter himself would have liked to make if he had a free hand and was responsible only to himself. Historical pictures are documents first, and works of art second, or third, or fourth."[11]

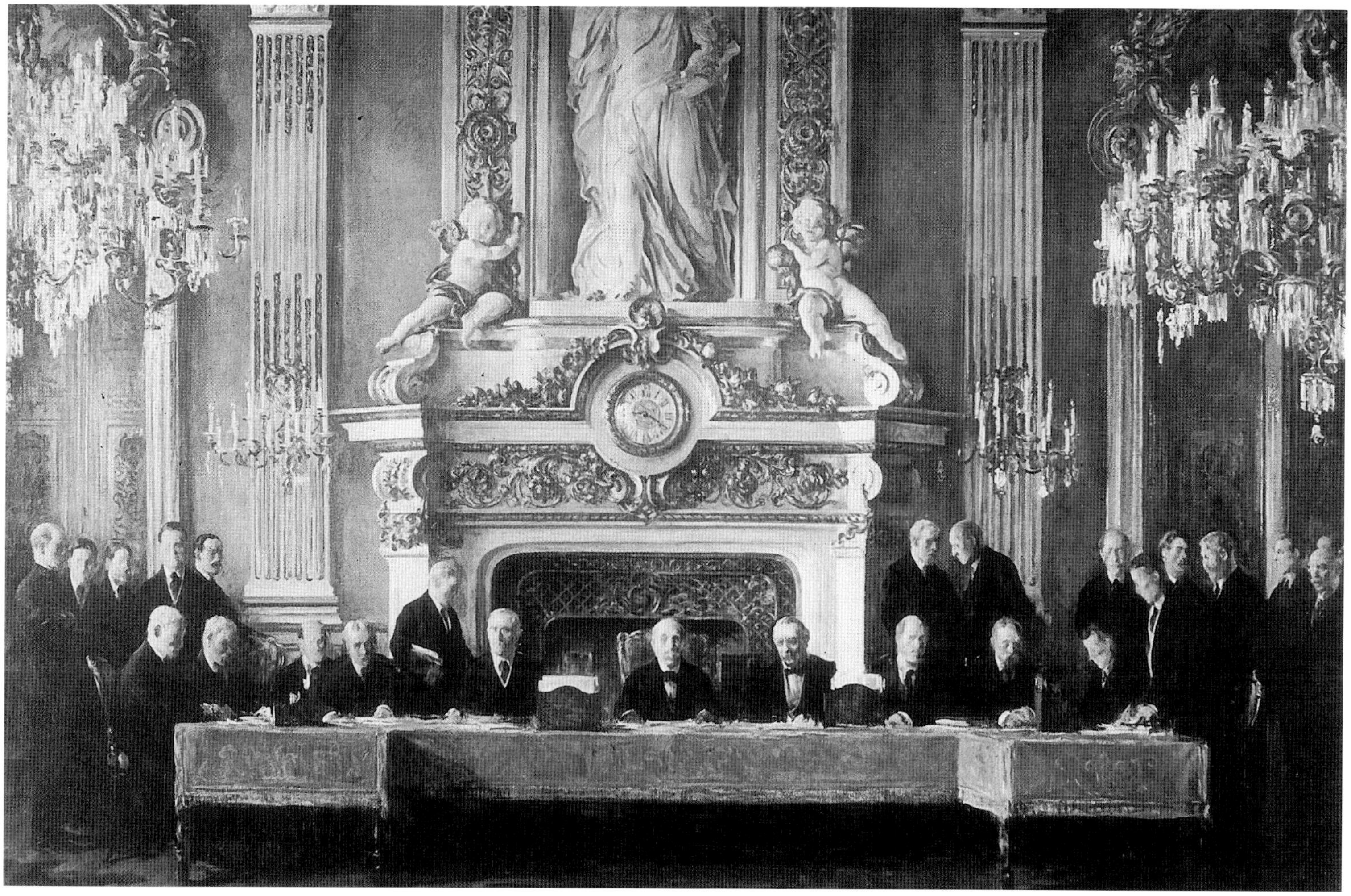

Fig. 77 *The Council of Ten* (*La Salle d'Horloge*), 1919. 48 x 72 in. (122 x 183 cm). Private collection

Two individual portraits resulted from the Versailles commission—those of Sir Robert Laird Borden, Prime Minister of Canada (fig. 78), and Sir Arthur William Currie, Commander of the Canadian Forces in France (fig. 79). Both were completed in 1920,[12] probably in Canada, and both belong to the informal, not heroic, style that characterized most of the portraits in the touring exhibition.[13]

The exhibition as a whole did not fare well with the critics. The reviewer for *American Art News* wrote: "The group is distinctly disappointing, so disappointing, in fact, that the wonder grows in studying the canvases that such able American portraitists as Miss Cecilia Beaux, Irving Wiles, Douglas Volk, Edmund C. Tarbell and even Joseph DeCamp should have so 'fallen down,' to use a colloquialism, in their productions ....'Premier Borden' and 'Gen. Currie' are serious, well painted half-lengths, admirably drawn and truthful likenesses, but neither are DeCamp."[14] A second critic found the portraits "sadly lacking" in inspiration, the result of their having been "painted to order."[15]

In 1918 DeCamp had painted the portrait of another high-ranking member of the military—Lt. Col. Paul Azan (fig. 80), Chief of the French Military Mission to Harvard University that year. Azan's full-length figure stands confidently against a backdrop of war clouds and a single, forlorn sprig of a tree. The work was unveiled at the Harvard Club in June, but DeCamp was unable to attend "due to illness."[16] Nineteen eighteen may, in fact, have marked the beginning of the artist's serious decline in health.[17]

The flow of portrait commissions continued unabated, however. Among the portraits executed in or about 1918 were those of Joseph Story, a copy after Charles Osgood's portrait of the former Chief Justice of the Supreme Court (Essex Institute, Salem, Massachusetts); Robert Archey Woods (Newton Theological School, Andover, Massachusetts);[18] and Lewis Parkhurst, a trustee of Dartmouth College (Hood Museum of Art, Dartmouth College, Hanover, New Hampshire).[19] The latter received the critics' usual plaudits for incisive characterization. "The seated figure, the head in full face with some shadow on the right side, carries a suggestion of mental and physical alertness

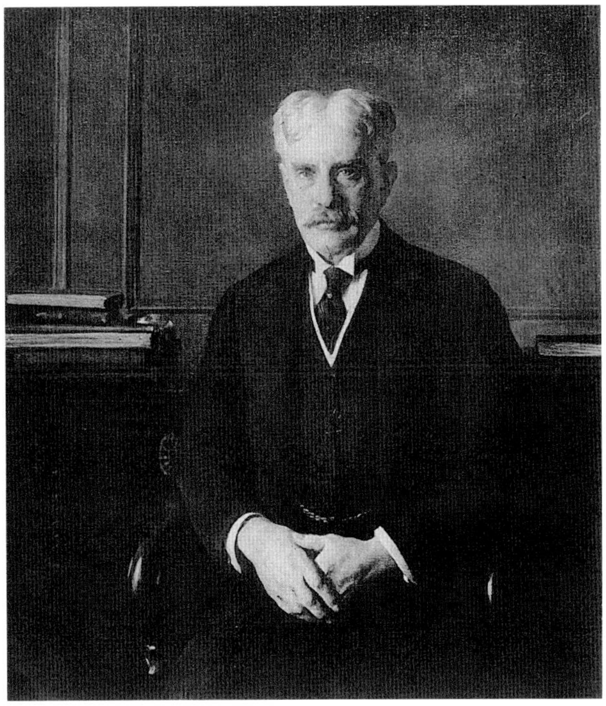

Fig. 78 *Sir Robert Laird Borden*, 1920. 44⅛ x 38⅛ in. (112 x 97 cm). Gift of the National Art Committee, National Museum of American Art, Smithsonian Institution, Washington, D.C.

that was surely intentional," wrote the reviewer for the *Boston Sunday Herald*.[20]

In 1919 the commissions included John King Lord, a trustee and professor of Latin at Dartmouth College (Hood Museum of Art, Dartmouth College, Hanover, New Hampshire);[21] Donald McKay Frost, a wealthy Boston lawyer and bibliophile (unlocated);[22] a pastel drawing of Peggy Wood (fig. 81),[23] and Edward Tuck, a banker of enormous wealth who eventually settled in a chateau in France surrounded by an art collection that may have included the tapestry shown in DeCamp's painting (fig. 82).[24]

The year 1920 saw not only the Borden and Currie portraits completed, but also those of DeCamp's son-in-law Alexander White Moffat as a naval officer (private collection); Eric Brown, Director of the National Gallery of Canada, Ottawa, a very painterly rendering in the style of John Singer Sargent, still owned by the gallery;[25] and the actor John Drew, a charcoal drawing now in the collection of the Players Club of New York. The following year brought commissioned portraits of, among others, Simon Flexner, a celebrated pathologist of the Rockefeller Institute;[26] Frederick Taylor Gates, a Congregational minister and a president of the Rockefeller Institute (both Rockefeller Institute for Medical Research, New York);[27] and Howard Clark Hollister, U.S. District Judge for Southern Ohio (U.S. District Court, Cincinnati).[28] The artist's last commissioned portrait, painted in 1922, was of Burton H. Wright, a businessman of Worcester, Massachusetts (State Mutual Life Assurance Company, Worcester).

These portraits of DeCamp's last years, displaying the loose, confident brushmarks of an artist who had worked in the genre for some twenty years, were rarely exhibited. Of the eighteen portraits executed from 1918 to 1922, only the Drew, Lord, Tuck, and, of course, the Borden and Currie pictures appeared in national shows. As a group, they display a certain perfunctoriness on the part of the artist, as though their chief purpose was to pay for the upkeep of two homes, servants, and a secretary/model. His more ambitious efforts at this time were clearly the interior scenes.

With few exceptions, DeCamp's last "portrait pictures" maintained his highest standards of excellence. "Reddy" Pearson was the model for all the remaining pictures, aside from *The Steward* of about 1919 (plate 36), for which George Washington Lewis, an

Fig. 79 *General Sir Arthur William Currie*, 1920. 44 x 38⅛ in. (112 x 97 cm). Gift of the National Art Committee, National Museum of American Art, Smithsonian Institution, Washington, D.C.

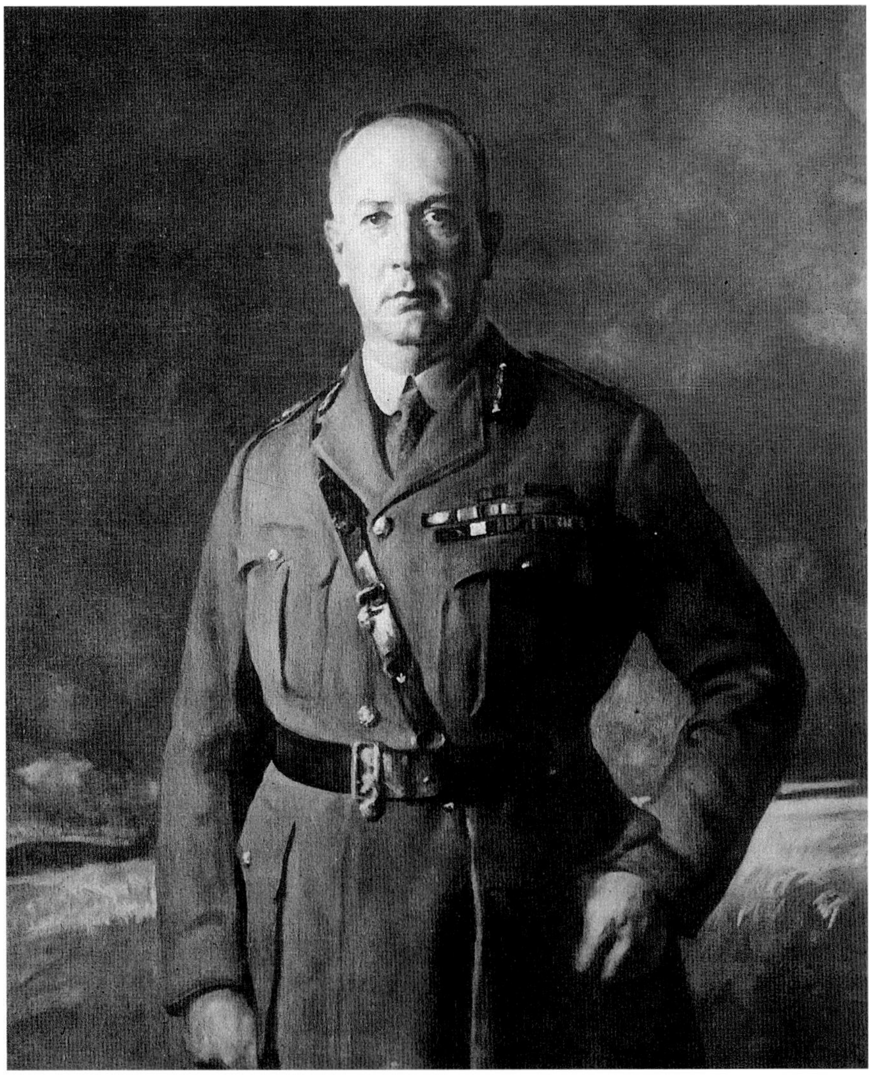

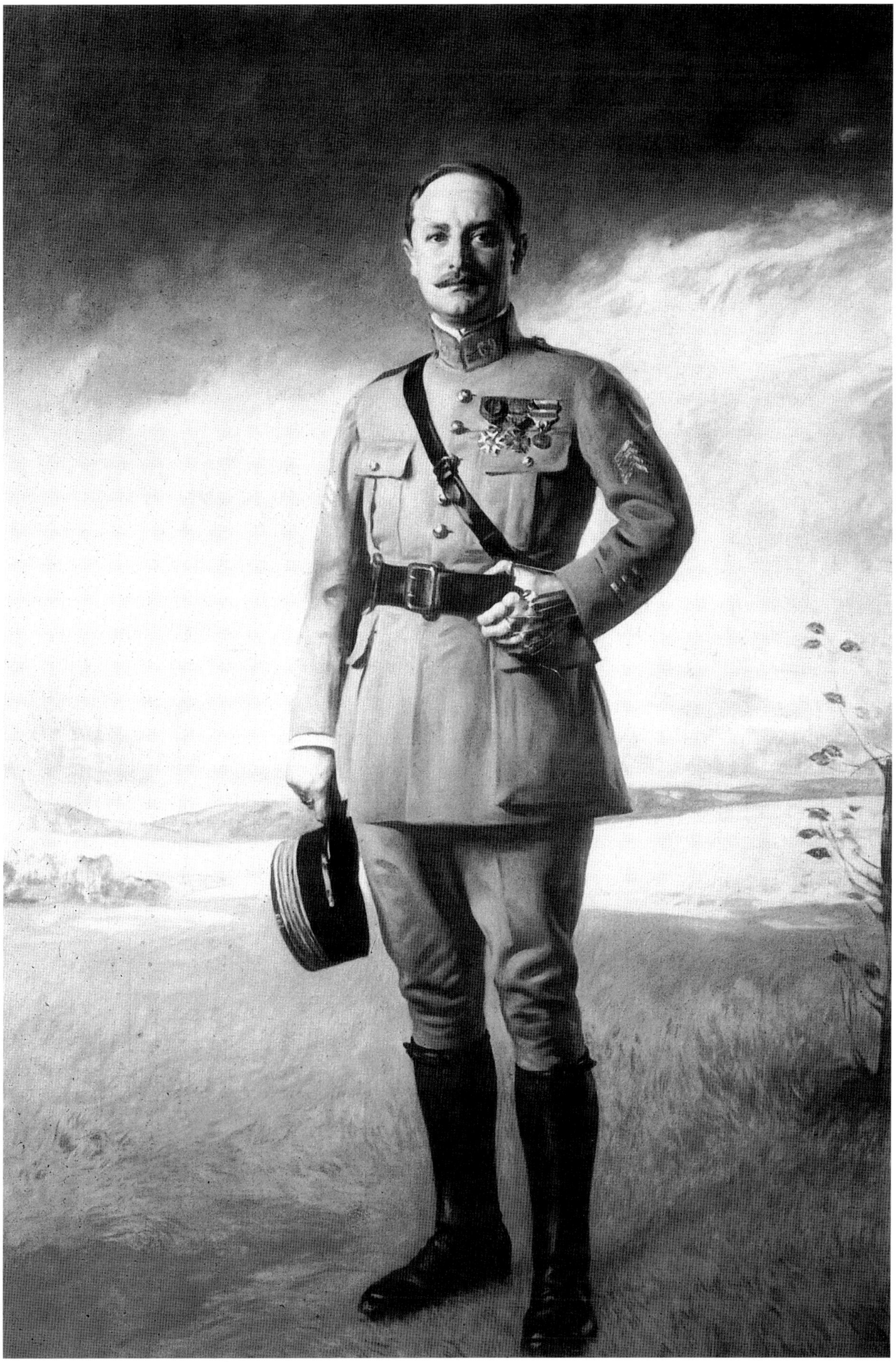

Fig. 80
Lieutenant Colonel Paul Azan,
1918.
93 x 57 in. (236 x 145 cm).
Private collection

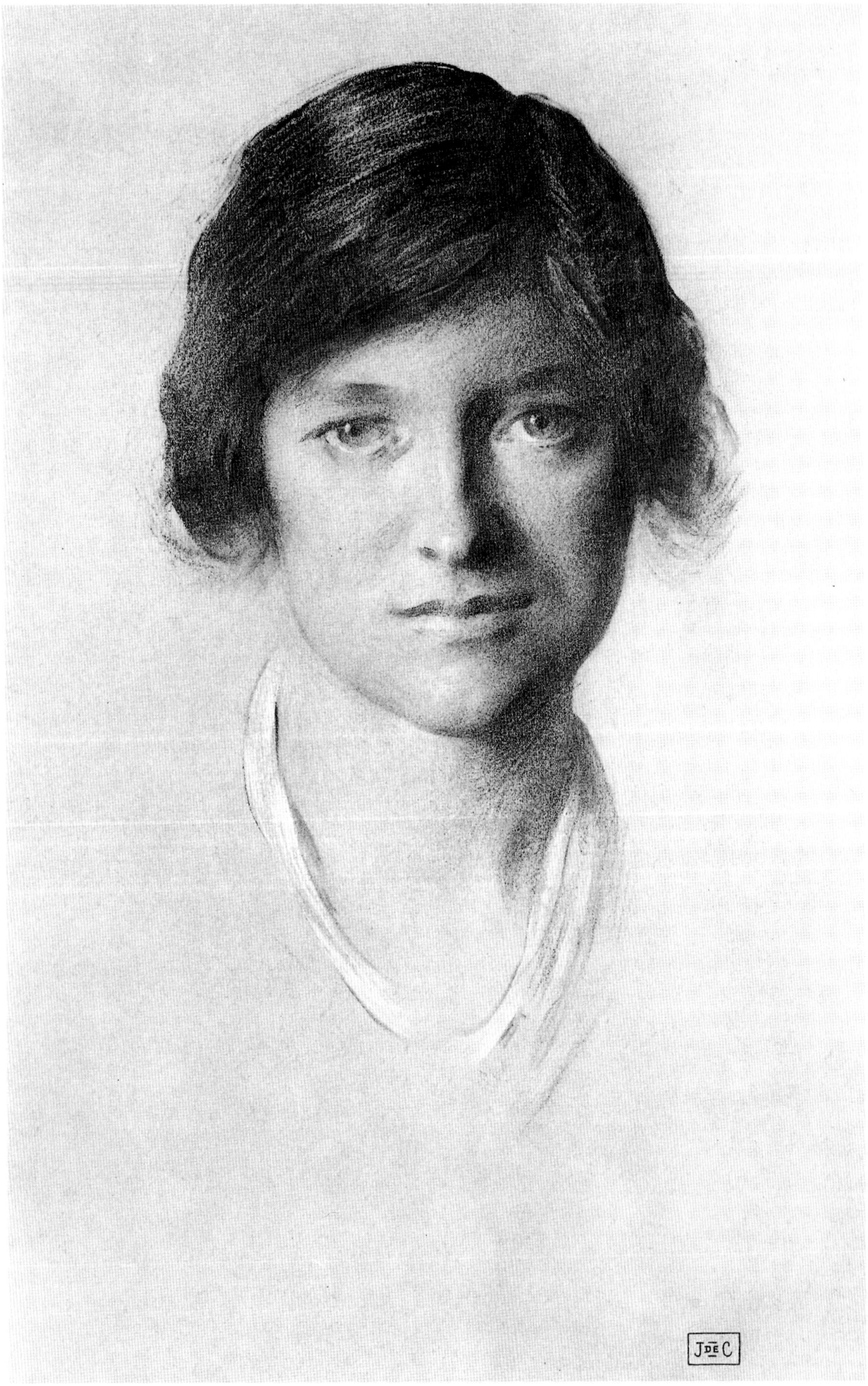

Fig. 81
Peggy Wood, ca. 1919.
Pencil and pastel on paper,
21 x 13½ in. (53.5 x 34.5 cm).
Collection of Susan and Herbert Adler

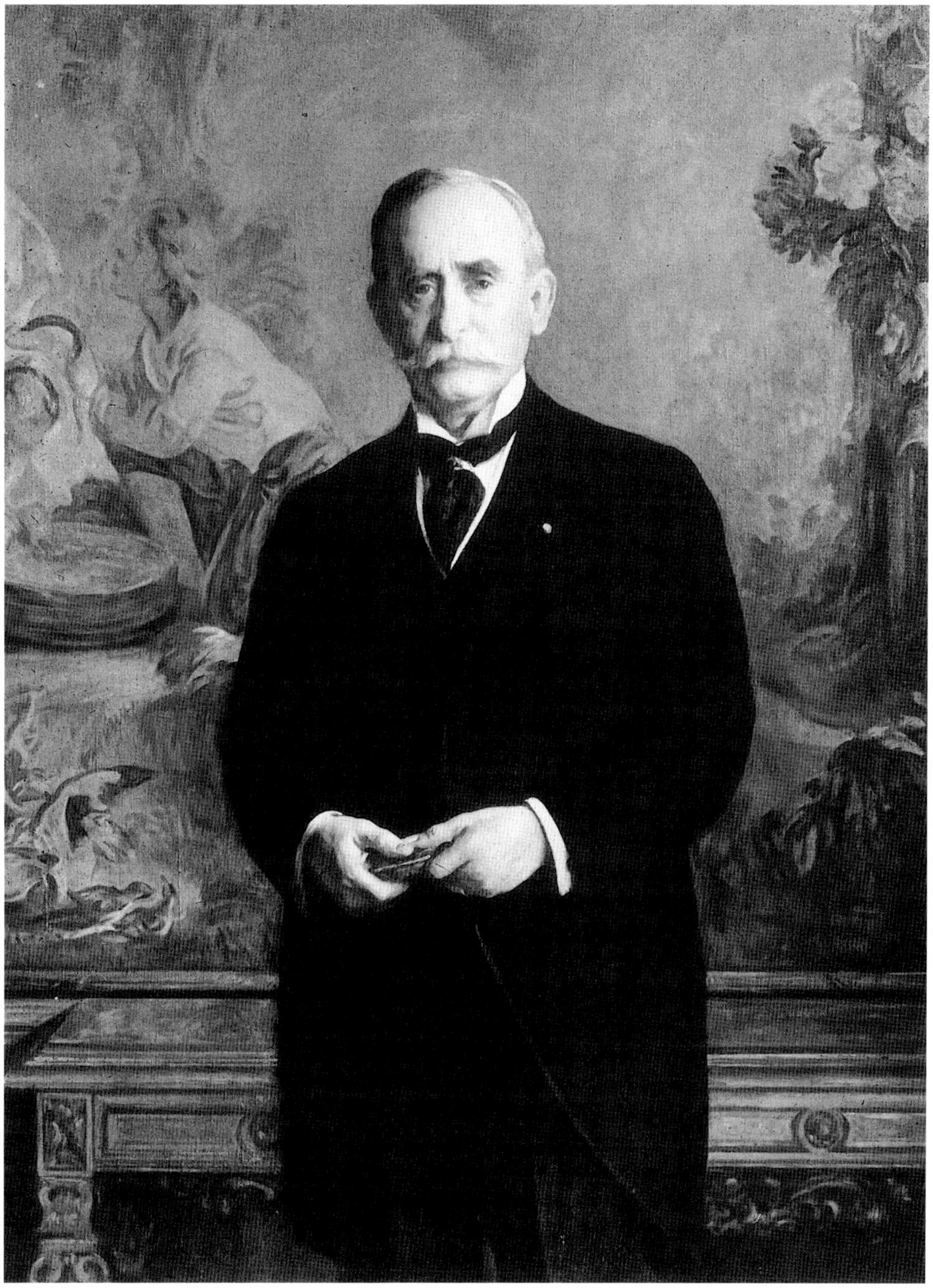

Fig. 82
Edward Tuck, 1919.
49½ x 40½ in.
(125.5 x 103 cm).
Hood Museum of Art,
Dartmouth College,
Hanover, New Hampshire;
Gift of Edward Tuck,
class of 1862

employee of Harvard's exclusive Porcellian Club, posed.[29] DeCamp succeeds in dignifying his sitter despite the scenario of a black servant presenting the main course of a meal to the viewer. According to Henry Louis Gates, Jr., African-Americans were rarely individualized in portraits until after 1940.[30] Rather, artists were apt to stereotype them as "grotesque buffoons, servile menials, comic entertainers, and threatening subhumans."[31] Only with the work of Winslow Homer and Thomas Eakins had an attempt been made to break with formulaic precedents in images of the African-American. DeCamp's warm and sympathetic character portrayal of Lewis clearly stands as another prime example.

Yet DeCamp might be said to have followed many of his fellow artists in producing paintings that enshrine another stereotype—the association of women with what Bram Dijkstra calls "caged creatures," such as goldfish and birds.[32] Dijkstra notes that images using this disparaging analogy were particularly numerous in the early years of the century and explains them as representations of women trapped in domestic interiors, unable to partake of the world beyond rearing children and maintaining the home. Here too, however, DeCamp breaks with tradition. In *Blue Bird* of about 1918 (plate 37) he places the figure next to an empty bird cage, with the freed creature perched on a finger of her hand—hardly the image of a trapped woman.

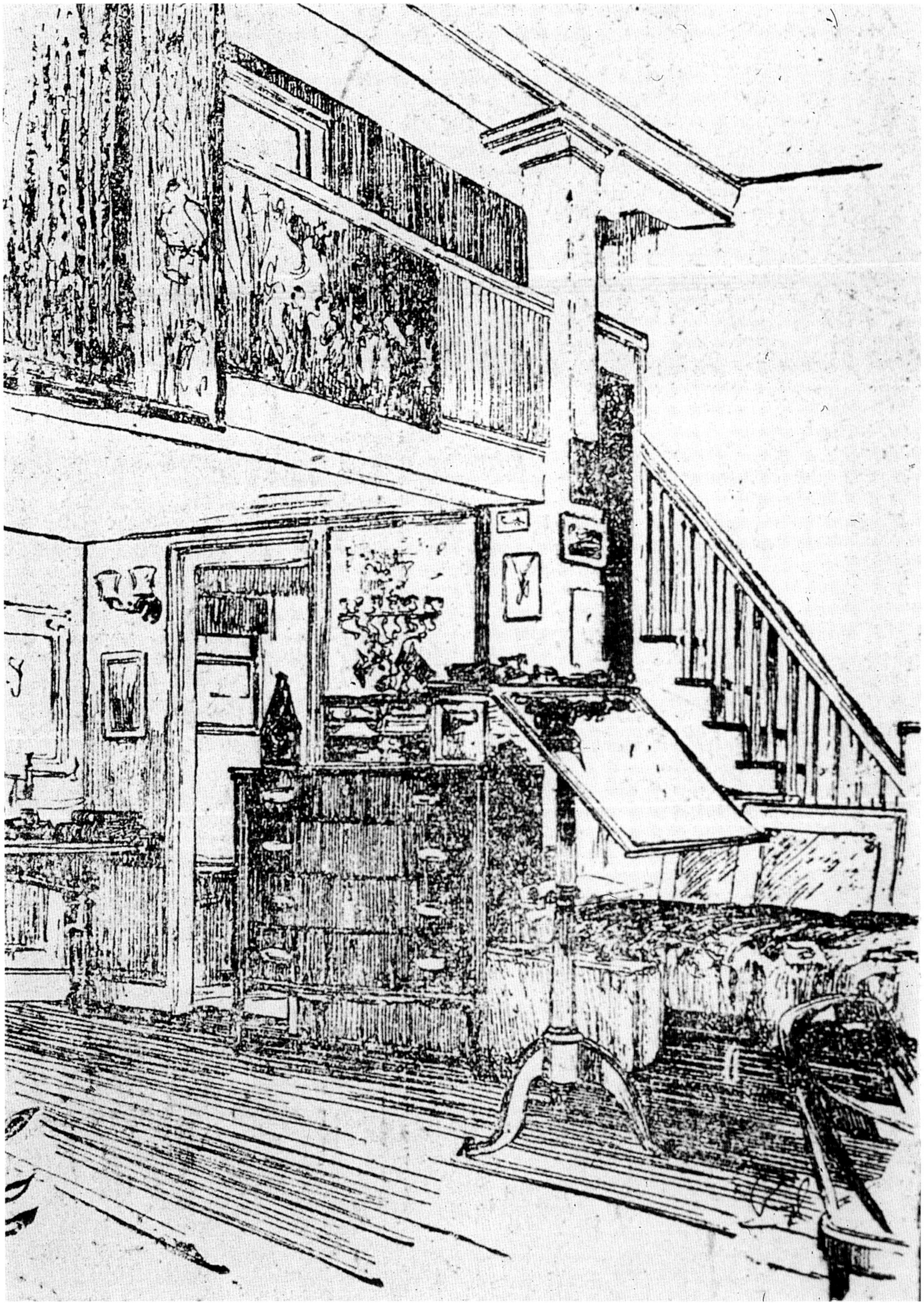

Fig. 83 The artist's Fenway studio, Boston. From *Boston Sunday Herald*, March 1, 1914

The choice of a blue bird may relate to the popularity at this time of Maurice Maeterlinck's play *L'Oiseau bleu* (1908), in which the blue bird possesses curative powers.[33]

The cage is also empty in *Red Kimono* of around 1919 (fig. 85), in which model "Reddy" Pearson again watches over the tiny bird, this time perched on the edge of a shallow glass dish of water. Bernice Leader examines this painting with a feminist approach similar to Dijkstra's; for Leader, the bird is a metaphor of the woman's limited freedom: "The bird's gilded cage perhaps symbolizes that the price of comfort for the leisure class woman is often domestic confinement. She is protected from the bustling city below, which is visible through the large window in the background and is contrasted with the secluded interior. That the woman is sadly aware of her loss of freedom is indicated by her slack, resigned pose and melancholy expression."[34]

DeCamp can scarcely have intended to convey such meanings. Certainly, no corresponding statements by him have survived and contemporary press reports are silent on the matter. It seems more likely that the artist was presenting women, not as trapped individuals, but as icons of beauty, juxtaposing them with other beautiful "objects" in quiet, aesthetically refined surroundings. The bowl in *Red Kimono* holds flowering narcissus bulbs, named for the egocentric youth of Greek mythology—an appropriate underscoring of the private world depicted in the painting. The nurturing of bulbs—then as now, a popular way of gardening indoors in the winter—was a feature of the oriental way of life. Virtually all DeCamp's last "portrait pictures" bear witness to the artist's fascination with the Orient: exquisite, colorful kimonos, for example, now became the costume of choice in which to clothe his models.

The wintry backdrop in *Red Kimono* would seem to be a view from the window of the artist's Boston studio at the time, at 120 Riverway, where he worked from 1916 until his death. After the 1904 Harcourt Street fire, DeCamp had moved his studio to 336 Boylston for a short time, but soon he settled in at the St. Botolph Studios, staying there from 1906 to 1910. The Fenway was a much heralded workshop for artists and it was here that DeCamp painted from 1911 to 1915, his studio being one of those illustrated (fig. 83) and described in a *Boston Sunday Herald* article of 1914: "DeCamp's skillful, vigorous portraits of well known men stand about the studio; an unfinished one is on the easel, with model stand and palet [*sic*] table in place for work. A Chinese hanging, a few Japanese prints and a few reproductions of old masters, some collected treasure, on the top of an old chest of drawers and a paintable, comfortable couch give charm to his workshop."[35]

Red Kimono was first shown at the 1919 Corcoran exhibition of the Ten American Painters, and subsequently was entered in ten other shows, including the Pennsylvania Academy of the Fine Arts annual of 1920, at which it won the Walter Lippincott Prize. The writer for *Academy Notes*, reviewing the picture when it was shown at the Albright Art Gallery in Buffalo, New York, in 1919, perceptively noted the brilliant coloration as "a new departure for the artist."[36]

This intensified color scheme also characterizes *Red and Gold* (private collection) and *The Window Blind* (plate 38), both of 1921, which show the same model ("Reddy" Pearson) and the same costume as *Red Kimono*. When exhibited at the Cincinnati Art Academy annual of 1922, *The Window Blind* was called an "interesting study of light."[37] Indeed, DeCamp had now returned for the last time to the Vermeeresque treatment of light, with a soft glow cast over the outline of the figure, her dress, the picture frame, and the upholstered chair to her left. The use of blinds to regulate the illumination of an interior harks back to Tarbell's series earlier in the century, but the full-length standing figure, quietly posed within a shallow interior space, recalls similar work by Frank W. Benson, such as *Figure in a Room* (New Britain Museum of American Art, Connecticut).

In October 1922 DeCamp underwent two operations at Boston's Massachusetts General Hospital. Family accounts differ on the cause of illness, but all agree that the artist finally succumbed to peritonitis, an inflammation of the membrane that lines the abdominal wall.[38] A last series of letters was exchanged between the DeCamps and Joseph H. Gest, director of the Cincinnati Art Academy. Edith alerted their friend to her husband's condition in November:

> I know that you will rejoice with us all to know that we brought Mr. DeCamp home from the hospital last Saturday. He is so happy to be at home and tho' he is pitifully weak still—he is coming back. We must be very patient and realize that he really practically died and has come back. Of course you know that he had two severe operations. Three blood transfusions—pneumonia and finally an abcess under his wound that is still being drained. The doctors say he is a perfect marvel but I have lived with him so long and know his endless courage and vitality and tho' I lost courage a bit when he was blind from loss of blood I really felt all the time that we couldn't let him go.... Mr. DeCamp is much interested to know whether the blood of three young medical students who gave their blood to him will alter his style![39]

Perhaps to promote the artist's recovery, Gest apparently asked him to be a visiting critic at the academy at some point in the future. DeCamp was able to respond in a legible hand in late January:

> Thank you for your letter of kind wishes. You have given me a good many important things to think about and in my still crippled condition, being as yet unable to write, I shall need a little time. Apparently my nerves had a considerable shock and I am being sent in a few days to Florida, in the hopes that a trip to a warmer climate will hasten my full recovery. The question of my making an occasional visit to Cincinnati is easy enough to settle, but to find a young and capable man to send to you is not so easy. I am feeling as well and cheerful as anyone could, and when my nerves coordinate as well as my

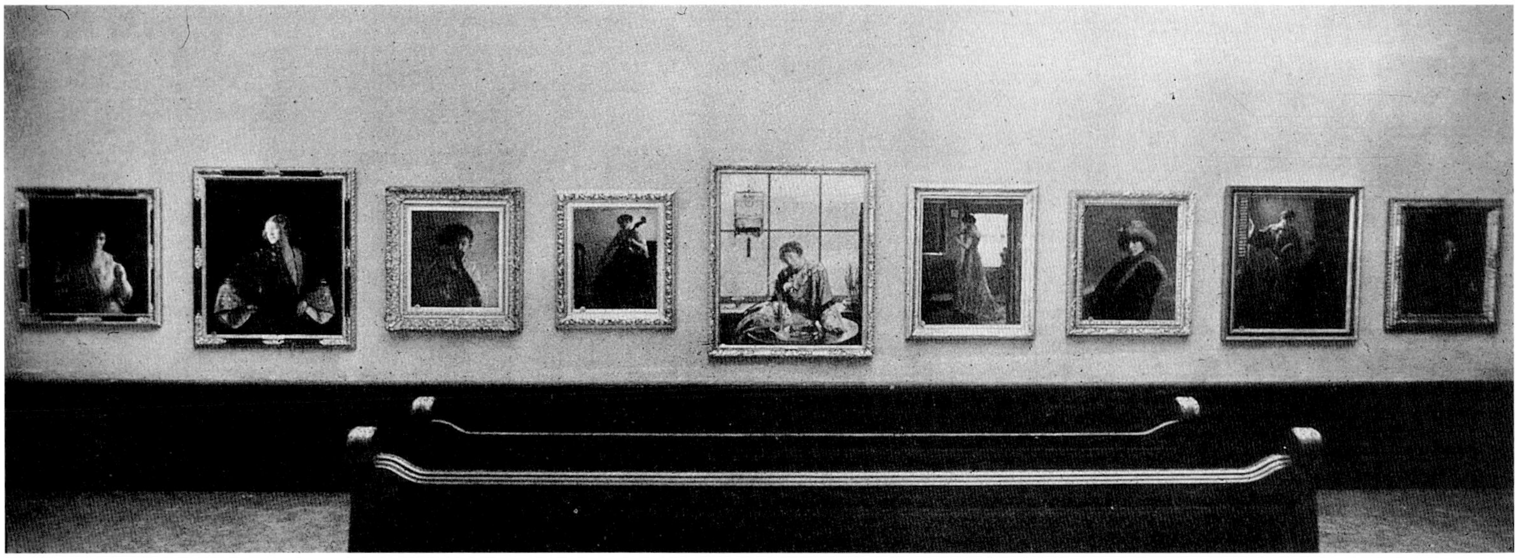

Fig. 84 View of the artist's memorial exhibition at the Albright (now Albright-Knox) Art Gallery, Buffalo, New York, 1924

digestion I shall be entirely happy. The various blood transfusions, as yet have shown no Cubist tendency.[40]

Soon after, DeCamp was taken by his daughter Sally and her husband to Boca Raton, Florida. In an age without antibiotics, however, his condition worsened, and he died on February 11, 1923. A memorial wreath was immediately placed beneath DeCamp's last painting, *The Blue Mandarin Coat* (plate 39), then hanging in the annual show of the Pennsylvania Academy of the Fine Arts. Unlike in the earlier kimono pictures, DeCamp focused on just the upper torso of the model, celebrating perhaps as never before the penetration of light into the scene—through the garment and the figure itself—even detailing the light coming through her nostrils and ear lobes. Rose V. S. Berry, after describing the painting in detail, concluded:

> As the attention of the observer returns to the head in the interesting survey it is notable that the predominating keynote is the red-gold, the hair, the eyebrows, the lips, the yellow inside of the coat, and more than all else the illuminating light which transforms the face into something indescribably fascinating. There is tenderness, resignation, and a consuming sadness expressed in the eyes which seek in pitiful appeal something from the impenetrable beyond. Some way she will always be associated in her sweetness with the funereal wreath which has been hung beneath her frame. And again the whole is perfect; there is not one discordant note in the brown, bronzed leaves of the wreath, and the formal, purple, velvet bow, which tells without words that DeCamp's "last picture is painted."[41]

Although the newspapers immediately pronounced the need for a memorial exhibition for DeCamp, it would be almost another year before such a show was organized. Appropriately, it opened at the St. Botolph Club in Boston, where DeCamp had spent so many hours. The display of fifty pictures (see p. 155) offered many reviewers a chance to see a full range of the artist's works for the first time. "Particular interest will be attached," wrote Harley Perkins, "to several early works [he mentions *Italian Girl* and 'a landscape made in Italy' (*Venetian Boat Yard*)] which will be a revelation to many who are more familiar with the later canvases such as won honors in contemporary exhibitions of American art."[42] "There are large numbers of younger men and women who have benefited by his periods of teaching at the Museum of Fine Arts School and the Massachusetts Normal Art School," Perkins stated in a later article, "and who will welcome the opportunity to obtain a glimpse of works which featured some time ago in local exhibitions, and have lately passed into museum and private collections in other parts of the country."[43]

In April the show, now comprising a mere dozen exhibits, traveled to the Albright Art Gallery in Buffalo, New York, where it shared billing with works by the expatriate James Shannon, who had also died in 1923. An installation photograph of the display, highlighting *Red Kimono*, appeared in the gallery's *Academy Notes* of July–December 1924 (fig. 84).[44] Further reduced to ten pictures when shown at the Memorial Art Gallery in Rochester in the summer of 1924, the exhibition provided at least one critic with the opportunity to compare the work of Shannon and DeCamp. "DeCamp is a more solid painter than Shannon, with excellent effects of light and shade. His figures have mass as well as form and are perfect foils for the pretty Shannon women hung around them."[45] Once again, DeCamp's works were seen as more academically constructed than those of his peers—in this case, in comparison to the more painterly vision of Shannon.

Eight paintings were added to the DeCamp section in October when the show moved on to the city of the

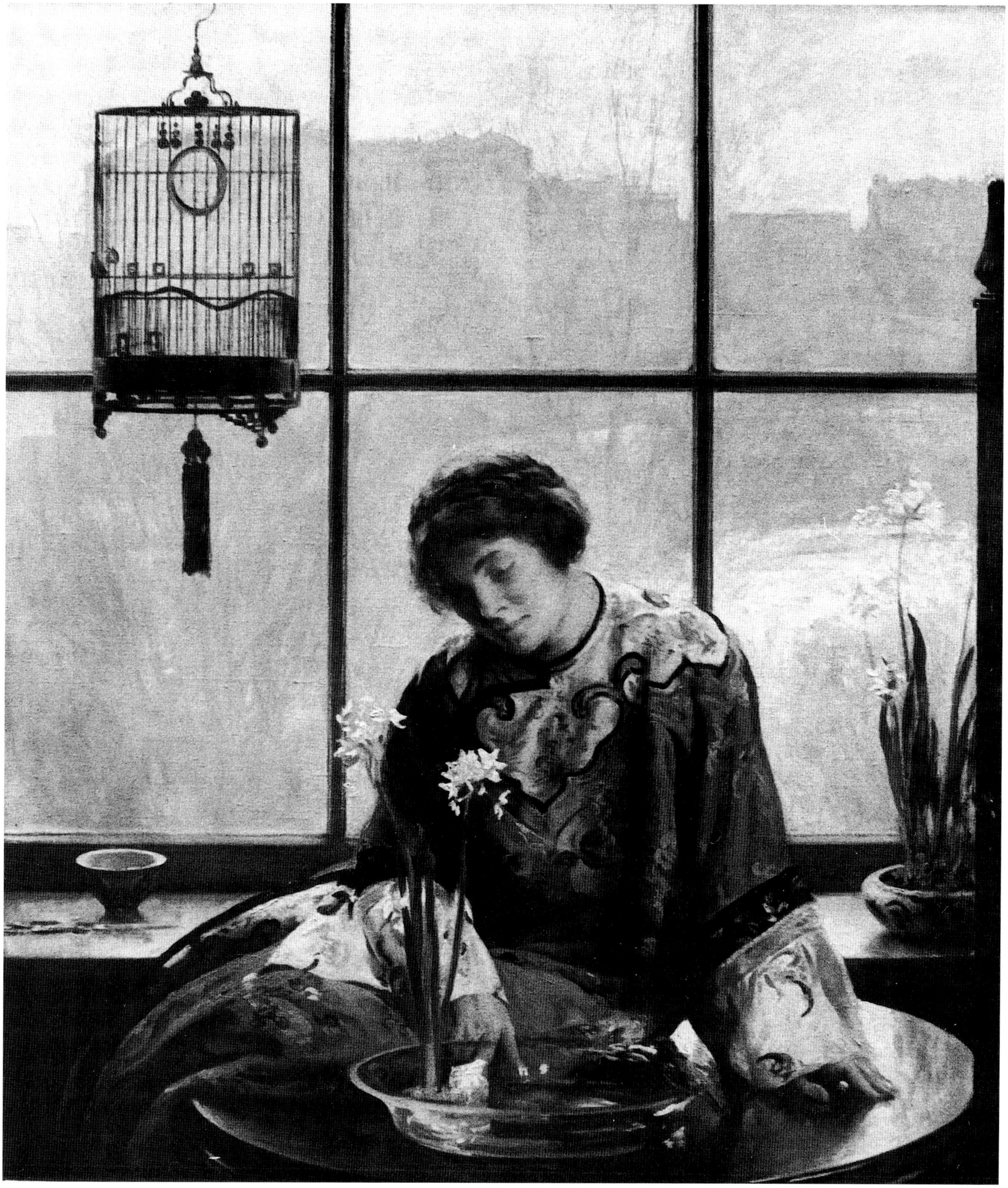

Fig. 85 *Red Kimono*, ca. 1919. 48¼ x 40¼ in. (122.5 x 102 cm). Cummer Museum of Art and Gardens, Jacksonville, Florida; Museum Purchase, 1975

artist's birth, Cincinnati, where, understandably, it received much attention. Mary L. Alexander's review speaks for all: "[DeCamp's] sincerity and ability are thoroughly established in the canvases contained in this memorial exhibition. It is paint for paint's sake—beautiful, mellow, rich, like old wine or seasoned wood. It has timbre and dignity; it is unostentatious and without the pyrotechnics of the less sincere. In it you feel incorporated the best traditions of the art of painting. In the handling of his lighted interiors there is a suggestion of Vermeer; they are carefully planned, beautifully and sincerely executed. He presents the thing as a whole rather than in parts.... DeCamp was considered by many artists of his day to be the finest American portraitist, especially in his portraits of men."[46]

From this point on, the DeCamp show was separated from the Shannon memorial. In November ten works were displayed at the Herron Art Institute in Indianapolis; in December the same paintings traveled to the Art Institute of Chicago; and in January 1925 eight works were shown at the Gallery of Fine Arts in Columbus. Correspondence between the organizers and the participating museums mentions two other venues—Cleveland and Akron, Ohio—but there is no evidence that these exhibitions actually took place. DeCamp's career had come to an abrupt end, but it is to the credit of the directors of these various institutions that his place in the history of American art was secured, if initially for only a brief moment.

There can be little doubt that, despite his continual technical experimentation, DeCamp would not have fared well had he lived into the vastly different world of the 1930s. Women were now pictured in the workplace, in the streets, and in other less than genteel situations. DeCamp would surely have survived as a painter of commissioned portraits, but the moment had passed for his and his contemporaries' vision of an idealized woman, protected from the harsher realities of life. Indeed, as early as the 1910s, the realist subjects of Robert Henri and his circle, and the formalist innovations of early Modernism, had begun to make the kind of art practiced by DeCamp seem part of history.

In the late 1950s, as Donald Moffat surmised in the passage quoted in the Preface to this book, the art world was not yet ready for a retrospective of DeCamp's work. It is only since then, with the spread of less dogmatically Modernist attitudes, that the art of DeCamp and his contemporaries has been deemed worthy of reappraisal. What impresses us today in DeCamp's oeuvre, aside from the image it presents of some aspects of turn-of-the-century American life, is the artist's virtuosity in the handling of paint and the continual infusion of new ideas into his work. As Paul Thomas wrote of DeCamp in 1908: "Scorning bravura, he insists on virtuosity. To translate his most salient characteristics into terms of the stringed instruments he so loves to put in his compositions, he has a marvelous 'singing bow,' an infinite breath, his themes are maestoso, con tenerezza, con amore."[47]

Notes

1 W[illiam]. H[owe]. D[ownes]., "The Ten Americans," *Boston Evening Transcript*, April 6, 1917, p. 4.

2 "Notes of the Studios and Galleries," *Arts and Decoration* 7 (April 1917), p. 336.

3 C. Powell Minnigerode to Joseph DeCamp, January 4, 1919; DeCamp files, Corcoran Gallery of Art, Washington, D. C.

4 DeCamp to Minnigerode, telegram of January 6, 1919; *ibid.*

5 DeCamp to Minnigerode, letter of January 6, 1919; *ibid.*

6 Minnigerode to DeCamp, January 8, 1919; *ibid.*

7 Members of the prestigious committee included the Honorable Henry White, Mrs. E. H. Harriman, J. Pierpont Morgan, and Charles P. Taft. DeCamp would paint the latter's portrait in about 1921.

8 Herbert L. Pratt to DeCamp, March 1919; quoted in Donald Moffat, "Joseph Rodefer DeCamp: Biographical Sketch," unpublished typescript, Frick Art Reference Library, New York, 1955–57, p. 39.

9 W[illiam]. H[owe]. D[ownes]., "The Fine Arts," *Boston Evening Transcript*, April 16, 1919, sect. 2, p. 4.

10 R. H. Ives Gammell, *The Boston Painters: 1900–1930* (Orleans, Mass.: Parnassus Imprints, 1986), p. 62.

11 W[illiam]. H[owe]. D[ownes]., "The Fine Arts," *Boston Evening Transcript*, February 4, 1922, sect. 1, p. 10. The other exhibitions to which the painting was sent were the 1922 annuals of the Detroit Institute of Arts, the Toledo Museum of Art, and the City Art Museum, St. Louis.

12 Borden dated his sitting for DeCamp to the "latter part of October and the first weeks of November" 1920; Henry Borden, ed., *Robert Laird Borden: His Memoirs*, vol. 2 (Toronto: McClelland and Stewart Ltd., 1969), p. 249.

13 Michael Quick, "Achieving the Nation's Imperial Destiny: 1870–1920", in *American Portraiture in the Grand Manner*, exh. cat. (Los Angeles: Los Angeles County Museum of Art, 1981). p. 73.

14 "War Portraits at Museum," *American Art News* 19 (January 22, 1921), p. 1.

15 James B. Townsend, "Annual Pa. Academy Exhibit," *American Art News* 19 (February 12, 1921), p. 1.

16 "Harvard Club Unveils Azan Portrait," *Boston Evening Transcript*, June 27, 1918, p. 4.

17 DeCamp is described as being in poor health around 1920 by Robert C. Vitz, in "The Eclipse of Cincinnati's Golden Age in Art," *Cincinnati Historical Society Bulletin* 27 (Winter 1969), p. 314.

18 For information on Woods, see Dumas Malone, ed., *Dictionary of American Biography*, vol. 20 (New York: Charles Scribner's Sons, 1936), pp. 503–04.

19 See Edward K. Robinson, "Lewis Parkhurst, Trustee," *Dartmouth Alumni Magazine* (March 1941), pp. 15–19, 86–87, and "Lewis Parkhurst Dies," *Dartmouth Alumni Magazine* (May 1949), pp. 25–26.

20 "News of the World of Art," *Boston Sunday Herald*, April 6, 1919, sect. 3, p. 8.

21 See Eric P. Kelly, "Old Families of Hanover," *Dartmouth Alumni Magazine* (December 1937), pp. 13–16.

22 See Marcus A. McCorison, "Donald McKay Frost—A Collector of Western Americana," *Western Historical Quarterly* 3 (January 1972), pp. 67–76.

23 See Catherine Gilbert, "Catherine Gilbert on Johnson, Alexander, Sterner, DeCamp, Hale and Kroll," in Elizabeth Johns, ed., *Seeing Women: Students Select from the Susan and Herbert Adler Collection of American Drawings and Watercolors*, exh. cat. (Danville, Ky.: Norton Center for the Arts, Centre College, 1992), pp. 14–18.

24 See Francis Lane Childs, "Mr. Tuck 75 Years After Graduation," *Dartmouth Alumni Magazine* (June 1937), pp. 9–12. It is unlikely that DeCamp painted the picture, which is dated 1919, in Europe. A highly detailed drawing exists for the work, however, and this may have been done a year earlier, while the artist was still abroad.

25 DeCamp painted Brown in Ottawa in October and November of 1920, at the same time as he completed the portraits of Borden and Currie for the National Art Committee. My thanks to Michael Pantazzi, Associate Curator of European Art at the National Gallery of Canada, Ottawa, for this information.

26 See Elmer Bendiner, "Simon Flexner: His 'Rock' Was for the Ages," *Hospital Practice* (April 15, 1988), pp. 213–20, 225–26, 230, 232, 237–38, 242, 244, 247–48, 253–54, 259, 262, 264–66.

27 Harris Elwood Starr, "Frederick Taylor Gates," in Allen Johnson and Dumas Malone, eds., *Dictionary of American Biography*, vol. 4 (New York: Charles Scribner's Sons, 1931), pp. 182–83.

28 "Howard Clark Hollister," in *History of Cincinnati and Hamilton County, Ohio* (Cincinnati: S. B. Nelson & Co., 1894), p. 608.

29 For information on Lewis, see Patricia H. Rodgers, Charles M. Sullivan, *et al., A Photographic History of Cambridge* (Cambridge, Mass.: MIT Press, n. d. [ca. 1984]), p. 83.

30 See Henry Louis Gates, Jr., "The Face and Voice of Blackness," in Guy C. McElroy, *Facing History: The Black Image in American Art, 1710–1940* (San Francisco: Bedford Arts, 1990), pp. 19–42.

31 *Ibid.*, p. 29.

32 Bram Dijkstra, *Idols of Perversity: Fantasies of Feminine Evil in Fin-de-Siècle Culture* (New York and Oxford: Oxford University Press, 1986), p. 185.

33 See "'Blue Bird' Built on Folklore of France," *Boston Sunday Herald*, April 4, 1915, p. 6.

34 Bernice Kramer Leader, "The Boston Lady as a Work of Art: Paintings by the Boston School at the Turn of the Century," Ph. D. diss., Columbia University, 1980, p. 128.

35 Barbee Babson: "Some Who Have Made Boston Famous in the World of Art," *Boston Sunday Herald*, March 1, 1914, special features, p. 3.

36 "The Thirteenth Annual Exhibition of Selected Paintings by American Artists at the Albright Art Gallery," *Academy Notes* 14 (January–October, 1919), p. 77.

37 M. R. C., "The Week in Art Circles," *Cincinnati Enquirer*, June 4, 1922, p. 13.

38 One of the most common causes of peritonitis is a ruptured appendix, which one family member maintains was the source of DeCamp's illness; another claims it to have been ulcers. Attempts to recover the hospital records have been unsuccessful.

39 Edith DeCamp to Joseph H. Gest, November 1922; Cincinnati Art Museum.

40 J. DeCamp to Joseph H. Gest, January 1923.

41 Rose V. S. Berry, "Joseph DeCamp: Painter and Man," *American Magazine of Art* 14 (April 1923) pp. 187–88.

42 H[arley]. P[erkins]., "The Fine Arts," *Boston Evening Transcript*, December 31, 1923, sect. 1, p. 15.

43 Harley Perkins, "Joseph DeCamp: The Man and the Artist, as Shown by His Works," *Boston Evening Transcript*, January 5, 1924, p. 8.

44 See "Eighteenth Annual Exhibition of Selected Paintings and Small Bronzes by American Artists, at the Albright Art Gallery," *Academy Notes* 19 (July–December 1924), p. 85.

45 Thurston V. Darling, "Gallery Exhibit Contrasts Work of Two Artists," *Democrat and Chronicle*, August 10, 1924; clippings files, Memorial Art Gallery of the University of Rochester, New York.

46 Mary L. Alexander, "Fine Exhibits Mark Opening of Art Museum," *Daily Times-Star*, October 1, 1924; clippings file, Cincinnati Art Museum, p. 56.

47 Paul K. M. Thomas, "The Art of Joseph DeCamp, Painter," *Cincinnati Times-Star*, March 13, 1909; Joseph DeCamp scrapbook, family of the artist.

Exhibitions

This list contains all exhibitions in which DeCamp is known to have shown work. Complete information on each exhibition—title, place, dates—is given where possible; imprecise or unascertainable data is indicated by square brackets and/or a question mark. Titles given at the end of each entry are those of works by DeCamp; they are printed here as they appear in the checklist or catalogue of the respective exhibition, or as gleaned from contemporary reviews.

1875

Seventh Annual Exhibition of the School of Design of the University of Cincinnati, June 16–19, #102 *Large Frame*

Cincinnati Industrial Exposition, Ohio Mechanics Institute, [dates?], Wood Carving

1876

Eighth Annual Exhibition of the School of Design of the University of Cincinnati, June 14–17, #60 *Ornamental Design*, #92 *Carved Gothic Stand*, #144 *Carved Bracket*

1877

Ninth Annual Exhibition of the School of Design of the University of Cincinnati, June 13–16, #16 *Figure (From Life)*, #31 *Head (After Coutoure [sic])*, #34 *Sketch (From Nature)*, #35 *Study of Trees (After Calame)*, #112 *Anatomical Figure (Cast)*, #237 *Carved Picture Frame*, #249 *Carved Picture Frame*

1881

Special Exhibition of Paintings by American Artists at Home and in Europe, Philadelphia Society of Artists, Pennsylvania Academy of the Fine Arts, Philadelphia, Nov. 7–Dec. 26, #98 *Street Scene, Venice*, $250

1883

[Paintings by Young Cincinnati Artists], A. B. Closson's Gallery, Cincinnati, Feb. 7[8?]–21, *Portrait of Lambert DeCamp, Self-Portrait, Calle Stretto, After the Rain, On the Lagoons*

Sixth Annual Exhibition of the Society of American Artists, American Art Gallery, New York, Mar. 26–Apr. 28, #34 *S. Vio*

Sixth Annual Exhibition of the Society of American Artists, Museum of Fine Arts, Boston, May 7–June 3, #34 *S. Vio*

Cincinnati Industrial Exposition, Sept., *Portrait*

1885

[Exhibition], Chase Gallery, Boston, [opened ca. Feb. 13], [3 portraits]

Fifth Annual Exhibition of Contemporary American Art, Museum of Fine Arts, Boston, May 5–June 2, #19 *Portrait of E. C. Cabot*

1886

Prize Fund Exhibition, American Art Association, Museum of Fine Arts, Boston, Feb.–Mar., #51 *St. John the Baptist*, $1,200

1887

Thirty-Fifth Exhibition of Oil Paintings, Boston Art Club, Jan. 14–Feb. 12, #103 *Marsh and Sand* [oil]

1888

Sixty-Third Annual Exhibition of the National Academy of Design, New York, Apr. 2–May 12, #485 *A Murky Day*

Tenth Annual Exhibition of the Society of American Artists, New York, [dates?], #38 *Moreland, Cape Ann*

First Annual Exhibition of American Pictures, Art Institute of Chicago, May 28–June 30, #31 *Moorland-Cape Ann*, #55 *Head*

Ohio Centennial Exposition, Columbus, Sept. 4–Oct. 19, #303 *Moorland, Cape Ann*, $500

1889

Annual Exhibition of the Boston Art Club [dates?], DeCamp on Selection Committee

Eleventh Exhibition of the Society of American Artists, Fifth Avenue Art Galleries, New York, May 13–June 15, #55 *Portrait of Miss J.*

1890

Seventeenth Triennial Massachusetts Charitable Mechanics Association, Boston, Oct. 1–Nov. 29, #84 *A Cape Anne Lane*

[Exhibition], St. Botolph Club, Boston, Jan. 27–Feb. 8, #40 *Medford Marshes*, #64 *Landscape*

Twelfth Exhibition of the Society of American Artists, Fifth Avenue Art Galleries, New York, Apr. 28–May 24, #60 *At the Piano*

Third Annual Exhibition of American Oil Paintings, Art Institute of Chicago, June 9–July 13, #56 *At the Piano*

[Exhibition], St. Botolph Club, Boston, Dec. 29–Jan. 17 [1891], #27 *The Mill Pond*, #42 *On the Marsh, Medford*

1891

Thirteenth Exhibition of the Society of American Artists, Fifth Avenue Art Galleries, New York, Apr. 27–May 3, #73 *Portrait*, #74 *Mill-Pond, Cape Ann*

Exhibition of Oil Paintings, St. Botolph Club, Boston, Dec. 24–Jan. 11 [1892], #8 *Portrait*, #13 *Bay Bushes*, #28 *The Dying Tree*, #44 *Misty Calm*

1892

Sixty-Second Annual Exhibition, Pennsylvania Academy of the Fine Arts, Philadelphia, Jan. 21–Mar. 5, #72 *A New England Garden*

Fourteenth Exhibition of the Society of American Artists, Fifth Avenue Art Galleries, New York, May 2–28, #64 *Landscape*, #65 *Arrangement in Black and Red*, #66 *Bay Bushes*

Eighteenth Triennial Exhibition of the Massachusetts Charitable Mechanics Association, Boston, Oct. 5–Dec. 3, #34 *Carnation and Black*

Fourth Annual Exhibition of the Art Club of Philadelphia, Nov. 14–Dec. 25, #86 *In the Arbor*, #109 *September Afternoon*

Exhibition of Oil Paintings, St. Botolph Club, Boston, Dec. 26–Jan. 14 [1893], *The Driveway*, *Portrait of a Lady*, *Bay Bushes*

1893

Massachusetts Fine Art Exhibit, Massachusetts Charitable Mechanics Association Building, Boston, Jan. 16–28, #39 *Carnation and Black*, $500

Forty-Seventh Exhibition, Boston Art Club, Jan. 20–Feb. 18, #46 *The Hammock*

Fifteenth Exhibition of the Society of American Artists, American Fine Arts Society, New York, Apr. 17–May 13, #12 *New England Garden* $300, #26 *The Hammock* $1,000, #143 *Study, September Morning* $200, #194 *Portrait of J[ohn]. L[eslie]. B[reck].*

World's Columbian Exposition, Chicago, May 1–Oct. 31, #1236 *Carnation and Black*

Fifth Annual Exhibition of Oil Paintings and Sculpture of the Art Club of Philadelphia, Nov. 23–Dec. 31, #86 *In the Arbor*, #109 *September Afternoon*

Sixty-Third Annual Exhibition, Pennsylvania Academy of the Fine Arts, Philadelphia, Dec. 18–Feb. 24 [1894], #94 *The Hammock*

1894

An Exhibition of Paintings by Joseph DeCamp, Dawson Watson, F. W. Benson, Philip Hale, E. C. Tarbell, F. P. Vinton, Theodore Wendel, and Mrs. L. C. Perry, St. Botolph Club, Boston, Jan. 29–Feb. 17, #8 *The Mirror* $1,000, #9 *Portrait of J[ohn]. L[eslie]. B[reck].*, #10 *The Hillside* $350, #11 *September Morning* $250, #12 *September Afternoon* $250

Forty-Ninth Exhibition, Oil Paintings, Boston Art Club, Jan. 20–Feb. 17, #64 *In the Arbor*

Sixteenth Exhibition of the Society of American Artists, American Fine Arts Society, New York, Mar. 12–Apr. 14, #93 *The Mirror*, #199 *The Hillside*

Sixty-Ninth Annual Exhibition of the National Academy of Design, New York, Apr. 2–May 12, #151 *In the Arbor*

Sixty-Fourth Annual Exhibition of the Pennsylvania Academy of the Fine Arts, Dec. 17–Feb. 23 [1895], DeCamp on Jury of Selection and Hanging Committee, #100 *The Dying Tree*, #101 Sleep, #102 *The Mirror*

1895

Fifty-First Exhibition, Oil Paintings and Sculpture, Boston Art Club, Jan. 19–Feb. 16, #144 *The Gold-Fish*

First Annual Exhibition of the Cleveland Art Association, [dates?], #284 *In the Arbor*

Seventeenth Annual Exhibition of the Society of American Artists, American Fine Arts Society, New York, Mar. 25–Apr. 27, #22 *Sleep*, #59 *Edge of the Orchard*, #155 *Girl with a Globe*

First Annual Exhibition and Art Loan Under the Auspices of the Art Club of Detroit, May 18–June 1, #204 *The Mirror* [Gold Medal]

Summer Exhibition, St. Botolph Club, Boston, [opened June 17], [entries?]

Seventh Annual Exhibition of Oil Paintings and Sculpture of the Art Club of Philadelphia, Nov. 18–Dec. 16, #25 *Edge of the Cliff*, #26 *Portrait*, #? *Miss X*

International Exposition of the Cotton States, Atlanta, Georgia, Sept. 18–Dec. 31, #155 *The Hammock* [Bronze Medal, oil], #156 *In the Arbor*

Sixty-Fifth Annual Exhibition, Pennsylvania Academy of the Fine Arts, Dec. 23–Feb. 22 [1896], #93 *The Hill-Side*, #94 *September Afternoon*, #92 *Girl with a Globe*

1896

Fifty-Third Exhibition, Oil Paintings and Sculpture, Boston Art Club, Jan. 13–Feb. 15, #26 *Sleep*

Exhibition of Paintings by Boston Artists, St. Botolph Club, Boston, Mar. 2–23, #19 *Landscape*

Eighteenth Annual Exhibition of the Society of American Artists, American Fine Arts Society, New York, Mar. 28–May 2, #174 *Head of a Young Woman*

A Group of Portraits, Cincinnati Museum Association, June 1–Dec. 31, #571 *Portrait of a Lady*

Eighth Annual Exhibition of Oil Paintings and Sculpture of the Art Club of Philadelphia, Brighton Street Gallery, Nov. 23–Dec. 21, DeCamp Chairman of the Exhibition Committee and Chairman of Jury of Admission and Hanging Committee, #31 *Magdalen*

1897

A Comparative Exhibition of Paintings in the Art Museum, Eden Park, Cincinnati Museum Association, Dec., #610 *Nude*

1898

Ten American Painters, Durand-Ruel Galleries, New York, Mar. 31–Apr. 16, #9 *The Reflections*, #10 *Magdalene*

Ten American Painters, St. Botolph Club, Boston, Apr. 25–May 14, #20 *Magdalene*, #23 *Reflections*

Fifth Annual Exhibition of Works by American Artists, Cincinnati Museum Association, May 21–July 5, #1 *Head of a Young Woman*

Greater America Exposition, Omaha, Nebraska, July 1–Nov. 1, #776 *Magdalene*

Fifteenth Annual Exhibition, Saint Louis Exposition and Music Hall Association, Sept. 14–Oct. 29, #114 *Head of a Young Woman*

1899

Sixty-Eighth Annual Exhibition, Pennsylvania Academy of the Fine Arts, Philadelphia, Jan. 16–Feb. 25, #17 *Woman Drying Her Hair*

Exhibition of the Society of Arts and Crafts Together with a Loan Collection of Applied Art, Copley and Allston Halls, Boston, April 4–[22 or 27?], #205a *Scheme for Decorative Panel*, #205b *Scheme for Decorative Panel*

Ten American Painters, Durand-Ruel Galleries, New York, Apr. 4–15, *Girl Sleeping*, *The Looking Glass*, *Girl Drying Her Hair*

Sixth Annual Exhibition of American Art in the Art Museum, Cincinnati Museum Association, May 20–July 10, #71 *Woman Drying Her Hair* [Temple Gold Medal], #72 *Sleep*, #73 *Sketch for Decoration in Public Dining Room*, #74 *Sketch for Decoration*

Sixteenth Annual Exhibition, Saint Louis Exposition and Music Hall Association, Sept. 11–Oct. 14, #103 *Sleep*, #104 *A Glimpse of the Sea*, #105 *Summer*

Twelfth Annual Exhibition of Oil Paintings and Sculpture by American Artists, Art Institute of Chicago, Nov. 6–Dec. 17, #81 *Sleep*

Exhibition of Sculpture by Charles R. Harley and of Pictures by Several Boston Artists, St. Botolph Club, Boston, Nov. 20–30, #4 *Landscape*

Exhibition of the Prang Collection, Copley Hall, Boston,

Nov. 23 [for one week, then sold at auction by Frank A. Leonard, beginning Dec. 1], [entries?]

1900

Sixty-First Exhibition, Boston Art Club, Jan. 6–Feb. 3, #31 *Sleep*

Sixty-Ninth Annual Exhibition, Pennsylvania Academy of the Fine Arts, Jan. 15–Feb. 24, #38 *Sleep*

Ten American Painters, Durand-Ruel Galleries, New York, Mar. 17–31, *Portrait of J. Eastman Chase*

Ten American Painters, St. Botolph Club, Boston, Apr. 16–30, #4 *Portrait of J. Eastman Chase*

Fine Arts Exhibition, United States of America, Paris Exposition of 1900, Apr. 25–Nov. 16, #179 *Woman Drying Her Hair*

Twenty-Fifth Anniversary Exhibition: 1875–1900, The Art Students' League of New York, May 10–19, #83 *Portrait*

Seventh Annual Exhibition of American Art, Cincinnati Museum Association, May 19–July 9, #54 *Girl with a Red Shawl*

[Exhibition], Hotel Rockaway, Rocky Neck, Mass., August, [entries?]

Inaugural Exhibition of the Syracuse Museum of Fine Arts, New York, [opened Nov. 20], #55 *Magdalene* $300

First Annual Boston Art Students' Association, New Gallery Exhibition of Contemporary American Art, Copley Hall and Alston Hall, Boston, Nov. 21–Dec. 18, #33 *Portrait of J. Eastman Chase*, #34 *The Green Shawl*

1901

Oil Paintings and Sculpture, Sixty-Third Exhibition, Boston Art Club, Jan. 5–Feb. 2, #7 *Arrangement in Pink, Black and Gold* [oil]

Seventeenth Annual Exhibition, Pennsylvania Academy of the Fine Arts, Philadelphia, Jan. 14–Feb. 23, #50 *Girl with Green Shawl*, #84 *Portrait*

Ten American Painters, Durand-Ruel Galleries, New York, Mar. 28–30, *Arrangement in Pink and Blue, The Green Shawl*

Twenty-Fifth Anniversary Exhibition of the School of the Museum of Fine Arts, Boston, April 6–28, #97 *Wharf, Gloucester*, #98 *The Green Shawl*

Eighth Annual Exhibition of American Art, Cincinnati Art Museum, May 18–July 8, #232 *Girl with Green Shawl*, #233 *At Gloucester*

Third Annual Exhibition of Oil Paintings, Worcester Art Museum, Mass., June 3–Oct. 14, #101 *The Girl with Green Shawl*

First Exhibition of Paintings, Loan Exhibition of American and Foreign Painters, Museum of Fine Arts, Syracuse, New York, [dates?], [entries?]

Thirteenth Annual Exhibition of Oil Paintings and Sculpture of the Art Club of Philadelphia, Nov. 18–Dec. 15, #59 *The Water Pier*, #83 *The Pink Settee*

1902

Sixty-Fifth Exhibition of Oil Paintings and Sculpture, Boston Art Club, Jan. 4–Feb. 1, #45 *June Sunlight*

Seventy-First Annual Exhibition, Pennsylvania Academy of the Fine Arts, Philadelphia, Jan. 20–Mar. 1, DeCamp on Jury of Selection, #147 *At the End of My Garden*

Ten American Painters, Durand-Ruel Galleries, New York, Mar. 30–Apr. 12, #18 *September Afternoon*, #19 *Ferry Landing—Low Tide*, #20 *Head of a Young Girl*, #21 *June*

Ten American Painters, St. Botolph Club, Boston, Apr. 21–May 10, #12 *Head of a Young Girl*, #13 *Ferry Landing, Low Tide*, #14 *June*, #15 *September Afternoon*

Ninth Annual Exhibition of American Art, Cincinnati Art Museum, May 17–July 7, #247 *Ferry Landing*, #238 *September Afternoon*

Fourth Annual Exhibition of Oil Paintings, Worcester Art Museum, Mass., May 29–Sept. 15, #159 *The Violin*

Summer Exhibition of Paintings by Boston Artists, Williams & Everett Galleries, Boston, [opened ca. June 7], *Lady in a Green Shawl*

Second Annual Exhibition of Contemporary Art, Copley Society, Boston, Nov. 19–Dec. 16, *Portrait*

Ninth Annual Exhibition, The Artists' Club, Denver, Dec. 10–21, #16 *The Reflection*

1903

Seventy-Second Annual Exhibition, Pennsylvania Academy of the Fine Arts, Philadelphia, Jan. 19–Feb. 28, #121 *The New Gown*, #154 *Portrait*, #430 *Portrait of a Boy*

Tenth Annual Exhibition of American Art, Cincinnati Art Museum, May 23–July 6, #53 *Portrait of Joseph Baker (Draughtsman)*, #54 *Portrait of A. P. DeCamp*, #55 *Portrait of a Boy*

Sixth Annual Exhibition of Oil Paintings, Worcester Art Museum, Mass., May 29–Oct. 4, #107 *June Sunshine*, #115 *On the Sea-wall*

Ten American Painters, Durand-Ruel Galleries, New York, [opened Apr. 18 or 20?], #22 *Portrait of a Boy*, #23 *Portrait of Joseph Baker, draughtsman*, #24 *Portrait of William Burpee*

Ninth Annual Summer Exhibition of American Oil Paintings, Worcester Art Museum, Mass., [opened ca. June 4], [entries?]

Summer Exhibition of Boston Artists, Williams & Everett Galleries, Boston, June 27–end of August, *Summer Day by the River's Brink*

Ninth Annual Exhibition of Paintings by Prominent Artists at the Poland Spring Art Gallery, Maine State Building, South Poland, Maine, summer, #65 *Girl with the Green Shawl*

Paintings and Sculpture Exhibited at the St. Botolph Club, Boston, Nov. 2–21, #6 *The Little Hotel*, #15 *Mother and Child*

Eighth Annual Exhibition, Carnegie Institute, Pittsburgh, Nov. 5–Jan. 1 [1904], DeCamp on Jury of Award, #32 *Joseph E. Baker, Draughtsman*, #33 *Portrait of a Boy*, #34 *The Sea Wall: September*

1904

Seventy-Ninth Annual Exhibition of the National Academy of Design, New York, Jan. 2–30, #37 *Portrait*

Seventy-Third Annual Exhibition, Pennsylania Academy of the Fine Arts, Philadelphia, Jan. 25–Mar. 5, #78 *Portrait of Joseph E. Baker, draughtsman*, #92 *The Little Hotel*

Ten American Painters, Durand-Ruel Galleries, New York, Mar. 19–Apr. 2, #5 *Portrait of Albert Baker, Esq.*, #6 *The Little Hotel*, #7 *The Blue Locket*

Ten American Painters, O'Brien's Gallery, Chicago, [before Apr. 17] [entries?]

Exhibition of Boston Artists, National Arts Club, New York, [opened ca. Apr. 12], *June Sunshine*

[Exhibition], Bradford Academy, Mass., [opened ca. Apr. 21], [entries?]

Louisiana Purchase Exposition, Saint Louis, Apr. 30–Dec. 1, #191 *Reading*, #192 *The Sea Wall, September*, #193 *Portrait of A. P. DeCamp*

Summer Exhibition of Paintings by Boston Artists, Williams & Everett Galleries, Boston, [opened ca. Apr. 21], [entries?]

Loan Exhibition, Museum of Fine Arts, Boston, [opened ca. July 7], *Portrait of J. Eastman Chase*

1905

Exhibition of Portraits—Present and Past Members, St. Botolph Club, Boston, Jan. 3–14, #51 *John L. Breck*, #53 *Robt. A. Boit*, #109 *Benj. Kimball*

One Hundredth Anniversary Exhibition [Seventy-Fourth Annual], Pennsylania Academy of the Fine Arts, Philadelphia, Jan. 23–Mar. 4, DeCamp on Jury of Selection, #229 *Portrait*, #495 *Portrait*, #626 *June Sunshine*

[Exhibition], Rowland Gallery, Boston, [opened ca. Jan. 28]–

Feb. 5, *Woman in the Green Shawl*, [nude], [portrait]

Ten American Painters, Montross Gallery, New York, Mar. 25–Apr. 13, *Portrait—Benjamin Kimball, In the Studio, The Heliotrope Gown*

Ten American Painters, St. Botolph Club, Boston, Apr. 26–May 13, *Portrait—Mr. Benjamin Kimball, In the Studio, The Heliotrope Gown*

Twelfth Annual Exhibition of American Art, Cincinnati Art Museum, May 20–July 10, #252 *Portrait of Albert Baker, Esq.*, #253 *In the Studio*

The Inaugural Loan Collection of Paintings, The Buffalo Fine Arts Academy, Albright Art Gallery, May 31–July 1, #74 *Woman Drying Her Hair*

Loan Exhibition of Paintings from Public and Private Collections, The Buffalo Fine Arts Academy, Albright Art Gallery, [opened ca. June 5], *Magdalene*

Summer Exhibition of Works by American Artists, The Copley Society of Boston, Copley Hall, June 19–Oct. 4, #27 *Girl with the Green Shawl*, #28 *June Sunshine*, #29 *Portrait*, #? *Joseph E. Baker*

Exhibition of the Works of Boston Artists, Columbus Art Association, [ca. Nov.], [entries?]

Tenth Annual Exhibition, Carnegie Institute, Pittsburgh, Nov. 2–Jan. 1 [1906], #59 *In the Studio*

1906

101st Annual Exhibition, Pennsylvania Academy of the Fine Arts, Philadelphia, Jan. 22–Mar. 3, #14 *In the Studio*, #67 *Self-Portrait*, #325 *La Penserosa*

Ten American Painters, Rhode Island School of Design, Providence, Feb. 5–27, *Portrait of Joseph E. Baker, Girl with Green Shawl, June Sunshine*

Ten American Painters, Montross Gallery, New York, Mar. 14–31, #8 *Self Portrait*, #9 *La Penserosa*, #10 *A Girl with a Book*

First Exhibition of Paintings by Boston Artists, Twentieth Century Club, Boston, Apr. 5–28, #10 *Portrait of Self*, #11 *Portrait Study*

Three of the Ten Americans, Rowland Gallery, Boston, Apr. 9–22, *Portrait of Mr. Munroe, Penseroso*

Collection of Paintings by Modern American Artists, Museum of Fine Arts, Boston, [opened ca. Apr. 15], *Portrait of J. Eastman Chase*

Ninth Annual Exhibition of Oil Paintings, Worcester Art Museum, Mass., May 31–Sept. 23, #3 *La Penserosa*

Twelfth Annual Exhibition of Paintings by Prominent Artists, Poland Spring Art Gallery, Maine State Building, South Poland, Maine, June 7–Oct. 6, #29 *In the Studio*

Ten American Painters, Kimball Gallery, Boston, Nov. 6–17, *In the Studio, Portrait of Dr. Forscheimer*, [2 unspecified entries]

Inaugural Exhibition, Art Association of Indianapolis, The John Herron Art Institute, Nov. 20–Dec. 31, #56 *The Sea Wall, September*

Ten American Painters, Rhode Island School of Design, Providence, [opened Nov. 21], *La Penserosa, Girl with Book, In the Studio*

Ten American Painters, Detroit Institute of Arts, Dec. 16[?]–25[?], June, *La Penserosa, Girl with a Book, In a Studio*

Ten American Painters, O'Brien's Gallery, Chicago, [opened Dec. 29], [entries?]

1907

Exhibition of Pictures by Boston Painters, St. Botolph Club, Boston, Jan. 9–26, #12 *Portrait*

Ten American Painters, Bresler Gallery, Milwaukee, Jan. 19–29[?], [entries?]

102nd Annual Exhibition, Pennsylvania Academy of the Fine Arts, Jan. 21–Feb. 24, DeCamp on jury, #103 *Portrait of Dr. Horace Howard Furness*

First Annual Exhibition of Oil Paintings by Contemporary American Artists, Corcoran Gallery, Washington, D.C., Feb. 7–Mar. 9, #108 *Portrait of Colonel Myron M. Parker*

Ten American Painters, J. J. Gillespie Galleries, Pittsburgh, Feb. 18–Mar. 4, [entries?]

Annual Exhibition of the Paint and Clay Club of New Haven, Young Men's Christian Association, [dates?], *In the Studio*

Ten American Painters, McClees Galleries, Philadelphia, Mar. 11–23, #8 *June*, #9 *La Penserosa*, #10 *Girl with Book*, #11 *In the Studio*

Ten American Painters, Montross Gallery, New York, Mar. 19–Apr. 6, #7 *Woman Braiding Her Hair*, #8 *Sally*

Exhibition of Paintings and Sculpture by American Artists, Swain Free School of Design, New Bedford, Mass., [dates?], [entries?]

Ten American Painters, Saint Louis Museum of Fine Arts, Feb. 1–14, [entries?]

[Exhibition], Rowland Gallery, Boston, May 1–20, *Sally, Girl Braiding Her Hair*

Fourteenth Annual Exhibition of American Art, Cincinnati Art Museum, May 18–July 17, #75 *Portrait of A. H. Chatfield, Esq.*, #76 *Portrait of Dr. F. Forchheimer*, #77 *Sally*, #78 *La Penserosa*

Tenth Annual Exhibition of Oil Paintings, Worcester Art Museum, Mass., May 31–Sept. 22, #135 *Girl with Book*, #159 *In the Studio*

Thirteenth Annual Exhibition of Paintings by Prominent Artists, Poland Spring Art Gallery, Maine State Building, South Poland, Maine, June 23–Oct. 1, #61 *June*

Third Summer Exhibition, Loan Collection of Paintings by American Artists, The Copley Society of Boston, Copley Hall, Boston, July 1–August [?], #2 *Girl Braiding Her Hair*

Twenty-Third Annual Exhibit, Art Association of Indianapolis, John Herron Art Institute, Dec. 8–Jan. 2 [1908], #22 *Dr. Howard Horace Furness*

1908

[Exhibition], Rowland Gallery, Boston, [opened Jan. 13], *In the Studio, June*

Twentieth Century Club, Boston, [opened Jan. 20], *In the Studio*

103rd Annual Exhibition, Pennsylvania Academy of the Fine Arts, Jan. 20–Feb. 29, #232 *Portrait of William S. Read*, #303 *Sally*, #702 *Girl with a Book*

Pictures by Boston Painters, St. Botolph Club, Boston, Jan. 28–Feb. 15, #13 *Die Lautenspielerin*

Eighth Annual Exhibition of Paintings, Drawings and Sculpture, The New Haven Paint and Clay Club, Mar. 5–28, #12 *In the Studio*

Ten American Painters, Montross Gallery, Mar. 17–Apr. 4, #10 *Guitar Player*, #11 *The Brown Veil*, #12 *The Cellist*, #13 *Portrait of Benjamin Kimball*

Ten American Painters, Pennsylvania Academy of the Fine Arts, Apr. 11–May 3, #20 *The Guitar-player*, #21 *The Pink Feather*, #22 *Sally*, #24 *La Penserosa*, #25 *Mr. Gilbert*, #26 *In the Studio*, #27 *The Green Shawl*, #28 *Girl with Book*, #29 *Magdalene*

Spring Exhibition of Boston Artists, Bigelow-Kennard Gallery, Boston, Apr. 23–June 1, *June*

[Exhibition], Rowland Gallery, Boston, [opened ca. May 14], *The Cellist*

Sixth Annual Exhibition, Bradford Academy, Mass., May 21 [for 2 weeks], [entries?]

Fifteenth Annual Exhibition of American Art, Cincinnati Art Museum, May 23–July 20, #14 *The Guitar Player*, #15 *The Pink Feather*, #16 *Portrait of Mr. Frederick Gilbert*, #17 *Portrait of Mr. C. L. Harrison*

Eleventh Annual Exhibition of Oil Paintings, Worcester Art Museum, Mass., May 29–Sept. 20, #37 *The Cellist*, #82 *Sally*

[Exhibition], Copley Gallery, Boston, [ca. Sept. 30–ca. Nov. 15], *Girl with Book, The Cellist*

Twenty-First Annual Exhibition of Oil Paintings and Sculpture by American Artists, The Art Institute of Chicago, Oct. 20–Nov. 29, #78 *The Pink Feather*

Fitchburg Women's Club Exhibition, Mass., Wallace Library, Nov. 15–25, *In the Studio*

Second Exhibition of Oil Paintings by Contemporary American Artists, Corcoran Gallery, Washington, D.C., Dec. 8–Jan. 17 [1909], #77 *The Pink Feather*, #81 *The Guitar Player* [silver medal], #86 *The Cellist*, #367 *Portrait of President Roosevelt*

Opening Exhibition of Paintings, Whistler House, Lowell, Mass., [opened Dec. 19], [entries?]

1909

104th Annual Exhibition, Pennsylvania Academy of the Fine Arts, Philadelphia, Jan. 31–Mar. 14, #421 *Portrait*

[Exhibition], Copley Gallery, Boston, Feb. 11–17, *Portrait of Roosevelt*

Esposizione Internazionale d'Arte della Citta di Venezia, [opened May], #13 *La Violoncellista*

Fourth Annual Exhibition, Brockton Women's Club, Mass., Mar. 17–20, *June Sunshine*

Ten American Painters, Montross Gallery, New York, Mar. 17–Apr. 7, #6 *The Blue Cup*

Ten American Painters, Copley Society, Boston, Apr. 12–24, *Girl with Guitar, Blue Cup*

Fourth Annual Exhibition of Selected Paintings by American Artists, Buffalo Fine Arts Academy, Albright Art Gallery, May 10–Aug. 30, #55 *Portrait of Dr. Horace Howard Furness*, #56 *The Blue Cup*

Twelfth Annual Exhibition of Oil Paintings, Worcester Art Museum, Mass., May 28–Sept. 19, #13 *Sally*, #15 *Girl with Book*

Summer Exhibition, Copley Gallery, Boston, [opened May 27], [entries?]

Fourth Annual Exhibition of Selected Paintings by American Artists at the Forest Park Art Building, The City Art Museum of Saint Louis, [opened Sept. 12], #55 *Portrait of Dr. Horace Howard Furness*, #56 *The Blue Cup*

1910

Exposicion Internacional de Arte del Centenario, Buenos Aires, Argentina, and Santiago, Chile, May 25–Sept. 30, #23 *La Violoncelista*

105th Annual Exhibition, Pennsylvania Academy of the Fine Arts, Philadelphia, Jan. 23–Mar. 20, #459 *The Blue Cup*, #476 *The Fur Jacket*

Loan Exhibition of Pictures, Franklin Union, Women's Municipal League, Boston, [ca. Jan. 29]–Feb. 24, *In the Studio*

Exhibition of Paintings by American Artists, Art Association of Columbus, Columbus Public Library under the auspices of the Columbus School of Art, Feb. 12–26, #17 *Girl with a Book*

Ausstellung Amerikanischer Kunst, Königliche Akademie der Künste zu Berlin, [opened ca. Mar. 19], [entries?]

General Exhibition, St. Botolph Club, Boston, Mar. 17–31, #5 *Cellist*, #12 Portrait *[Rev. Daniel Merriman, D.D.]*

Ten American Painters, Montross Gallery, New York, Mar. 24–Apr. 16, #8 *Roses*, #9 *The Fur Jacket*, #10 *Portrait of Frederick Winthrop, Esq.*

Fifth Annual Exhibition of Selected Paintings by American Artists, The Buffalo Fine Arts Academy, Albright Art Gallery, May 11–Sept. 1, #64 *Roses*

Seventeenth Annual Exhibition of American Art, Cincinnati Art Museum, May 21–July 20, #208 *Fur Jacket*, #209 *Blue Cup*

Sixteenth Annual Exhibition of Paintings by Prominent Artists at the Poland Spring Art Gallery, Maine State Building, South Poland, Maine, June [?]–Oct. 3, *Girl with Book*

Thirteenth Annual Exhibition of Oil Paintings, Worcester Art Museum, Mass., June 3–Sept. 19, #16 *The Little Seamstress*, #37 *Portrait [Rev. Daniel Merriman]*

Fifth Annual Exhibition of Selected Paintings by American Artists, The City Art Museum of Saint Louis, Sept. 15–Nov. 15, #64 *Roses*

Catalogue of Paintings, Rhode Island School of Design, Providence, Oct. 4–25, #7 *Portrait of Dr. Daniel Merriman*

Twenty-Third Annual Exhibition of Oil Paintings and Sculpture by American Artists, The Art Institute of Chicago, Oct. 18–Nov. 27, #64 *The Blue Cup*, #65 *The Fur Jacket*

1911

106th Annual Exhibition, Pennsylvania Academy of the Fine Arts, Philadelphia, Feb. 5–Mar. 26, #308 *Portrait of Dr. James Tyson*, #312 *Portrait of Dr. Louis Storr*

[DeCamp One-Man Exhibition], St. Botolph, Boston, Feb. 27–Mar. 10, 1911, #1 *Self-Portrait*, #2 *Polly*, #3 *Sally*, #4 *The Violinist*, #5 *The Window*, #6 *Francis I. Amory*, #7 *Daniel Merriman, D.D.*, #8 *Joseph E. Baker*, #10 *Albert Baker*, #11 *Charles P. Curtis*, #15 *The Fur Jacket*, #16 *Frank Duveneck*, #?s *Colonel Roosevelt, Girl with Book, La Penserosa, Pink Feather, The Blue Cup*

Fourth Annual Exhibition, Canadian Art Club, Toronto Art Museum, Mar. 3–25, #65 *Girl with Book*

Ten American Painters, Montross Gallery, New York, Mar. 17–Apr. 18, #4 *The Window*, #5 *Portrait–Francis I. Amory*

Collection of Pictures and Sculpture in the Pavilion of the United States of America at the Roman Art Exposition, Rome, Mar. 27–Nov. 1, #8 *Magdalen*

Sixth Annual Exhibition of Selected Paintings by American Artists, Buffalo Fine Arts Academy, Albright Art Gallery, May 12–Aug. 28, #33 *The Pink Feather*, #34 *The Fur Jacket*

Fourteenth Annual Exhibition of Oil Paintings by American Painters, Worcester Art Museum, Mass., May 28–Sept. 18, #15 *The Blue Cup* $3,500

Seventeenth Annual Exhibition of Paintings and Sculpture by Prominent Painters and Sculptors, Poland Spring Art Gallery, Maine State Building, South Poland, Maine, [dates?], #53 *Mr. Albert Baker*, #54 *Mr. Joseph Baker*

Summer Exhibition of Paintings, Copley Society, Boston, [opened ca. July 15], *Mother and Child, Girl with a Fur*

Canadian National Exhibition, Toronto, Aug. 26–Sept. 11, #65 *Girl with Book*

Sixth Annual Exhibition of Selected Paintings by American Artists, City Art Museum of Saint Louis, Sept. 17–Nov. 17, #29 *The Pink Feather*, #30 *The Fur Jacket*

Exhibition of Paintings by American Artists, Rhode Island School of Design, Providence, Sept. 21–Oct. 17, #4 *The Grey Turban*

Twenty-Fourth Annual Exhibition of American Oil Paintings and Sculpture, The Art Institute of Chicago, Nov. 14–Dec. 27, #91 *The Gray Turban*

1912

Eighteenth Annual Exhibition of Original Oil Paintings, Water Colors, and Sculpture by American and Foreign Artists, The Nebraska Art Association, Jan. 6–28, #25 *The Blue Cup*

The Inaugural Exhibition, The Toledo Museum of Art, Jan. 17–Feb. 12, #23 *The Pink Feather*

Annual Exhibition, Boston Art Club, Jan. 20–Feb. 10, *The Fur Jacket*

107th Annual Exhibition, Pennsylvania Academy of the Fine Arts, Philadelphia, Feb. 4–Mar. 24, #153 *Francis I. Amory* [Carol H. Beck Gold Medal], #425 *Three Friends*, #434 *The Window*, #623 *Portrait of Miss Agnes Woodbury*

Fifth Annual Exhibition, Canadian Art Club, Toronto, [opened Feb. 8], #207 *The Pink Feather*

Exhibition of Contemporary American Art under the auspices of the Peabody Institute and Charcoal Club, Peabody Institute Galleries, Baltimore, Feb. 27–Mar. 17, #88 *The Little Hotel*

Ten American Painters, Fifteenth Annual Exhibition, Montross Gallery, New York, Mar. 15–Apr. 6, #8 *The Violinist*

Spring Exhibition, Whistler House, Lowell, Mass., [opened Apr. 3], *The Fur Jacket*

Seventh Annual Exhibition of Selected Paintings by American Artists, Albright Art Gallery, Buffalo Fine Arts Academy, May 21–Sept. 2, #47 *The Gray Turban*, #48 *Pauline*, #49 *The 'Cellist*

Nineteenth Annual Exhibition of American Art, Cincinnati Art Museum, May 25–July 27, #88 *The Violinist* $3,000

Fifteenth Annual Exhibition of Oil Paintings, Worcester Art Museum, Mass., June 7–Sept. 15, #15 *Portrait of Albert Baker*

Special Summer Exhibition of Paintings by Prominent American Artists, The Portland Society of Art, L. D. M. Sweat Memorial Art Museum, Portland, Maine, July–August, #73 *June Sunshine*

First Annual Exhibition of the Art Association of Newport, R.I., The Studio Building, [opened ca. July 25], *La Penserosa*

Canadian National Exhibition, Toronto, Aug. 24–Sept. 9, #207 *The Pink Feather* $3,000

Seventh Annual Exhibition of Selected Paintings by American Artists, City Art Museum of Saint Louis, [opened Sept. 15], #34 *Pauline*

Exhibition of Paintings, Rhode Island School of Design, Providence, Oct. 4–27, #10 *June Sunshine* $2,000

Twenty-Fifth Annual Exhibition of American Oil Paintings and Sculpture, The Art Institute of Chicago, Nov. 5–Dec. 8, #75 *Portrait–Frank Duveneck*, #76 *The Violinist*

Twenty-Eighth Annual Exhibition of Oil Paintings by American Artists, Art Association of Indianapolis, The John Herron Art Institute, Dec. 17–Feb. 3, #19 *The Violinist*

Fourth Exhibition, Oil Paintings by Contemporary American Artists, Corcoran Gallery of Art, Washington, D.C., #139 *Portrait of Frank Duveneck*

1913

Ten American Painters, Empire Art Gallery, Rochester, New York, Jan. 22–31, *Blue Cup*

[Exhibition of Work by Instructors and Alumni of the Massachusetts Normal Art School], [opened ca. Feb. 5], *The Blue Cup*

108th Annual Exhibition, Pennsylvania Academy of the Fine Arts, Philadelphia, Feb. 9–Mar. 30, #311 *Portrait of Frank Duveneck*

Nineteenth Annual Exhibition of the Artists' Club of Denver, Together with the Traveling Exhibition of Oil Paintings Assembled by The American Federation of Arts, Denver Public Library, Feb. 28–Mar. 11, #15 *The Violinist*

The American Painters, Montross Gallery, New York, Mar. 12–Apr. 5, #10 *The Blue Lady*, #40 *Drawing*, #41 *Drawing*, #42 *Drawing*

Eighth Annual Woman's Club of Brockton, Mass., Mar. 24–[28 or 29?], *The Fur Jacket*

Ten American Painters, Copley Gallery, Boston, Apr. 14–May 5, *The Blue Lady*, *Portrait of Frank Duveneck*, *Three Nude Drawings*

Loans to the Museum, Rhode Island School of Design, Providence, May–May [1913], *The 'Cellist*

Eighth Annual Exhibition of Selected Paintings by American Artists, Albright Art Gallery, The Buffalo Fine Arts Academy, May 10–Aug. 31, #134 *Sally*

Twentieth Annual Exhibition of American Art, Cincinnati Art Museum, May 24–July 26, #121 *Portrait of Frank Duveneck*, #122 *The Blue Lady* $3,500

Nineteenth Annual Exhibition of Paintings and Sculpture by Prominent Painters and Sculptors at the Poland Spring Art Gallery, Maine State Building, South Poland, Maine, [summer?], #55 *June Sunshine*

Summer Exhibition, Portland Society of Art, L.D.M. Sweat Memorial Art Museum, Portland, Maine, July 1–Sept. 15, #124 *The Cellist*

Canadian National Exhibition, Toronto, Aug. 23–Sept. 8, [entries?]

[Exhibition], Copley Gallery, Boston, Oct. 6–20, *The Cellist*

[Pictures by Artists Who Are to Hold One-Man Shows Later in the Season], [opened ca. Oct. 7], [entries?]

[Exhibition], National Institute of Arts and Letters, [opened ca. Nov.], *The Blue Lady*

Twenty-Sixth Annual Exhibition of American Oil Paintings and Sculpture, The Art Institute of Chicago, Nov. 14–Dec. 25, #108 *The Blue Lady*

1914

Twenty-Ninth Annual Exhibition of Paintings and Sculpture, Art Association of Indianapolis, John Herron Art Institute, Jan. 1–Feb. 1, #22 *The Blue Lady*

The Friends of American Art, Loan Exhibition of American Paintings at the Art Institute of Chicago, Jan. 8–28, #7 *Portrait*

109th Annual Exhibition, Pennsylvania Academy of the Fine Arts, Philadelphia, Feb. 8–Mar. 29, #301 *Portrait–Frank Webster*

Fifth Annual Exhibition of Contemporary American Art under the auspices of the Charcoal Club and the Peabody Institute, Peabody Institute Galleries, Baltimore, Feb. 10–Mar. 10, #54 *The Fur Jacket*

Portraits by Living Painters, Loan Collection, The Copley Society of Boston, Copley Hall, Mar. 3–24, #50 *Miss W*, #? *Francis I. Amory*

Ten American Painters, Montross Gallery, New York, Mar. 18–Apr. 7, #22 *The Flirt*

Drawings by Painters, St. Botolph Club, Boston, Mar. 28–Apr. 10, #1 *Study*, #5 *The Mirror*, #8 *Study for the 'Pink Feather,'* #13 *Study*, #45 *'Cellist*, #46 *Study*, #52 *Study for 'The Blue Cup,'* #54 *Girl with 'Cello*, #59 *Study*, #60 *Girl with 'Cello*

[Exhibition], Copley Gallery, Boston, [opened ca. Mar. 24], *Amy Morris Homas*

[Selected Paintings by American Artists], [opened ca. Apr. 3], [entries?]

Exhibition of Contemporary American Paintings Owned in Worcester County, Worcester Art Museum, Mass., [opened ca. Apr. 29]–May 10, [entries?]

Ninth Annual Exhibition of Selected Paintings by American Artists, Albright Art Gallery, The Buffalo Fine Arts Academy, May 16–Aug. 31, #35 *The Little Hotel*

Third Annual Exhibition of Pictures by American Painters, Art Association of Newport, R. I., July 20–30, #29 *The Pink Feather*

Anglo-American Exposition, Shepherd's Bush, Fine Arts Palace, London, [August?], *The Fur Jacket*

Ohio Painters Exhibition, The Toledo Museum of Art, [first 2 weeks of Oct.], #277 *The Cellist*

Autumn Exhibition, Rhode Island School of Design, Providence, Oct. 25–Nov. 23, #10 *Portrait of Colonel A. George Bullock*

First General Exhibition, Guild of Boston Artists, Boston, Nov. 1–14, *Pink Feather*

1915

Annual Members' Exhibition of the Philadelphia Art Club, Feb. 21–Mar. 5, *Silver Waist*

Ohio Painters Exhibition, Gallery of Fine Arts and Art Association of Columbus, Columbus Public Library, Jan. 10–Feb. 1, #9 *The Cellist* $2,500

Panama-Pacific International Exposition, San Francisco, Feb. 20–Dec. 4, #3903 *Portrait of Frank Duveneck*

Ten American Painters, M. Knoedler & Co., New York, Mar. 15–27, #11 *The Silver Waist*, #12 *Portrait of Benjamin A. Kimball*

Sixtieth Annual Exhibition of Contemporary American Art, Boston Art Club, Apr. 3–May 1, #22 *The 'Cellist*

First Annual Exhibition of Selected Paintings by American Artists, Detroit Institute of Arts, Apr. 9–May 31, #15 *The Blue Lady*, #17 *The Silver Waist*

Tenth Annual Exhibition of Selected Paintings by American Artists, Albright Art Gallery, The Buffalo Fine Arts Academy, May 22–Aug. 30, #53 *The Silver Waist*

Twenty-Second Annual Exhibition of American Art, Cincinnati Art Museum, May 22–July 31, #57 *Portrait of William Gilbert*

Guild of Boston Artists Travelling Exhibition, Worcester Art Museum, Mass., Oct. 3–24, #9 *The Blue Lady*

A Collection of Paintings, Miniatures, and Sculpture from the Guild of Boston Artists, The Memorial Art Gallery, Rochester, New York, Oct. 30–Nov. 28, #52 *The Blue Lady* $3,500

National Association of Portrait Painters Annual Exhibition, Vanderbilt Gallery of the Fine Arts Building, New York, November, [entries?]

Twenty-Eighth Annual Exhibition of American Oil Paintings and Sculpture, The Art Institute of Chicago, Nov. 16–Jan. 2 [1916], #97 *The Silver Waist*

An Exhibition of Paintings, Miniatures and Sculpture by Members of the Guild of Boston Artists, Albright Art Gallery, The Buffalo Fine Arts Academy, Dec. 5–Jan. 2 [1916], #9 *The Blue Lady*

Portraits by Joseph DeCamp, Guild of Boston Artists, Dec. 28–Jan. 8 [1915], #1 *Rev. Daniel Merriman*, #2 *Sally*, #3 *A. G. Bullock, Esq.*, #4 *President Sanford*, #5 *Miss [Amy Morris] Homans*, #6 *A. F. Estabrook, Esq.*, #7 *Frank G. Webster, Esq.*, #8 *Charles H. Taylor, Esq.*, #9 *Francis I. Amory, Esq.*, #10 *Robert Saltonstall, Esq., and Son*, #11 *Benjamin A. Kimball, Esq.*, #12 *Dr. F. C. Shattuck*, #13 *Charles Sprague, Esq.*

1916

The Guild of Boston Artists, The Toledo Museum of Art, Jan., #209 *The Blue Lady*

Post-Exposition Exhibition in the Department of Fine Arts, Panama-Pacific International Exposition, San Francisco, Jan. 1–May 1, #5653 *The Fur Jacket*, #5654 *Portrait of Frank Duveneck*, #5655 *The 'Cellist*, #5663 *Girl with a Book*, #5665 *Penseroso*

Exhibition of Paintings, Miniatures and Sculpture by Members of the Guild of Boston Artists, The Detroit Institute of Arts, Feb., #9 *The Blue Lady*

111th Annual Exhibition, Pennsylvania Academy of the Fine Arts, Philadelphia, Feb. 6–Mar. 26, #308 *Portrait–Pauline*

Nineteenth Annual Exhibition of the Denver Artists' Club Together with the Traveling Exhibition of Oil Paintings assembled by The American Federation of Arts, Denver Public Library, [opened Feb. 26], *Violinist*

Exhibition of Paintings, Miniatures and Sculpture by Members of the Guild of Boston Artists, The Art Institute of Chicago, March, *The Blue Lady* [?]

Ten American Painters, M. Knoedler & Co., New York, Mar. 6–18, #4 *Charles Sprague*

Exhibition of Paintings, Miniatures and Sculpture by Members of the Guild of Boston Artists, Museum of Fine Arts, Boston, Mar. 7–Apr. [2 or 3?], *The Silver Waist*

Second General Exhibition, Guild of Boston Artists, Evans Memorial Galleries, Museum of Fine Arts, Boston, Apr. 3–21, *Mrs. Frank G. Webster*

An Exhibition of Paintings, Miniatures and Sculpture by Members of the Guild of Boston Artists, Milwaukee Art Institute, Apr., *Blue Lady* [?]

An Exhibition of Paintings, Miniatures and Sculpture by Members of the Guild of Boston Artists, City Art Museum of Saint Louis, [opened May 7], #9 *The Blue Lady*

Guild of Boston Artists, Ben Foster Paintings, Charles Haag Sculpture, Anna V. Hyatt Sculpture, Special Exhibitions, The Chicago Art Institute, Mar. 9–Apr. 2, #9 *The Blue Lady*

Exhibition of Paintings by Boston Artists, The National Arts Club Galleries, New York, Mar. 29–Apr. 27, #33 *The Fur Jacket*

Catalog of Exhibits, Milwaukee Art Society, Apr., [entries?]

Twenty-Second Annual Exhibition of Paintings and Sculpture by Prominent Painters and Sculptors at the Poland Spring Art Gallery, Maine State Building, South Poland, Maine, summer, #69 *Pauline*

An Exhibition of Paintings, Miniatures and Sculpture by Members of the Guild of Boston Artists, Cleveland Museum of Art, Oct. 5–29, *The Blue Lady*

Ten American Painters, Tilden-Thurber Gallery, Providence, Nov., [entries?]

Exhibition of Paintings, Miniatures and Sculpture by Members of the Guild of Boston Artists, Mattatuck Historical Society, Conn., Nov. 1–30, *The Fur Coat*

Twenty-Ninth Annual Exhibition of American Oil Paintings and Sculpture, The Art Institute of Chicago, Nov. 2–Dec. 7, #84 *Pauline*

Exhibition of Paintings, Miniatures and Sculpture by Members of the Guild of Boston Artists, Utica Public Library, Ohio, Nov. 5–22, #9 *The Blue Lady*

Exhibition of Paintings, Miniatures and Sculpture by Members of the Guild of Boston Artists, Free Public Library, New Bedford, Mass., [opened ca. Dec. 13], #5 *The Fur Jacket*

Sixth Exhibition of Contemporary Oil Paintings, Corcoran Gallery of Art, Wash., D.C., Dec. 17–Jan. 21 [1917], #90 *The Seamstress*, #104 *The Silver Waist*

1917

Panama-Pacific Exposition, Palace of Fine Arts, [opened ca. Jan. 17], #8 *Portrait–George Chadwick*, #9 *Portrait–Robert Treat Paine 2nd*, #10 *Three Silver Point Drawings*

Second General Exhibition, Guild of Boston Artists, Evans Memorial Galleries, Museum of Fine Arts, Boston, Apr. 3–21, *Mrs. Frank Webster*

Ten American Painters, Sculpture by Albert H. Atkins, St. Botolph Club, Boston, Apr. 9–20, #6 *Portrait–Robert Treat Paine, 2nd*, #12 *Portrait–George Chadwick*, #22 *Silver Point Drawing*, #25 *Silver Point Drawing*, #31 *Silver Point Drawing*

Exhibition of Oil Paintings by Boston Artists, National Arts Club, New York, April 11[?]-27, [entries?]

Annual Exhibition of Paintings by Contemporary Boston Artists, John-Esther Gallery, Abbott Academy, Andover, Mass., May 19–June 12, *The Blue Lady*

Twenty-Fourth Annual Exhibition of American Art, Cincinnati Art Museum, May 26–July 31, #65 *The Reader*, #66 *George Whitefield Chadwick*

Thirtieth Annual Exhibition of American Oil Paintings and Sculpture, The Art Institute of Chicago, Nov. 8–Jan. 2 [1918], #57 *Portrait of George Chadwick*

1918

113th Annual Exhibition, Pennsylvania Academy of the Fine Arts, Philadelphia, Feb. 3–Mar. 24, #340 *Portrait–George Chadwick*, #436 *The Blue Bird*

Exhibition of Painting and Sculpture by Members, St. Botolph Club, Boston, Feb. 18–Mar. 1, #12 *Portrait* (unfinished)

Fourth Annual Exhibition of Selected Paintings by American Artists, Detroit Institute of Arts, Apr. 9–May 30, #68 *The Reader*

Twelfth Annual Exhibition of Selected Paintings by American Artists, Albright Art Gallery, The Buffalo Fine Arts Academy, May 11–Sept. 9, #22 *The Fur Jacket*

Twenty-Fifth Annual Exhibition of American Art, Cincinnati Art Museum, May 25–July 31, 1918, #9 *The Blue Bird*

Annual Exhibition of Selected Paintings by American Artists, The Toledo Museum of Art, [opened June 9]–end of summer, #173 *The Reader*

General Exhibition of Paintings, Sculpture and Miniatures of Members of the Guild of Boston Artists, Dec. 30–Jan. 18 [1919], *Blue Bird*

1919

Ten American Painters, Corcoran Gallery of Art, Wash., D. C., Feb. 6–27, #9 *Red Kimono* $6,000, #10 *Blue Bird* $4,500

Thirty Paintings by Thirty Artists, Macbeth Gallery, New York, [?]–March, *The Red Kimono*

[Exhibition], Guild of Boston Artists, [opened Apr. 1], *Benjamin A. Kimball, Lewis H. Parkhurst*

Fifth Annual Exhibition of Selected Paintings by American Artists, Detroit Institute of Arts, Apr. 16–May 31, #94 *The Bluebird*

Thirteenth Annual Exhibition of Selected Paintings by American Artists and A Group of Small Selected Bronzes by American Sculptors, Albright Art Gallery, The Buffalo Fine Arts Academy, May 24–Sept. 8, #30 *The Red Kimona*

Eighth Annual Exhibition of Selected Paintings by American Artists, The Toledo Museum of Art, June–August, #19 *The Bluebird*

Fourteenth Annual Exhibition of Paintings by American Artists, City Art Museum of Saint Louis, Sept. 14–Oct. 28, #34 *The Red Kimona*

Exposition d'Artistes de l'Ecole Américaine, Musée National du Luxembourg, [opened Oct. 1]–Nov., #107 *La Jaquette de Fourrure*

Seventh Exhibition of Oil Paintings by Contemporary American Artists, Corcoran Gallery of Art, Wash., D.C., Dec. 21–Jan. 25 [1920], #58 *The Steward*, #93 *Portrait–George W. Chadwick, Esquire*

1920

Exhibition of Paintings and Sculpture by Members, St. Botolph Club, Jan. 2–19, *Red Kimono*

An Exhibition of Important Works by a Number of America's Leading Painters, Albright Art Gallery, The Buffalo Fine Arts Academy, Jan. 10–Feb. 15, #18 *Woman Drying Her Hair*, #19 *Roses*, #20 *The Gray Turban*

115th Annual Exhibition, Pennsylvania Academy of the Fine Arts, Philadelphia, Feb. 8–Mar. 28, #222 *The Red Kimono* [Walter Lippincott Prize], #239 *Portrait–Prof. J. K. Lord*

Exhibition of Works by Boston Artists under the auspices of The Copley Society, Museum of Fine Arts, Boston, Mar. 11–Apr. 5, #34 *Walter C. Baylies*

Exhibition of Works by Boston Artists Through the Courtesy of The Copley Society, Algonquin Club, Boston, Apr. 9–25, #21 *Blue Bird*

Sixth Annual Exhibition of Selected Paintings by American Artists, The Detroit Institute of Arts, Apr. 20–May 31, #46 *The Red Kimona*

[Exhibition], Copley Gallery, Boston, [opened ca. May 30], [entries?]

Ninth Annual Exhibition of Selected Paintings by American Artists, The Toledo Museum of Art, June–August, #323 *The Red Kimona*

Spring Exhibition of the Guild of Boston Artists, June 5–15, [entries?]

Eighteenth Water Color Exhibition, Pennsylvania Academy of the Fine Arts, Philadelphia, Nov. 7–Dec. 12, #325 *Portrait of John Drew* (charcoal)

Exhibition of Paintings, New Bedford Art Club, Mass., Dec. 5 [for one week], [entries?]

1921

Exhibition of Paintings, Sculpture and Etchings by Boston Artists, Dartmouth College, Hanover, N.H., Jan. 8–16, *Portrait of Professor John K. Lord, Portrait of Edward Tuck*

Exhibition of Etchings and Drawings in Monochrome by Boston Artists, St. Botolph Club, Boston, [opened Jan. 17], *Portrait Head, Silverpoint*

Exhibition of War Portraits, The Metropolitan Museum of Art, New York, Jan. 18–Feb. 10 or 11[?], *Robert Laird Borden, Arthur William Currie*

116th Annual Exhibition, Pennsylvania Academy of the Fine Arts, Philadelphia, Feb. 6–Mar. 27, #283 *The Window Blind*

General Exhibition of Paintings, Sculpture and Miniatures, Guild of Boston Artists, ?–ca. Feb. 10, *The Window Blind*

Loan Exhibition of Paintings Owned by Members of the Algonquin Club, Algonquin Club, Boston, [opened ca. Feb. 14], *The Blue Cup*

Special Exhibition of Paintings by Contemporary American Artists, The Cleveland Museum of Art, Feb. 16–Mar. 27, *The Red Kimono*

Exhibition of War Portraits, Rhode Island School of Design, Providence, March, *Robert Laird Borden, Arthur William Currie*

Seventh Annual Exhibition of Paintings, Sculpture and Miniatures, Guild of Boston Artist, Mar. 12–[for a month], [entries?]

Sixteenth Annual Exhibition of the Woman's Club of Brockton, Mass., Mar. 21–Apr. 3, *The Bluebird*

Exhibition of War Portraits, Pennsylvania Academy of the Fine Arts, Philadelphia, Apr. 2–30, *Robert Laird Borden, Arthur William Currie*

Twentieth Annual International Exhibition of Paintings, Carnegie Institute, Pittsburgh, Apr. 28–June 13, #78 *The Window Blind*

Ninth Annual Exhibition, The National Association of Portrait Painters, May 2–14, #8 *Lewis of the Porcellian*

Exhibition of War Portraits, Signing of the Peace Treaty, 1919, and Portraits of Distinguished Leaders of America and of the Allied Nations Painted by Eminent American Artists for Presentation to The National Portrait Gallery, National Gallery of Art, Washington, D.C., May, *Robert Laird Borden, Arthur William Currie*

Eighth Annual Exhibition, Mystic Art Association, Conn., Aug. 11–24, [entries?]

Exhibition of War Portraits Organized by The National Art Committee, The Cleveland Museum of Art, Oct. 1–Nov. 14, *Robert Laird Borden, Arthur William Currie*

Exhibition of War Portraits, Albright Art Gallery, The Buffalo Fine Arts Academy, Dec. 10–Jan. 3 [1922], *Robert Laird Borden, Arthur William Currie*

Exhibition of the Work of Boston Painters, St. Botolph Club, Dec. 12–24, #12 *Red and Gold*, #20 *Place de la Concorde*

Eighth Exhibition of Oil Paintings by Contemporary American Artists, Corcoran Gallery of Art, Wash., D.C., Dec. 18–Jan. 22 [1922], #161 *The Window Blind*

Paintings by Members of the Guild, Guild of Boston Artists, Dec. 27–Jan. 7 [1922], [entries?]

1922

Exhibition of Paintings by Boston Artists, Carnegie Institute, Pittsburgh, Jan. 23–Feb. 25, #9 *The Red Kimono*, #10 *The Blue Bird*, #11 *The Silver Waist*

117th Annual Exhibition, Pennsylvania Academy of the Fine Arts, Philadelphia, Feb. 5–Mar. 26, #63 *The Council of Ten*, #239 *Red and Gold*

Exhibition of War Portraits Organized by The National Art Committee, The Detroit Institute of Arts, Apr. 5–26, *Robert Laird Borden, Arthur William Currie*

Eighth Annual Exhibition, The Detroit Institute of Arts, April 11–May 31, #36 *The Council of the Ten*

The Twenty-Ninth Annual Exhibition of American Art, Cincinnati Museum of Art, May 27–July 31, #2 *The Window Blind*

Eleventh Annual Exhibition of Selected Paintings by American Artists, The Toledo Museum of Art, June–August, *The Council of the Ten*

Loans to the Museum, Rhode Island School of Design, Providence, June 1–June 1 [1923], *Red and Gold*

Fifteenth Annual Summer Exhibition of Paintings by American Artists, M. Knoedler & Co., [opened ca. July 12], #3 *The Blue Bird* $5,000

Eleventh Annual Exhibition, Newport Art Association, R.I., [opened ca. July 15]–end of July, *Red and Gold*

Seventeenth Annual Exhibition of Paintings by American Artists, City Art Museum of Saint Louis, Sept. 15–Oct. 25, #32 *The Council of Ten*

Autumn Exhibition, Rhode Island School of Design, Providence, Oct. 10–Nov. 5, #10 *Red and Gold* $3,000

Thirty-Fifth Annual Exhibition of American Paintings and Sculpture, The Art Institute of Chicago, Nov. 2–Dec. 10, #56 *The Council of the Ten*

An Exhibition of Paintings by Pittsburgh & Contemporary American Artists, Carnegie Institute, Pittsburgh, Dec. 4–Jan. 6 [1923], #7 *Blue Kimona*

1923

118th Annual Exhibition, Pennsylvania Academy of the Fine Arts, Philadelphia, Feb. 4–Mar. 25, #270 *The Blue Kimono*

Exhibition of Paintings by Local Artists, St. Botolph Club, Mar. 12–24, #15 *the Red Kimona*, #16 *Red and Gold*

Ninety-Eighth Annual Exhibition of the National Academy of Design, Mar. 17–Apr. 15, #275 *The Silver Waist*

Loan Exhibition of Paintings by Former Cincinnati Artists, Cincinnati Art Museum, Apr. 7–23, *Portrait of E. F. Bliss, Esq.*, *Portrait of Charles P. Taft*

Seventeenth Annual Exhibition of Selected Paintings and Small Bronzes by American Artists, Albright Art Gallery, The Buffalo Fine Arts Academy, Apr. 8–June 18, #57 *The Blue Kimona*

Summer Exhibition of Contemporary American Paintings and Small Bronzes, The Memorial Art Gallery, Rochester, New York, July–Sept., #24 *The Blue Mandarin Coat*

Collection of Drawings Lent by Mr. and Mrs. Anson C. Goodyear, The Buffalo Arts Academy, Albright Art Gallery, Sept. 29–Oct. 21, #22 *Nude Reclining*

Autumn Exhibition, Rhode Island School of Design, Providence, Oct. 16–Nov. 11, #7 *The Blue Bird* $3,000

1924

Memorial Exhibition of the Work of Joseph Rodefer DeCamp: 1858–1923, St. Botolph Club, Boston, Jan. 7–[26 or 28?], #1 *Italian Girl*, #2 *Young John the Baptist*, #3 *The Seamstress*, #4 *The Blue Mandarin Coat*, #5 *Walter Baylies, Esq.*, #6 *Red and Gold*, #7 *Sally*, #8 *Ted*, #9 *Guitar Player*, #10 *Silver Waist*, #11 *The Fur Jacket*, #12 *William Dexter, Esq.*, #13 *The Blue Cup*, #14 *The Blue Veil*, #15 *Venetian Boat Yard* (1878), #16 *Frank Webster, Esq.*, #17 *Joseph Baker, Esq.*, #18 *The Blue Bird*, #19 *Nude*, #20 *Robert Saltonstall, Esq., and Son*, #21 *Albert Baker, Esq.*, #22 *Girl Reading*, #23 *Armistice Day, Paris*, #24 *Frank Duveneck*, #25 *The Gray Turban*, #26 *Red Kimono*, #27 *The 'Cellist*, #28 *The Pink Feather*, #29 *Study for Decoration*, #30 *Girl with the Book*, #31 *George W. Chadwick, Esq.*, #32 *Il Pensieroso*, #33 *Charles P. Taft, Esq.*, #34 *Pauline*, #35 *Lewis*, #36 *Mother and Daughter*, #37 *Landscape*, #38 *Woman Drying Her Hair*, #39 *Mari Moffat*, #40 *Baby Head*, #41 *Portait of a Naval Officer*, #42 *The Window Blind*, #43 *The Green Shawl*, #44 *Artist and Model*, #45 *Sketch for Decoration*, #46 *Group of Drawings*, #47 *Group of Drawings*, #48 *Group of Drawings*; added later: *Decoration–School of Philosophy*, *Little Hotel*

Eighteenth Annual Exhibition of Selected Paintings and Small Bronzes by American Artists; A Group of Paintings by the Late Sir James J. Shannon, R.A., 1862–1923, and A Group of Paintings by the Late Joseph R. DeCamp, 1828–1923, Albright Art Gallery, The Buffalo Fine Arts Academy, Apr. 20–June 30, #60 *The Gray Turban*, #61 *The Blue Mandarin Coat*, #62 *Il Pensieroso*, #63 *The Cellist*, #64 *Nude*, #65 *Red and Gold*, #66 *The Green Shawl*, #67 *The Red Kimono*, #68 *The Window Blind*, #69 *The Blue Bird*, #70 *The Violinist*, #71 *Sketch*

Annual Exhibition of Contemporary American Paintings and Sculpture and Memorial Collections of Portraits by the Late Sir James J. Shannon, R.A., 1862–1923 and Joseph R. DeCamp, 1838–1923, The Memorial Art Gallery, Rochester, New York, July–Sept., #31 *Red and Gold* $1,500, #32 *The Blue Bird* $2,500, #33 *Nude* $3,000, #34 *The Red Kimona* $2,500, #35 *The Cellist* $1,500, #36 *Il Penserosa* $1,500, #37 *Mother and Daughter* $2,000, #38 *The Window Blind* $2,500, #39 *The Green Shawl* $2,000; added later: *The Violinist* $1,000

The Work of Joseph DeCamp, Cincinnati Museum of Art, [opened Oct. 1], #1 *Il Pensieroso*, #2 *The Cellist*, #3 *Nude*, #4 *Red and Gold*, #5 *The Green Shawl*, #6 *The Red Kimono*, #7 *The Window Blind*, #8 *The Blue Bird*, #9 *The Violinist*, #10 *Sketch 1–10*, #11 *The Gray Turban*, #12 *The Blue Mandarin Coat*, #13 *Portrait of Frank Duveneck*, #14 *Woman Drying Her Hair*, #15 *At Gloucester*, #16 *Decorative Panel–Study*, #17 *Portrait of Eugene F. Bliss*; added later: *Seamstress*

Special Exhibition of the Work of Joseph DeCamp, Indianapolis Museum of Art, Nov. 9–30, #3911.24 *Il Pensieroso*, #3905.24 *The Cellist*, #3903.24 *Nude*, #3906.24 *Red and Gold*, #3909.24 *The Green Shawl*, 3910.24 *The Red Kimono*, #3908.24 *The Window Blind*, #3902.24 *The Blue Bird*, #3907.24 *The Violinist*, #3904.24 *Sketch*

Joseph DeCamp Memorial Show, Art Institute of Chicago, Dec., [10 entries?]

1925

Joseph DeCamp Memorial Exhibition, Gallery of Fine Arts, Columbus, Jan. 4–Feb. 1, [10 entries?]

Selected Bibliography

Aside from the large number of contemporary reviews of the artist's work as it appeared in exhibitions throughout his career, the literature on DeCamp is anything but extensive. This bibliography lists only writings of a more substantial nature that have a direct bearing on DeCamp's life and art.

American Portraiture in the Grand Manner, 1720–1920. Exh. cat. Los Angeles County Museum of Art, 1981. Text by Michael Quick, William H. Gerdts, *et al.*

Berry, Rose V. S. "Joseph DeCamp: Painter and Man." *American Magazine of Art* 14 (April 1923), pp. 182–89.

Boone, M. Elizabeth. "Gilded Age Values and a Golden Age Painter: American Perceptions of Jan Vermeer." *Rutgers Art Review* 12–13 (1991–92), pp. 47–67.

The Bostonians: Painters of an Elegant Age, 1870–1930. Exh. cat. Museum of Fine Arts, Boston, 1986. Text by Trevor J. Fairbrother.

Caffin, Charles H. "Some American Portrait Painters." *Critic* 44 (January 4, 1904), pp. 31–48.

Court, Lee. W., ed. *Joseph DeCamp: An Appreciation.* Boston: Student Association of the Massachusetts Art School, 1924.

DeCamp, Graydon, ed. *Record of the Descendants of Ezekiel and Mary Baker DeCamp of Butler County, Ohio.* Cincinnati: privately printed, 1976.

Downes, William Howe. "Joseph DeCamp and His Work." *Art and Progress* 4 (April 1913), pp. 918–25.

Gammell, R. H. Ives. *The Boston Painters: 1900–1930.* Orleans, Mass.: Parnassus Imprints, 1986.

———. *Twilight of Painting.* New York: G. P. Putnam's Sons, 1946.

The Golden Age: Cincinnati Painters of the Nineteenth Century Represented in the Cincinnati Art Museum. Exh. cat. Cincinnati Art Museum, 1979.

Harlow, Alvin F. *The Serene Cincinnatians.* New York: E. P. Dutton & Co., 1950.

Hartmann, Sadakichi. "The Tarbellites." *Art News* 1 (March 1897), pp. 3–4.

Hiesinger, Ulrich W. *Impressionism in America: The Ten American Painters.* Munich: Prestel, 1991.

Hoeber, Arthur. "DeCamp: A Master of Technique." *Arts and Decoration* 1 (April 1911), pp. 248–50.

Leader, Bernice Kramer. "The Boston Lady as a Work of Art: Paintings by the Boston School at the Turn of the Century." Ph. D. diss. Columbia University, New York, 1980.

———. "Antifeminism in the Paintings of the Boston School." *Arts Magazine* 56 (January 1982), pp. 112–19.

Moffat, Donald. "Joseph Rodefer DeCamp: Biographical Sketch," "Joseph Rodefer DeCamp: Chronology," and "A Partial List of the Paintings of Joseph Rodefer DeCamp, 1858–1923." Unpublished typescripts. Frick Art Reference Library, New York, 1955–57.

Morris, Harrison S. *Confessions in Art.* New York: Sears Publishing Co., 1930.

Painters of the Harcourt Studios. Exh. cat. Lepore Fine Arts, Newburyport, Mass., 1992.

Perkins, Harley. "Joseph DeCamp: The Man and the Artist, as Shown by His Works." *Boston Evening Transcript,* January 5, 1924, p. 8.

Robinson, Morris R. "Some Artists Who Called 'Squam, Lanesville, and the Folly Home." Unpublished MS. Annisquam Historical Society, Mass., 1973.

Ten American Painters. Exh. cat. Spanierman Gallery, New York, 1990. Text by William H. Gerdts, Sheila Dugan, Ronald G. Pisano, *et al.*

Vitz, Robert C. "Cincinnati Art and Artists, 1870–1920." M. A. thesis. Miami University, 1967.

———. "The Eclipse of Cincinnati's Golden Age in Art." *Cincinnati Historical Society Bulletin* 27 (Winter 1969), pp. 304–19.

List of Illustrations of Works by DeCamp

Index of Names

Numerals in *italics* refer to pages with illustrations

Photograph Credits

Photographs were provided by the author and the institutions named in the captions. Individual credits are as follows:

American Academy of Arts and Letters, New York: fig. 34
Mr. and Mrs. Jeffrey Brown: fig. 22
Courtesy Brown-Corbin Fine Art, Lincoln, Massachusetts: fig. 22
Geoffrey Clements, Inc.: figs. 43, 81
Roger Core: plate 38
Michael Fischer: plates 9, 24; figs. 18, 46, 51, 64
John G. Hagan: plate 39; fig. 73
Thom Hindle: figs. 1, 16
Stephen Kovacik: fig. 17
Rick Lucas: plate 22
M. S. Rezny Photography, Inc.: plate 3
M. Rodrigo del Pozo: plates 16, 27
Clive Russ: plates 20, 30, 39; figs. 47, 50, 73
Jim Strong, Inc.: plate 32; fig. 76